Claiming Compensation for Criminal Injuries

Tolley Publishing Company Limited

Claiming Compensation for Criminal Injuries

by Dennis Foster LLB, Solicitor,

Advocate to the Criminal Injuries Compensation Board

Tolley Publishing Company Limited

A member of the Reed Elsevier plc group

ISBN 0 85459 946-0

First published 1991, as *Claiming on the Criminal Injuries Compensation Board*

Second edition 1997

Published by
Tolley Publishing Company Ltd
Tolley House
2 Addiscombe Road
Croydon
Surrey
CR9 5AF
0181-686 9141

Typeset in Great Britain by
Action Typesetting Limited, Northgate Street, Gloucester

Printed and bound in Great Britain by
Hobbs the Printers, Southampton

Foreword to the first edition

In the first full year of its operation the Criminal Injuries Compensation Board had 4 Members. It received 2,452 applications and paid out £400,000 in compensation.

At the present time CICB has 43 Members, it receives over 50,000 applications a year and will pay out over £100 million in compensation in the current year.

It is by any test 'big business' and it is, therefore, essential that all legal practitioners who hold themselves out to give general legal advice should have a knowledge of its workings and its scope.

Mr Foster has for many years been an active lawyer on the staff of the Board, advising on cases and presenting them at hearings. In this admirable book he has now produced a thoroughly professional and authoritative account of the workings of the Scheme which will be of great practical help to all practitioners.

He goes carefully through the various provisions of the Scheme, gives reference to those High Court decisions which are relevant on its interpretation, and deals with the various cases where the decisions of the Board have been subject to judicial review.

Whilst recognising that the Board is not bound by precedent in what is largely a discretionary Scheme, he has usefully drawn together the 'case law' which the Board has itself formulated over the years and which is at the moment to be found scattered amongst its various Annual Reports.

This book will, I believe, be of great assistance to many practitioners and as Chairman of the CICB I have no hesitation in commending it to them.

Lord Carlisle of Bucklow Q.C.
March 1991

Preface

This second edition is really the third. The original second edition, with the provisions of the 1994 Tariff Scheme, never saw the light of day as the decision of the House of Lords in February 1995 regarding that Scheme nipped it in the bud.

On a personal note I wish to thank my wife Morag and my daughter Emily for all the work that they have done on this second edition and its predecessor, and to dedicate this book to them, to the other members of my family – the Foster Sunday Eleven – and to my friends and colleagues on the staff of the Board and the Authority with whom I have enjoyed working during my years as an advocate to the Board.

I particularly wish to thank those of my senior colleagues, lawyers and administrators, who have an unrivalled knowledge of the workings of the 1990 and 1996 Schemes, whose suggestions have helped to reduce the number of errors and misconceptions on my part in my commentary on the two concurrent Schemes.

It is appropriate to state, however, that the views herein expressed are my own and do not in any way represent an 'official' view or statement of policy of the Criminal Injuries Compensation Authority, or the Appeals Panel or the Board.

Dennis Foster

Contents

		page
Introduction		1
Chapter 1:	**Jurisdiction**	8
	1. Time limit for application	9
Chapter 2:	**Applications arising from a crime of violence**	12
	1. Crime of violence	12
	2. 'Sustained personal injury'	26
	3. 'Directly attributable'	30
Chapter 3:	**Other applications for compensation**	45
	1. Apprehension of an offender (para 4(b) 1990; para 8(c) 1996)	45
	2. Railway incidents (para 4(c) 1990; para 8(b) 1996)	51
Chapter 4:	**Minimum award and maximum award**	54
	1. Minimum award in 'old' Scheme cases	55
	2. Minimum award – the 1996 Scheme	60
Chapter 5:	**Eligibility to receive compensation**	63
	1. Introduction	63
	2. Informing the police without delay	66
	3. Co-operating with the police in bringing the offender to justice	68
	4. Giving all reasonable assistance to the Board (1990 Scheme) and to the Authority or Appeals Panel (1996 Scheme)	80
Chapter 6:	**The effects of character and conduct on compensation awards**	82
	1. Criminal convictions	82
	2. The applicant's 'conduct before, during or after the events giving rise to the claim'	91
	3. Children playing dangerous games	97

Chapter 7: **Further constraints on compensation awards** 98
1. The possibility of benefiting the offender 98
2. Members of the same household 99

Chapter 8: **Awards to minors and to persons under disability – special arrangements – structured settlements** 104
1. The powers of the Board under the 1990 Scheme 104
2. The powers of the Authority's claims officer under the 1996 Scheme 106

Chapter 9: **Rape and other sexual offences** 108
1. Victims of rape or other sexual assaults 108
2. Sexual offences against minors 113

Chapter 10: **Personal injury attributable to 'traffic offences' (1990 Scheme) or 'to the use of a vehicle' (1996 Scheme)** 117
1. Introduction 117
2. Paragraph 11 of the 1990 Scheme 117
3. Paragraph 11 of the 1996 Scheme 120

Chapter 11: **Assessment of compensation – 1990 Scheme** 121
1. Introduction 121
2. General principles of assessment 122
3. Cases of serious injury 125
4. Future loss of earnings 128
5. Medical evidence and interim awards 132

Chapter 12: **Limitations on assessment of compensation – 1990 Scheme** 138
1. Lost earnings or earning capacity (para 14) 138
2. Duplication of payment from public funds (para 19, 1990 Scheme) 144
3. Pension payments (para 20, 1990 Scheme) 148
4. Damages and other court orders (para 21, 1990 Scheme) 151

Chapter 13: **Assessment of compensation – 1996 Scheme** 153
1. Types and limits of compensation 153
2. Compensation for loss of earnings 154
3. Compensation for special expenses 166
4. Standard amount of compensation 173

Chapter 14: **Death of the victim – 1990 Scheme** 181
1. Death in consequence of the injury (para 15, 1990 Scheme) 181
2. Death otherwise than in consequence of the injury (para 16, 1990 Scheme) 196

	3. Deductible benefits (para 19, 1990 Scheme)	196
	4. The effect of pensions on the amount of compensation awarded (para 20, 1990 Scheme)	198
	5. Apportionment of awards and deductions under the 1990 Scheme	199
Chapter 15:	**Compensation in fatal cases – 1996 Scheme**	201
	1. Introduction	201
	2. The spouse of the deceased	203
	3. The parent of the deceased	204
	4. A child of the deceased	205
	5. The amount of compensation payable	206
Chapter 16:	**Procedure for determining applications**	215
	1. Introduction	215
	Part A: Rules preserving applicant's rights in 'old' Scheme cases	217
	Part B: Applications under the 1990 Scheme	221
	1. Commencement of application	221
	2. Referral to an oral hearing	224
	3. Entitlement to an award	225
	4. Hearings	227
	Part C: Procedure for determining applications under the 1996 Scheme	243
	1. Introduction	243
	2. The initial decision	243
	3. Review of the decision	244
	4. Appeals against review decisions	247
	5. Oral hearing of appeals (paras 72–78 and 79–82 (1996))	256
	6. Rehearing of appeals	259
Chapter 17:	**Reconsideration of a case after a final award**	262
	1. Reopening cases – para 13 of the 1990 Scheme	262
	2. Reopening cases – paras 56 and 57 of the 1996 Scheme	264
Chapter 18:	**Reconsideration of decisions**	266
Appendix 1:	Judicial Review of the Board's decisions – summaries of selected cases	268
Appendix 2:	Criminal Injuries Compensation Scheme – 1990 Scheme	307
Appendix 3:	Criminal Injuries Compensation Scheme – 1996 Scheme	315
Index		348

Table of Cases

page

Alcock and others v Chief Constable of South Yorkshire Police [1992] 1 AC 310 .... 33, 38
Associated Provincial Picture Houses v Wednesbury Corporation [1948] 1 KB 223; [1947] 2 All ER 680 83
Auty and others v National Coal Board [1985] All ER 930; [1985] 1 WLR 784 131

Bolton Metropolitan District Council v Secretary of State for the Environment [1995] JPL 1043 86
British Transport Commission v Gourley [1956] AC 185; [1955] 3 All ER 796; [1956] 2 WLR 41 .... 129, 142

Commissioner of Police for the Metropolis v Caldwell [1982] AC 341; [1981] 1 All ER 961; [1981] 2 WLR 509 15
Corbett v Barking, Havering and Brentwood Health Authority [1991] 2 QB 408; [1991] All ER 498; [1990] 3 WLR 1037 189
Coward v Comex Houlder Diving Ltd (1988) unreported 186
Cresswell v Eaton [1991] 1 All ER 484; [1991] 1 WLR 1113 189
Croke v Wiseman [1981] 3 All ER 852; [1982] 1 WLR 71 127

Donnelly v Joyce [1974] QB 454; [1973] 3 All ER 475, [1973] 3 WLR 514 .... 127, 273
DPP v Parmenter, *see* R v Savage; DPP v Parmenter 15

Harris v Empress Motors [1983] 3 All ER 561 186
Hay v Hughes [1975] QB 790; [1975] 2 WLR 34 189
Hayden v Hayden [1992] 1 WLR 986, [1992] PIQR Q111; [1993] 2 FLR 16 189
Housecroft v Burnett [1986] 1 All ER 332 .... 127, 172
Hunt v Severs [1994] 2 AC 350 127

McLoughlin v O'Brian [1983] AC 410; [1982] 2 All ER 298; [1982] 2 WLR 982 .... 26–28, 30, 33–36, 58, 276
Malyon v Plummer [1963] 2 All ER 344 186
Mehmet v Perry [1977] 2 All ER 332 189

O'Dowd v Secretary of State for Northern Ireland (1982) 9 NIJB 35, 36, 39

Parry v Cleaver [1970] AC 1; [1969] 1 All ER 555; [1969] 2 WLR 821 .... 143, 148

R v Bradshaw (1878) 14 Cox CC 83 15
R v Burstow [1996] The Times, 30 July 30
R v Chan-Fook [1994] 2 All ER 552; [1994] 1 WLR 689 303
R v Chief Constable of Cheshire, ex parte Berry
(1985) unreported......................... 236, 281, 283, 287, 300, 301
R v Criminal Injuries Compensation Board, ex parte Aston
[1994] PIQR P460; [1994] COD 500................................. 291
R v Criminal Injuries Compensation Board, ex parte Avraam
(1995) unreported.. 300
R v Criminal Injuries Compensation Board, ex parte Baptiste
(1971) unreported.. 270
R v Criminal Injuries Compensation Board, ex parte Barrett
[1994] 1 FLR 587; [1994] JPIL 150; [1994] PIQR Q44 ...... 200, 289
R v Criminal Injuries Compensation Board, ex parte Blood
(1982) unreported.. 278
R v Criminal Injuries Compensation Board, ex parte Brady
[1987] The Times, 11 March 237, 283
R v Criminal Injuries Compensation Board, ex parte Brown
(1987) unreported.. 284
R v Criminal Injuries Compensation Board, ex parte C (1996)
unreported.. 305
R v Criminal Injuries Compensation Board, ex parte Carr
[1980] Crim LR 643 275
R v Criminal Injuries Compensation Board, ex parte Clowes
[1977] 3 All ER 854; [1977] 1 WLR 1353 .... 35, 272, 282, 286
R v Criminal Injuries Compensation Board, ex parte Cobb
[1995] PIQR P90; [1995] COD 126....................................293
R v Criminal Injuries Compensation Board, ex parte Comerford
(1980) unreported.. 274
R v Criminal Injuries Compensation Board, ex parte Cook
[1996] 2 All ER 144; [1996] 1 WLR 1037
....86, 184, 294, 297, 298, 301, 305
R v Criminal Injuries Compensation Board, ex parte Cragg
(1982) unreported.. 278
R v Criminal Injuries Compensation Board, ex parte Crangle
[1981] The Times, 14 November 276, 284
R v Criminal Injuries Compensation Board, ex parte Crowe
[1984] 3 All ER 572; [1984] 1 WLR 1234
....86, 87, 90, 281, 291, 295, 299
R v Criminal Injuries Compensation Board, ex parte
Cummins [1992] PIQR Q81; [1992] COD 297 288
R v Criminal Injuries Compensation Board, ex parte
Dickenson (1995) unreported.. 11, 290
R v Criminal Injuries Compensation Board, ex parte
Dickson [1996] The Times, 19 July 304
R v Criminal Injuries Compensation Board, ex parte Earls
(1982) unreported.................................... 136, 226, 234, 280
R v Criminal Injuries Compensation Board, ex parte Emmett
(1988) unreported.. 285

R v Criminal Injuries Compensation Board, ex parte Fox (1972) unreported........ 270
R v Criminal Injuries Compensation Board, ex parte Gambles [1994] PIQR P134; [1994] JPIL 66...... 86, 87, 290, 291, 298, 299, 302
R v Criminal Injuries Compensation Board, ex parte Gould (1989) unreported........ 286
R v Criminal Injuries Compensation Board, ex parte Gray (1992) unreported........289
R v Criminal Injuries Compensation Board, ex parte Hopper (1995) unreported........ 86, 87, 298
R v Criminal Injuries Compensation Board, ex parte Ince [1973] 3 All ER 808; [1973] 1 WLR 1334 ....31–35, 38, 39, 48, 271, 276
R v Criminal Injuries Compensation Board, ex parte Jobson (1995) unreported........ 298
R v Criminal Injuries Compensation Board, ex parte Johnson [1994] The Times, 11 August........ 37–39, 292
R v Criminal Injuries Compensation Board, ex parte Lain [1967] 2 QB 864; [1967] 2 All ER 770; [1967] 3 WLR 348 ....234, 268, 280
R v Criminal Injuries Compensation Board, ex parte Lawton [1972] 3 All ER 582; [1972] 1 WLR 1589........ 270
R v Criminal Injuries Compensation Board, ex parte Letts (1989) unreported........ 286
R v Criminal Injuries Compensation Board, ex parte Lloyd (1980) unreported........ 275, 279
R v Criminal Injuries Compensation Board, ex parte Maxted (1994) unreported........ 86, 87, 291
R v Criminal Injuries Compensation Board, ex parte McGuffie and Smith [1978] Crim LR 160........ 200, 273
R v Criminal Injuries Compensation Board, ex parte Milton [1995] The Times, 12 December........ 299
R v Criminal Injuries Compensation Board, ex parte Parsons [1982] The Times, 25 November........ 37–39, 276, 292
R v Criminal Injuries Compensation Board, ex parte Parsons (1990) unreported........ 287, 300, 301
R v Criminal Injuries Compensation Board, ex parte Penny [1982] Crim LR 298........ 21, 278
R v Criminal Injuries Compensation Board, ex parte Powell [1994] PIQR P77........ 86, 87, 255, 295
R v Criminal Injuries Compensation Board, ex parte Prior (1982) unreported........ 279
R v Criminal Injuries Compensation Board, ex parte R (1996) unreported........ 303
R v Criminal Injuries Compensation Board, ex parte RJC (An infant) (1978) 122 SJ 95; [1978] Crim LR 220........ 273
R v Criminal Injuries Compensation Board, ex parte Richard C (1981) unreported........ 276

R v Criminal Injuries Compensation Board, ex parte Richardson (1973) 118 SJ 184; [1974] Crim LR 99 .... 142, 270, 271
R v Criminal Injuries Compensation Board, ex parte Schofield [1971] 2 All ER 1011; [1971] 1 WLR 926 .... 35, 46, 269
R v Criminal Injuries Compensation Board, ex parte Scott (1995) unreported.. 296
R v Criminal Injuries Compensation Board, ex parte Sorell (1987) unreported.. 283
R v Criminal Injuries Compensation Board, ex parte Staten [1972] 1 All ER 1034; [1972] 1 WLR 569............................ 270
R v Criminal Injuries Compensation Board, ex parte Thomas [1995] PIQR P99; [1995] COD 210.................................. 294
R v Criminal Injuries Compensation Board, ex parte Thompstone [1984] All ER 572, [1984] 1 WLR 1234.. 86, 87, 90, 281, 291, 295, 299
R v Criminal Injuries Compensation Board, ex parte Tong [1977] 1 All ER 171; [1976] 1 WLR 1237 .... 272, 280
R v Criminal Injuries Compensation Board, ex parte Townend (1970) unreported.. 268
R v Criminal Injuries Compensation Board, ex parte W (An Infant) (1981) unreported.. 275
R v Criminal Injuries Compensation Board, ex parte WEB (1982) unreported.. 277
R v Criminal Injuries Compensation Board, ex parte Warner [1987] QB 74; [1986] 2 All ER 478; [1986] 3 WLR 251 .... 13, 51, 276, 282
R v Criminal Injuries Compensation Board, ex parte Webb [1987] 1 QB 74 33
R v Criminal Injuries Compensation Board, ex parte Westrop (1980) unreported..274
R v Criminal Injuries Compensation Board, ex parte Whitelock (1986) unreported.. 282
R v Criminal Injuries Compensation Board, ex parte Wilson (1991) unreported.. 288
R v Criminal Injuries Compensation Board, ex parte Young (1995) unreported.. 299, 305
R v Cunningham [1957] 2 QB 396; [1957] 2 All ER 412; [1957] 3 WLR 76 15
R v Hull Visitors, ex parte St Germaine [1979] 1 WLR 140 294
R v Ireland [1996] The Times, 22 May 30, 302
R v Lawrence [1981] Crim LR 421 CA 286
R v Parker [1977] 2 All ER 37; [1977] 1 WLR 600................. 273
R v Savage; DPP v Parmenter [1991] 3 WLR 914................. 15, 303
R v Spratt [1991] 2 All ER 210 15
R v Venna [1976] QB 421; [1975] 3 All ER 788; [1975] 3 WLR 737 15
Regan v Williamson [1976] 2 All ER 241; [1976] 1 WLR 305 .... 189, 190
Roberts v Johnstone [1988] 3 WLR 1247 127

RP & TG v Home Secretary and Criminal Injuries Compensation Board (1994) unreported 11, 290

Smith v Manchester City Council (1974) 118 SJ 597 125
Spittle v Bunney [1988] 3 All ER 1031; [1988] 1 WLR 847 .... 189, 190
Stanley v Saddique [1992] QB 1; [1991] 1 All ER 529; [1991] 2 WLR 459 189
Stapley v Gypsum Mines Ltd [1953] AC 663; [1953] 2 All ER 478; [1953] 3 WLR 279 35
Stubbings V Webb [1993] 1 All ER 322 11

Wells v Wells (1996) unreported 131

Introduction

This Second Edition incorporates the substantial changes brought about by the new Scheme which came into operation on 1 April 1996.

The 1996 Scheme commences with these words:

> 1. This Scheme is made by the Secretary of State ...

The Scheme expressly affirms in para 84 that applications received before 1 April 1996 are entitled to be considered under the terms of the 1990 Scheme, or, in the case of some older or reopened cases, earlier Schemes. In view of the fundamental changes made by the 1996 Scheme, the preservation of applicants' entitlement to have their applications considered under the old rules is of the greatest importance.

The principal change which took effect in relation to all applications made on or after 1 April 1996 was to alter the basis of assessment of compensation. In all applications made prior to 1 April 1996 compensation was and is based upon common law damages (1990 Scheme para 12). In applications on or after 1 April 1996, awards will be the 'standard amount of compensation ... shown in respect of the relevant description of injury in the Tariff appended to this Scheme, which sets out ... a scale of fixed levels of compensation ...' (para 25).

By fixing the amount of compensation according to a tariff of awards that are intended to reflect the seriousness of the injury, the 1996 Scheme removed the need to consider the principles of common law damages in relation to the 'pain, suffering and loss of amenity' suffered by the applicant and the widely varying degrees of severity, as between one case and another, which the common law endeavours to accommodate and distinguish. Instead one takes the essence of the injury in simple form and reads off the tariff figure for that injury. Thus to take one example from the 'Tariff of Injuries':

'Head: burns: minor	Tariff level 3	Standard Amount: £1,500'
or 'Head: burns: moderate	Tariff level 9	Standard Amount: £4,000'
or 'Head: burns: severe	Tariff level 13	Standard Amount: £10,000'

To the lawyer this change is something of a culture shock. To everyone having dealings with the Scheme it is intended to be a simplification of the process of evaluating the thousands of applications for compensation made every month.

A common law assessment of damages includes as separate heads of claim the 'general damages' for the injury itself, plus any future financial loss, and 'special damages' for past financial loss incurred up to the date of assessment of the claim. It had been the Government's intention under the abortive 1994 Tariff Scheme that the one tariff figure 'to reflect the severity of the injury sustained' would be substituted for all these heads of claim.

The Government White Paper published in December 1993 set out the Government's then proposals in relation to changes in the CICS – the Scheme had stood largely unchanged since its inception in 1964 – and also gave the reasons why those changes were being made. Paragraphs 2 and 3 of the White Paper stated:

> It is widely accepted that there is no objectively 'right' sum of money which can compensate an individual for the pain and suffering which he or she has endured as a result of an injury. In deciding on the appropriate level of damages to award to an individual in a civil suit, the courts could take into account a number of different factors and attempt the almost impossible task of assessing how the injury has affected that particular individual in all of the circumstances which apply. Similarly under the current Criminal Injuries Compensation Scheme the Criminal Injuries Compensation Board attempts to make these judgements. This is a complex and time-consuming process with much inevitable uncertainty for the applicant. The Government remains committed to providing a tangible measure of help to blameless victims of crimes of violence in recognition of the hurt which they have suffered, but it no longer believes that the best way of doing this is by attempting an individual assessment in each case which can, in any event, only arrive at an essentially artificial sum of money.
>
> Accordingly, the Government has decided to introduce a new system of payment to the victims of crimes of violence. The main features of the new arrangements are:
>
> (i) compensation will no longer be assessed on the basis of common law damages;
> (ii) injuries of comparable severity will be grouped or banded together in a tariff of awards, and each band will attract a single lump sum payment;
> (iii) there will be 25 tariff levels, with awards ranging from £1,000 to £¼ million;
> (iv) tariff levels will be based on the Board's past award levels;
> (v) the average claimant should be no worse off than under the current scheme;
> (vi) no separate payment will be made for loss of earnings or medical expenses;
> (vii) the basic rules for eligibility will remain largely as before;
> (viii) the new scheme will apply to all applications lodged on or after 1 April 1994.
> (ix) cases lodged before April 1994 will be cleared by the present Board under the current rules.

The above extract from the 1993 White Paper sets out the purposes of the changes later effected by the 1994 Tariff Scheme. The implementation of the latter was declared unlawful by a decision of the House of Lords in February 1995, and therefore the amendments to the Scheme proposed in the 1993 White Paper had to go back to the drawing board. It will be noted, however, that only item (vi) of the above proposals has not survived in the 1996 Scheme, paras 30 to 34 of which allow certain claims for loss of earnings and paras 35 and 36 of which permit compensation for 'special expenses'.

The preservation of the rules of the 1990 or earlier Schemes as the basis for deciding entitlement to compensation and also for assessing the amount of such compensation in all cases lodged with the Board before 1 April 1996 means that a dual system is in operation from that date and will remain in operation for some time whilst pre- 1 April 1996 cases are considered and resolved. Applicants and their advisers will have to be clear from the outset which set of rules applies to their particular application. This is simple. Any application received by the CICB before 1 April 1996 will be governed by the 1990 (or earlier) Scheme and compensation will be assessed on the basis of common law damages. All applications received on or after that date will be governed by the 1996 Scheme and the amount of awards will be fixed by reference to the tariff appended to that Scheme and the rules of that Scheme permitting payment for certain defined loss of earnings and 'special expenses'. Rules governing eligibility remain substantially unchanged, although there are some changes.

The White Paper of December 1993 refers to a period of 'around two years' to allow the CICB to finalise all 'old Scheme' cases. Having regard to the heavy caseload of the CICB at the date of commencement of the 1996 Scheme, it is expected that the dual system will have to remain in operation for at least that period to clear all cases. It is estimated that all old Scheme cases will be initially decided on the papers by the CICB within about a year, but there are currently about 20,000 old Scheme cases in which applicants have requested and been granted the right to a hearing. All these applicants will still be entitled to a hearing under the terms of the 1990 or earlier Schemes.

As will be apparent from the chapters in this book dealing with the working of the CICA after 1 April 1996, the 1996 Scheme contains a number of important procedural changes for deciding applications. The 1990 Scheme contained provision for the Board, which under that Scheme and earlier Schemes had been 'entirely responsible for deciding what compensation should be paid in individual cases', to delegate decisions to 'such members of the Board's staff as the Board may designate' (para 3 of the 1990 Scheme).

The 1996 Scheme now creates a new structure and a new Authority for dealing with claims for compensation. Paragraphs 1, 2 and 3 of the 1996 Scheme read as follows:

> 1. This Scheme is made by the Secretary of State under the Criminal Injuries Compensation Act 1995. Applications received on or after 1 April 1996 for the payment of compensation to, or in respect of, persons who have sustained criminal injury will be considered under this Scheme.

Administration of the Scheme

2. Claims officers in the Criminal Injuries Compensation Authority ('the Authority') will determine claims for compensation in accordance with this Scheme. Appeals against decisions taken on reviews under this Scheme will be determined by adjudicators. Persons appointed as adjudicators are appointed as members of the Criminal Injuries Compensation Appeals Panel ('the Panel'). The Secretary of State will appoint one of the adjudicators as Chairman of the Panel. The Secretary of State will also appoint persons as staff of the Panel to administer the provisions of this Scheme relating to the appeal system.
3. Claims officers will be responsible for deciding, in accordance with this Scheme, what awards (if any) should be made in individual cases, and how they should be paid. Their decisions will be open to review and thereafter to appeal to the Panel, in accordance with this Scheme. No decision, whether by a claims officer or the Panel, will be open to appeal to the Secretary of State.

The first change to note is that the CICB, which had administered the Scheme and decided all questions of entitlement to compensation since the inception of the Scheme in 1964, ceased to have responsibility for the Scheme from 1 April 1996, save only in respect of applications received by the Board before that date.

From 1 April 1996 the newly constituted Criminal Injuries Compensation Authority (CICA) took on that responsibility. Earlier Schemes provided that the Board, consisting of Queen's Counsel and experienced solicitors appointed to the Board by the Secretary of State, would be 'assisted by appropriate staff', the latter being civil servants appointed by the Home Office and the Scottish Office to assist the Board members as the persons responsible for the Scheme in its administration. From 1 April 1996, however, those civil servants are officers of the CICA; indeed they are the CICA. Members of the CICB have no part to play in the operation of the 1996 Scheme by the CICA. All decisions on entitlement under the 1996 Scheme will be made by civil servants as officers of the CICA, including the review of such initial decisions where the applicant does not accept the initial decision.

Paragraph 60 of the 1996 Scheme provides that 'all applications for review' of the initial decisions 'will be considered by a claims officer more senior than' the one who made the original decision. Under para 61, if the applicant does not accept the outcome of the review, he/she may appeal to the Panel. As has been mentioned above, para 2 of the 1996 Scheme states that 'Appeals against decisions taken on reviews under this Scheme will be determined by adjudicators', who will be appointed members of the Criminal Injuries Compensation Appeals Panel.

The Appeals Panel is an entirely new creation. Its members will include senior lawyers but not exclusively so as with the CICB. The Authority and the Panel replace the CICB in relation to all cases received after 31 March 1996. The Appeals Panel is entirely independent of the Authority which administers the Scheme. This differs from the situation under the old

Scheme whereby appeals were heard by two or three members of the Board other than the single member who made the initial decision. The Panel will have a secretariat which is quite separate from the Authority.

The Appeals Panel will deal only with appeals against decisions of the Authority so that it will only hear cases arising under the 1996 Scheme. A decision by the Appeals Panel is final in that 'no decision' by the Panel 'will be open to appeal to the Secretary of State' (para 3, 1996 Scheme).

The CICB will continue after 1 April 1996 to hear appeals under the old Schemes. However, para 85 of the 1996 Scheme provides for a 'transfer date', a date yet to be fixed by the Secretary of State. On the transfer date, the CICB will cease to exist and all outstanding 'old Scheme' cases will be transferred to the Authority, but with the proviso (para 86) that decisions which would have been made under the old Scheme by a single member of the Board or by 'at least two Members of the Board' may be made by 'a single legally qualified member of the Panel' or by 'at least two legally qualified members of the Panel'. This effectively preserves the right of applicants whose applications fall to be considered under the old Scheme to a hearing under its terms even after the Board has ceased to exist. The practical effect of these administrative changes will be dealt with in detail in the chapters which follow.

The change from the common law basis of assessment of awards to a fixed tariff sum is by far the most important change effected by the 1996 Scheme. The rules of eligibility of entitlement under the Scheme have (in the words of the 1993 White Paper) 'stood the test of time and have worked well in practice'. Although there are some important changes in the rules of eligibility, advisers already familiar with the basic rules of the earlier Schemes will note that those principles will, for the most part, continue to apply to applications for compensation for the foreseeable future.

Thus the familiar questions which will still need to be asked and answered are referred to briefly in para 26 of the White Paper in the following words:

(i) was a crime of violence involved;
(ii) was the crime reported to the police;
(iii) did the conduct of the applicant help cause the incident;
(iv) does the character and conduct of the applicant make an award, or a full award, inappropriate; and
(v) would damages exceed the minimum threshold?

Applicants and advisers should note the new time limit of two years within which applications must be lodged after the incident (para 17). Under earlier Schemes the time limit was three years, in line with the time limit for court claims for personal injury. Paragraph 17 also states that a claims officer may waive this time limit where he considers it reasonable and in the interests of justice to do so. It is to be hoped that the Authority will be flexible in interpreting this time limit, at least until the change in the rule becomes more widely known, not least to accommodate applicants whose injury was already two years old on 1 April 1996 and who had, until the change effected on that date, another year before their application would have been out of time under the old Scheme.

Two further important changes made by the 1996 Scheme which should be noted relate to:

(i) accidental injuries suffered by persons engaged in 'activity directed to containing, limiting or remedying the consequences of a crime' (para 12); and

(ii) the Scheme's requirements relating to claims for 'mental injury alone' (para 9).

In respect of (i) above – cases where accidental injuries are suffered in 'containing, limiting or remedying' the consequences of a crime – para 12 provides that no compensation will be payable unless it can be proved that an 'exceptional risk' was taken 'which was justified in all the circumstances'. Previously this requirement of 'exceptional risk' applied only to accidental injuries sustained in the law enforcement activities referred to in para 4(b) of the 1990 Scheme, now set out in para 8(c) of the 1996 Scheme. It is thought that this extension of the 'exceptional risk' rule will particularly affect applications by firefighters and other rescue services engaged in fighting fires started by arson.

Regarding (ii) above – 'nervous shock' cases where mental injury alone is suffered – applications are regulated by para 9 of the 1996 Scheme. This paragraph defines the factors which must be established before compensation will be payable 'for mental injury alone'. These requirements specify some recognised common law principles regarding the relationship between the applicant and the injured party necessary to entitle the applicant to compensation, and the proximity of the applicant to the incident and its immediate aftermath.

The 1996 Scheme expressly states two principles which were not previously written into the Scheme but which were nevertheless always applied.

Paragraph 64 provides that 'the standard of proof to be applied by the Panel in all matters before it will be the balance of probabilities', i.e. the standard of proof in civil cases, not the heavier burden of proof 'beyond reasonable doubt' applicable in criminal cases. This paragraph also provides that 'it will be for the appellant to make out his case'. The burden of proof is on the appellant.

The second principle likewise affirmed is in para 10 of the 1996 Scheme which states that for the purpose of eligibility under the Scheme 'it is not necessary for the assailant to have been convicted of a criminal offence'. This has always been the case under earlier Schemes.

The 1996 Scheme, like its predecessors, gives the Authority and the Panel discretionary powers, largely similar to those exercised by the CICB, to reduce or refuse awards. These discretionary powers will continue to arise in those cases where the victim has not conducted himself according to the principles of good citizenship on which the rules of entitlement are based, such as informing the police promptly of the circumstances of the injury and not having himself provoked or voluntarily engaged in the violence which resulted in his or her injury. The rules governing entitlement to an award in cases where the victim has died as a consequence of the injury have also been substantially altered by the 1996 Scheme. These rules are set out in paras 37 to 44 of the 1996 Scheme.

Chapter 1

Jurisdiction

The 1996 Scheme (para 8 and 'Note 1') restates the geographical limits of the Scheme's jurisdiction in largely similar terms to para 4 of the 1990 Scheme. For an application to the Board to fall within the Scheme the injury must have been 'sustained in Great Britain'. The first significance of 'sustained in Great Britain' is that it excludes incidents occurring in Northern Ireland, the latter being covered by a separate Scheme under the provisions of the Criminal Injuries (Compensation) Northern Ireland Order 1988. The scope of the Scheme which is considered here is that which applies only to England, Scotland and Wales.

The person sustaining such an injury may be of any nationality and need not be resident in Great Britain. A foreign visitor thus comes within the Scheme. The Board from time to time deals with applications resulting from violence in this country between persons who are nationals of two different foreign countries. The Scheme thus reflects the general principle of the law that anyone within the realm is entitled to enjoy the protection of 'the Queen's peace' whilst going about his affairs.

A national or resident of Great Britain who is injured in a crime of violence committed outside Great Britain is not within the Scheme.

Many other countries have schemes for compensating the victims of violent crimes. Their varieties of approach, in particular in relation to reciprocity, cannot be dealt with here. It should be noted, however, that the United Kingdom has ratified the European Convention on the Compensation of Victims of Violent Crime, which came into force for the United Kingdom on 1 June 1990. Ratification provides benefits of reciprocity in countries where schemes, unlike ours, are not open to anyone injured within their jurisdiction.

Although 'sustained in Great Britain' is a sufficient definition of jurisdiction for nearly all applications, the definition also includes injury sustained on a British ship, aircraft or hovercraft. This is an important provision as the ship, aircraft or hovercraft could be anywhere in the world. Provided it is British, however, the injury sustained thereon is within the jurisdiction of the Scheme. Also included is injury sustained 'on, under or above an installation in a designated area within the meaning of section 1(7) of the Continental Shelf Act 1964 or any waters within 500 metres of such an installation'. Oil rigs in British waters are thus brought within the Scheme.

Note 1 to the Scheme states that 'in Great Britain' includes:

(a) 'in a lighthouse off the coast of Great Britain' (the 1990 Scheme wording is 'off the coast of the United Kingdom'; the 1996 wording is thus more consistent with the confinement of claims to those arising 'in Great Britain' in both Schemes); and

(b) 'that part of the Channel Tunnel designated part of Great Britain by the Channel Tunnel Act 1987' or in the control zones defined by the Channel Tunnel (International Arrangements) Order 1993 (SI No 1813).

The inclusion of part of the Channel Tunnel within the Scheme, however, applies only to a person 'injured by a UK officer' in the exercise of his duties and to any UK 'officer injured in the exercise of his duties'. The term 'UK officer' is defined in the Protocol made under the Channel Tunnel Treaty.

Note 2 to the 1996 Scheme defines the meaning of 'British aircraft' and 'British hovercraft' by reference to the Civil Aviation Act 1982 and the Hovercraft Act 1968. 'British ship' means any vessel used in navigation which is wholly owned by British citizens or 'bodies corporate incorporated under the law of some part of, and having their principal place of business in, the United Kingdom' or Scottish partnerships or 'one of Her Majesty's ships'. Her Majesty's aircraft, hovercraft or ships, which 'belong to, or are exclusively used in the service of, Her Majesty in right of the government of the United Kingdom', are included.

Although an injury sustained anywhere in the world on a British ship, aircraft or hovercraft as defined above is within the Scheme, a British Embassy in a foreign country is not 'Great Britain' for this purpose, nor is an overseas British military establishment. Accordingly, an injury inflicted in any of these types of establishment is not within the Scheme. Whatever status these establishments may respectively enjoy under English or international law, for the purposes of criminal injury compensation they are in each case 'part of a foreign field' which remains just that. When the possibility of bringing these two exceptions within the Scheme was considered by the review of the Scheme published in 1978, leading to the publication of the amended 1979 Scheme, the working party undertaking the review considered that there was not a sufficiently strong case for extending eligibility to diplomats, civil servants and members of the armed services stationed abroad, whilst leaving outside the scope of the Scheme the many British civilians travelling or residing abroad. Under the 1996 Scheme this situation is unchanged.

1. Time limit for application

The 1996 Scheme reduces the time period within which applications must be lodged from three years to two years. Paragraph 17 of the 1996 Scheme provides that applications 'must be received by the Authority within two years of the date of the incident'. This is not an absolute rule, and para 17 continues:

> A claims officer may waive this time limit where he considers that, by reason of the particular circumstances of the case, it is reasonable and in the interests of justice to do so.

The time limit under the 1990 Scheme was regulated by para 4 of that Scheme and stated:

> Applications for compensation will be entertained only if made within 3 years of the incident giving rise to the injury, except that the Board may in exceptional cases waive this requirement. A decision by the Chairman not to waive the time limit will be final.

Under the 1996 Scheme the Authority is unlikely to apply the time limits strictly in the period immediately following the commencement of the new Scheme on 1 April 1996. To do so would exclude many applications in which the incident may have occurred more than two years before 1 April 1996 but the applicant or his adviser believed there was up to another year before the application had to be lodged to avoid being refused as out of time. Some leniency is expected up to 1 April 1997. Applicants and their advisers should comply strictly with the two-year time limit wherever possible and in any event lodge the application with the Authority as soon as they possibly can. Paragraph 17 expressly states that an application 'should be made as soon as possible after the incident giving rise to the injury'.

The 'particular circumstances' in which the time limit may be waived are not defined or restricted to any particular category of case. Apart from cases which need to be considered in relation to the transition from a three-year time limit to a two-year time limit, cases for waiver have, in practice, mostly been those involving persons under a legal disability, particularly minors. Prior to the commencement of the 1996 Scheme, the Board received many applications on behalf of abused children where the offences against them commenced years before the application was made. Late applications made by young persons on attaining their majority, in respect of injury sustained in childhood, should be made as soon as possible after reaching full age. These cases have generally been considered sympathetically under the 1990 Scheme and the time limit may be waived where there is a good reason why the application could not have been made before, and substantial injustice would result from not waiving the time limit. The reasons for the time limit must be kept in mind, however, especially the practical difficulties of obtaining reliable evidence long after the event.

These observations are based on the view taken by the Board under the 1990 Scheme. The policy of the Authority under the 1996 Scheme may well be similar, but the shorter time limit will put delayed applications at greater risk of being disallowed.

Persons having parental rights over children, including in appopriate cases the social services departments of local authorities, are encouraged to make applications on behalf of minors even if the offences of which they are aware are partly or wholly outside the time limit. Such applications should be made as soon as possible after the circumstances become known.

In cases where the victim and the offender were living together as members of the same family at the time of the offence, and the offence was before 1 October 1979, neither the Board nor the Authority can consider the case at all, as the Scheme in operation before that date excluded such offences. In a 1994 decision, the High Court upheld this rule (*RP and TG v Home Secretary and Criminal Injuries Compensation Board*, Court of Appeal, 4 May 1994). If the abuse complained of continued over a period of time partly before and partly after that date, abuse during the latter period may be considered within the Scheme.

Ignorance of the existence of the Scheme is frequently put forward as the reason for the delay in making the application. This is not a sufficient ground for treating a late application as an exceptional case. A 1995 decision of the High Court has emphasised that the Chairman of the Board has a wide discretion under the 1990 Scheme. The decision accepted that there had to be regard to the practical difficulties of obtaining reliable evidence long after the event (*R v Criminal Injuries Compensation Board, ex parte Dickenson*, Queen's Bench Division, 22 February 1995).

The Board's twenty-fifth report (1989) cites a case in which the then three-year time limit was not waived. The applicant had pursued a civil claim for the injury sustained and, on this proving unsuccessful, applied to the Board out of time. In refusing the application the Chairman stated:

> The Board does not accept and never has accepted that pursuit of a civil claim is a valid reason for not applying to the Board within the limitation period.

Applicants must be advised to comply strictly with the new two-year time limit under the 1996 Scheme so far as possible, because the discretion available under para 17 may not be exercised in their favour should they fail to do so.

The Board's original time limit of three years was said to be based on the same time limit in the courts for instituting personal injury claims. That rule was itself the subject of a House of Lords decision in 1993 (*Stubbings v Webb* [1993] 1 All ER 322) which decided that civil claims for damages based on rape or indecent assault were subject to a six-year time limit rather than three years. The case turned on a point of interpretation of the Limitation Act 1980. Whilst this case appears to have no obvious bearing on the interpretation of either the 1990 or 1996 Schemes, it may prove of some assistance in attempting to argue for the 'time limit' discretion to be exercised in favour of a claim lodged outside the Scheme's time limit provision.

Chapter 2

Applications arising from a crime of violence

1. Crime of violence

The 1996 Scheme, like all versions of the Scheme which preceded it, has as its central purpose the compensation of innocent victims of crimes of violence. Paragraph 8 of the 1996 Scheme defines the several categories of 'criminal injury' for which compensation may be claimed. As in the 1990 Scheme, the majority of claims will be for personal injuries directly attributable to a crime of violence (including arson, fire raising or an act of poisoning). Paragraph 8(a) includes this familiar basic definition.

Paragraphs 8(b) and (c) likewise re-establish the now familiar categories of personal injuries directly attributable to an offence of trespass on a railway (first included as a new provision (para 4(c)) in the 1990 Scheme) and personal injuries directly attributable to the apprehension or attempted apprehension of an offender or a suspected offender, the prevention or attempted prevention of an offence, or the giving of help to any constable who is engaged in any such activity.

Paragraph 8 further provides that the 'criminal injury' must be an injury sustained in Great Britain. The geographical limitation of the Scheme's jurisdiction to injury 'sustained in Great Britain' has been dealt with in the preceding chapter and is defined in Note 1 to the 1996 Scheme.

The 1990 Scheme, which will continue to apply to applications lodged with the Board before 1 April 1996, provided in para 4 of the Scheme:

> The Board will entertain applications for ex gratia payments of compensation in any case where the applicant ... sustained ... personal injury directly attributable ... to a crime of violence ...,

with para 4(b) and (c) including personal injury directly attributable to the apprehension of an offender or to an offence of trespass on a railway. In these respects, therefore, para 4 of the 1990 Scheme and para 8 of the 1996 Scheme match each other.

From 1 April 1996 the 1996 Scheme will be administered by the Criminal Injuries Compensation Authority whose officers, referred to in the 1996 Scheme as 'claims officers', will determine claims for compensation in accordance with that Scheme. The claims officer is under a duty to consider whether the applicant made a full and prompt report of the incident to the police, co-operated with the police in bringing the offender to justice and does not himself have such a serious criminal record that an award out of public funds would be inappropriate. The applicant's conduct in relation to the incident must also be considered.

These powers of discretion, whereby the claims officer *may* withhold or reduce compensation after considering the applicant's actions and conduct in relation to the requirements of para 13 of the 1996 Scheme (para 6 of the 1990 Scheme) illustrate the fundamental purpose of the Scheme to compensate the innocent victim who has not brought the injury upon himself by his own actions and who has also fulfilled the reasonable expectations of his fellow citizens by making every reasonable effort to enable the police to bring the assailant to justice. These important powers are considered in detail in Chapters 5 and 6.

'Crime of violence' is not defined in the Scheme itself – nor has it been defined by the courts. However, it has been the subject of judicial interpretation by the High Court in cases where an applicant has sought judicial review of a decision by the Board. The Scheme itself specifically includes the offences of arson and poisoning within the range of crimes of violence.

Offences which can be identified easily as crimes of violence include assault occasioning actual bodily harm (Offences Against the Person Act 1861, s 47), wounding or grievous bodily harm (s 20), wounding with intent (s 18), as well as murder, attempted murder and manslaughter.

The Scheme avoids listing offences which are crimes of violence. What is or is not a crime of violence remains a matter of interpretation by the claims officer in each particular case.

In *R v Criminal Injuries Compensation Board, ex parte Warner* (1986) – noted in the Appendix (page 282) – a train driver had suffered psychiatric injury as a consequence of someone committing suicide by standing on the railway line as the train approached. It was argued for the appellant that the person killed had committed a crime, namely the offence under section 34 of the Offences Against the Person Act 1861 of 'endangering the safety of any person conveyed or being in or upon a railway', and that the appellant's injury, namely psychiatric illness, was 'directly attributable' to the commission of that crime. To come within the Scheme, however, the applicant had also to establish that the crime to which the injury was attributable was a 'crime of violence'. In this he failed. This case preceded the addition of the words 'an offence of trespass on a railway' by the 1990 Scheme and repeated in the 1996 Scheme. Such circumstances have therefore been within the Scheme since 1990 but only because a special category of injury, not resulting from a crime of violence, was created by para 4(c) of the 1990 Scheme and which is now to be found in para 8(b) of the 1996 Scheme.

The judgment of Lawton LJ in that case still helps to clarify what is and what is not a crime of violence:

> In my judgement counsel's submission that what matters is the nature of the crime, not its likely consequences, is well founded. It is for the Board to decide whether unlawful conduct because of its nature, not its consequences, amounts to a crime of violence.

> The nature of a crime is different from its consequences.
>
> If consideration of probable consequences is what makes a crime one of violence, a motorist who leaves his vehicle in a dangerous position contrary to section 24 of the Road Traffic Act 1972 commits a crime of violence.
>
> The meaning of 'crime of violence' is very much a jury point. Most crimes of violence will involve the infliction or threat of force but some may not. I do not think it prudent to attempt a definition of words of ordinary usage in English which the Board as a fact-finding body have to apply to the case before them. They will recognise a crime of violence when they hear about it, even though as a matter of semantics it may be difficult to produce a definition which is not too narrow or so wide as to produce absurd consequences, as in the case of the Road Traffic Act 1972 to which I have referred.

References to 'the Board' in the judgment quoted above are to the Criminal Injuries Compensation Board. The same would apply to cases considered by claims officers of the Criminal Injuries Compensation Authority or the Appeals Panel in deciding what is or is not a crime of violence for the purposes of the 1996 Scheme.

Cases which have frequently caused the Board to ask itself the question 'Where is the crime of violence in this case?' are those in which injury to the applicant has been sustained as a consequence of physical contact between the injured party and another but the element of intent required by the criminal law is absent. It is sometimes argued that the element of hostility is a necessary element in the crime of assault.

Injury resulting from an accident is not within the Scheme. If A, while walking normally along the pavement, accidentally bumps into B causing B to fall and break his arm, there is no crime of violence, or indeed any crime at all – as A had no intention of assaulting B, and neither was he reckless in so doing. The principle of the criminal law that in order to prove a crime one has to establish not only the wrongful act but also the guilty mind – the intent – applies. A mere accidental injury will not fall within the Scheme.

The position is different where, intending to assault A, the assailant causes injury to B to whom he intended no harm. Thus if one man intentionally swings a punch or beer glass at another but misses the intended victim and instead hits and causes injury to a third party, the latter may make a claim under the Scheme.

Another situation which would generally be within the Scheme is one in which a dangerous and reckless action aimed at no specific victim causes injury to another. The throwing of a beer glass across a crowded public house where the circumstances indicate the likelihood of injury to someone present would generally be regarded as a reckless act and a crime of violence.

It is appropriate in relation to this latter type of case, where recklessness is a factor, to look at the principles of the criminal law which need to be applied. Although in many instances the crime of violence will comprise the violent or guilty act and the guilty intent, in others the assailant does not intend the harmful result but is reckless as to the consequences of his action. The crime may thus be made out, comprising the act and the recklessness rather than the act and the intent.

R v Cunningham [1957] 2 QB 396 decided that for the purpose of an offence under section 47 of the Offences Against the Person Act 1861 (occasioning actual bodily harm), 'recklessness' required the accused to have foreseen that the particular kind of harm might be done as a result of his action and yet he had nevertheless gone on to take the risk of it.

In *R v Venna* [1976] QB 421, the court said 'We see no reason in logic or law why a person who recklessly applies physical force to the person of another should be outside the criminal law'. This was also a case of assault occasioning actual bodily harm. The much earlier case of *R v Bradshaw* (1878) 14 Cox CC 83 had decided that the element of *mens rea* (the guilty mind) in the offence of battery was satisfied by proof that the defendant intentionally or recklessly applied force to the person of another.

In *Commissioner of Police for the Metropolis v Caldwell* [1982] AC 341, Lord Diplock said that a person was reckless (as to the destruction or damaging of property) if

> (1) he does an act which in fact creates an obvious risk that property would be destroyed or damaged and (2) when he does the act he either has not given any thought to the possibility of there being any such risk or has recognised that there was some risk involved and has nonetheless gone on to do it.

The principles of recklessness may have differences of application in relation to crimes involving damage to property or reckless driving. In relation to assault occasioning actual bodily harm (the section 47 offence with which the Board or Authority is most frequently concerned), *R v Spratt* [1991] 2 All ER 210 decided that a defendant who failed to give thought to the possibility that his actions might give rise to a risk of causing another person actual bodily harm was not guilty of an offence under section 47 of the 1861 Act. The test of recklessness was said in such cases to be that laid down in *R v Cunningham*, that the accused had foreseen that the particular kind of harm might be done and yet had gone on to take the risk of it.

These principles have been considered further in the House of Lords cases of *R v Savage; DPP v Parmenter* [1991] 3 WLR 914, with the court stating at page 924 'where the defendant does not advert to the possibility of harm there would be no assault, let alone assault occasioning actual bodily harm'.

It is, however, sufficient in order to establish the offence of assault occasioning actual bodily harm contrary to section 47 of the 1861 Act for the Crown to show that the defendant committed an assault and that actual bodily harm was occasioned by the assault; the Crown is not obliged to prove that the defendant intended to cause some actual bodily harm or was reckless as to whether such harm would be caused. The Board, or claims officer or Appeals Panel, must apply the principles of the criminal law in deciding whether a crime of violence has been committed.

In the remainder of this chapter references to 'the Board' may also be regarded as references to the 'claims officer' and 'the Appeals Panel', as the principles which govern the proper interpretation of 'crimes of violence' are the same under the 1990 and 1996 Schemes. It is therefore considered that the interpretation applied by the Board over many years is the best guide to the future.

The cases mentioned above necessarily involved, amongst other things, a decision by the court as to fact in relation to the state of the defendant's mind at the time he acted in such a way as to cause injury or damage. In many cases the assailant, the person whose intent or recklessness is relevant to the question whether a crime of violence has been committed, is never identified or apprehended. Paragraph 10 of the 1996 Scheme provides expressly that 'it is not necessary for the assailant to have been convicted of a criminal offence in connecton with the injury'. This has always been the case under the 1990 and earlier Schemes.

This being so, the Board has to arrive at the justice of the case before it by applying its experience to those facts of the case which are established, drawing a proper and reasonable inference from those facts as to the actions and intentions of the unknown assailant.

The difference in the burden of proof required of the applicant before the Board, being the balance of probabilities (paras 19 and 64 of the 1996 Scheme) – as opposed to the burden on the prosecution in a criminal trial of proving the guilty act and intent or recklessness of the accused beyond reasonable doubt – enhances the prospects of an applicant succeeding before the Board where parts of the jigsaw of fact which would be essential in a criminal trial are wholly missing.

Many applications which are refused by the Board, on the grounds that the applicant has not satisfied the Board that there was a crime of violence, are those in which the alleged assailant may have been acting in self-defence. As self-defence is a complete defence to the alleged crime, there is no crime by the person who inflicted the injury where self-defence is established. The onus in this respect, as in all others, is upon the applicant to satisfy the Board that the alleged assailant was not acting in self-defence. It may be that the injured applicant had himself been the aggressor. The attack on the injured applicant might, in those circumstances, have been no more than sufficient force to repel the attack by the applicant. If so, the applicant will not succeed as the injuries he suffered were the consequences of an act of self-defence by the other party.

In cases before the Board where self-defence is relevant, the question of the applicant's conduct under para 6 of the 1990 Scheme (para 13(d) of the 1996 Scheme) will often be the deciding factor; once the evidence indicates that the applicant was himself the aggressor, he will generally be outside the Scheme as a consequence of his own 'conduct' under para 6

(1990) or para 13 (1996) without the need to decide points of law relating to self-defence.

Quite different problems arise in those cases in which the applicant is able to give the Board very little information regarding the incident. His statement might read as follows:

> I had spent the evening drinking with friends. As it was Saturday I'd been drinking at lunch-time as well. In the evening I suppose I drank 7 or 8 pints. My friends went home before me and I started walking home alone at about 11.15 pm. I remember leaving the pub and getting to the corner of the street. The next thing I remember is waking up in hospital with head and face injuries. I had been attacked.

There may be little additional evidence to assist the Board in deciding how such injuries came about. The police evidence and the hospital medical report may assist. There may have been witnesses who found the applicant lying injured in the road. The nature of the injuries may throw some light on how they were caused, whether they were more consistent with, say, a traffic accident than with being struck by some sort of weapon. The views of the doctor who treated the injuries may be obtained on this aspect.

Although the Board will examine all the available evidence with great care, it is for the applicant to make out his case in all respects (para 25 1990, para 64 1996) and establish to the Board's satisfaction that on the balance of probabilities his injuries were attributable to a crime of violence.

Although proof before the Board is the civil burden of proof – the balance of probabilities – and not the criminal burden of proof – beyond reasonable doubt – the Board will not make an award where the cause of injury is simply not established at all, and remains merely a matter of conjecture.

(a) Injuries in the course of sport

The fact that an injury is sustained in the course of participation in sport does not necessarily take it outside the Scheme. Where the playing of the game itself carried the clear risk of injury, and injury is sustained in the ordinary course of the game, there is generally no crime and the injured party is deemed to have accepted that risk. Although one cannot generalise, it would perhaps be reasonable to expect that a batsman who is injured by a 'bouncer', and a footballer (rugby or soccer) who is injured in a tackle while he had the ball, would be unsuccessful if they applied to the Board in respect of those injuries.

The Board may, however, make an award where the injury is sustained as a consequence of a criminal assault, even if it is on the field of sport and whether or not the injury arose from an incident which might be regarded as a commonplace of the sport in question.

Accordingly the Board made an award to a player in a football match where a number of incidents in the course of the game gave rise to the assailant punching the applicant. When both parties were being restrained by team-mates, the assailant kicked the applicant in the face causing a broken nose. The incident was corroborated by the referee. The Board was satisfied that the attack was a crime of violence, and there was no question of such conduct coming within the scope of implied consent or acceptance of the risk. The fact that sport happened to be the context in which the crime occurred in no way negated the criminal nature of the assailant's actions.

(b) Conviction of assailant

The conviction of the assailant for a crime of violence against the applicant will be accepted by the Board as establishing that aspect of the applicant's claim, although the applicant still has to satisfy the Board on all other issues which may be material to his application, which may include the applicant's own conduct or convictions, and whether or not the injury merits at least the minimum award (of £1,000) which can be made under the Scheme. These aspects are all considered in subsequent chapters. In the case of sexual offences the assailant may have been convicted of indecent assault, but the application is founded upon an allegation of rape or buggery. In such cases the applicant has to make out the more serious offence before the Board if compensation is to be assessed on that basis.

(c) Immunity at law of the offender

It is convenient to consider in this context the matter of the legal incapacity of the alleged assailant in relation to the crime of violence upon which the applicant relies. Paragraph 10 of the 1996 Scheme reads as follows:

> It is not necessary for the assailant to have been convicted of a criminal offence in connection with the injury. Moreover, even where the injury is attributable to conduct within paragraph 8(a) in respect of which the assailant cannot be convicted of an offence by reason of age, insanity or diplomatic immunity, the conduct may nevertheless be treated as constituting a criminal act.

Paragraph 4 of the 1990 Scheme stated this principle as follows:

> In considering for the purposes of this paragraph whether any act is a criminal act a person's conduct will be treated as constituting an offence notwithstanding that he may not be convicted of the offence by reason of age, insanity or diplomatic immunity.

In its guidance Statement, published in April 1987, the Board commented by way of guidance on this part of the Scheme in relation to the immunity of an offender attributable to his youth:

> In cases where people are injured in assaults by children the police often take no action due to the age of the offender, for in law children below 10 years of age in England (8 years in Scotland) are considered incapable of

> committing a crime. Victims of such incidents may, however, be within the scope of the Scheme. The Board consider in each individual case whether the acts of the offender would constitute an 'assault' or some other crime of violence but for the offender's age. Much may turn upon whether the child knew what he was doing was wrong, but nevertheless went on to do it.

In relation to immunity of the offender attributable to his insanity, the Board's Statement comments that:

> as with young children, claims for injuries inflicted by persons whose state of mind makes them at law incapable of being guilty of a crime will be allowed if the act which caused the injury would have been a crime of violence if it had been committed by a sane person.

Regarding injuries inflicted by young children, the offender clearly has to be capable of the wrongful act; the inference of the above sentence of the Board's Statement in relation to child offenders appears to be that the circumstances must show that the child also had the intent to commit the wrongful act.

It should be borne in mind in these 'immunity' cases, both in respect of child offenders and offenders suffering from mental incapacity, that the Scheme does not alter the nature of 'crime' required to bring the injury within the Scheme. In particular it does not say that the wrongful act on its own will suffice. The provision in the Scheme states that the wrongful act 'will be treated as constituting an offence notwithstanding' the incapacity.

It is argued, however, that the wrongful act should only be 'treated as constituting an offence' if all the evidence of the wrongful act taken together would be sufficient to enable the Board to infer the guilty intent if the offender had the capacity to form that intent. A simple question in relation to the evidence in such cases may be sufficient: would this action if committed by an adult (or by a person of sound mind) have constituted a crime of violence? If the answer is affirmative, para 4 (1990) enables the Board – and para 10 (1996) enables the claims officer and the Appeals Panel – to find the application within the terms of the Scheme.

In considering cases where injuries are caused by the actions of children, a realistic distinction needs to be made between acts of exuberance which may arise, for example, in the course of vigorous playground games, and actions which, were they the actions of adults, would constitute crimes of violence.

From time to time, the Board considers incidents of playground injury where such a test must be applied. A rough chasing and catching game between children of similar age and size may well result in injury which would not be within the Scheme. Sometimes, however, the context of a game is used, perhaps by a bigger child, as an excuse to assault and injure a smaller child in an act of bullying or aggression. Such circumstances have to be looked at on their individual merits as they could well be within the Scheme.

Having considered the Board's treatment of 'crimes of violence' by persons who may not be convicted by reason of age, it is appropriate to look further at cases in which the offender cannot be convicted 'by reason of insanity'. Applicants whose cases fall to be considered under this part of para 4 (1990) or para 10 (1996) are most frequently nurses or other staff working in mental hospitals whose injury is sustained through the actions of patients.

The Board receives many applications from hospital staff injured by the aggressive actions of mental patients. Common examples include nurses who are punched or kicked by patients in the course of what would be regarded as deliberate assaults were it not for the mental incapacity of the assailant. These assaults come within the terms of the Scheme. Often the applications describe the assailant as a patient who is known to be aggressive and inclined to lash out at staff unprovoked.

The Board made an award to a hospital cleaner who was injured when two male mental patients were fighting in the day room, resulting in one of them falling against the door behind which the applicant was carrying out her duties. The door struck the applicant and injured her. The Board decided that the injuries were directly attributable to a crime of violence by one or other of the fighting patients.

More difficult are cases where the actions of the patient are indiscriminate due to the patient's disturbed condition, rather than a result of his intention which may be inferred (if somewhat artificially) from a seemingly deliberate attack.

Nursing cases frequently involve injury to nursing staff when bodily lifting a patient into or out of bed and into or out of the bath. In many such cases the injury is to the back, caused by some sudden action of the patient objecting to what is happening. Such cases are some of the most difficult for the Board to decide. If the actions of the patient could reasonably be construed as aggressive and comparable with an action which, if carried out by a person of sound mind, would constitute an assault, the applicant may well succeed. Where, however, the evidence indicates that the patient's action is due to, for example, the involuntary thrashing of arms or legs arising entirely from the patient's mental and physical condition, and is not in any way an action which could reasonably be described as aggressive towards or aimed at the applicant, the application would be unlikely to succeed.

As in the cases involving under-age assailants, the Scheme does not permit the applicant to succeed simply by showing that injury resulted to the applicant from the actions of a person who is immune from prosecution, without the circumstances of that injury also indicating that the actions of the offender amounted to a crime of violence, albeit by an offender who could not be convicted by reason of incapacity. For the applicant to succeed it must be appropriate for the Board or claims officer or the Appeals Panel to infer an intention (or recklessness) on the part of the person causing the injury.

The Board's twentieth report refers to a case in which a nurse sustained a broken nose when she was allegedly butted by a handicapped child aged thirteen. The single member refused the application, not being satisfied that the injury resulted from a crime of violence as opposed to an accident. At the hearing the Board was informed that the applicant was nursing the mentally subnormal child on her lap when he turned, looked at her and brought his head up into her face. She said that the child was very active and could become agitated and would then bite and butt. He could not speak and had very poor sight and hearing. At the hearing the Board rejected the application for the reason given by the single member.

The Scheme is not intended to provide compensation in cases where injury is sustained by nurses in the day-to-day care of patients whose mental state results in their acting in a violent or unpredictable way. Each individual case must be treated on its merits. A nurse who is injured by the action of a mental patient will very often be familiar with the particular patient and his or her habits and dislikes and reactions to various daily routines. An applicant's statement of facts to the Board might read as follows:

> I was working on St John's ward which is a male ward for mentally ill patients. I had worked on that ward for about six months. John Smith is one of the patients. He is a heavy man, about 15 stone. He is always aggressive and awkward at bedtime and has to be helped into bed by one of the staff. On this occasion I was helping him into bed. He was shouting and cursing and waving his arms about. When he was partly on the bed and while I was still supporting him he suddenly went inert so that his full body weight fell on me. He does this sometimes to make it difficult to get him into bed as he is so heavy. I felt a severe pain in my back. I was unable to continue work on that shift and have been off work since because of back pain.

Do these facts amount to a 'crime of violence'? With regard to the injury being caused by the offender going inert, in a different context of a police officer being injured by a prisoner under arrest going inert whilst being held by the police officer, in circumstances which indicated that the prisoner's action was deliberate and intended to injure the officer, the facts would amount to an assault. The difficulties in establishing a technical assault in such cases and whether a crime of violence has been made out were considered by the Court of Appeal in *R v Criminal Injuries Compensation Board, ex parte Penny* [1982] Crim LR 298, which is noted in Appendix 1.

In the case of the injured nurse in the example given above, the Board may conclude that the actions of the patient amounted to a crime of violence, there being evidence to indicate that the action which caused injury was intentional rather than merely involuntary or accidental and, were it the action of a person of sound mind, would be an assault.

Such cases, however, contain many variations of fact and the Board will not infer intent or recklessness where the evidence on balance of probabilities does not support it. The 'crime of violence' still has to be made out. The immunity from prosecution has to be distinguished from the crime itself not being established.

(d) Motoring and 'crime of violence'

Paragraph 11 of the 1990 Scheme deals with injuries 'attributable to traffic offences'.

Paragraph 11 of the 1996 Scheme deals with injuries 'attributable to the use of a vehicle'.

These are discussed in detail in Chapter 10. The basic principle is to exclude injuries caused by a vehicle unless the latter is used deliberately to inflict injury on any person.

(e) Dog bites

In the Guide to the (1990) Scheme published in 1994, para 15 of the Guide commented as follows:

> Injury caused by animals.
>
> Sometimes applications are made which involve attacks by animals, usually dogs. Such cases are not covered by the Scheme unless what has happened amounts to an assault as, for example, where the person in charge of a dog deliberately sets the dog upon some person, or whose failure to control a dog whom he knows to be vicious amounts to criminal recklessness, as opposed to mere negligence or carelessness.

Failure to keep a dog under control is not, in itself, a crime of violence even when injury is caused and the failure amounts to an offence – unless the applicant can satisfy the Board that the dog was, in effect, used as a weapon and was deliberately set upon the victim by the person having control of it, or, as the Guide points out, that person's actions amounted to criminal recklessness in failing to control an animal known to be vicious.

Thus an applicant who establishes that, in the course of an argument or a fight with another, the latter's dog joined in on its master's behalf and bit the applicant causing him injury, will not be entitled to an award on those facts alone. The Board has, however, made awards where the dog has been used intentionally as a means of inflicting injury. A police officer who was injured in attempting to make an arrest received an award where the owner of the dog, in resisting arrest, gave repeated and clear words of command to his dog to 'Get him Toby, get him'. The obedient Toby bit the officer in the leg causing a painful injury and a scar.

The reason behind this requirement is that where there is no crime of violence there can be no compensation even though a crime has been committed and injury has resulted. In dog-bite cases the Board or claims officer must be satisfied that the owner or controller of the dog has assaulted the applicant by means of the dog's directed attack, or by the controller's criminal recklessness, as opposed to mere carelessness or negligence.

(f) Injuries arising from arson

Paragraph 8 of the 1996 Scheme and para 4 of the 1990 Scheme expressly include arson as a crime of violence. Many applications are made by firefighters injured in the course of fighting a fire caused by arson. As arson is often very difficult to prove, such applications are assisted by the burden of proof being on the balance of probabilities, so that where there has been no prosecution of the arsonist – nor even the cause of the fire established beyond reasonable doubt – the injured firefighter can establish his claim if the evidence on balance of probabilities indicates that the fire was deliberately or recklessly started 'by persons unknown'.

The 1996 Scheme, however, makes important changes in the application of the Scheme to such cases. Paragraph 12 of the 1996 Scheme provides:

> Where an injury is sustained accidentally by a person who is engaged in:
>
> (a) any of the law-enforcement activities described in paragraph 8(c); or
>
> (b) any other activity directed to containing, limiting or remedying the consequences of a crime,
>
> compensation will not be payable unless the person injured was, at the time he sustained the injury, taking an exceptional risk which was justified in all the circumstances.

Thus the requirement of 'exceptional risk' in cases where the injury is accidental and the activity is 'directed to containing, limiting or remedying the consequences of a crime' in (b) above will catch firefighters and other persons engaged in rescue services at a fire. This will put them in a similar position to policemen or others injured accidentally while 'engaged in ... the law-enforcement activities described in paragraph 8(c)'. Paragraph 12(a) is not new as paras 4(b) and 6(d) of the 1990 Scheme already required persons injured accidentally whilst engaged in law enforcement activities to show that they were 'taking an exceptional risk which was justified in all the circumstances'. Paragraph 12(b) of the 1996 Scheme is, however, an entirely new provision.

As the treatment of applications in respect of accidental injuries arising from arson will be substantially different under the 1990 and 1996 Schemes, it is appropriate to consider them separately.

(i) Applications before 1 April 1996: the 1990 Scheme – It has to be remembered that the 1990 or earlier Schemes will govern applications lodged before 1 April 1996. The following commentary is still 'current law' so far as the Scheme is concerned in relation to pre- 1 April 1996 cases. The narrative therefore refers to the 'Board' rather than the Authority or claims officers as it is the Board which will decide cases already in the system before 1 April 1996.

Before the 1990 Scheme came into force the 1979 Scheme operated. In 1987 the Board published a 'Statement', the purpose of which was similar to the 'Guide' to the 1990 Scheme subsequently published, namely to clarify the Board's policy in certain types of cases. The Board's 1987 Statement commented in relation to arson:

> accidental injuries suffered whilst fighting a fire or escaping from a fire

> or rescuing people from a building are within the Scheme if the fire was started deliberately or recklessly.

The Statement did not form part of the Scheme; it had no legal status and did not bind the Board in deciding cases. Its purpose, stated in the headnote to it, was to provide applicants and their advisers with:

> a guide as to how the Board are likely to determine applications ... However it is emphasised that each application will be decided on its merits and what is said in this statement does not limit the discretion of an individual Board member or Board members at a hearing.

As a matter of policy, the Board has, in 'firefighter' cases, tended to interpret fairly widely the attributability of injury to the crime of arson. Many injuries to firefighters derive from falls where they are fighting the fire from positions made precarious or dangerous by the fire or by the effects of fighting the fire, such as timbers or surfaces made slippery and dangerous by quantities of water or foam from the fire-fighting appliances.

The Board's twenty-fifth report cites an application by a firefighter who attended a blaze in a lock-up garage started by arson. While fighting the fire he fell, sustaining concussion and back injuries. The single member made a full award.

The indication in the 1987 Statement that 'accidental injuries suffered whilst fighting a fire' are within the Scheme gives the individual applicant much scope for arguing his case, but it is for the Board to decide in each case when and where 'fighting a fire' started and finished. It could be argued that from hearing the alarm and sliding down the pole to his return to the station after the fire, the fire officer could be regarded as fighting a fire, and that any accidental injury which he may suffer between those two events is within the Scheme. The Board would not accept that this is a proper interpretation. Most cases before the Board involve injury to the firefighter at the scene of the fire while actively engaged in his duties of fighting the fire or rescuing persons in the affected building. The Board takes a common-sense view of the scope of the words 'fighting a fire' in each case.

In a 1989 case, a fire officer had attended the scene of a fire at a football ground. A number of appliances had attended the fire which turned out to be a minor one. When the applicant and his colleagues arrived, they ran out their hoses across the football ground in readiness but the hoses were not brought into use as the fire had already been dealt with. The applicant was walking across the grass to return to the appliance and to supervise the winding-in of the hoses when he slipped on the grass and fell, injuring his back. The Board made no award. The injury was not directly attributable to a crime of violence. The words 'directly attributable' apply to injuries attributable to arson as well as to any other crime of violence; where an injury is sustained accidentally, to come within the Scheme it must arise 'while fighting a fire' or 'rescuing persons from a building', according to the ordinary accepted meaning of tho words.

(ii) *Applications on or after 1 April 1996: The 1996 Scheme* – These cases will now be governed by para 12 of the 1996 Scheme. This provision substantially alters the situation of persons, usually officers in the fire service, who are injured accidentally while fighting fires caused by arson. They will not, as previously, merely have to prove the 'crime of violence' (arson) as the cause of the fire and that the injury was sustained in the course of fighting that fire or escaping from or rescuing people from that fire. When the injury is 'accidental', which in the nature of things many fire-fighting injuries are, such as falling or slipping in the course of fire-fighting activities, the applicant must now show that he was 'taking an exceptional risk which was justified in all the circumstances'.

'Exceptional risk' has been a requirement in respect of accidental injuries incurred in the course of law enforcement activities since the 1990 Scheme came into operation. Board members have frequently made the observation in relation to applications by police officers injured by, for example, a fall when pursuing an offender:

> The applicant's injuries were sustained accidentally. Although I can see that the officer was taking a risk (in the particular case) I cannot see how that risk can be regarded as exceptional. I therefore make no award.

The Board has taken the view in such cases that normal policing activities will frequently contain some element of risk of physical injury. When taking that 'normal level of risk', the injury resulting from it is not enough to bring the applicant within the Scheme. The risk must be 'exceptional', in some way out of the ordinary run of routine activities demanded of police officers in the course of carrying out their duties.

It is likely that claims officers of the Authority and the Appeals Panel will take a similar view in para 12(b) cases – which will for the most part be injured firefighters or persons whose jobs involve them in 'containing, limiting or remedying the consequences of a crime'.

As with accidental law enforcement cases under the 1990 Scheme, the exceptional risk must be 'justified in all the circumstances'. By way of illustration the requirements of para 12(b) would presumably be met by a firefighter who, whilst fighting a fire caused by arson, is faced with a situation in which there is known to be a person trapped within a burning building, and there is only one very dangerous course open to him with any prospect of rescuing that person, and the firefighter takes that course, sustaining accidental injury in so doing.

Far more difficult to decide will be cases where the circumstances of the fire itself make fighting it particularly difficult and hazardous and the firefighter sustains accidental injury whilst carrying out his duties according to the standard procedures of the fire service. If, for example, the injury was sustained in a fall from a slippery or precarious foothold this may not be within the Scheme as not being an 'exceptional risk'. Each case will hinge upon its own facts.

It must be kept in mind that the 'exceptional risk' rule applies only to 'accidental' injuries. If the firefighter is injured by a falling wall or timber whilst fighting a fire started by arson, or by exploding material in the burning premises, such injury would not be 'accidental' but within para 8(a) of the 1996 Scheme as 'directly attributable to a crime of violence'.

The question of 'exceptional risk' in relation to the law enforcement activities of paras 8(c) and 12(a) of the 1996 Scheme is dealt with in Chapter 3.

2. 'Sustained personal injury'

The Scheme is intended to compensate for 'personal injury'. Paragraph 17 of the 1990 Scheme, which governs all applications received by the Board before 1 April 1996, excludes damage to 'any property whatsoever arising from the injury unless the Board are satisfied that the property was relied upon by the victim as a physical aid'. The Board thus allows claims under the 1990 Scheme for such items as spectacles and hearing aids. Paragraph 35(a) of the 1996 Scheme allows, under the heading 'special expenses', compensation in respect of 'property or equipment ... on which [the applicant] relied as a physical aid, where the loss or damage was a direct consequence of the injury'.

(a) Personal injury

Personal injury includes mental injury as well as physical injury. For an applicant to succeed in relation to 'mental injury', distress and emotional upset arising from a frightening and unpleasant experience are not in themselves sufficient. In *McLoughlin v O'Brian* [1983] AC 410, Lord Bridge stated:

> The first hurdle which a plaintiff claiming damages (for nervous shock) ... must surmount is to establish that he is suffering not merely grief, distress or any other normal emotion, but a positive psychiatric illness.

The 1990 Scheme included mental injury as well as physical injury. That Scheme did not, however, provide a definition of mental injury and the Board is guided by common law decisions, such as the case cited above, in applications governed by that Scheme. The 1996 Scheme, however, sets out expressly in para 9 the precise scope and limitations of 'mental injury' cases, traditionally referred to as 'nervous shock' cases by the common law. The rules set out in para 9 of the 1996 Scheme govern such cases.

It is appropriate to observe that the changes effected by the 1996 Scheme in the basic principles of deciding compensation for criminal injury were arrived at in two stages. The now-abortive 1994 Tariff Scheme would, if it had been effectively brought into operation, have achieved a clean break from the common law basis of all previous Schemes up to and including the 1990 Scheme, and put in its place a rigid but hopefully clear-cut set of rules by which the amount of compensation for specified injuries was fixed.

The abortive 1994 Tariff Scheme attempted not only a codification of common law damages, so that the amount of compensation for a particular injury could be decided by reference to a fixed tariff of awards, but also would have swept away the need under earlier Schemes for complex common law rules to be considered. The many heads of claim under the common law would have been replaced in their entirety by the one fixed figure for the injury.

The 1994 Scheme was attacked at two different levels:

(i) the political argument which claimed that it was unfair in its treatment of innocent victims of violent crime, and

(ii) the legal challenge on the grounds that it had been unlawfully brought into effect.

The political attack gathered momentum during the twelve months or so that the legal challenge took to proceed through the Court of Appeal and finally the Judicial Committee of the House of Lords, whose decision in February 1995 rejected the means of implementation of the 1994 Tariff Scheme as unlawful. By the time of this final decision killing off the 1994 Scheme, the political debate in the media and in Parliament had reached a point at which a number of alterations would have been needed to render a new Scheme in its place generally acceptable. The result is the 1996 Scheme, which brings back, in more or less codified form, certain loss of earnings and expenses, including future loss and cost of care. These are dealt with in a later chapter.

The 1990 and earlier Schemes did not attempt any definition of 'mental injury' but the Board has adopted the above statement of Lord Bridge in *McLoughlin v O'Brian* as the proper test in cases where applicants claim compensation for mental injury under the Scheme. There must be 'a positive psychiatric illness' proved by medical evidence.

(b) Mental injury – requirements under the 1996 Scheme

The 1996 Scheme has gone a step further by defining the Authority's requirements if a claim 'for mental injury alone' is to succeed. The relevant conditions for such a claim to succeed are set out in para 9 of the 1996 Scheme in the following terms:

> For the purposes of this Scheme, personal injury includes physical injury (including fatal injury), mental injury (that is, a medically recognised psychiatric or psychological illness) and disease (that is, a medically recognised illness or condition). Mental injury or disease may either result directly from the physical injury or occur without any physical injury, but compensation will not be payable for mental injury alone unless the applicant:
>
> (a) was put in reasonable fear of immediate physical harm to his own person; or

(b) had a close relationship of love and affection with another person at the time when that person sustained physical (including fatal) injury directly attributable to conduct within paragraph 8(a), (b) or (c), and
  (i) that relationship still subsists (unless the victim has since died), and
  (ii) the applicant either witnessed and was present on the occasion when the other person sustained the injury, or was closely involved in its immediate aftermath; or

(c) was the non-consenting victim of a sexual offence (which does not include a victim who consented in fact but was deemed in law not to have consented); or

(d) being a person employed in the business of a railway, either witnessed and was present on the occasion when another person sustained physical (including fatal) injury directly attributable to an offence of trespass on a railway, or was closely involved in its immediate aftermath. Paragraph 12 below does not apply where mental injury is sustained as described in this sub-paragraph.

Paragraph 9 concludes by stating that para 12 does not apply to mental injury claims under sub-para (d) – railway cases – so that where the mental injury has been 'sustained accidentally' in such cases it does not have to be shown that the injured party was 'taking an exceptional risk' in order to come within the Scheme.

The 1996 Scheme follows the common law requirement that a medically proved mental illness must be established if compensation is to be paid for the mental aspect of injury.

Each part of para 9 will be examined in due course.

It is necessary with this as with other parts of the Scheme to look at both the 1990 and the 1996 Schemes, as they are not the same in all respects.

(c) Mental injury or nervous shock – requirements under the 1990 Scheme

At 31 March 1996 there were about 100,000 applications with the Board awaiting a decision, either by the single member or at a hearing. As the 1990 Scheme applies to these pre- 1 April 1996 applications, the law as it stands under the 1990 Scheme needs to be examined side by side with the 1996 Scheme rules. The next part of this chapter looks at the law in relation to 1990 Scheme cases.

The law relating to personal injury claims involving 'nervous shock', as the common law has always termed them, or 'mental injury' as is now more appropriate in cases considered under the Criminal Injuries Compensation Scheme, has developed rapidly in recent years. The case of *McLoughlin v O'Brian* was a House of Lords decision in 1982. Since then, numerous cases have further refined the law of damages for nervous shock. Disasters such as the sinking of the *Herald of Free Enterprise* at Zeebrugge, the Kings Cross fire and the Hillsborough football tragedy have resulted in much litigation and a decision of the House of Lords that sets out the law in respect of relatives of persons killed or injured who have suffered mental illness as a result.

In such cases, medical evidence has been adduced of mental illness suffered by survivors whose symptoms included depression, flashbacks, inability to cope with work or domestic tasks, complete loss of interest in previous hobbies and activities and 'survivor guilt' – the sense of guilt at having survived a disaster when loved ones have been killed. The term 'post-traumatic stress disorder' is used to described this type of illness.

For claims which have in the past been categorised as nervous shock cases to come within the Scheme as an injury, the grief and distress must exceed what would be regarded as normal grief and distress caused by, for example, the death of a loved one, and must, in the words of Lord Bridge quoted on page 26 above, amount to a positive psychiatric illness. This will be a question of fact for the Board to decide, based upon the medical and other evidence of the applicant's mental condition.

Victims of violence very often suffer symptoms of diminished self-confidence and capacity to enjoy life in social and recreational activities. Statements such as 'I no longer go out in the evenings'; 'I never go out after dark unless I am with a friend'; 'I have given up sporting activities as I no longer have the confidence'; 'I am always nervous when I am out as I now know that this can happen'; 'I freeze if someone is following me' appear in applications over and over again. It is one of the effects of violent crime that the emotional and social damage lingers long after the physical cuts and fractures have healed.

In 1990 Scheme cases the type of loss indicated by the above comments will form part of the overall damage compensated under the legal heading of 'pain and suffering and loss of amenity', although the measure of damage will not generally be greater than the level of compensation deemed appropriate for the physical injury suffered, as this level of emotional and social loss is an almost inevitable consequence of a violent unprovoked attack resulting in physical injury.

Outside this majority category, however, are the cases where a distinct mental illness is established by medical evidence. In such cases the Board can assess and award the compensation appropriate to that injury (provided of course that it is directly attributable to a crime of violence), whether or not physical injury has also been suffered.

A 40-year-old divorced woman made application to the Board in relation to several incidents over a period of three years. Because of the nature of the incidents, the Board treated them as one application. On one occasion her flat was entered, all her clothes were slashed and her furniture damaged. She received death threats and as a result, twice entered hospital for psychiatric treatment. She moved house to escape the harassment but without success. She received a false telephone call to say that her son was ill. Her windows were smashed. Her dog was poisoned. She was subjected to continual harassment. The applicant suffered a nervous breakdown and again entered hospital for psychiatric treatment. The incidents had throughout been reported to the police. The Board regarded the threats to kill as a crime of violence under section 6 of the Offences Against the Person Act 1861 and made a full award.

Recent (1996) decisions in the criminal courts based upon allegations of 'stalking' and 'harassment' have shown that, as the law now stands, no crime, and certainly no crime of violence, is made out unless these activities amount to a recognised offence such as grievous bodily harm, with the mental injury being proved. In *R v Burstow*, Court of Appeal, Criminal Division, reported in *The Times*, 30 July 1996, the Court of Appeal held that a 'stalker' could be convicted of a section 20 (grievous bodily harm) offence where he had not inflicted physical violence and the grievous harm was of a psychiatric nature.

In *R v Ireland*, decided on 14 May 1996, the Court of Appeal Criminal Division commented upon the principles whereby the making of telephone calls may constitute an assault for the purposes of section 47 of the Offences Against the Person Act 1861. (See Appendix 1.)

Where the applicant has proved a mental injury directly attributable to the crime of violence, there will be compensation in 1990 Scheme cases for 'pain and suffering and loss of amenity' as in cases of physical injury.

(d) Mental injury – the test applied by the 1990 and 1996 Schemes

It has been seen that both the 1990 and 1996 Schemes apply the same medical test for establishing the existence of the mental injury. The 1996 Scheme states that mental injury is 'a medically recognised psychiatric or psychological illness'. This is essentially a re-statement of the *McLoughlin v O'Brian* test laid down by Lord Bridge and adopted by the Board in 1990 Scheme cases. In both 1990 Scheme cases and 1996 Scheme cases, the Board and the Authority and the Appeals Panel are working on the same definition of mental injury.

3. 'Directly attributable'

For an injury to qualify for compensation it must be directly attributable to a crime of violence or to the apprehension of an offender or the attempted prevention of an offence or to the giving of help to a constable engaged in any such activity or to an offence of trespass on a railway.

In the day-to-day working of the Scheme the words 'directly attributable' are given their normal meaning in everyday language. The words are clearly meant to require a clear causal link between the crime of violence and the injury which is suffered by the applicant. The term 'directly attributable' is not a term of art in the common law, which speaks of 'remoteness of damage' and whether the damage suffered was 'reasonably foreseeable' as a consequence of the action complained of. The Board had to decide, when the Scheme came into existence, the meaning of 'directly attributable' in each case before it without guidance from the courts.

In the Board's 1977 Statement issued for guidance in the interpretation of the 1969 Scheme, the Board commented as follows:

1. Personal injury is directly attributable to any of the matters set out in paragraph 5 of the (1969) Scheme (crime of violence; apprehension of an offender) if such matter is, on the basis of all the relevant facts, a substantial cause of personal injury. It does not need to be the sole cause. The word 'substantial' means that 'the relationship between the particular cause and the personal injury is such that a reasonable person applying his common sense would fairly and seriously regard it as being a cause'.
2. If an intervening cause is the negligence or wrongful act of the applicant or a third party, the injury may still be attributable to the original event and give rise to a claim for compensation. It only ceases to be so when the intervening event is so powerful a cause as to reduce the original offence to a piece of history.

The wording of the guidance Statement at that time took into account the decision of Lord Denning, then Master of the Rolls, in *R v Criminal Injuries Compensation Board, ex parte Ince* [1973] 3 All ER 808 (see also Appendix 1, page 271). In that case, the death of a police officer in a car accident while proceeding to investigate a reported burglary was held to be directly attributable to the attempted prevention of an offence, even though the accident was the result of his own carelessness and, as it transpired, the information was false and only a lesser offence was about to be committed.

In its report issued in 1986 on the proposals for a statutory scheme, the working party commented: 'Following the decision of the Court of Appeal in *R v CICB ex parte Ince* it is clear that the word "directly" has become virtually without effect'. It recommended that the then proposed statutory Scheme should include a more stringent test of remoteness 'which clearly conveys the need for a very close and immediate link between the offence and the consequent injury'.

This recommendation has not been brought into operation. Both the 1990 and 1996 Schemes, like their predecessors, include the words 'directly attributable' as the only specific wording in the Scheme to assist the Board and the Authority and applicants regarding the tests of remoteness and causation which must be applied in every case.

The Board and the Authority must occasionally consider the proper limits of a claim by an applicant who, having suffered an injury from an act of criminal violence, obtains medical advice or treatment which is erroneous and exacerbates rather than improves the situation.

Where such a situation arises in an action for damages brought in the courts in respect of the initial injury, for example by an employee suing his employers for failure to provide a safe system of work or by a motorist injured as a consequence of the negligence of another driver, the court has to decide whether the element of medical error arising in the subsequent treatment of the initial injury constitutes a major new intervening factor (*novus actus interveniens*) for which the original wrongdoer should not be liable, or is merely a risk of medical complication, including, for example, the risk of error in diagnosis or treatment, which essentially arises as one of the risks created by the original injury.

The common law test whether the further damage or injury is recoverable from the original wrongdoer is the test of remoteness of damage. The authorities on the common law test of remoteness suggest that in terms of medical error the culpable negligence of a surgeon - for example in removing the wrong finger or limb - would not be regarded as a risk to which the injured party was exposed by the original injury. The consequences of such gross negligence by the surgeon might not be recoverable, it seems, as this aspect of the loss would flow from the later supervening negligence of the surgeon (*novus actus interveniens*) which would break the chain of causation between the original injury and the loss resulting from the subsequent negligence of another party.

The common law test is one of foreseeability, which is not the same as the test of 'direct attributability' under the Scheme. The common law has to consider in such cases whether the new supervening act, negligent or otherwise, of the third party is such that the chain of causation between the original wrongful act and the further loss flowing from the subsequent action of the third party is broken. If it is, the further loss is too remote and not reasonably foreseeable as a risk created by the original wrongful act.

On the other hand, if the subsequent event, negligent or otherwise, of the third party is not such a supervening act, but is to be regarded as an occurrence, the risk of which was itself reasonably foreseeable as a consequence of the original wrongful act, then the loss flowing from the subsequent event is not too remote, and damages for that loss are recoverable from the original wrongdoer in addition to damages for the original injury or loss.

Under the Scheme, however, the Board and the Authority must decide whether each and every loss subsequent to the original criminal injury is directly attributable. A series of High Court decisions has made it clear that the Board, and this applies equally to the Authority and the Appeals Panel, is to reach its decision on the basis of whether the injury was *directly attributable* to the crime of violence and not whether the injury was *reasonably foreseeable* as a consequence of the crime of violence.

It might fairly be argued that the requirement of direct attributability is a narrower and stricter test in deciding the scope of the loss for which compensation is payable under the Scheme than the common law test of foreseeability. A consequence further down the chain of events which follows the original incident may well not be regarded in common-sense terms as directly attributable to the original incident, but may nevertheless be regarded as reasonably foreseeable, in that the original incident has created a new situation in which the victim is exposed to new foreseeable risks, such as medical error in the treatment of the original injuries.

The case of *Ince* (see above) and others discussed later in this chapter indicate that the word 'directly' is, in certain circumstances at least, to be construed widely – and that supervening negligence by a third party or even of the injured party himself will not necessarily exclude the injury resulting from that subsequent act from being 'directly attributable' to the original incident which brought the claim within the terms of the Scheme, and thus recoverable by way of compensation under the Scheme.

(a) Decisions under the 1990 Scheme in relation to nervous shock

In the first edition of this book under the heading 'nervous shock' a number of leading cases were considered in detail as these gave some guidance on the common law principles which assisted the Board and applicants and their advisers on the application of the words 'directly attributable' to cases where the applicant has suffered mental injury. It was acknowledged that whilst the wording of the Scheme, in stating that compensation was payable in respect of personal injury 'directly attributable' to a crime of violence, was putting forward a different principle from the common law test which requires the injury to be 'reasonably foreseeable', there was some common ground as well as differences between the two principles. The Board therefore looked to the common law in such cases for guidance on what were the limits of 'directly attributable' injuries properly compensatable under the Scheme.

The case of *McLoughlin v O'Brian* has already been referred to in relation to the legal definition of what is a 'mental injury'. That case also defined the principles on which common law claims for mental injury arising from witnessing or coming upon the injury of another should be decided. These rules were based upon the common law principle of what was or was not 'reasonably foreseeable' as a consequence of the original wrongful act of the defendant in that case. They were also the subject of a decision of the House of Lords in the Hillsborough case of *Alcock v Chief Constable of South Yorkshire Police* [1992] 1 AC 310.

The Board must decide on the facts of each case whether the injury is directly attributable – and in interpreting the wording of the Scheme, the Board should take into account the particular circumstances of the applicant's injury and whether or not it falls within the purpose and spirit of the Scheme. It has been observed judicially that the 1990 and earlier *ex gratia* Schemes are not statutes and should not be treated or interpreted as if they were (Lawton LJ, *R v CICB, ex parte Webb* [1987] 1 QB 74) The decision of the Board in one case does not constitute a precedent in another. Any Board decision which is referred to when considering another case can, at best, be only an indication of how the Board saw the facts of that particular case in the context of the Scheme.

The argument that 'directly attributable' is narrow and restrictive if one considers the ordinary use of the word 'direct' in everyday language must contend with the decision of the Court of Appeal in *R v CICB, ex parte Ince* in which Lord Denning made clear that 'directly attributable' did not mean 'solely attributable' and that an injury might still be attributable and give rise to a claim for compensation even if the intervening cause was the negligence or wrongful act of the injured person or a third party.

The view has been expressed that the very considerable scope thus given to the words 'directly attributable' has resulted in the word 'directly' becoming virtually redundant. It is submitted that this is not the effect of *Ince*.

The decision in *Ince* was a clear indication from the Court of Appeal that in certain circumstances an intervening act, such as the negligence of the applicant or a third party, did not prevent an injury from being 'directly attributable' to the particular cause which would bring the application within the terms of the Scheme – which in *Ince* was the investigation by a police officer of a reported burglary.

The difficulties in deciding what is or is not directly attributable in such cases as nervous shock remain. It is submitted that the Board is not required by the decision of *Ince* to regard the word 'directly' as adding little to the meaning of 'attributable'.

The Board has still to apply the test of directness. Although as a Court of Appeal decision *Ince* cannot be regarded merely as a decision on its own particular facts, it should also not be regarded as having established more than the principle that 'directly' attributable does not mean 'solely' attributable, and that the presence of another cause in the events resulting in injury does not remove the primary cause from being what a layman might call the 'real' cause. In *Ince* the court decided that the real cause of the applicant's injury was his being called upon to 'apprehend a suspected offender', in the course of which he came by his injuries.

In an application decided by the Board in 1988 the mother of a murdered child sought compensation for nervous shock. The medical evidence established that she suffered a prolonged depressive adjustment reaction – 'a positive psychiatric illness' – which satisfied that aspect of a nervous shock claim. The circumstances were that the child, aged five years, had disappeared from a funfair on 24 June and her decomposing body was found on 18 July, having laid at the point where it was found for four to five days.

The single member of the Board who decided the case on the papers made no award and stated:

> In order to found a claim in respect of reaction to the death of a relative it is necessary to show either that the applicant was within sight or sound of the event or present in the immediate aftermath.
>
> Grief upon learning of the death of a relative, however tragic the circumstances, cannot found an independent claim.

The Board member had applied the *McLoughlin v O'Brian* test which is a test based upon the question of foreseeability. The decision would appear to indicate that the Board member found as a fact that not only had the applicant not received her injury as a consequence of being within sight or sound of the event, but also had not come upon the 'immediate aftermath' as had the mother in that other case.

The applicant requested a hearing. Counsel for the applicant submitted that the common law tests of foreseeability and duty of care were not the appropriate ones and that the two questions needing to be asked under the Scheme were:

(i) Is the applicant suffering from an 'injury' within the meaning of the Scheme? and

(ii) If so, is it 'directly attributable' within the meaning of the Scheme?

He referred to *O'Dowd v Secretary of State for Northern Ireland* (1982). In that case the applicants for compensation were close relatives of persons murdered in a shooting incident; as a result, they had suffered nervous shock. The case turned upon the meaning of the words 'directly attributable', which are also contained in the Scheme for criminal injury compensation applying to Northern Ireland. The cases reviewed by the Appeal Court included *McLoughlin v O'Brian* and three High Court decisions where a decision of the Board had been the subject of judicial review: *R v CICB ex parte Clowes* (1977), *R v CICB ex parte Ince* (1973) and *R v CICB ex parte Schofield* (1971) – these are all considered in more detail in Appendix 1.

The questions posed for the decision of the Appeal Court of Northern Ireland were:

(i) whether under the provisions of the Scheme an injury can only be considered as *directly attributable* to a criminal offence if the applicant for compensation was present at the scene of the crime at the time of the commission of the crime and was directly injured physically or was injured mentally or emotionally by personal perception of the crime;

(ii) if the answer to question (i) is no, whether the applicant was on the facts of the case entitled to compensation.

The arguments against the injuries of the applicants being regarded as directly attributable were largely based upon the public policy consideration that unless the court limited 'direct attributability' to injury directly caused by personal perception of the crime ('within sight and sound'), 'the area of compensatability would be indefinitely and unacceptably extended'.

However, the arguments for the applicants carried the day. The court found that in the authorities before it 'the learned judges ... were ... speaking of the effective cause and not, in principle, confining their outlook to the 'immediate' cause, as meaning the proximate cause with no act intervening between the *causa causans* and the damage' (*per* Lord Lowry).

On the question of the need in terms of public policy in any given case to reconcile the logic of causation with the need to draw the line beyond which liability does not run, Lord Lowry continued:

> This brings me to *McLoughlin v O'Brian* ... I resist the temptation to comment at length on the interesting and thought-provoking speeches of their lordships; the main point for present purposes is that, *even at common*

> *law* (where the need to prove *foreseeability* and the possible resort to *public policy* considerations confront a plaintiff *in a way in which they cannot obstruct a criminal injury claimant*) the need for the claimant's initial presence at the scene of the disaster in nervous shock cases has been consigned to the lumber room of rejected legal fallacies.

Quoting Lord Reid in *Stapley v Gypsum Mines Ltd* (1953), Lord Lowry continued:

> If there is any valid logical or scientific theory of causation it is quite irrelevant in this connection. In a court of law this question must be decided as a properly instructed and reasonable jury would decide it ... The question must be determined by applying common sense to the facts of each particular case ...
>
> It is safe to say that an act can be an effective cause (*causa causans*) of damage, even if it is preceded, accompanied or followed by another act (whether negligent or not) of the injured party or a third party; whether the act complained of is a *causa causans* is a question of fact and degree.

This last passage appears to incorporate the principle established by Lord Denning's judgment in *Ince* already referred to above.

His lordship in *O'Dowd* also made clear that the authorities prevented him from placing a limit on the 'ambit of compensatability'. To do so would be contrary to the authorities, and his lordship could 'discover from the language of the legislation no criterion by which to decide what is the limit to be imposed on the meaning of the words "directly attributable". If a limit is to be prescribed it must therefore be devised by Parliament and not guessed at by the court'.

The Board hearing the application of the mother of the murdered girl, having considered the authorities and arguments submitted on her behalf, decided that the application came within the Scheme and made a full award.

The decision in *O'Dowd v Secretary of State for Northern Ireland* is not an English authority, being a decision of the Appeal Court of Northern Ireland in respect of an application under the compensation scheme applying in Northern Ireland. It is, however, a judicial decision upon the meaning of the words 'directly atttributable' which are common to both schemes. In arriving at its decision the court reviewed the decisions of the English courts by way of judicial review in relation to the Scheme applying in Great Britain, as well as the leading English cases relating to nervous shock, remoteness and causation.

The Northern Ireland court decided that it was not appropriate to place limits upon the 'ambit of compensatability'. It was also the court's view that as criminal injury compensation claims were not restricted by the common law rule of foreseeability and the questions of public policy which confront a plaintiff at common law, there were even fewer obstacles in the way of the applicant under the Scheme (regarding such matters as remoteness and causation) than faced a common law plaintiff. Moreover, common law plaintiffs now have the benefit of the broad scope of liability firmly established by their lordships in *McLoughlin v O'Brian*, so that a restricted class of near relatives can recover damages for nervous shock resulting from either directly experiencing the injury to a child or a spouse (within sight or sound of the incident), or coming upon the immediate aftermath which for this purpose is regarded as part of the incident itself.

More recently the Divisional Court in July 1994 decided in the case of *R v CICB, ex parte Johnson* that the court was bound by a decision of the Court of Appeal in November 1982, *R v CICB, ex parte Parsons*, and that had it been necessary in deciding the case, should have viewed the case of *O'Dowd* (referred to above) 'as authority of the most persuasive kind'.

The judgment in *Johnson's* case has given a clear indication that the Board has to decide what is or is not 'directly attributable' to the original crime of violence and that tests of reasonable foreseeability are not the proper basis of the Board's decisions under the Scheme.

In that case the applicant had suffered a shock-induced psychiatric illness as a consequence of discovering the recently murdered body of a friend lying on the floor in the friend's home. She had a key and let herself in to her friend's home and found that her friend 'had been violently killed' with signs of a violent struggle. The initial decision by the single Board member was stated as follows:

> I am not satisfied that the applicant's illness was directly attributable to a crime of violence - para 4(a).

The applicant requested a hearing and lodged a psychiatric report. On reconsidering the case the single board member again refused the application stating:

> The report from the psychiatrist does not affect the question of attributability. The applicant's illness has been caused by the discovery of her friend's body and was therefore, in my opinion, only indirectly attributable to the crime of violence.

The applicant was still dissatisfied with this decision and through her solicitors requested a hearing in the following terms:

> We respectfully submit that the member of the Board who adjudicated over our client's application has erred in his finding that our client's illness is only indirectly attributable to the crime of violence. Undoubtedly, had the applicant not discovered her friend's brutally murdered body, she may not have suffered the psychiatric condition catalogued by the medical report but certainly if the murder had never taken place it would appear our client was unlikely to have suffered from any condition at all. In our view the act of finding the body is not so removed from the murder itself so as to break the causal link between the actual violence committed upon our client's friend and our client's subsequent psychiatric condition.

The applicant accepted that if the finding of the body was of itself an act so unconnected with the murder as to be a supervening act which therefore broke the causal link between the initial violence and the applicant's condition, the condition suffered would not directly be attributable to the murder. The applicant, however, did not accept that this was the case and contended that it was only reasonable to assume, following a murder where the victim is left lying on her own living room floor, that the body is likely to be discovered, and that such discovering was an integral part of the whole murder scenario – so much so, it was submitted, that it must be linked directly and form part of the initial violence.

The renewed application was heard by three members of the Board. The application was again refused. The hearing Board's decision was given in the following terms:

> The applicant claimed to have suffered psychiatric illness as a result of finding the body of a murdered woman sometime after the crime had been committed. Having considered the authorities placed before the Board, they concluded that in the light of *Alcock and others v The Chief Constable of South Yorkshire Police* that where the injury alleged is psychiatric, in order that it should be directly attributable to a crime of violence it is necessary to consider whether the victim has a sufficiently proximate relationship with the immediate victim of the crime within the definition provided by the case. On the evidence the Board were not so satisfied.

The applicant in *Johnson's* case also cited the decision of the Court of Appeal in *R v CICB, ex parte Parsons*, reported in *The Times* on 25 November 1982. In that case the applicant had suffered a shock-related psychiatric condition following his discovering the decapitated body of a man who had committed suicide by lying on the line on which he was driving his train. In their written reasons for their decision in the *Parsons* case the Board stated that one of its conclusions was that:

> We were not satisfied that it was reasonably foreseeable that a person who found the dead man's body, which may have been lying on the line for a considerable time, would suffer personal injuries in the form of nervous shock or depression as a result of doing so. Accordingly we considered that these injuries were too remote a cause of and were not directly attributable to a crime of violence,

and thus not within the Scheme. The court considered in detail the earlier Court of Appeal case of *R v CICB, ex parte Ince* and the judgments of Lord Denning and Megaw LJ in that case on the meaning of 'directly attributable'. Megaw LJ had stated in the case of *Ince* (at page 815):

> First, there is the question of the meaning of the phrase 'directly attributable to'. In my judgment, personal injury is directly attributable to any of the matters (crime of violence, arrest of an offender, attempted prevention of an offence, or any of the other matters set out in paragraph 5 of the [1969] Scheme), if such matter is, on the basis of all the relevant facts, a substantial cause of personal injury. It does not need to be the sole cause. By the word 'substantial' I mean that the relationship between the particular cause and the personal injury is such that a reasonable person, applying his common sense, would fairly and seriously regard it as being a cause.

Counsel for the Board in the Divisional Court in the *Parsons* case conceded that reasonable foreseeability was not a test under the Criminal Injuries Compensation Scheme and that the Scheme was not on all fours with the liability at common law. The court accepted that this was so,

Glidewell J commenting:

> It may be thought strange that it is not, but the Scheme could specifically so be worded as to ensure that it was if that were the intention of those responsible for the administration of the Scheme, but quite clearly the phraseology of the Scheme does not attempt to import the criteria for liability in tort.

The Divisional Court concluded 'that in this case the Board were wrong and that they should have concluded that the injuries to this applicant were directly attributable to the crime of violence, in other words, that it was not too remote' and accordingly quashed the Board's decision. The Court of Appeal upheld the decision of Glidewell J.

It has to be said that the case of *Parsons* was a 'railway suicide' case which also involved argument on whether an offence of 'endangering the safety of any person conveyed ... upon a railway' under section 34 of the Offences Against the Person Act 1861 was a 'crime of violence for the purpose of the Scheme, which point was later ruled on by the Court of Appeal and finally resolved by the addition, in the 1990 Scheme, of para 4(c), so that injuries directly attributable 'to an offence of trespass on a railway' were within the Scheme.

The *Parsons* case, however, in citing the case of *Ince*, made very clear that common law rules of foreseeability did not apply to the Scheme. In *Johnson's* case, Kay J decided that he was bound by the decision of the Court of Appeal in *Parsons* that 'the test of foreseeability plays no part in that Scheme' (quoting Cumming-Bruce LJ in that case). The learned judge having concluded that he was bound by the decision in *Parsons*, and having regarded *O'Dowd* 'as authority of the most persuasive kind', concluded that 'it is quite impossible to distinguish the facts in the present case (*Johnson*) in any way that would permit a different outcome' from the decision in the *Parsons* case and quashed the Board's decision 'since there had been an error on a point of law' and sent the application back to the Board for reconsideration.

One further observation of the learned judge in *Johnson's* case is of particular interest in this context. Having restated the need to establish firstly the injury, the psychiatric illness, and secondly that that illness 'was caused by the finding of the body', the learned judged stated:

> Whilst foreseeability is in no way the test for entitlement to compensation, clearly the less foreseeable a consequence of an event is, the more difficult it may be to establish the necessary causal link. Thus it would not be improper for the Board to have in mind foreseeability in determining whether the evidence established causation in a case such as this.

The reference to causation in this passage of the judgment is, it is submitted, by way of emphasising the principles of 'causation' made clear in the cases of *Parsons* and *Ince* already discussed.

If one were to attempt a summary of essential meaning of 'directly attributable', one could not do better than to refer to the passage in the judgment of Megaw LJ in *Ince's* case already quoted.

(b) *Provisions of the 1996 Scheme in relation to mental injury or nervous shock*

As has already been stated, the 1996 Scheme, para 9, goes further towards a definition of what will be a compensatable mental injury than any previous scheme, all of which required principles of common law to be drawn in to clarify the Scheme's effect.

The 1996 Scheme, para 9, defines the scope and the conditions of claims for mental injury from 1 April 1996:

1. The mental injury must be a 'medically recognised psychiatric or psychological illness'. In practice the Authority will require medical evidence which fully makes out such injury to be present before an award will be made in respect of it. Showing some of the symptoms consistent with mental injury will not be sufficient unless the medical evidence establishes in clear terms the existence of an attributable recognised psychiatric illness.
2. The mental injury may result from the physical injuries suffered by the applicant himself or herself, or occur without any physical injury.
3. Where the 'mental injury alone' is suffered, i.e. without accompanying physical injuries, the 1996 Scheme, para 9 lays down specific rules which the evidence must satisfy before an award for that mental injury can be made.
4. The conditions which must be satisfied before compensation can be awarded for 'mental injury alone' are in four categories.
   (a) The first category comprises cases where the applicant must have been put in reasonable fear of immediate physical harm to his or her own person.
   (b) The second category includes cases where the applicant has a close relationship of love and affection with another person who sustains a physical injury (including fatal injury) directly attributable to a crime of violence within para 8(a) (or to law enforcement activity or trespass on a railway within para 8(b) or (c)).
   For this category of applicant to succeed, he or she must either have witnessed and been present on the occasion when the other person sustained the injury or been closely involved in its immediate aftermath.
   (c) The third category of case in which 'mental injury alone' is sufficient comprises those applicants who are the non-consenting victims of sexual offences, subject to the exclusion of 'a victim who consented in fact' but was deemed in law not to have consented.
   (d) The fourth category includes 'a person employed in the business of a railway' who:
      (i) either witnessed and was present on the occasion when

another person sustained physical injury (including fatal injury) directly attributable to an offence of trespass on a railway, or

(ii) was closely involved in its immediate aftermath.

Paragraphs 1 and 2 above are clear and straightforward. The rules relating to 'mental injury alone' in 3 and 4 may be clarified by further comments.

The first important point to note is that the categories of cases in which compensation may be paid for 'mental injury alone' (i.e., the claimant himself not having also suffered physical injuries) are exclusively the six categories of cases set out below. Unless a person who suffers 'mental injury alone' can show that his injury comes within one of these six categories the application for compensation will fail. The six categories are:

(i) (at 4(a) above) – primary victim is not physically injured but is made ill by fear of physical injury to his own person (para 9(a));

(ii) (at 4(b) above, first leg) – victim is present and witnesses physical injury to a loved one (para 9(b)(ii));

(iii) (at 4(b) above, second leg) – victim is not present but is closely involved in the immediate aftermath of a loved one being physically injured (para 9(b)(ii)). Such cases might include the mother of an injured child coming upon her or him shortly after the incident and giving first aid or discovering or identifying the child's body;

(iv) (at 4(c) above) – victim is the non-consenting victim of a sexual offence (which the Scheme states does not include a victim who consented in fact but was deemed in law not to have consented) (para 9(c));

(v) (at 4(d) above, first leg) – victim is employed in the business of a railway and is present and witnesses someone sustaining physical injury (fatal or otherwise) directly attributable to an offence of trespass on a railway (which includes the so-called 'railway suicide' cases) (para 9(d));

(vi) (at 4(d) above, second leg) – victim is employed in the business of a railway and, although the victim is not 'present'; he or she is closely involved in the 'immediate aftermath' of the event in question (para 9(d)).

Thus, on the face of the words used by the Scheme at para 9(b)(ii), it would appear that the mother who becomes mentally ill on learning that her child has been sexually abused but not physically injured is not within the Scheme, even if the child is also suffering a psychiatric illness as a result of the abuse. However, the disclosure of the past abuse may possibly be regarded as the 'immediate aftermath' where the mother is then 'closely involved' with her child in the medical and legal procedures which follow the disclosure. The parent who becomes mentally ill through fear for a child's safety where a child is threatened with physical harm in the parent's presence, or is abducted, but in fact suffers no physical injury, is also, on the face of it, outside the Scheme on the basis that mental injury induced by fear of immediate physical harm to another, even a loved one, is not within the express wording of the 1996 Scheme. Again, the Authority may regard actions which represent the threat of physical harm to the child as crimes of violence and sufficient to bring the application within the terms of the Scheme.

The Passenger on the platform who becomes mentally ill after seeing a 'railway suicide' is outside the Scheme unless he is a railway employee.

Paragraph 9(a) covers the 'primary' victim who is himself made mentally ill by fear of himself being injured. Examples include a woman who escapes from a man who attempts to rape her whilst she is walking home alone at night by fighting him off and running home to safety. She sustains no physical injury but subsequently develops a psychiatric illness proved by medical evidence to be directly attributable to the attack. The fear must be 'reasonable'; an appropriate reaction on the part of the applicant to the situation in which she finds herself. The fear must be of 'immediate' physical harm – such as a householder threatened by an armed burglar in his home, or a cashier threatened by a firearm in the course of a robbery.

Paragraph 9(b) refers to the 'secondary' victim. The first leg of para 9(b) refers to someone who is physically present within sight and sound of physical injury being sustained by someone with whom the secondary victim has 'a close relationship of love and affection'. Examples of the latter will include husband and wife and parent and child, although other relationships not necessarily involving a family tie may be included if, on the facts, the strong emotional tie is proved. It may well be that authorities by way of decisions in the courts will be cited by applicants and their advisers to flesh out this brief definition of relationships which come within the scope of this provision. A 'close relationship of love and affection' is a question of fact to be established by evidence in each case. A grandparent, for example, may be on close affectionate terms with the victim and thus qualify, but equally may be a grandparent whose life and affections have been quite unconnected with the victim who would therefore not qualify. In addition, the relationship must have been 'a close relationship of love and affection' *at the time* when the person sustained the injury and *must still subsist* at the time of the application to the Authority and decision by the Authority or Appeals Panel unless the victim has since died.

Under this first leg of para 9(b) the secondary victim must be 'present', sufficiently physically close to the injurious event suffered by the primary victim to see or hear the primary victim being injured.

The second leg of para 9(b), which also requires the close relationship of love and affection, covers the case where the secondary victim is not physically present when the primary victim sustains his or her injury but 'was closely involved in its immediate aftermath'. For the involvement of the secondary victim in the aftermath to be 'immediate', it would seemingly have to be very proximate in time and space to the injury to the primary victim. The use of the words 'involved in' also suggests an early discovery of, or coming upon the injuries of the primary victim such as to 'involve' the secondary victim in those events.

Coming upon or discovering the injurious event and the injury to the primary victim more than an hour or two after it had occurred might not seem to be within this provision, however horrific the impact on the secondary victim, as the latter would not be 'closely involved in the immediate aftermath' of the injurious event. It is necessary, however, to consider the context as well as look at the ordinary meaning of the words in order to assess whether a given situation satisfies these conditions. A wife who visits her injured husband or child in hospital, perhaps some hours after or many miles from the scene of the injury and suffers a mental illness as a result, may be regarded as sufficiently proximate in time and place to be 'closely involved' in the 'immediate aftermath'. Likewise a husband or wife or son or daughter or brother who returns home after being away for some weeks to find the body of wife or husband or parent or sibling in the home, even if the fatal injury was incurred some weeks before, as the discovery of the loved one's body would probably be regarded as 'close involvement' and sufficiently 'immediate' in such circumstances.

It must also be remembered that under the 1996 Scheme the 'aftermath' extension of 'witnessed and was present' applies only where the secondary victim has a 'close relationship of love and affection' with the primary victim. Mental injury resulting from, for example, finding the body of a stranger who has been murdered is not within the 1996 Scheme, nor is the applicant who is present when someone other than a loved one is murdered or injured.

Learning of the death or injury of a loved one by being told of it by a third party or by television or radio – even close to, or at the time of the event – would not, it seems, fulfil either of the legs of para 9(b), as the secondary victim was not physically present at the time and place of the injury nor was he or she 'closely involved in its immediate aftermath'.

Although these conditions of entitlement are intended to be reasonably self explanatory, it will be noted by applicants and advisers who are familiar with common law principles on this subject, and the leading cases in damages for so-called nervous shock, that the 1996 Scheme uses some familiar phrases, the precise meaning of which has been extensively considered by the courts. It has to be kept in mind, however, that the Scheme states its own rules and it is those rules which govern questions of entitlement under the Scheme.

Paragraph 9(c) refers to 'the non-consenting victim of a sexual offence'. This provision ensures, for example, that the many victims of childhood sexual abuse who suffer mental illness as a result and whose claims are recognised by the 1990 Scheme are also within the 1996 Scheme. This provision is not confined to child victims. Any person suffering mental illness as a direct consequence of their being the primary victim of a sexual offence may claim. This provision makes clear, however, that 'a victim who consented in fact' is not within the Scheme even if for the purpose of the general law the victim cannot give consent by reason of age or mental infirmity. It is unlikely that the apparent factual consent by a child under the age of, say, twelve years would affect entitlement to an award. Although there is no provision in para 9(c) to include any 'secondary' victim, such as the mother of an abused girl who becomes mentally ill on discovery of her daughter's abuse, the mother's close involvement in the legal and medical procedures following immediately after and as a result of such disclosure may entitle her to an award under para 9(b) above.

Paragraph 9(d) provides that applicants who suffer mental illness directly attributable to an offence of trespass on a railway are only entitled to claim if they are 'employed in the business of a railway'. This provision excludes, for example, a passenger who became mentally ill as a result of seeing someone commit suicide by jumping under an approaching train. Railway employees such as train drivers or guards who either 'witness and are present' on the occasion or who are 'closely involved in its immediate aftermath', and who become mentally ill as a result, may claim.

The test of whether the railway employee is 'present' and 'witnesses' the occurrence and what is or is not the 'immediate aftermath' will probably be the same factual test as in those cases involving 'a close relationship of love and affection' between primary and secondary victim already discussed, as the wording used is the same. It is likely that where the applicant is the first to discover the victim's body, even where there is some lapse of time between the incident causing injury and the discovery of the body, he will come within the Scheme as being involved in the immediate aftermath if he has to deal with the situation personally and suffers mental illness as a result.

Every case will depend upon its own facts and these words in the Scheme will be interpreted according to their ordinary everyday meaning. It bears repeating that 'witnessed and was present' will require the applicant to have been in the immediate vicinity and to have seen or heard the occurrence of the injury and that, failing this, the victim must have been 'closely involved' in the 'immediate' aftermath. The latter would presumably include, for example, a train guard who has to investigate an emergency halt by the driver and himself has to take part in the rescue of an injured person, but probably not another railway employee who sees the rescue activities after the incident but is not actively involved in them.

Just who is or is not 'a person employed in the business of a railway' is not explained in the Scheme. This will be interpreted in a common-sense way. The choice of words suggests a wider meaning than the more restrictive 'employed by a railway company' which could have been used. The more general definition chosen is perhaps the most appropriate with the prospect of privatisation of the railway system bringing with it a multiplicity of involved parties and companies in that industry.

The final sentence of para 9(d) makes clear that the requirement that the applicant must have been taking an 'exceptional risk' for certain 'accidental' injuries to qualify for an award (para 12, 1996 Scheme) does not apply to these railway employee cases.

Chapter 3

Other applications for compensation

Paragraph 8(c) of the 1996 Scheme and para 4(b) of the 1990 Scheme both provide that personal injury directly attributable to certain law enforcement activities is within the Scheme.

Paragraph 8(c) of the 1996 Scheme provides that a personal injury directly attributable to 'the apprehension or attempted apprehension of an offender or a suspected offender, the prevention or attempted prevention of an offence, or the giving of help to any constable who is engaged in any such activity' is within the Scheme.

Applications received before 1 April 1996 fall to be considered under the terms of the 1990 Scheme; those received on or after that date are governed by the 1996 Scheme. As in respect of this particular category the rules are the same under both Schemes, the observations which follow apply in all cases. For convenience the respective paragraphs are referred to by the abbreviations '4(b) 1990' and '8(c) 1996'.

1. Apprehension of an offender (para 4(b) 1990; para 8(c) 1996)

These paragraphs are concerned with injury directly attributable to the apprehension of an offender, or to the prevention of an offence or to the giving of help to any constable who is engaged in any such activity.

Many applications are made to the Board and the Authority by police officers for consideration under para 4(b) 1990, and 8(c) 1996, the injury sustained being directly attributable to the applicant's activities in relation to law enforcement, either the apprehension or attempted apprehension of an offender or suspected offender, or the prevention or attempted prevention of an offence.

Civilians also make claims under para 4(b) 1990, 8(c) 1996 where their injury is directly attributable to the 'giving of help to any constable who is engaged in any such activity', or where they have acted on their own and sustained injury whilst apprehending an offender.

A police officer is regarded as being engaged in the apprehension or attempted apprehension of an offender or a suspected offender from the time he or she is first called to act in relation to the offence or suspected offence. The duration of the activity of apprehension on the part of the police officer may then continue through the period of his or her going to the incident, the action of arresting the alleged offender and even after the latter has been taken into custody.

These observations on the meaning of para 4(b) 1990, 8(c) 1996 are based upon the Board's 1987 'Statement', an informal commentary on the Board's interpretation of the 1979 Scheme, the wording of which was similar to the 1990 and 1996 Schemes in this regard. The Statement also points out that an 'accidental' injury incurred in one of these activities has to satisfy a further condition explained below.

Many cases falling to be considered under para 4(b) 1990, 8(c) 1996 involve injuries suffered accidentally by police officers, either while going to the scene of the incident or while giving chase to the offender. These particular cases have to be looked at in the light of para 6(d) 1990 or 12 1996 which provide for certain conditions to be satisfied before an injury sustained *accidentally* in an 'apprehension' or 'prevention' activity can be the subject of an award.

Before commenting on the particular rules which apply to *accidental* injuries arising from law enforcement activities under the 1990 Scheme and, under para 12 of the 1996 Scheme, activities 'directed to containing, limiting or remedying the consequences of a crime' it is helpful to consider the position of the innocent bystander who is injured in the course of 'apprehension' or 'prevention' activities.

The scope of the 'crime of violence' and the questions of intention and recklessness on the part of the assailant have already been considered. The example of assailant A intending to strike B but hitting C by mistake illustrates the point that C may claim successfully under the Scheme for his injuries, as A has committed a crime of violence and C has suffered an injury directly attributable to that crime. Such cases fall within para 4(a) of the 1990 Scheme and para 8(a) of the 1996 Scheme.

There is another category of 'innocent bystander' to be considered under para 4(b) 1990, 8(c) 1996 where the injury to the innocent bystander is 'directly attributable to the apprehension or attempted apprehension of an offender or a suspected offender, the prevention or attempted prevention of an offence, or the giving of help to any constable who is engaged in any such activity'. It is helpful to look at the development of the position of the innocent bystander, who is injured in the mêlée of an attempt to arrest or in the pursuit of an offender, as a result of a High Court decision in 1971 and then by way of amendments made to the Scheme in 1979 which have been carried also into the 1990 and 1996 Schemes.

In *R v Criminal Injuries Compensation Board, ex parte Schofield* [1971] 2 All ER 1011, the applicant who was shopping was accidentally knocked down and injured when the store detective was chasing a man suspected of shoplifting (see Appendix 1). It was not clear who had knocked the applicant down. The court held that there was nothing in the Scheme (in the way that the equivalent to para 4(b) 1990, 8(c) 1996 was then worded) to limit compensation to cases where the applicant was himself arresting or attempting to arrest an offender. The innocent bystander who was accidentally injured by such activity was thus within the Scheme as it then stood.

The 1978 report of the interdepartmental working party recommended in the light of the *Schofield* decision that the Scheme be amended so that bystanders who were victims of an assault which is either intentional or as a result of recklessness would be within the Scheme but 'those who are injured because their attention is distracted or because some other person's attention is distracted by the incident so as to cause an accidental injury would not'.

The 1979 Scheme, which contained amendments based upon these recommendations, included for the first time a provision now contained in para 12 1996 (para 6(d) 1990) which provides that compensation will not be payable in the case of an application under para 8(c) 1996 (4(b) 1990) where the injury was sustained accidentally, unless the applicant was at the time taking an exceptional risk which was justified in all the circumstances.

If the bystander has truly been the victim of a crime of violence, intentional or reckless, the application falls within para 8(a) 1996 (4(a) 1990).

If he or she is injured in a para 8(c) 1996 (4(b) 1990) situation directly attributable to an 'apprehension or attempted apprehension', for example is accidentally knocked down by the pursuer or the pursued, the application is outside the Scheme unless he or she was 'taking an exceptional risk'. This is considered below.

Another variation which has to be considered in this context is the innocent bystander who sees the situation as an 'apprehension or attempted apprehension' and lends assistance, for example tries to stop a shoplifter who is running away from a pursuing store detective. Such a case is reported in the Board's twenty-fifth report in 1989. The applicant fell and was injured when he assisted a store detective in stopping a suspected shoplifter. The applicant deliberately put himself in the path of the suspect who ran into him and the impact caused injuries to the applicant's shin and elbow and a prolapsed intra-vertebral disc, leaving a permanently twisted back. The application in this case fell squarely within the then equivalent provision to para 8(c) 1996. The injuries were directly attributable to the attempted apprehension of a suspected offender. Had the Board considered that the injuries were suffered accidentally, the applicant could probably have successfully argued that, as he was 'having a go', he was taking an exceptional risk and was therefore within the Scheme on that basis.

Many applications from police officers who are injured in the course of their duty are a result of assault – these cases are dealt with under para 8(a) 1996 (4(a) 1990). A large number of applications involving injuries to police officers arise from circumstances which fall within the terms of para 8(c) 1996 (4(b) 1990) – i.e., the injury is 'directly attributable to the apprehension of an offender' but is sustained accidentally, for example while chasing the suspect in order to apprehend him. In these circumstances, in 1990 Scheme cases para 6(d) operates in conjunction with para 4(b), and in 1996 Scheme cases para 12 applies.

As already stated, para 6(d) 1990 provides that:

> ... compensation will not be payable in the case of an application under paragraph 4(b) above where the injury was sustained *accidentally*, unless the Board are satisfied that the applicant was at the time taking an *exceptional risk* which was justified in all the circumstances. (Author's italics.)

Paragraph 12 applies the same conditions to 1996 Scheme cases of accidental injury arising from 'law-enforcement activities'. It also extends the application of the 'exceptional risk' principle to include for the first time any other activity directed to 'containing, limiting or remedying the consequences of a crime'. Thus accidental injury in the course of pursuing an offender is not within the Scheme, save in those exceptional cases. The interpretation of the word 'exceptional' gives rise to difficulties. It may be argued that the pursuit of criminals or suspected criminals is such an integral part of the duty of a police officer that an accidental injury in the course of such pursuit would only rarely be regarded as the result of taking an exceptional risk.

The requirements of 'exceptional risk' were introduced for the first time in the 1979 Scheme. Before that requirement was introduced, the interpretation of the term 'directly attributable' by the Board and by the court in *Ince* had brought accidental injuries within the scope of the Scheme to an extent not envisaged when the Scheme first came into operation. The Scheme was never intended to compensate accidental injury where, for example, a lady had fallen over a piece of furniture which had been moved by a burglar, or the applicant had suffered accidental injury through some occupational hazard – such as pursuit of the offender by a police officer.

The amendment was an attempt to re-establish the need for a closer link between the injury sustained and the criminal event. Paragraph 6(d) 1990 (first included in 1979) thus introduced two new requirements for accidental injury in the course of 'apprehension' to come within the Scheme. The first was that the applicant must have been 'taking an exceptional risk'. The second was that such risk had to be 'justified in all the circumstances'. These two requirements are incorporated, in the same wording, in the 1996 Scheme (para 12).

Although the majority of applications which fall to be considered under the combined terms of paras 4(b) and 6(d) 1990 (paras 8(c) and 12 1996) involve injuries to police officers where the activities giving rise to the injuries come more or less within the terms of the occupation of the applicant, the Board also receives applications where civilians have assisted in such activities and sustained accidental injury. The Authority will have to consider the new category of cases caught by para 12(b) 1996 which will mainly comprise firefighters injured while 'containing, limiting or remedying' the consequences of the crime of arson.

The 1986 report of the interdepartmental working party on a then proposed statutory Scheme drew a clear distinction between the case of the police officer injured accidentally while acting in the scope of his em, ment in the law enforcement field and the case of the member of the pu injured while attempting to prevent an offence or apprehend an offenc -, the latter being an activity which is 'not their job, and if they do not receive compensation under the Scheme they will not receive it from any other source'. The report suggested changes in relation to these two different categories of accidental injury. It is not helpful to consider these arguments further at the present time, however, as these changes have not been effected, and the 1990 and 1996 Schemes continue on the same basis as the 1979 Scheme, with the requirement that accidental injury in the 'apprehension' situation (and 'containing, limiting, or remedying' situation in 1996 Scheme cases) must meet the conditions as to 'exceptional risk' and must also be 'justified in all the circumstances'.

The Board's 1987 Statement gives some guidelines which are still helpful where the terms of the 1979, 1990 and 1996 Schemes are similar, as in this context. The Statement gives examples of situations which might or might not amount to an 'exceptional risk'. The mere act of falling and suffering injury while in pursuit of an offender on foot will not in itself be an exceptional risk. Jumping or climbing over things such as walls or fences will usually not be taking an exceptional risk, although jumping over an obstacle where one cannot see what is on the other side, especially at night, may be. Where the pursuit involves running over rough unlit ground at night, those factors may be sufficient if taken together, to bring the case within the Scheme as an 'exceptional risk'. The point often raised when questioning an officer in such cases is: 'I can see that the officer took a risk, but I cannot say that it is an exceptional risk'. In making out his case, it is for the applicant to establish that the risk is exceptional. In every case, however, the exceptional risk has to be 'justified in all the circumstances'. Where the evidence establishes that the officer had a choice of route in the pursuit and took the more hazardous one without justification, or took a risk which was not appropriate to the offence or the danger to the public with which the officer was dealing at the time of the accidental injury, the claim may fall outside the Scheme as a risk which was not 'justified in all the circumstances'.

Cases noted in the Board's twenty-fourth report in 1988 and twenty-fifth report in 1989 and twenty-eighth report in 1992 serve to illustrate the Board's approach.

Case 1

The applicant, a police officer, was called to a building society office to deal with a man suspected of deception. As he arrived at the office, the suspected man came out of the door and, pushing the applicant aside, ran off down the street. The applicant gave chase. As he drew close to the man he suddenly slipped and fell. He got up, and went to help another officer who was in the process of arresting the man. There was a struggle at this point. Later on that day, the applicant's left wrist became swollen, and on investigation it turned out he had a scaphoid fracture of his wrist. In this case the member disallowed the application and commented:

> The applicant slipped and fell on the road while chasing the alleged assailant. He sustained his injuries as a result of his fall. He sustained no injuries from being pushed aside beforehand. I cannot find that his running along the road in pursuit of the applicant was taking an exceptional risk.

The applicant requested a hearing on the grounds that he could not be sure whether he was injured when he slipped over or when he subsequently helped to arrest the suspect. This latter possibility had not been emphasised in the original application.

At the hearing, the Board of three members decided that on the balance of probabilities the applicant received his injury when he fell over. It also decided that the applicant could not be said to have been taking an exceptional risk in the circumstances of this pursuit. Accordingly it upheld the decision of the single member.

Case 2

A police officer was chasing a young man whom he suspected of being involved in a car theft. The suspect had abandoned the car and taken off on foot, and the officer followed. It was just after midnight on a December night, and the chase took place along a beach on the south coast. While running along the foreshore the officer slipped and fell heavily on his back. The young man ran on but was eventually arrested by other officers.

The applicant was treated in hospital, where he complained of pain in his back between the shoulder blades. An X-ray revealed a fracture of the body of a thoracic vertebra, for which he was given analgesia and told to rest. He was off work for two weeks, and then returned only to light duties.

The single member disallowed the application on the grounds that the applicant had not at the time been taking an exceptional risk. The applicant requested a hearing before the Board at which he emphasised that the ground he had been running on was uneven, and was wetter than he had expected, not thinking that the tide came up that far. It was a poorly maintained path, and there was no lighting.

On the evidence before it, the Board concluded that the applicant had been taking an exceptional risk, and made a full award.

Case 3

A 30-year-old police constable was pursuing a suspect down an alleyway on foot late at night, but in a well-lit area. At the end of the alley was situated a white painted metal barrier which the applicant attempted to avoid. He was unsuccessful and caught his upper arm against the barrier, causing him to fall to the ground and lose consciousness. Skull X-rays showed that the officer had sustained a depressed left parietal fracture. His application to the Board was disallowed, the single member observing as follows:

> I have now seen photographs of the barrier with which the applicant collided. The injury sustained was accidental rather than being due to a crime of violence. Since I am not satisfied that the applicant was at the time taking an exceptional risk, no award can be made under para 6(d) of the Scheme. (Paragraph 6(d) 1990 is similar in its terms to para 12(a) 1996.)

Case 4

A man, aged 51, was at home one evening when he heard the sound of breaking glass coming from a neighbour's house. He went out to investigate, saw a man jumping out of the ground floor window and gave chase. Dim light made it difficult to see the terrain and, while attempting to apprehend the intruder, the applicant slipped and fell, sustaining a fracture of the humerus. The Board member allowed the application.

Case 5

The applicant, a police officer, was off duty when he was informed by a neighbour that intruders were breaking and entering another house. While in pursuit of the intruders he had to climb over a car which was blocking his way. The applicant fell and injured his foot. The incident occurred at 16.35 hours. The Board disallowed the application under para 4(b) and 6(d) 1990 (in similar terms to para 12(a) 1996). Since the incident happened in daylight and was accidental, there was no exceptional risk.

2. Railway incidents (para 4(c) 1990; para 8(b) 1996)

Paragraph 4(c) was an entirely new provision in the 1990 Scheme, effective from 1 February 1990. It is continued in similar wording by para 8(b) 1996. Thus in addition to injury directly attributable to a crime of violence (para 4(a) 1990, 8(a) 1996) or to the apprehension of an offender (para 4(b) 1990, 8(c) 1996), para 4(c) 1990 (8(b) 1996) provides for personal injury directly attributable 'to an offence of trespass on a railway.' This brief provision was the culmination of much litigation and political debate.

R v Criminal Injuries Compensation Board, ex parte Warner [1987] QB 74 brought to a conclusion in England and Wales the applications which had been made to the Board in the preceding years by a number of train drivers who had suffered psychiatric injury as a consequence of persons committing suicide by placing themselves on the railway line in the path of oncoming trains. This case has already been considered in relation to the comments of the Court of Appeal on the meaning of 'crime of violence' under the Scheme, which concluded that whether a crime was to be regarded as a crime of violence depended upon the nature of the crime and not upon its likely consequences. Thus trespass on a railway, which constitutes a statutory offence, could properly be described as a crime but is not a crime of violence, even though the consequences are the death of one party and the illness through shock of another.

Many train drivers, some of whom had lost their livelihoods as a consequence of the experience, thus found that their applications were outside the Scheme and no compensation could be paid by the Board in respect of their injuries and financial loss.

The final adjudication of these cases in England and Wales, by the decision of the Court of Appeal in *Warner*, coincided with the deliberations of politicians, lawyers and others with regard to the then proposed statutory Scheme. The position of the railwaymen in these suicide cases was debated along with the many other matters relating to possible amendments to the Scheme. The amendments to the Scheme which came into operation on 1 February 1990 included the addition of para 4(c) which had the effect of reversing the decision in *Warner*. The 1996 Scheme includes the same provision.

Paragraph 28 of the 1990 Scheme, however, which governed implementation of what was then a new provision, stated that para 4(c) of that Scheme was effective only in relation to applications in respect of injuries incurred after 1 February 1990. Therefore, all train drivers injured in this way before 1 February 1990 in England and Wales remain outside the Scheme.

The Board's twenty-eighth Report (1992) states in relation to para 4(c) 1990 (8(b) 1996) cases:

> Trespass on a railway
>
> It is important to note in these cases, as in all others in which the applicant claims to have suffered stress as a result of an incident, that the Board [this applies equally to the Authority and the Appeals Panel] can only make an award if he has suffered some recognised mental illness. The normal stress associated with such an incident would not generally amount to such a condition and would not, therefore, attract an award.

Two examples of decided cases are then given:

> *Case 1:* The applicant, a 40 year-old train driver, tried to stop his train when he saw a youth ahead trying to climb an embankment. The youth, who fell on to the line, was fatally injured. The driver attended to him until the emergency services arrived at which time the youth's mother also appeared on the scene and in a state of distress she accused the driver of causing her son's death. The applicant suffered from severe shock and psychological distress and he received an award.
>
> *Case 2:* The applicant, a 55 year-old train driver, suffered post traumatic stress disorder when the train he was driving struck a man who had deliberately put his body on the railway line to commit suicide. An award was made.

An interesting case in the Board's twenty-ninth Report (1993) illustrates that if the 'trespass on a railway' is an act of sabotage which the Board is satisfied was intended to cause an accident and injury it can also be a 'crime of violence'.

The applicant, a 34 year-old train driver, tried to stop his train when he saw a car parked on a level crossing. Unfortunately, he was unable to stop the train in time and the car was pushed 40 yards down the track. The police established that the car was deliberately abandoned on the track with the intent to cause an accident. The application met the requirements of para 4(a) of the 1990 Scheme (8(a) (1996) and the applicant was awarded compensation for the psychological injuries he sustained. It can be seen that the award could equally have been made under para 4(c) 1990 (8(b) 1996) as the circumstances also constituted trespass on a railway.

The Board's thirty-second report (1996) cites a decision where the presence of the person on the railway was not 'an offence of trespass on a railway' and the application which relied upon para 4(c) (1990) was refused.

The applicant was a train driver and suffered trauma after an incident on the railway caused him to carry out an emergency stop. The alleged 'offender', however, was crossing the track by means of an authorised foot crossing and was thus not trespassing on the railway. Police advised that the youth had been acting absent-mindedly and that he failed to realise the train was approaching. No offence was identified. The application was refused, therefore, under para 4(c) of the Scheme.

Chapter 4

Minimum award and maximum award

The Scheme was never intended to compensate victims who suffer minor injury only. The Scheme has always had a minimum award provision, whereby only injuries warranting compensation of at least the minimum award are within the Scheme. Paragraph 24 of the 1996 Scheme provides:

> The injury must be sufficiently serious to qualify for an award equal at least to the minimum amount payable under this Scheme in accordance with paragraph 25.

The 1996 Scheme operates according to a number of 'Levels'. The lowest award is Level 1 which is the minimum award of £1,000 (the same as under para 5 of the 1990 Scheme). The highest level in the Scheme, Level 25, is an award of £250,000. Thus from April 1996 the Scheme has for the first time a maximum award for injury as well as a minimum award. This maximum 'standard amount of compensation' at Level 25 may, however, be exceeded where the provisions of para 22 apply, but para 23 provides that 'the *total* maximum amount payable in respect of the same injury will not exceed £500,000'. (Author's italics.)

All applications received by the Authority on or after 1 April 1996 are governed by the rules of the 1996 Scheme and are thus awarded the fixed sum of money set out in the appropriate level in the Tariff for the particular injury suffered.

Applications received by the Board before 1 April 1996 are wholly governed by the 1990 or earlier Schemes. These applications are subject to the same minimum award of £1,000 as under the 1996 Scheme but, unlike 1996 Scheme cases, pre- 1 April 1996 cases are not subject to the maximum award of £250,000 (or in certain cases £500,000) fixed by the 1996 Scheme. It had always been a feature of the Scheme until the 1996 Scheme came into operation that the Board had the same unlimited jurisdiction in awarding compensation under the Scheme as the High Court has in terms of damages. This meant that cases of very serious injury involving such items as substantial future loss of earnings or substantial costs for future care would receive the same sum, calculated on the same common law principles, as would a successful plaintiff with similar injuries and loss in the High Court.

These very substantial claims represented only a small minority of claims to the Board prior to 1 April 1996. The Board's thirty-second Report for the year ended 31 March 1996, states that in the financial year 1995/96 the Board resolved a total of 76,225 applications. Of these, 44,036 received monetary awards. The 1996 Report states that 12 cases received payments in excess of £500,000.

All applications received before 1 April 1996, however, have no maximum or 'ceiling' figure. They are governed only by the minimum award of £1,000. The 1990 Scheme fixed this at £750 from 1 February 1990, and then the figure was increased to the present £1,000 with effect from 6 January 1992.

Although all cases are therefore subject to the same minimum award, the approach to the assessment of minor injury is now different under the 1990 and 1996 Schemes, and these are dealt with separately below.

1. Minimum award in 'old' Scheme cases

The first part of para 5 of the 1990 Scheme reads:

> Compensation will not be payable unless the Board are satisfied that the injury was one for which the total amount of compensation payable ... would not be less than the minimum amount of compensation.

The amount of the minimum award has been increased from time to time to take account of the effect of inflation in the award of damages, so that the Scheme more or less maintains a constant level at which particular injuries qualify for an award. The original minimum award was £50; this has been increased in several stages to £400 (for applications between 1982 and November 1986); £550 (up to February 1990); £750 (from February 1990); and £1,000 from January 1992.

In its origins, the Scheme was the expression of public sympathy for persons suffering serious injury from criminal violence; the inclusion of minor injuries within the Scheme would have greatly increased the number of applications and the cost of administration.

The particular injury which has always occupied a position on the borderline of the minimum award is 'undisplaced nasal fracture' – the broken nose. Up to now the victim who suffers this injury has been just within the Scheme. The guideline figure for this particular injury in the figures published by the Board in 1984 (when the minimum award stood at £400) was £450.

Three years later, in June 1987, the Board reconsidered its guidelines for this and other injuries, and increased the award for undisplaced nasal fracture to £550. In November 1986, shortly before this revision of the guidelines by the Board, the minimum award under para 5 of the Scheme had been increased to £550 so that this injury was again just within the Scheme. Subsequent revision of the Board's guidelines put undisplaced nasal fracture at £650 when the current minimum award was £750; a broken nose was thus unlikely to be sufficient on its own to justify an award under para 5, even if the circumstances of the application in all other respects met the requirements of the Scheme. There are two factors to be borne in mind, however, in considering whether this particular injury or any other relatively minor injury taken on its own is sufficient to merit an award under the old Scheme. One is that while Parliament may vary the minimum award figure from time to time, the Board has responsibility in pre- 1 April 1996 applications for assessing the appropriate compensation in each and every application on its individual merits. The second is that in many cases the application reveals other minor injuries and financial loss which could make the difference between a nil award and a minimum award.

Advisers who assist injured persons in preparing applications should always keep in mind the minimum award provision. There are thousands of injuries suffered every year which are painful and distressing and, for a while, unsightly, such as black eyes, bloody noses, scratches and abrasions, but which do not qualify for an award under the Scheme. To encourage persons to apply to the Board or the Authority where the minor level of injury offers no prospect of an award being made raises false hopes which, when disappointed by being refused, serve to aggravate the sense of grievance at having not only suffered the injury but been refused compensation for that injury. Good advice at the outset can help reduce both the disappointment to victims and the number of 'hopeless' cases which the Board or Authority has to deal with.

In respect of pre- 1 April 1996 cases, para 5 speaks of 'the total amount of compensation' having to reach the minimum figure – this means, as well as compensation for the physical injury, any loss of earnings or other recoverable out-of-pocket items.

Thus for the applicant who has suffered minor injuries which in terms of common law damages would merit an award of, say, £800 (and therefore less than the minimum award) but was off work for a week and suffered a loss of net earnings of £150, and had to replace his spectacles, broken in the course of the assault, at a cost of £105, his 'total amount of compensation payable' would be £1,055 and therefore would be within the Scheme. (As is discussed below, 1996 Scheme cases do not include loss of earnings in the first 28 weeks. Therefore, a few weeks' loss of earnings cannot be added to bring a case within the Scheme where the level of award for the injury alone does not merit an award; it will be noted also that para 35 of the 1996 Scheme allows certain 'special expenses' to be added to the 'standard amount of compensation' under para 22. Unlike para 5 of the 1990 Scheme, however, the applicant has to suffer at least a 'Level 1' injury to come within the Scheme. He cannot add 'special expenses' to a below Level 1 injury to qualify.)

The only deduction which may be made in order to arrive at the 'total amount of compensation' for the purpose of deciding whether an applicant is entitled to at least the minimum award under para 5 of the 1990 Scheme is the amount of any social security benefits, deductible under para 19 of the 1990 Scheme. Compensation awarded, for example, by the magistrates' court when the assailant was convicted is not deductible for the purpose of para 5 calculation, even though it is deductible (under para 21 of the 1990 Scheme) from any award which may be made.

Take, for example, an applicant whose 'total amount of compensation' is assessed as follows:

		£
(i) injury		900
(ii) loss of net earnings		125
(iii) replacement of hearing aid		85
	Total	£1,110

It might be that he received a Department of Social Security payment of £80 in respect of the injury and was awarded (and recovered) £150 compensation payable by the assailant in the magistrates' court.

His 'paragraph 5' calculation under the 1990 Scheme would thus be:

		£
(i) award for injury		900
(ii) loss of net earnings		125
(iii) replacement of hearing aid		85
	Sub total	£1,110
Deduct:		
(iv) Social security benefit		80
	Total	£1,030
Ignore (for the purpose of para 5 only):		
(v) Criminal court compensation		£150

The 'paragraph 5' calculation would therefore in this case be £1,030, which is above the Scheme's minimum figure.

The award which the applicant would receive, however, would be £880, as any criminal court compensation received by the applicant is deducted from the award even though it is ignored for the purpose of the para 5 minimum award calculation.

It is for the applicant to make out his case. Although the Board's staff make initial enquiries of the doctor or hospital where the applicant states in his application form he received treatment, it is often the case where the applicant received only minor injuries that he received no medical attention. It is difficult to assess injuries without any corroboration by way of a medical report. If there are photographs taken shortly after the incident showing the immediate effect of the injuries, or a statement from a witness to the incident or a member of the applicant's family describing the nature and extent of the injuries, this assists the Board in deciding both on the genuineness of the claim and on the assessment of the appropriate compensation, including whether or not the injuries justify at least the minimum award.

The police report obtained by the Board's staff will sometimes indicate that the applicant was found by the police at the scene of the incident having suffered certain injuries.

However, where an applicant gives a description of only minor injuries and there is no medical evidence, the application will be likely to fail under para 5, even if in other respects the conditions of the Scheme are fulfilled.

In its twenty-third report (1987), the Board commented:

> In general terms the lower limit would exclude most minor injuries, e.g. cuts, bruises or sprains where it is clear that there has been a complete recovery within two or three weeks leaving no scar. It would also exclude cases of transient shock which is the normal consequence of any unpleasant experience (such as a mugging), though the Board is likely to take a more generous view of the effect on an elderly person who has sustained other minor injuries.

In relation to pre- 1 April 1996 cases one must also bear in mind that even though physical injuries are minor or non-existent, an applicant who suffers a mental illness which is directly attributable to a crime of violence will be within the Scheme if the mental injury is sufficiently serious. The principle stated by Lord Bridge in *McLoughlin v O'Brian* (1982) will apply in such cases:

> The first hurdle which a plaintiff claiming damages [for nervous shock] must surmount is to establish that he is suffering not merely grief, distress or any other normal emotion, but a positive psychiatric illness.

Thus in cases where mental illness is claimed to be the injury suffered, medical evidence to establish that to be the case is essential for the applicant to succeed.

In a case governed by the 1990 Scheme the applicant had suffered stress and depression as a result of finding out that her young children had been sexually assaulted by a trusted male relative. One of the children had told her what had happened. The applicant had to be present with each of her children while they made detailed statements to the police regarding the abuse they had each suffered. This had been a stressful and distressing experience for the applicant. The Board considered *McLoughlin v O'Brian* and decided that the applicant's distress and other symptoms, although genuine, did not meet the requirements laid down in that case. Like the common law, the 1990 Scheme does not compensate for the emotional distress which any normal person experiences in situations involving injury to a loved one. Anxiety and depression, said Lord Bridge in *McLoughlin*, are normal human emotions. The applicant has to show by medical evidence a positive psychiatric illness. There was no such evidence in the present case. The Board made no award.

The question of mental injury is discussed in more detail in Chapter 2 which deals with the meaning of the term 'personal injury'. Under both the 1990 Scheme and 1996 Scheme 'personal injury' includes mental injury provided that it satisfies the *McLoughlin v O'Brian* test of a 'medically recognised psychiatric or psychological illness' (para 9 of the 1996 Scheme).

Three cases are quoted, by way of illustration, of the Board's approach to the assessment of the minimum award under the 1990 and earlier schemes.

In the Board's twenty-eighth report (1992) the offender, who was the husband of the applicant, returned home after a night out with his wife and in a drunken state attacked her, hitting her with a telephone directory, dragging her round the house by her ankles and eventually throwing her out causing bruising and swelling to her nose, right eye, forearm and knee. The applicant sought no medical treatment and stated she was fully recovered. The application was disallowed under para 5 because the Board was not satisfied that the injuries would attract the minimum level of award.

In the Board's twenty-fifth report (1989) a man aged 27 was walking home with a friend in the early hours of the morning when they were attacked by a number of youths for no apparent reason. The applicant sustained bruising and a small laceration along his right ear where he had been bitten. Four sutures were given and the scar healed well, being hidden within the fold of the ear. No award was made.

A 28 year-old man was shopping with his wife and mother in a DIY store. While they were waiting in the queue for the checkout, his wife was continually bumped by the trolley of the man behind them. Words were exchanged and, as the applicant turned to leave the shop, he was punched in the face. A further assault took place outside the shop by the assailant's companion. Although the applicant's injuries were relatively minor, he had for some time been suffering from agoraphobia and claimed that this had been aggravated by the assault. After considering the medical evidence obtained by the Board, the single member disallowed the application on the grounds that the agoraphobia pre-dated the incident and that the remaining injuries did not attract the minimum award of compensation.

The question of minimum award will in certain circumstances be decided in favour of an applicant of tender years or an elderly applicant where it is to be expected that the impact of a frightening experience would be greater than with most adults. Thus, for example, an 80 year-old living on her own who disturbs a burglar in her home at night and, while suffering no physical injury, suffers shock and is unable, through nervousness and fear that such an intrusion might be repeated, to continue to live on her own, would probably receive an award. Although there is no principle which states that burglary as such, where no physical violence to the person occurs, is a crime of violence, the Board will consider sympathetically the impact of fear of violence from a burglar who is disturbed by the applicant where the threat of violence is a real one and the impact of fear upon the householder, especially a vulnerable elderly person, is considerable.

Each case has to be considered on its individual merits. In refusing an application where the applicant has, for example, received punches to the face and suffered minor bruises and abrasions, a Board member may comment that although the applicant has had a painful and unpleasant experience, his injuries are not such that a court would award at least the minimum award. No award can be made in such a case.

In many cases of minor injury such as bruising and scratches, or black eyes or a bloody nose, the evidence of injury in the medical report extends only to the physical injury – if this is insufficient on its own to merit at least the minimum award, none can be made.

2. Minimum award – the 1996 Scheme

As has already been stated, the minimum award in all cases under the 1996 Scheme, or (since 6 January 1992) under the 1990 Scheme, is £1,000. Both Schemes require the amount of compensation to reflect the severity of the injury, and minor injuries remain outside the Scheme. Under the 1996 Scheme if the injury does not merit the minimum award fixed by Level 1 of the Tariff no award can be made. Levels of compensation are fixed according to Levels 1 to 25 which are set out in table form in the 1996 Scheme.

The Tariff specifies 27 injuries which merit a Level 1 award of £1,000. These are listed as follows:

1. Head: ear: fractured mastoid
2. Head: ear: temporary partial deafness lasting 6–13 weeks
3. Head: ear: tinnitus (ringing noise in ears) – lasting 6–13 weeks
4. Head: eye: blurred or double vision – lasting 6–13 weeks
5. Head: facial: temporary numbness/loss of feeling, lasting 6–13 weeks
6. Head: nose: deviated nasal septum
7. Head: nose: undisplaced fracture of nasal bones
   (these two previously 'borderline' injuries to the nose are therefore expressly within the 1996 Scheme)
8. Head: teeth: fractured/chipped tooth/teeth requiring treatment
9. Head: teeth: chipped front teeth requiring crown
10. Head: teeth: fractured tooth/teeth requiring crown
11. Head: teeth: damage to tooth/teeth requiring root-canal treatment
12. Head: teeth: loss of one tooth other than front
13. Head: teeth: slackening of teeth requiring dental treatment
14. Lower limbs: minor damage to tendon(s)/ligament(s) (full recovery)
15. Lower limbs: sprained ankle – disabling for at least 6–13 weeks
16. Medically recognised illness/condition (not psychiatric or psychological) – significantly disabling disorder where the symptoms and disability persist for more than six weeks (up to 13 weeks) from the incident/date of onset
17. Minor injuries: multiple (examples are given in the Notes to the Tariff at the end of the Tariff tables – see below, at the end of this list)
18. Neck: strained neck: disabling for 6–13 weeks
19. Neck: whiplash injury: effects lasting 6–13 weeks

20. Physical abuse of children: minor abuse: isolated or intermittent assault(s) beyond ordinary chastisement resulting in bruising, weals, hair pulled from scalp etc.
21. Sexual abuse of children: minor isolated incidents - non-penetrative indecent acts
22. Sexual assault (single assault: victim any age): minor indecent assault - non-penetrative indecent physical act over clothing
23. Shock (including conditions attributed to post-traumatic stress disorder and depression); disabling, but temporary mental anxiety, medically verified
24. Torso: back: strained back - disabling for 6–13 weeks
25. Torso: fractured rib
26. Upper limbs: minor damage to tendon(s)/ligament(s) (full recovery)
27. Upper limbs: sprained wrist - disabling for 6–13 weeks.

(i) Minor injuries - multiple

Example of injuries qualifying under item 17 above are given in the Notes to the Tariff as follows:

(a) grazing, cuts, lacerations (no permanent scarring);
(b) severe and widespread bruising;
(c) severe soft tissue injury (not permanent disability);
(d) black eye(s);
(e) bloody nose;
(f) hair pulled from scalp;
(g) loss of fingernail.

The applicant must have suffered at least three such minor injuries, at least one of which must have had 'significant residual effects' for at least six weeks and necessitated at least two visits to or by the doctor within that six-week period. As (a) to (g) above are given as examples of qualifying injuries, it seems that other minor injuries may be added to make up the three injuries to qualify.

It is in the nature of a tariff that it is fixed and therefore does not have the flexibility which has always been the nature of the common law as a whole and not least in the matter of assessing common law damages for personal injury.

Awards will be made to reflect the nature and severity of the injury sustained in accordance with the Tariff of injuries appended to the Scheme. The injury must be sufficiently serious to attract 'a standard amount of compensation determined by reference to the nature of the injury in accordance with paras 25 to 29' (para 22 1996 Scheme). Paragraph 28 provides that any injury not listed in the Tariff which appears to the Authority sufficiently serious to qualify for at least the minimum award payable shall be referred by the Authority, having first consulted the Panel, to the Secretary of State for direction as to the Tariff level into which the injury should fall. Such referral and consultation will exclude the circumstances of any individual case and be limited to a description of the injury alone by reference to the relevant medical reports.

Paragraph 26 provides that minor multiple injuries will be assessed in accordance with Note 1 to the Tariff already dealt with above. It further provides that an award for more serious but separate multiple injuries will be the Tariff award for the highest rated injury plus 10 per cent of the Tariff value of the second most serious injury and, where there are three or more injuries, 5 per cent of the Tariff value of the third most serious injury.

Under the abortive 1994 Tariff Scheme the fixed award appropriate to the injury would have been the only award, as all other possible heads of claim such as loss of earnings, past or future, and costs of medical care and other expenses were wholly removed from the terms of compensation. The 1996 Scheme defines the 'standard amount of compensation' in paras 25 to 29, 'compensation for loss of earnings' in paras 30 to 34, 'compensation for special expenses' in paras 35 and 36. 'Compensation in fatal cases' in paras 37 to 43, and compensation where the victim has died 'otherwise than in consequence of the injury' in para 44.

These separate heads of claim and methods of fixing compensation in all applications made under the 1996 Scheme are set out in para 22 of that Scheme under the heading 'Types and limits of compensation'. Each of these headings is dealt with fully in later chapters. The immediately following chapters will deal first, however, with eligibility.

Chapter 5

Eligibility to receive compensation

1. Introduction

In the 1996 Scheme under the subheading 'Eligibility to receive compensation' is para 13 which provides as follows:

> A claims officer may withhold or reduce an award where he considers that:
>
> (a) the applicant failed to take, without delay, all reasonable steps to inform the police, or other body or person considered by the Authority to be appropriate for the purpose, of the circumstances giving rise to the injury;
>
> or
>
> (b) the applicant failed to co-operate with the police or other authority in attempting to bring the assailant to justice; or
>
> (c) the applicant has failed to give all reasonable assistance to the Authority or other body or person in connection with the application; or
>
> (d) the conduct of the applicant before, during or after the incident giving rise to the application makes it inappropriate that a full award or any award at all be made; or
>
> (e) the applicant's character as shown by his criminal convictions (excluding convictions spent under the Rehabilitation of Offenders Act 1974) or by evidence available to the claims officer makes it inappropriate that a full award or any award at all be made.

This substantially repeats the parallel provision of the 1990 Scheme, para 6(a), (b) and (c). As the many thousands of applications received by the Board before 1 April 1996 are governed by the terms of the 1990 Scheme, it is necessary to keep these terms in mind. Paragraph 6 of the 1990 Scheme commences as follows:

> The Board may withhold or reduce compensation if they consider that –
>
> (a) the applicant has not taken, without delay, all reasonable steps to inform the police, or any other authority considered by the Board to be appropriate for the purpose, of the circumstances of the injury and to co-operate with the police or other authority in bringing the offender to justice; or
>
> (b) the applicant has failed to give all reasonable assistance to the Board or other authority in connection with the application; or
>
> (c) having regard to the conduct of the applicant before, during or after the events giving rise to the claim or to his character as shown by his

> criminal convictions or unlawful conduct and, in applications under paragraphs 15 and 16 below [where the victim has died], to the conduct or character as shown by the criminal convictions or unlawful conduct, of the deceased and of the applicant – it is inappropriate that a full award, or any award at all, be granted.

The continuance of the familiar prerequisites for a successful claim under the 1996 Scheme is consistent with the statement in the White Paper published by the Home Office in December 1993 that 'these basic criteria have stood the test of time and have worked well in practice. No fundamental changes to current rules are therefore proposed'.

In discussing these provisions in relation to cases considered by the Authority and the Appeals Panel after 1 April 1996 and by the Board in relation to cases lodged before that date, there is therefore no need to treat the two systems separately. There is every reason to expect that the continuance of essentially similar provisions will mean a continuance of broadly the same policy in their interpretation by the Authority and Appeals Panel as has been established over the years by the Board up to 1996. There must also be taken into account the decisions of the High Court on judicial review of Board decisions where the court has ruled in particular on the test of 'reasonableness' which applies to the exercise of the discretion which these provisions give the decision-making authority under the 1996 Scheme as well as the Board in pre- 1 April 1996 cases.

In this chapter, therefore, the effect of these parallel provisions in the two Schemes will be dealt with together, making such distinctions as variation of wording between them makes necessary. For ease of reference, para 6 of the 1990 Scheme and para 13 of the 1996 Scheme will be referred to as 'para 6/13'.

Likewise, where the comment is based upon the decisions and statements of the Board up to 1996 and it is expected that the Authority and the Appeals Panel will follow a similar line, reference is made to 'the Board' only. This is appropriate as there is as yet no body of decisions or statements by the Authority or Appeals Panel to draw upon.

Paragraph 6/13 is in some respects the heart of the Scheme. Its provisions indicate very clearly that under the Scheme there is a direct relationship between the performance of certain duties as a citizen and entitlement to an award. The origin of the Scheme was the expression of sympathy felt by society at large for the innocent victims of crimes of violence. In para 6/13 society is saying to each applicant in simple terms, 'if you have done your bit by us, we will do our bit by you'.

Unlike the 1990 Scheme (para 4) the 1996 Scheme does not expressly state that applications for *ex gratia* payments of compensation will be 'entertained'. The 1996 Scheme commences by stating that the Scheme

> ... is made by the Secretary of State under the Criminal Injuries Compensation Act 1995 and that applications received on or after 1 April 1996 for the payment of compensation to, or in respect of, persons who have sustained criminal injury will be considered under this Scheme.

Although the 1990 Scheme is non-statutory and the 1996 Scheme is made by the Secretary of State on the authority of statute, the discretionary provisions in para 6/13 will apply in all cases.

The Board (as already explained, the use of this term in the paragraphs which follow should be deemed to include the Authority and the Appeals Panel) is required to decide on the information before it whether the injury suffered by the applicant is attributable to a crime of violence. If the Board is satisfied that this is so, such a finding is not sufficient in itself to enable the Board to make an award. It must also satisfy itself that on the information and evidence before it, the applicant has fulfilled the criteria of para 6/13, which are:

(i) Has the applicant informed the police *promptly* and *fully* of the circumstances in which the injuries were sustained?

(ii) Has he *fully* co-operated with the police in bringing the offender to justice?

(iii) Has he given *all* reasonable assistance to the Board in connection with the application?

(iv) Was the applicant's conduct such that he was not a totally blameless victim?

(v) Has the applicant a record of criminal convictions?

If the applicant's case fails any of these criteria, which are questions of fact to be decided by the Board, there arises a discretion which the Board must exercise.

Paragraph 6/13 states that in such cases the Board 'may withhold or reduce an award'.

In exercising that discretion the Board must consider whether, having regard to the applicant's failure to fulfil one or more of the five criteria set out above, it should make:

- a full award; or
- a reduced award and, if so, the extent of such reduction; or
- a nil award.

The Board must consider the merits and faults of the applicant's case under the rules of the Scheme in the exercise of its discretion under para 6/13. The Board's finding as a question of fact that, for example, the applicant delayed in informing the police of the circumstances of his injury, or that his conduct before sustaining the injury was provocative, does not legally preclude the applicant from receiving compensation. Such shortcomings in the application do not bring about a bar to compensation as such, but they do place a duty on the part of the Board to consider the merits as well as the failings of the applicant's case so that its decision to make a full award or a reduced award or a nil award is arrived at by an informed and fair exercise of the discretion, thereby producing a decision which is appropriate to the circumstances of the particular case. Recent decisions of the High Court in relation to the exercise of the Board's discretion are considered in Chapter 6.

In the year to 31 March 1993, the Board resolved 58,688 cases. In that same year 4,069 cases were refused for failure to comply with the requirements of para 6/13 regarding informing and co-operation with the police, 2,888 cases on the grounds of the applicant's own conduct and a further 1,888 cases on the grounds of the applicant's criminal convictions. With similar circumstances frequently presenting themselves for consideration and decision by the Board, it would be surprising if the Board did not have some broadly agreed policy in dealing with such cases.

Decisions on the papers are taken by the Board or an authorised officer of the Board or by a claims officer of the Authority, with oral hearings or appeals decided by the Board or the Appeals Panel. It is important that there should be a broadly similar approach to deciding cases which present broadly similar sets of circumstances in order to be fair as between one applicant and another. Broad considerations of policy, however, must not fetter the proper exercise of the discretion given to the decision maker by para 6/13. In each and every case, therefore, the individual merits of the case must be considered and an informed and fair discretion exercised in deciding whether to make a full award, a reduced award or no award at all. Such decisions must be arrived at after proper consideration of the merits of the individual case. If the decision making officer or the hearings Board or the Appeals Panel express themselves to be bound by a particular policy relating to cases of, for example, 'non co-operation' or 'conduct', this would be a wrongful fettering of their discretion in arriving at their decision in the case and that decision might therefore be challenged in the court on a point of law.

The remainder of this chapter addresses the requirements in para 6/13 in respect of informing the police, co-operating with the police in bringing the offender to justice, and assisting the Board.

2. Informing the police without delay

Paragraph 6 of the 1990 Scheme states:

> The Board may withhold or reduce compensation if they consider that … the applicant has not taken, without delay, all reasonable steps to inform the police, or any other authority considered by the Board to be appropriate for the purpose, of the circumstances of the injury.

Paragraph 13 of the 1996 Scheme is similar in its effect, but uses the words 'failed to take' all reasonable steps instead of 'has not taken'. The same considerations therefore apply in all cases. 'Failure' perhaps implies a sense of duty on the party of the applicant more than did the 1990 Scheme wording.

In making his report to the police, it is important that the victim reports all the relevant circumstances. If he deliberately leaves out important information his application would probably fail, and if he gives the police false information this would be regarded as non-co-operation with the police, another aspect of para 6/13. It is the applicant/victim who must personally fulfil the obligation to inform the police. A report made by a third party, whether or not that person knows the full circumstances of the injury, does not satisfy the requirement.

In the great majority of cases it is the police to whom the applicant must report. 'Other authority' is appropriate in only a narrow class of cases, and reports to employers or trade union officials will not fulfil the requirements of para 6/13 except in certain cases discussed below.

Where, for example, the police have reason to believe that the applicant knew the identity of his assailant but declined to give that name to the police, and the Board accepts that this is the case, the application would probably fail, as the applicant has not only failed to inform the police of all material facts within his knowledge but has also failed to co-operate with the police in bringing the offender to justice.

The applicant may have informed the police of the circumstances of his injury without delay, but if he refuses to make a complaint the Board would probably make no award. The applicant must be a willing prosecution witness from the outset and sustain that willingness, if required, through to the conclusion of the alleged assailant's trial.

The Scheme speaks of informing and co-operating. Merely giving information without making complaint, which enables the police to carry out their further investigation of the matter with the knowledge that they have a complainant who will make a statement and in due course will give evidence at the trial of the offender, falls short of the overall requirement under para 6/13 of 'informing' and 'co-operating', and subject to the considerations mentioned below, the Board would be unlikely to make an award.

In the most serious cases such as wounding with intent or attempted murder, the seriousness of the crime may cause the police to pursue their investigation regardless of the absence of a complaint by the injured party. Where serious injury totally incapacitates the injured party from giving any information to the police, the failure to inform the police and make a complaint of assault will not be regarded as failure by the injured party to comply with the Scheme. The Board will, however, consider whether the injured applicant has given all possible information and assistance to the police as soon as his capacity to do so is restored.

Applications frequently fail where the police have been informed of the incident, but not by the applicant himself. The fact that the police know that there has been an incident does not mean that they have knowledge of the applicant's injuries or precisely how these came about. It is the duty of the applicant personally to give all possible assistance to the police if he wishes to make a claim to the Board.

When an application is received, one of the first steps taken by the Board's staff is to request a police report from the relevant police authority. The information received by the Board in response to that request is central to the Board's consideration of the requirements of para 6/13 in relation to an application.

3. Co-operating with the police in bringing the offender to justice

The Scheme requires that the applicant takes all reasonable steps to co-operate with the police with a view to the offender being apprehended and convicted. Failure to co-operate with the police usually results in no award being made.

The applicant may fail to co-operate simply out of indifference or because he considers that to do so would be a waste of time as he has little positive information to give, or because he and the assailant have made up their differences. None of these explanations will be acceptable to the Board as they constitute a failure to meet the applicant's obligations under para 6/13.

Refusal to make a written statement or attend an identification parade will be regarded as a refusal to co-operate.

In many cases the victim has good reason to fear reprisals from his assailant if he assists the police in the prosecution. This will not, however, be regarded by the Board as a generally acceptable reason for not co-operating with the police in the prosecution of the assailant.

The Board has indicated that a victim who wilfully fails to attend the trial of the alleged assailant to give evidence, or deliberately gives untrue evidence, for example failing to identify an assailant whom he is able to identify, will be regarded as having failed to co-operate with the police.

The information before the claims officer when the questions of reporting to and co-operating with the police are considered on the papers will usually consist of the applicant's own account of events included in his application and the contents of the police report on the incident.

The latter tells the Board or Authority amongst other things when, where and by whom the incident was first reported, the name of the assailant if known, any criminal proceedings arising from the incident and the outcome of such proceedings.

The report will also contain information regarding the applicant's willingness to inform the police of all the relevant circumstances and how he came by his injuries, and willingness to support a prosecution if the assailant could be identified and charged with an offence.

The application form requires the applicant to state whether he personally reported the incident to the police and, if so, where and when that report was made. If the applicant did not report the incident promptly or at all, he is asked to give an explanation for this in the application form.

The third document which will often assist the Board in resolving the questions of delay in reporting or apparent failure to co-operate with the police is the medical report, which is also obtained by the Board's staff at the initial enquiry stage. When the latter shows, for example, that the applicant was badly hurt and went straight to hospital for emergency treatment and was detained in hospital for several days, this may explain an apparent failure to report promptly or to co-operate with the police in their investigation of the incident.

It has to be said, however, that although the information in the medical report can sometimes assist the Board in the context of reporting and co-operating, the information on these matters in the police report and in the application form itself is always central to these questions.

The Board has stated that it attaches great importance to the duty of the applicant to make a prompt and full report to the police for three principal reasons:

(i) that prompt investigation of the circumstances by the police is the best means of establishing the truth of the facts alleged by the applicant and providing corroboration of his allegation of injury attributable to a crime of violence;

(ii) that such investigation is the Board's best, or indeed only, protection against fraudulent claims; and

(iii) that the Scheme requires as a matter of principle that the police are given every possible assistance by the applicant in identifying and prosecuting the offender so that society at large, whose taxes pay for the compensation, has the best possible chance of stopping the offender repeating the offence against other victims.

These principles can best be illustrated by examples. Although the examples below are not actual cases decided by the Board, they are typical of the situations which most often occur in applications to the Board.

The following are examples of applications which would be likely to fail under para 6/13 of the Scheme:

(i) Application form states that the applicant suffered a badly cut lip, a broken tooth and bruising to the face in a fight outside a pub. The applicant spoke to the police at the scene before he was taken to hospital by ambulance with another man also hurt in the fight which involved several other youths.

The applicant was treated in the casualty department where his lip was stitched and he then went home. He had no more contact with the police thereafter.

Police report states that the police were called by the licensee of the pub. The police found two youths on the scene; both had been injured. The applicant told police he was hurt in a fight. He refused to make a complaint and gave no particulars or identification of his assailants.

Comment: The refusal to make a complaint would result in there being no police investigation.

(ii) Application form states that the applicant was attacked by two youths when walking home alone at 11.00 pm. He remembers falling and being kicked and may have lost consciousness briefly. He was helped by a passer-by and taken to hospital by ambulance. He spoke to a police officer at the hospital who came to see him regarding the incident in which he was injured. He was in hospital for twenty-four hours for observation and then discharged.

Police report states that police went to the hospital one hour after the incident but were not permitted to see the applicant by the medical staff. The police returned to the hospital the next morning and interviewed the applicant regarding the incident. The applicant wanted no police action taken and signed a statement to that effect.

Comment: A 'retraction' statement will usually be regarded by the Board as in breach of the requirements of para 6/13. (See also page 75.)

(iii) Application form states that the applicant was struck and cut by a glass when fighting broke out between two groups of youths in a night club. The incident was on a Friday night. The applicant was taken to hospital by a friend. He had four stitches to his face and returned home. He 'felt rotten' during the weekend and did not go out of the house. He went to work on the Monday morning, and on Monday evening went to the police station where he reported the incident and made a statement.

Police report states that the incident was first reported by the applicant on Monday 6 October at 6.30 pm, the reported incident having occurred on Friday 3 October at 11.50 pm. The police had gone to the disturbance at the night club but had not seen the applicant and knew nothing of his injury until he reported it the following Monday.

Comment: A delay of two days after the applicant had returned home from hospital with evidence that the applicant was able to return to work in the meantime before reporting the incident would constitute 'delay' under para 6/13. The opportunity to investigate the matter would have been substantially prejudiced by the delay. The Board looks to the applicant's having taken the very earliest opportunity to communicate with the police, second only to any necessary emergency treatment of injury.

(iv) Application form states that the applicant had been leaving a football ground and walking with friends towards their car to go home. A group of youths ran up to them from behind and attacked them without provocation. The applicant, who was a supporter of the visiting team, believed that the youths who attacked him were home supporters. The applicant fell as a result of the attack and suffered a broken wrist. The attackers ran off. The answer to the question in the application form 'Was the incident reported to the police?' was 'No', and the reason for not reporting given as 'I had no idea who my attackers were and saw no point in telling the police as there was no hope of catching them'.

Comment: Under the Scheme it is the duty of the applicant to inform the police of the incident as soon as possible regardless of his personal view, however reasonably based, of the chances of successfully tracing and prosecuting the offenders.

(v) The same incident as in (iv) above, but the application form states that the incident was reported ten days later, the explanation for the delay being 'I spoke to a local policeman about the incident and he said I should report it and that I could make a claim to the Criminal Injuries Compensation Board. Until then I did not know about the Scheme and that the incident had to be reported'.

Comment: The application would probably fail as there was delay in informing the police. Ignorance of the Scheme's requirements or of the existence of the Scheme is, like ignorance of the law, no excuse.

The premise on which the requirements of para 6/13 are based is that it is reasonable to expect all adult citizens to realise that (a) a violent physical attack upon them causing them some injury is a crime, and (b) crime is essentially a matter for the police, who should accordingly be informed as soon as practically possible of the circumstances.

Many applicants state as the reason for failing to report the incident that they had no idea who their attackers were and 'saw no point in reporting it'. This explanation, though understandable, will usually result in there being no award. Only in a minority of such cases is the victim truly unable to give any information at all which would assist an investigation. The applicant is in no position to judge what other information the police may have from other sources of this or other incidents of a similar nature in the vicinity, thus making even fragmentary information from the applicant of some value. It is important not to lose sight of a principal element of the Scheme, which is the duty to report, to give all the information one can, however incomplete, and to do so as quickly as possible after the incident has occurred.

The Scheme says 'without delay'. It does not say 'immediately' but the examples given above illustrate the strictness with which the Board interprets 'delay'. The obligation to report is regarded as of the utmost urgency. A few hours could be too late. It is likely that the Authority will take a similar view.

When the applicant is seen by police at the scene of the incident a matter of minutes after it has occurred and, subject to any serious or disabling injury having been suffered, does not take that opportunity to inform the police as fully as he can of the circumstances of his injury, the application will be likely to fail. Often in such cases the applicant is speaking with police while waiting for an ambulance. If the applicant is able to communicate but declines there and then to assist the police regarding the incident, the application will be unlikely to succeed for failure to co-operate or to take all reasonable steps to inform the police of the circumstances.

When the injury is such that urgent treatment must precede the giving of a statement, the police will frequently see to the transporting of the applicant to hospital and inform the applicant that, as no statement can be obtained immediately, the applicant should contact the police as soon as he can after receiving treatment so that the statement can be obtained. Failure to follow this up on the applicant's part frequently leads to the refusal of an application under para 6/13.

When compensation has been refused by the Board on the papers on the grounds of delay in reporting, and the applicant requests and is granted a hearing, the Board will have more detailed evidence than appears on the papers alone regarding the sequence of events – commencing with the incident and finishing with the reporting of the incident to the police by the applicant (if he did so).

Under the 1996 Scheme procedure, the initial decision by a claims officer and the review by a more senior claims officer will be on papers only. Any appeal from the reviewing officer's decision is to the Appeals Panel which, like a Board hearing under the 1990 Scheme, is an oral hearing, when oral evidence from witnesses will supplement the documentary evidence.

All manner of circumstances may affect the applicant's actions, and the Board's assessment of those actions between incident and reporting.

To meet fully the requirements of para 6/13, the applicant has virtually to show that the point of time at which he reported the incident was the earliest at which it was physically possible for him to do so. Anything less and the application will be likely either to fail or the Board will make a reduced award.

The questions likely to be asked at a hearing include some of the following, which are intended to illustrate the factors which assist the Board in deciding firstly what point in time represented the applicant's earliest realistic chance to report the incident and the injury and, secondly, whether the applicant took that chance:

(i) Did the police attend the scene? Did you speak to the police? What was said? Did you tell the police what had happened? Did you know the assailant? Did you identify him to the police? Did you assist the police with a description?

(ii) Did you see the police when you were at the hospital? What was said by you and by the police? How was the matter left? Were you asked to contact the police again when you came out of hospital? Did you do so?

(iii) Did you tell the police you wanted no action taken? Did you sign a statement to that effect? What were your reasons for signing that statement? Why did you wish no investigation or prosecution? Did you not wish to assist in the prosecution of your assailant? Did the police say that they saw no prospect of catching the offender and request a statement to that effect? Would you have supported a prosecution if the police had been able to do so, or had arrested someone for the offence?

(iv) In your application you say that you did not see the police at the scene, you went to hospital to get treatment and went home to bed. You did not report the incident for three days. Were you alone when you were attacked? Was there a phone nearby? How far was the incident from the nearest police station? Do you live alone? Are you on the telephone at home? Why did you not phone the police? Did you ask your wife/flatmate to phone the police? Did you go out of the house the next day? When did you return to work? Why did you not go to the police station as soon as you were able to do so?

These questions illustrate the sort of information the Board will need in four different types of situation, to help it decide whether the applicant fulfilled the requirements of 'informing' and 'co-operating'. The claims officer of the Authority and the Appeals Panel will likewise seek answers to these questions in arriving at a fair decision on the issues of 'reporting' and 'co-operating'. Every case is in some way different from every other. The Board's duty is to exercise a discretion which takes account of those variations from one case to another. The Authority and Appeals Panel have a similar duty.

The requirements of para 6/13 may in some cases seem rather harsh. It is not surprising that the injured applicant will feel rotten and just want to go home to bed to sleep it off. Having done so he will often just want to stay indoors for the next few days. These understandable human reactions to being hurt or injured have, however, to be weighed by the Board against the clearly stated 'John Citizen' duty of the applicant to set the police on the trail of the assailant at the earliest possible moment, and with the maximum assistance by way of information which the applicant can give them.

Two categories of case should be distinguished from the majority. First, the seriously injured applicant who is detained in hospital and medically unfit to see the police for several days is not regarded as having delayed unreasonably. The decision of the hospital medical staff that the applicant was unfit to be interviewed would be accepted by the Board as it would be by the police. However, from the point at which the medical staff regarded the applicant as fit to be interviewed, the Board will need to be satisfied that the applicant co-operated fully with the police in bringing the offender to justice to whatever extent he was able.

The second category of applicant whose position under para 6/13 is somewhat different is the child victim or minor. It would not be realistic or appropriate to place upon a child of tender years any responsibility for immediately informing the police of an assault, and the Board does not do so.

However, where the injured party is between say, 15 and 18 years of age, the Board may examine the applicant's response to the alleged assault in terms of the requirements of para 6/13, not necessarily because the full obligations of that paragraph are required of the youthful applicant, which generally they are not, but because the fulfilment of the requirements of para 6/13 adds considerably to the weight of the evidence of the claim as a whole towards satisfying the Board that the requirements of para 4(a) (1990) or 8(a) (1996) – the crime of violence – are established. It is not unreasonable to ask why, say, a 17 year-old youth who has been attacked and injured did not report the attack to the police.

The Board's twenty-third report (1987) contains the following case report:

The applicant was 17 years old at the time of the incident. He alleged that he was inside a cafe when a fight developed. Although he claimed he was not involved, he was nevertheless struck above the left eye with a bottle. When the police arrived they took him to hospital. He made no formal complaint of assault, and signed a policeman's notebook to that end. Later on, the applicant's solicitor made the complaint to the police; but the enquiries the police then made were fruitless. The application was disallowed. The Board member commented:

> Paragraph 6(a) of the (1979) Scheme requires applicants for awards both to report alleged assaults to the police without delay and thereafter to co-operate with the police, so that prompt investigations may be made to bring the offenders to justice. In this case, the applicant at first refused to make any complaint or to co-operate with the police and signed a statement to this effect. It was much too late when some days later solicitors acting for the applicant sought to make a complaint, and in these circumstances an award of public funds is inappropriate.

The Board tends not to hold against a young minor applicant the failure of his parents to comply with the reporting requirement of para 6/13 where the parents appear to have taken responsibility for the matter.

Thus where for example a 14 year-old youth is attacked and injured and goes straight home to his parents, who fail to report the assault to the police promptly or at all, the Board would probably not refuse to make an award under para 6/13, as the failure of the parents to report the incident is not ascribed to the injured minor.

Non-reporting may, however, result in the application being more likely to fail under para 4(a) (1990), 8(a) (1996) if the absence of a police investigation results in the Board or Authority not being satisfied as to the circumstances of the injury.

A further illustration of the 'minor' applicant in the context of para 6/13 is contained in the following hypothetical application:

The application form states that the applicant, aged 13, was struck in the face by an older boy and suffered a broken nose. His elder brother, aged 16, took him to hospital where he was treated but not detained. The matter was not reported until ten days later when the boy's parents, who had been away on holiday, returned home and immediately went to the police station where the boy made a statement.

If the Board accepts the truth of the incident, the application would probably not be refused under para 6/13 as the Board does not expect from a minor the same level of responsibility in the matter of reporting as would be expected of an adult.

In cases of apparent failure to co-operate with the police, the Board is careful to distinguish between two types of situation. If the applicant refuses to co-operate with the police by, for example, refusing to make a statement, failing without reasonable excuse to keep appointments to be interviewed by the police, refusing to attend an identification parade or look at police photographs, refusing to name a known assailant or refusing or failing without reasonable excuse to attend court to give evidence against the assailant, the Board will be unlikely to make an award. Where, however, the applicant has given the police all the information and assistance he can and would have supported a prosecution had there been sufficient evidence, and it is the view of the police as well as the applicant that there is no basis on which to mount a prosecution, the absence of a formal statement by the applicant or formal complaint will not be 'refusal to co-operate'.

In the latter situation the applicant will sometimes have signed a brief formal statement that he wishes no police action to be taken. On the face of it this statement could be regarded as evidence of refusal to co-operate, but the Board seeks to establish which of two situations is the basis for such a statement.

Was it:

(a) the applicant's confirmation of his refusal to assist a prosecution?; or

(b) a statement requested by police so that they can close their file where the applicant has done all he can to assist?

Sometimes in the second situation where a prosecution is seen by police as a non-starter, the statement by the applicant to the effect that he wishes the police to take no action and would not support a prosecution is made at a police officer's request and is nothing more than a formal step to enable the police to close their file. There is nothing improper about such a course, but as it makes two totally different situations under the Scheme similar in outward appearance, the Board must establish by inquiry the true context in which the statement was made. If the true situation is (b) and not (a) above, the Board will not refuse an award on the grounds of non-co-operation. Nevertheless, it is essential, if the applicant is to succeed before the Board, that he should have reported the facts even if he takes the view that there is no prospect of a successful prosecution.

In the Board's twenty-third report (1987) the following case is reported: The applicant was a self-employed taxi driver. He was attacked by a group of skinheads and received various injuries. In his application form he wrote:

> I did not report the matter to the police because it seemed pointless. The youths had disappeared and I did not think there was any point whatsoever in the police looking for them because it would have been impossible.

His solicitors reiterated this in a letter. They also said that he had attended the local hospital, and suggested that a report to this authority was sufficient instead of a report to the police. The application was disallowed.

Sometimes where there has been a delay, it becomes clear that the only reason the offence was reported at all was because the applicant had become aware that reporting was necessary if he wished to claim compensation. Although the intended claim to the Board being the spur to make the report to the police is not in itself an obstacle, the delay in reporting would be material to the Board's decision.

Two cases reported in the Board's twenty-fourth report (1988) illustrate, in the first, the Board's view of the applicant who decides for his own reasons not to make a prompt report to the police, and in the second, the way in which the applicant's personal situation, particularly where the applicant is elderly and isolated, can modify the Board's view so that the discretion under para 6/13 can be properly exercised in the applicant's favour.

In the first case a young man made an application in which he stated that he had been assaulted while walking home in the early hours of the morning. He said he had been attacked by two men from behind, and as a consequence suffered bruising to his face and a broken jaw. He did not report the incident to the police for four days, and when asked to give his reasons for this said that he had not seen his assailants, and would not have been able to give a description of them. Furthermore, there were no witnesses.

The single member disallowed the application, explaining the decision as follows:

> The Board attaches great importance to prompt reporting to the police ... of any alleged assault. Thus and only thus can an applicant's allegations be thoroughly investigated by the police, and the chances of any assailant being brought to justice maximised. The applicant, without justification in my view, failed to report promptly to the police the incident in which he claims to have been assaulted and I disallow the application under paragraph 6(a) of the [1979] Scheme. On the available evidence – and the onus is on the applicant – I cannot say how he came by his injuries and thus that paragraphs 4 [crime of violence] and 6(a) are satisfied.

In the second case, a lady aged 78 was mugged by two young men. Her handbag was seized and she was thrown to the ground, landing on her right shoulder. After the attack she felt shocked and dazed, and went home. She did not go to the hospital until the next morning, where she was discovered to have a dislocated shoulder.

It was only after some persuasion that she reported the matter to the police, and this did not occur until three days after the incident. The application was disallowed by the Board on the grounds of delay in reporting.

The applicant requested a hearing. She wrote that she had delayed in reporting to the police because she had been shocked after the incident. She was not on the phone at home, and had never used a public call box. No one had helped her at the scene of the incident. It was only when her brother saw her that the report was made.

The Board considered all the circumstances, and decided that in this case there should be a full award.

The requirement of para 6/13 is that the 'police' be informed without delay. In certain cases, albeit a small minority, the reporting process to another 'body or person considered by the Authority to be appropriate for the purpose' may be accepted instead. The quoted wording is from para 13(a) of the 1996 Scheme. The equivalent wording in the 1990 Scheme is:

> ... or any other authority considered by the Board to be appropriate for the purpose.

The purpose and effect is similar under both Schemes.

The Board and the Authority regard the police as the authority to whom the applicant is expected personally to report the circumstances of his injury. With very few exceptions, reporting elsewhere but not to the police will generally result in compensation being refused. The Scheme itself does not give any guidance on what 'other authority' (in the 1990 Scheme cases) or 'other body or person' (1996 Scheme) may be considered appropriate.

The way in which the Board has approached this question under the 1990 and earlier Schemes will therefore provide a guide to the approach likely to be taken by the Authority and the Appeals Panel under the 1996 Scheme. Applicants will have reported the incident in many cases to trade union officials or to their employers or simply to the hospital where their injuries were treated. Many applicants state, in requesting a hearing, that they reported the assault to the hospital and believed that the hospital was obliged to inform the police. In the majority of cases, reporting only to the first or second of these supposed alternatives (union or employer) and not to the police will result in the application being refused; this will certainly be the case where the applicant merely informs the hospital where treatment was obtained. He will be deemed not to have met the reporting requirement of this part of the Scheme.

The exceptions are cases where the injuries are received in mental hospitals or prisons. The Board generally accepts that with regard to injuries received within these particular confined communities it would be inappropriate to require a report to the police, but it still looks for (a) the prompt and full reporting and recording of the incident and (b) its investigation by the internal authority of the mental hospital or prison within which the incident occurred.

In cases where, for example, a nurse in a mental hospital is injured by the aggressive action of a patient – or a prison officer, or another prisoner, is injured by the criminal action of a prisoner, the Board generally does not expect or require a report to the police as a condition of entitlement to an award. The Board will request copies of accident books, records of incidents, corroborative statements of any witnesses and a report by the mental hospital or prison authority on the result of any internal investigation into the incident. These documents will generally be sufficient to enable the Board to make a decision on an application made under the terms of the Scheme.

The Board may sometimes accept the internal reporting, recording and investigating procedures of schools and educational authorities where injury is caused to a young child by a fellow pupil – but only if there is sufficient evidence of investigation of the matter without the police becoming involved. The mere recording of an incident and injury would not be sufficient on its own unless that process established clear evidence of a crime of violence which meets the requirements of para 4(a) (1990), 8(a) (1996). Where the children concerned are older and the conduct of the assailant is more appropriately regarded as criminal than in the case of a younger child, the Board or Authority may consider that it is appropriate to involve the police even if the education authority undertakes its own investigation.

More difficult as a category is the injured employee who reports to his union official but not to the police. In the case of public transport employees, the injury is often sustained in the course of work where a ticket inspector or bus conductor is attacked and injured by a passenger. He or she will generally have reported the incident to the employer and to a union official. This will usually be in accordance with an established procedure between employers and employees for reporting and recording violent incidents affecting employees in the course of their work and will frequently result in the police being informed. The Board may refuse an application where, for example, a bus conductor is attacked and injured by a passenger and reports the incident to his employer or union official but the police are not informed. There is, as a result, no investigation of the matter by the police.

The Board expects the police to be informed of violent crimes. Incidents in prisons or 'closed' hospital units caring for mentally disturbed or geriatric patients are perhaps the only true exceptions to this basic rule, so that such hospital or prison authorities are the only examples of 'other body or person' or 'other authority' under the 1996 and 1990 Schemes likely to be an acceptable alternative to the police under para 6/13.

Mention needs to be made of situations which illustrate flexibility where this is necessary in the interests of justice. A young child who is attacked by a stranger or who is sexually abused by a member of the family will perhaps tell a parent or a social worker of the incident. No more can be expected of the victim in terms of compliance with para 6/13, but the Board still needs the benefit of a prompt police investigation of the incident. If the person to whom the child has reported the matter fails to inform the police promptly, the application to the Board may fail as the Board does not have sufficient evidence to be satisfied on the balance of probabilities that the incident occurred in the terms alleged.

Cases of sexual abuse of children are dealt with separately in Chapter 9, but with regard to the obligation to report 'without delay' very considerable flexibility is allowed by the Board in this type of case. In many cases the victim is a very young child - and as the person to whom a child would be expected to report so serious a matter is usually the mother, who in many cases is the wife of the abuser, the father or stepfather of the victim, there are no means whereby the victim can make the situation known. Often the truth of the victim's situation is made known long after the event by the victim informing either a close friend, a relative or schoolteacher in whom the child feels able or even compelled to confide. This may lead to an enquiry by the police which reveals a situation which has continued over a number of years, with many separate acts of abuse having occurred resulting in mental injury to the child. Once the facts are established by police investigation, and whether or not there has been a successful prosecution of the offender, the Board will usually treat the case history as one application.

If the abuse ended more than two years (1996 Scheme) or three years (1990 Scheme) before the application is made, the time limit provisions apply, although allowances are made if the application comes within a reasonable time of the victim attaining majority. The time limit applying to applications under the Scheme has already been considered in Chapter 1.

It has already been noted in Chapter 1 in relation to the time limit that the 1996 Scheme (para 17) imposes a two-year time limit after the incident for lodging the application with the Authority. It has also been noted that in the initial period - probably the first year of the 1996 Scheme, i.e. up to 1 April 1997 - the Authority will waive the two-year time limit, provided that the application received in that period meets the three-year time limit under earlier Schemes. After 31 March 1997 it is to be expected that applicants will be required to 'meet' the two-year time limit in lodging applications with the Authority.

There is one other provision which should be mentioned in this context, and that is the exclusion of any remedy for 'family violence', including sexual abuse, under the Scheme before 1 October 1979. Cases affected by this provision will become rarer with the passage of time, but might arise where the victim applies on attaining 18 years of age and the application includes abuse in early childhood, which could be before that date. Where the abuse started before that date but continued after it, only the latter may be the subject of compensation by the Board. This principle was confirmed as correct in law by a recent decision of the High Court upholding the

Board's refusal to award compensation for pre- 1 October 1979 sexual abuse within the family home. The words of exclusion in para 7 of the 1969 Scheme which preclude these cases read:

> Where the victim who suffered injuries and the offender who inflicted them were living together at the time as members of the same family no compensation will be payable.

4. Giving all reasonable assistance to the Board (1990 Scheme) and to the Authority or Appeals Panel (1996 Scheme)

The Authority and Appeals Panel need the full co-operation and assistance of the applicant in bringing the application to a state of readiness for a decision on the papers or, if there is a hearing, at the subsequent hearing.

The areas in which factual information is needed include the incident in which injury was suffered, the applicant's contacts with police and treatment of the injuries at a hospital or by his general practitioner. The application form which every applicant must complete covers these areas and gives the Authority's staff a start in gathering all material facts needed for a decision. In most cases there will be some additional information needed from the applicant, and the Authority's staff will write to the applicant requesting that information. If there is no response or co-operation, the application cannot be completed and submitted for decision.

The Board has not readily refused an award outright under para 6(b) of the 1990 Scheme except in the worst cases. It may reasonably be expected that the Authority will exercise its power along similar lines to refuse an application on the grounds that the applicant has 'failed to give all reasonable assistance to the Authority' under para 13(c) of the 1996 Scheme. More frequently, the failure on the part of the applicant to respond to requests for information from the Authority's staff will result in the application being treated as abandoned. This does not amount to a decision disallowing the application. It means that the Authority's staff will take no further action on the matter unless and until the applicant communicates with the Authority and produces a response on the outstanding matters of fact required from him.

Failure by the applicant to attend appointments for medical examination arranged by the Authority will create similar problems, and where the failure to co-operate is repeated, could lead to the application being treated as abandoned or disallowed. Where this situation arises, the Authority's staff will usually send a final warning letter by recorded delivery. If there is still no reply after a suitable interval and clearly no prospect of progress, the file is laid by. It is not destroyed in case the applicant gets in touch and is willing to assist the Authority in bringing the application to a conclusion at a later stage.

A situation which occurs with surprising frequency is the failure on the part of an applicant who has requested and been granted a hearing to attend the hearing on the appointed day. This is wasteful of valuable hearing time which might have been allocated to another case. Under para 25 of the 1990 Scheme, the Board may dismiss an application when the applicant fails to attend the hearing of his application and has offered 'no reasonable excuse for his non-attendance'. Similarly, under para 78 of the 1996 Scheme, the Appeals Panel may 'determine the appeal in his absence'. The Schemes also provide for possible reinstatement and rehearing of such an application in suitable cases. (See page 259 regarding para 78 (1996).)

Chapter 6

The effects of character and conduct on compensation awards

As the 1996 Scheme expressly preserves the provisions of the 1990 Scheme in respect of all applications outstanding at 31 March 1996 (over 100,000 cases at that date) it is necessary to look at the parallel provisions of the 1990 and 1996 Schemes in each aspect of the Schemes' operation. This chapter looks in turn at those parts of the two Schemes which deal with an applicant's 'convictions' and 'conduct'.

1. Criminal convictions

The wording of para 6(c) of the 1990 Scheme reads:

> The Board may withhold or reduce compensation if they consider that ...
>
> (c) having regard to the conduct of the applicant before, during or after the events giving rise to the claim or to his character as shown by his criminal convictions or unlawful conduct ... it is inappropriate that a full award, or any award at all, be granted.

There are two quite separate aspects covered by para 6(c): the applicant's convictions, and his conduct. Paragraph 13 of the 1996 Scheme separates these two entirely different provisions and reads:

> A claims officer may withhold or reduce an award where he considers that:
>
> ...
>
> (d) the conduct of the applicant before, during or after the incident giving rise to the application makes it inappropriate that a full award or any award at all be made; or
>
> (e) the applicant's character as shown by his criminal convictions (excluding convictions spent under the Rehabilitation of Offenders Act 1974) or by evidence available to the claims officer makes it inappropriate that a full award or any award at all be made.

These long-established requirements are thus continued under the new Scheme. The discretion vested in the persons responsible for making decisions on applications under para 13 of the 1996 Scheme means that the nature of these qualifying provisions to compensation remains the same as before, and is subject to the applicant in each case satisfying the claims officer or the Panel – as with the Board under earlier Schemes – that there has been no 'conduct' on the part of the applicant or 'criminal convictions' which would make a full award, or any award at all, inappropriate.

The test of 'appropriateness' means that entitlement is not so much a technical point of law as a weighing of the applicant's 'conduct' or 'convictions' in the scale of values of the public at large whose taxes have provided the funds from which an award would be made. 'Appropriateness' is an evaluation and enables or even requires the Authority to consider the reaction of the man in the street to those factors in the case which fall to be considered under these two heads. Neither the 1990 nor the 1996 Scheme lays down criteria in deciding such matters (although the Guide to the 1996 Scheme indicates a 'penalty points' system for evaluating convictions). The Authority or Panel is given a discretion which has to be exercised in a fair and reasonable way, after having the material evidence placed before it, so that it is an informed discretion. If, after it has considered the evidence in the case, the Authority or Panel decides to exercise its discretion in such a manner as any reasonable tribunal could not so decide on the evidence before it, the decision would be wrong in law and subject to judicial review by the High Court. The legal principle is known as the *Wednesbury* principle after the decision in *Associated Provincial Picture Houses v Wednesbury Corporation* [1948] 1 KB 223.

Cases involving judicial review of the decisions of the Board are summarised in Appendix 1.

Accepting that the law provides a means of challenging a decision of the Board, Authority or Panel 'at which no reasonable tribunal properly directing itself could have arrived' (the *Wednesbury* rule), one asks: what are the proper considerations to which the Board or Authority or Panel should apply its mind in deciding what factors make an award 'inappropriate' when considering 'character'?

The Scheme is, in a sense, a statement of a relationship between the applicant on the one hand and his fellow citizens on the other. The compensation is provided by Parliament and is therefore taxpayers' money.

The question which the Board or Authority or Panel has to ask itself is: is it appropriate to make an award to this applicant in respect of an injury he has suffered as an innocent victim of a crime of violence, in the face of his own record of convictions for crimes against the interests of his fellow citizens, they being the providers of the fund from which compensation would be paid? If a full award is deemed inappropriate, the Authority or Panel or Board must also consider whether a reduced award is also inappropriate or whether a reduction, rather than making no award at all, would meet the point.

Applicants who have been refused compensation under this provision and who ask for a hearing sometimes protest that they have no convictions for violent crime, or that they have paid the penalty for their crimes by way of fines or imprisonment, or that their own crimes should not mean that anyone else is entitled to attack them and 'get away with it'. The Board, the Authority or the Panel, in considering such representations, will ask itself whether the public at large would consider it appropriate that a Scheme established to compensate members of the public for injury suffered as a consequence of crime should be used to compensate someone who is, on this occasion, the victim but who on one or more recorded occasions has inflicted damage or loss or injury on his fellow citizens by his own deliberate criminal activity. The Board or Authority would also have in mind that individual fellow citizens were the victims on each occasion of such criminal activity and that the cost of each criminal trial has been borne by the same taxpayers whose taxes provide the compensation.

The Scheme may be unique in this concept of the worthy or unworthy applicant, but since 1990 it has contained an express requirement that the applicant's convictions be considered.

The Board's 1987 'Statement' and the 1990 'Guide' giving informal guidance as to the interpretation of the Scheme suggested that even one conviction for a serious crime of violence or other serious crime could result in the application being rejected completely. Where the applicant has in the past been convicted of murder or attempted murder or rape or an armed robbery, involving a substantial term of imprisonment, an award is most unlikely although there is no rule which would make that the case in all circumstances.

Where an applicant under the 1990 Scheme has numerous convictions for offences of violence, such as assault occasioning actual bodily harm, it is unlikely that he would receive an award, unless the last of these convictions was at least four or five years before the application. Where there has clearly been a substantial effort by the applicant to rehabilitate himself the Board may consider a substantial reduction, say 75 per cent, rather than a nil award, to encourage the process of rehabilitation which could be regarded as being in society's interests as well as the applicant's.

A change which has been effected by the 1996 Scheme is the express exclusion of 'spent' convictions under the Rehabilitation of Offenders Act 1974. Before 1 April 1996 the Scheme had no such express exclusion and the Board's practice was to take note of all convictions although it would generally attach little significance to 'old' convictions which did not, in the view of the Board, impinge upon its consideration of the appropriateness or otherwise of making an award. Now the 1996 Scheme precludes the consideration of 'spent' convictions under that Scheme.

In an effort to achieve a uniformity of approach to the difficult question of convictions under para 13(e) of the 1996 Scheme, the Authority's Guide to the 1996 Scheme indicates, in paras 8.15, 8.16 and 8.17 to the Guide, that in exercising its discretion to refuse or reduce an award on the basis of an applicant's character as shown by his or her convictions, ignoring spent convictions under the Rehabilitation of Offenders Act 1974:

> We will assess the extent to which convictions may count against an award by reference to the system of penalty points below. These points are based upon the type and/or length of any sentence imposed by the courts together

> with the time between date of the sentence and the receipt of the application. Any sentence imposed by a court after the application has been sent to us will also be taken into account.

The system of penalty points is then set out under three headings:

Sentence of the Court	*Period between date of sentence and receipt of application by CICA*	*Penalty points*

The penalty points are then totalled up and the total will attract a stated percentage reduction in the award.

The Guide then states, after certain 'Notes' to assist interpretation of the table:

> Having done that assessment, we will then consider any relevant mitigating factors such as where the injury resulted from the applicant's assistance to the police in upholding the law or from genuinely helping someone who was under attack.

The Guide is available from the Authority. The points table can be used to calculate (a) the penalty points attaching to each conviction and sentence, (b) the total penalty points for all 'unspent' convictions, and (c) the 'percentage reduction' attracted by that total number of penalty points. It is thus a mathematical exercise.

It is important to emphasise that this calculation does not bind the Authority. Indeed if the Authority decided the matter only on the calculation of penalty points and made its decision entirely on the percentage reduction table set out in para 8.16 of the Guide, it would be fettering its discretion under para 13 of the 1996 Scheme and thus open to challenge by way of judicial review. It is a legal requirement in all cases considered under para 13 of the 1996 Scheme, as with para 6 of the 1990 Scheme, that the Authority exercises its discretion whether to reduce or withhold compensation after considering all the merits of the individual case and should not regard itself as bound by a particular policy with regard to certain types of case.

The exercise of that discretion must not only be unfettered by considerations of general policy; the exercise of the Authority's or the Panel's discretion must involve a consideration of the alternatives open to the Authority or the Panel under the terms of the Scheme – that they *may* reduce or withhold an award – and involve a consideration whether a full award may be made and, if this is considered to be inappropriate, whether a reduced award should be made. If so, the appropriate level of reduction falls to be considered, having regard to the individual merits of the case. That level of reduction might be anything from a small reduction to a substantial one, or withholding compensation altogether where the Panel or the Authority in the exercise of its discretion considers that the facts of the case merit that decision.

Four recent court decisions on the exercise of the Board's discretion, as evidenced by the reasons given by the Board for its decisions, illustrate how the court has interpreted this important aspect of the Scheme. The cases of *R v CICB, ex parte Gambles* (*The Times* 5 January 1993) (since disapproved by the Court of Appeal in *R v CICB, ex parte Cook* (December 1995)), *R v CICB ex parte Powell* (decided 16 July 1993) and *R v CICB, ex parte Maxted* (decided 8 July 1994) relate to para 6(c) 1990 (conduct), 6(c) 1990 (convictions), 6(a) 1990 (informing the police and co-operating with the police) and 6(c) 1990 (convictions) respectively.

The Board's decision was quashed in *Gambles* and *Powell* and upheld in *Cook* and *Maxted*. In *Gambles* Sedley J concluded that the Board's reasons did not demonstrate that it had proceeded to arrive at its decision in three stages, by considering the following questions:

(a) Does the applicant's conduct make a full award inappropriate?
(b) If so, to what extent does the applicant's conduct impact on the appropriateness of an award?
(c) What award if any should the applicant consequently receive?

The Board's reasons should 'demonstrate ... that the conclusion had been reached by appropriate process of reasoning from the facts.'

In *Cook* the Court of Appeal (Aldous LJ) stated with regard to the above decision:

> I believe that the reasoning and the conclusion reached by Sedley J in *Gambles* is wrong. A decision that no award was appropriate out of public funds is equivalent to deciding that the award should be nil. The question that the Board had to ask was the equivalent of the third question suggested by the judge: Should the applicant receive an award and, if so, what amount? ... It is not incumbent upon the Board, as suggested by Sedley J, to demonstrate in their reasons that the conclusion has been reached by an appropriate process of reasoning from the facts. The reasons must be adequate and comply with the principles to which I have referred earlier in this judgment.

Earlier in his judgment Aldous LJ referred to para 22 of the 1990 Scheme and to the House of Lords case of *Bolton Metropolitan District Council v Secretary of State for the Environment* [1995] JPL 1043 and the earlier Board case of *R v CICB, ex parte Thompstone and Crowe* [1984] 1 WLR 1234. He stated:

> I believe it is clear that the Board's reasons should contain sufficient detail to enable the reader to know what conclusion has been reached on the principal important issue or issues, but it is not a requirement that they should deal with every material consideration to which it has had regard. If the reasons given are sufficient, they cannot be reviewed in judicial review proceedings unless the Board misconstrued its mandate or the decision is *Wednesbury* unreasonable.

In delivering judgment Aldous LJ also approved the decision of Buxton J in *R v CICB, ex parte Hopper* (unreported, 7 July 1995), which was decided after and distinguished *Gambles*, refusing an application to quash a decision of the Board which had been expressed in the following terms:

> The applicant's character and way of life as evidenced by the list of convictions and cautions makes it inappropriate that he should receive an award of compensation from public funds.

In the case of *Hopper*, Buxton J had cited the judgment of Sir John Donaldson MR in *Thompstone and Crowe*:

> In each case, although different categories of circumstances can be taken into account, the issue is the same. Is the applicant an appropriate recipient of an *ex gratia* compensation payment made at public expense? ([1984] 1 WLR 1234 at p 1239).

In *Cook* the Court of Appeal also had to decide whether the decision of the Board to refuse an oral hearing under para 24 of the 1990 Scheme was wrong. The Court of Appeal upheld the Board's decision and the appeal was dismissed.

Of the decision of Sedley J in *Gambles*, Hobhouse LJ observed in *Cook*: 'In my judgment, *Gambles* seeks improperly to extend the scope of judicial review from an assessment of the propriety of the decision to an evaluation of its merits', and that *Gambles* was 'inconsistent with the decision of the Court of Appeal in *R v CICB, ex parte Thompstone and Crowe*'.

In *Powell*, although the Board's evidence was that it had exercised its discretion on the merits of the case, the Board had indicated that the applicant's withholding from the police the name of his assailant 'precluded' an award. The court decided that the Board had fettered its discretion and decided the case according to a general policy of the Board in such cases and not on the merits of the case. The court quashed the Board's decision.

In *Maxted* the Board had refused an award on the grounds of the applicant's convictions and its reasons showed an evaluation of those convictions by the Board and the nature of its discretion, citing an earlier decision of the court that 'the Scheme is intended to afford the widest possible discretion to the Board in its administration of the Scheme'.

The Board's reasons, although fully set out, did not include the 'three stages' considered necessary by the court in *Gambles*. There is no reference to a process of reasoning starting with the question of whether or not a full award should be made and, if not, whether there should be a restricted award and, if so, the amount of that restriction. The court in *Maxted* concluded that the Board, having given its reasons for withholding compensation:

> ... were under no obligation to spell matters out further in their decision letter than they did. Their discretion is very wide ... This is one of those cases where the Board might have decided the case the other way but, as entitled, they chose not to do so. This court is not empowered to substitute its discretion for that of the Board and this application [to quash the Board's decision] fails.

Where an applicant with a serious criminal record is attacked and seriously injured as a direct consequence of his assisting the police in securing the prosecution and conviction for serious offences of his former criminal associates, the applicant would have some prospect of an award even though it would probably be substantially reduced.

It must be remembered that all these considerations are intended merely to illustrate how the significance of an applicant's conviction is weighed in the balance before the Panel or Authority decides in its discretion whether a full award or reduced award or a nil award is appropriate. Each case is considered on its merits. None of these factors is binding on the Panel or Authority, whose discretion is unfettered by the Scheme.

An important distinction between the consideration of convictions by the Panel or Authority and by the criminal court is that the latter, when dealing with sentence after conviction, will consider only those convictions recorded before the offence for which sentence is being imposed. The Panel or Authority, in contrast, considers all 'unspent' convictions before and after the incident in which the applicant sustained injury, up to the date of the Panel's or Authority's decision. Although the phrase 'previous convictions' is sometimes used as a term borrowed from the criminal courts, its use indicates a commonly held misunderstanding of the Board's or Authority's wider powers in considering *all* of the applicant's convictions before and after the incident in which the injury was sustained (save that the *Authority or Panel* may not consider 'spent' convictions).

An applicant whose application has been refused on the initial decision by the Board on the grounds of convictions will sometimes protest in his request for a hearing that, for example '... two of my three convictions for assault were after the incident when I was attacked'. If the applicant were addressing the bench before sentencing in the criminal court, legally he would have a good point. Before the Board or Appeals Panel, however, he is making not only a bad point in law but is also emphasising a factor which is likely to diminish his prospects of discretion being exercised in his favour.

Criminal offences by the applicant are not inherently better or worse for having been committed after, rather than before the incident which gives rise to the application for compensation. Subsequent convictions, however, are likely to be relatively recent, thus reducing the chances of a successful submission by the applicant that he is a reformed character, and, if those subsequent convictions involve violence, the Board is faced with clear evidence that, since being a victim of violence for which he seeks compensation, he has himself been guilty of violence against others, who may in their turn also be applicants for compensation. In these circumstances the discretion of the Board or Authority or Appeals Panel is less likely to be exercised in the applicant's favour.

The Board or Authority is not only concerned with convictions for offences involving violence when considering the applicant's convictions. An applicant with numerous convictions for dishonesty should not expect to succeed. Where these consist of several relatively minor shoplifting offences, there may be a reduced award rather than the withholding of an award altogether.

Burglary, which the law regards as a serious criminal offence, is similarly regarded under the Scheme, and a number of convictions for burglary will usually mean a nil award unless this criminal activity on the part of the applicant is sufficiently far in the past, and other evidence shows a genuine and sustained effort to reform. The exclusion of 'spent' convictions from the Authority's considerations has already been mentioned above.

Injury inflicted by one young adult male on another is the most common incident in applications under the Scheme. Where the victim/applicant is in his twenties and has convictions, they will not only probably be recent, but also, perhaps, numerous. If a youth engages in shoplifting and later commits a series of burglaries, he may have a lengthy and serious list of convictions by the time he is 21. If he is the victim of a crime of violence at, say, 25, he may make application under the Scheme as a young man who has committed no offence for four or five years, is married and has a young family, has been in regular employment during those four or five years and is getting a home together. His earlier convictions may be 'spent' under the terms of the 1996 Scheme.

The decision maker in such a case must balance the positive and negative aspects. The evidence of criminal activity being genuinely a thing of the past in such a case may be strong. Four or five years with no convictions would probably enable a reduced award to be made rather than no award at all. The seriousness of the offences – indicated by the seriousness with which the court imposing sentence viewed them – is crucial in such cases. The period for which the applicant has gone straight is also crucial. The Board or Authority or Appeals Panel must be satisfied that a real reform has taken place for an applicant with a bad record of recent convictions to stand any chance of even a much reduced award by the exercise of the discretion in the applicant's favour.

The line which has to be drawn in such cases is a very fine one. The discretion given by both Schemes to the decision maker has to be exercised in a 'reasonable' way for that decision to be lawful. It involves a choice between the relative merits of refusing altogether to make an award from public funds to someone with numerous convictions, and whose conduct has caused a great deal of anxiety and expense to the individual victims of his criminal activity as well as to society at large, and making an award, albeit substantially reduced, to bring to bear the unacceptability of the applicant's past conduct in the eyes of the public whilst acknowledging the value of the applicant's apparent reformed way of life to himself and to society and thus encouraging it to continue.

Convictions for offences involving fraud on the public, the 'con-man', will usually mean a nil award. In 1990 the Board refused to make an award to an applicant who had served a prison sentence for offences which involved defrauding the public of cash deposits. Similarly, where there is a conviction for smuggling or dealing in prohibited drugs, an award would probably be refused.

The cry of the applicant who is refused an award on the grounds of his convictions, 'my convictions had nothing to do with my being attacked and injured', is understandable but has no basis in law. The Scheme creates a duty to consider convictions – and the judicial review cases of *Thompstone and Crowe* (noted in Appendix 1) establish the unfettered discretion to consider whether convictions, even wholly unrelated to the incident, make an award 'inappropriate'.

Convictions for soliciting for purposes of prostitution have presented the Board with some difficulties in the past. An application by a prostitute with numerous convictions for soliciting has to be considered under para 6(c) 1990 (or para 13(e) 1996). The Board has generally taken the view that convictions for soliciting as a prostitute will not exclude an award altogether where a prostitute is raped or is attacked in some other way and injured.

When express reference to an applicant's convictions was first brought in by the 1990 Scheme it included with the words 'criminal convictions' the words 'or unlawful conduct'; the scope of the latter is unclear. The Board's Guide to the 1990 Scheme, 'Victims of Crimes of Violence', simply states with regard to the words 'unlawful conduct':

> An applicant injured in the course of committing a serious crime will usually receive no award.

Statements before the Board or Authority or Appeals Panel which have been taken by police will sometimes contain clear evidence of criminal activity on the part of the applicant in respect of which there is, for one reason or another, no conviction. The additional words are perhaps to be construed as enabling the decision under the Scheme to take account of such criminal activity, even though there is no conviction, if it is admitted by the applicant or the tribunal is satisfied of its truth.

The Guide to the 1996 Scheme, by setting out a points table which will be applied by claims officers in considering convictions, may seem inconsistent with the element of discretion which the Scheme contains. If the discretion is not exercised in addition to applying the points table, the decision may be challengeable. The practical working of this part of the Scheme has not yet been revealed by decided cases.

The situation is difficult where the evidence indicates that the applicant's life is conducted in a context of unlawful activity, for example that the applicant is a known drug dealer or is known to be a member of a violent criminal gang, but has avoided conviction for any offence. The words 'character as shown by his criminal convictions or unlawful conduct' may entitle the tribunal to decide whether it is satisfied on the balance of probabilities that the applicant has engaged in 'unlawful conduct' which would make it inappropriate to make a full or reduced award.

The 1996 Scheme (para 13(e)) does not include the words 'unlawful conduct' but speaks of 'evidence available' which may make an award inappropriate. The burden of satisfying the Board or Authority or Appeals Panel that an award is not 'inappropriate' rests upon the applicant (para

25 (1990), para 18 (1996)). Where there is evidence of unlawful conduct on the part of the applicant, he has to satisfy the tribunal either that the evidence on balance of probabilities is erroneous, or that, if true, is not of such a serious nature as to justify the reduction or withholding of an award. Where the evidence indicates that the applicant has a criminal charge outstanding and is awaiting trial for that alleged offence at the time of adjudication of his application, the application will usually be adjourned until the result of that trial is known.

2. The applicant's 'conduct before, during or after the events giving rise to the claim'

As noted at the beginning of this chapter, the provisions of both the 1990 and 1996 Schemes must be examined. This is mainly because at 31 March 1996 there were many thousands of current applications which must be decided according to the terms of the Scheme which was in operation before the 1996 Scheme came into effect on 1 April 1996. Resolution of all these 'old Scheme' cases will probably take at least two years. It is helpful to observe the way in which the Criminal Injuries Compensation Board applies the rules of the earlier Scheme as these are substantially similar to the equivalent provisions in the 1996 Scheme, and the White Paper which preceded the 1996 Scheme encouraged the view that the familiar rules of eligibility which had 'stood the test of time' would continue to be applied in the same way.

The commentary which follows is therefore primarily based upon the principles upon which the CICB has decided issues relating to the 'conduct' of the applicant 'before, during or after' the incident giving rise to the application. It is reasonable to expect that the Authority and the Appeals Panel, created by the 1996 Scheme, will similarly interpret the equivalent provision in the 1996 Scheme. The wording of para 6(c) of the 1990 Scheme which relates to the conduct of the applicant reads:

> The Board may withhold or reduce compensation if they consider that ... having regard to the conduct of the applicant before, during or after the events giving rise to the claim ... it is inappropriate that a full award, or any award at all, be granted.

As with all the other requirements of para 6 (1990) – those of informing the police, co-operating in the prosecution of the offender and consideration of any criminal convictions recorded against the applicant – the Board has a complete discretion and each case will ultimately depend upon its own particular facts. As has already been stated, the Board's discretion is bound only by the duty to exercise that discretion reasonably; it may not arrive at a conclusion which no reasonable tribunal, properly directing itself on the evidence before it, could have reached – the *Wednesbury* rule.

The conduct of the applicant which may be considered by the Board to be such that an award from public funds would be 'inappropriate' may be before, during or after the actual incident which caused the applicant's injury. The equivalent part of the 1996 Scheme is in para 13 which provides:

> A claims officer may withhold or reduce an award where he considers that ... (d) the conduct of the applicant before, during or after the incident giving rise to the application makes it inappropriate that a full award or any award at all be made.

Although the wording differs slightly, there is no material difference between the 'conduct' provisions of the 1990 and 1996 Schemes and they will therefore be considered together.

As the illustrations of this provision which follow in this chapter are based upon the decisions of the 'Board', it is the Board which is referred to rather than the Authority or the Appeals Panel. As already explained, there is reason to believe that largely the same interpretation will be placed upon this provision under the 1996 Scheme as the Board has done under the 1990 Scheme. Time will tell.

Typical examples of conduct 'before' the incident are provocative conduct by the applicant during the moments leading up to the incident, or the applicant engaging voluntarily in a fight or in a situation which clearly carried the risk of violence. The Board takes a firm line on the conduct of the applicant which makes him the author of his own misfortune or which encourages, provokes or exacerbates potentially violent situations. There are many tragic cases which come before the Board where the applicant has sustained grave injuries which have perhaps caused brain damage or other serious physical injury with consequent loss of career and the capacity to earn a living. In some of these the applicant has received no award because his injuries were the result of an attack on him which was provoked by his own conduct or were the result of his agreeing to engage in violence. The excessive response on the part of the assailant to the applicant's conduct is not generally considered material if the applicant's conduct was the initiating or exacerbating factor leading to that excessive response.

A serious insult which is met with a stabbing or 'glassing' as a response may result in the Board withholding or reducing any award for the injuries. The situation will be the same if the applicant invited the person who (or whose associates) caused the injury to 'go outside' and settle an argument by fighting. An applicant who says 'I know I invited him outside for a fight but that was one to one. His mates were outside, and they all set upon me and kicked me unconscious' should not expect to receive an award. If the applicant struck the first blow or in some other way was the first to cause the incident, which may have initially been verbal, to escalate into something physical (as the Board sometimes puts it – 'The applicant was the first to resort to violence'), an award would be unlikely. The applicant verbally insulting the assailant or the assailant's wife or girlfriend, or striking the first blow or inviting a fight or agreeing to a fight or voluntarily engaging in a fight which had already started between others, are all examples of 'conduct before' the incident which caused the applicant's injuries. Such conduct has to be 'wrong' or 'bad' conduct.

Although thoughtless and inconsiderate behaviour will sometimes provoke violence, it would not generally affect the injured party's prospects of compensation unless it amounted to conduct which was intended or calculated to provoke violence or was such that a violent response was likely.

Wearing a 'City' football scarf on the predominantly 'Rovers' terraces at a football match would not in itself be 'conduct', nor even would cheering loudly a 'City' goal. The risk of violence, however, may be regarded as higher in the charged atmosphere of sporting (or unsporting) rivalry, and if the conduct by word or deed of the lone City supporter erred towards wrongful deliberate provocation of the rival supporters, such as chanting insults, this could be 'conduct' which would affect an award.

If the surrounding circumstances suggest that the lone supporter had so placed himself for the purpose of provocation, his prospects of a full award in respect of an assault by rival supporters would recede. The throwing of a lighted match into a pool of petrol is an action which has to be distinguished from throwing it into a pool of water. The thrower of the lighted match must be expected to take account of the circumstances within which his actions are carried out and their likely effect.

In refusing an application under this paragraph the Board may give as the reason:

> The incident in which the applicant received his injuries resulted from the applicant's own aggressive and provocative conduct and an award of compensation is therefore inappropriate.

The Board looks at all the evidence and examines the violent incident from its very beginning. The insult, the aggressive face to face confrontation, the threat or readiness to strike a blow, the push, the finger poked in the chest, the first punch and so on may be apparent from the evidence. The applicant's conduct is examined closely in the sequence of words and actions from the beginning right through to the end – it is the applicant's conduct, not the assailant's which is central to the Board's deliberation.

The situations in which violence may flare up between individuals are infinitely various. The noisy party next door, the smacking of a neighbour's child for being a nuisance, the deliberate obstruction of one car driver by another in traffic and a thousand and one different human situations can and do lead to the face to face confrontation, the threat, the insult, the push, the punch and so on.

In all of these situations the Board has to examine the applicant's conduct. Did his conduct start the ball rolling towards confrontation and the risk of violence? Did his confronting his neighbour on his neighbour's front doorstep amount to aggressive or provocative conduct, even though the neighbour had allegedly struck his child? Did the applicant start the incident by deliberately obstructing the other driver? Did he provoke the fight by leaving his car and going over to the driver of the other car and confronting him?

The Scheme also requires the applicant's conduct *during* the incident to be examined. Once an incident has reached a point where physical violence is likely or violence has actually commenced the applicant's conduct continues to be under examination.

If the applicant did not provoke the violence, did he exacerbate it? When the assailant shouted an insult at him did the applicant go across the road to sort it out? Did the applicant willingly continue a confrontation in which there was a risk of violence? Did he swap insults? Did he, as the assailant may say, give the assailant a push, or a poke in the chest? Did the applicant ask the assailant to step outside? Did he accept the assailant's invitation to go outside to sort it out? The applicant's conduct has to survive the Board's scrutiny of all such aspects.

The main questions asked throughout are: did the applicant (i) start or (ii) provoke or (iii) exacerbate or (iv) voluntarily participate in the violence? If he did any of these, the withholding or reduction of an award will probably result.

Acting according to the 'code of the wild west' whereby a man must respond to an insult and accept a challenge to fight is so often a young man's undoing, especially when full of drink. It is his undoing both on the night when he faces his assailant and gets injured, and later when he faces the Board – as the law and the Scheme demand that a man must ignore an insult and must retreat from a fight or the threat of one.

The layman is often surprised to learn of the legal duty to retreat which applies in the law of assault and which the Board properly applies when examining the applicant's conduct. If violence is clearly about to start, or has already started, the Board will require of the applicant that any reasonable opportunity to remove himself from the scene should be taken. Even in a case in which the applicant is, up to that point, entirely blameless, if he fails to take an opportunity to depart from the violent situation and instead continues it the Board must take this into account.

Frequently the Board deals with cases in which a group are having a peaceful drink when another group take exception to them for no legitimate reason and attack them as they leave the pub. As an immediate initial response the group under attack, having no immediate alternative, fight back in self defence in order to escape from the surprise attack. After an initial skirmish, the applicant finds himself for a moment disengaged from the immediate fighting. He sees one of his attackers across the street. Some fighting is still going on nearby involving the applicant's friends and members of the group who attacked them. The applicant has a choice; to run away or to run again towards his erstwhile opponent. He decides to have another go at his attacker and gets injured in the fight which follows. His exercise of that choice becomes the focal point of the Board's consideration. The applicant would be unlikely to receive a full award and, depending on all the circumstances in the particular case, may receive no award.

In the chronological sequence of events which the Board has to examine where the applicant's conduct is in issue, this last example is somewhere near the join between 'conduct during' and 'conduct after'.

The 'conduct after' which most frequently causes the application to be refused is the revenge attack or reprisal by the applicant following the incident in which he was himself injured. As in the previous example, the applicant may be entirely blameless for the commencement of hostilities but his reaction to being attacked must also pass the test. He may even be blameless up to and including the point at which he is injured, but if his reaction is to engage in a later reprisal attack his application would probably be refused.

Neither the law nor the requirements of the Scheme permit the applicant to take the law into his own hands.

It is not part of the Board's function to judge sexual morals or the private ethical standards of individuals or the religions to which they may adhere. The Board is concerned with what a reasonable person of any persuasion would regard as provocative or aggressive conduct towards another.

If a wife admits to her husband that she has been unfaithful to him and is, as a result, beaten up by her husband, she would not on the basis of the adultery or of the admission of it be outside the Scheme. If, however, she accompanies the confession with gratuitous insults and taunts of a sexual nature the Board might take a different view.

The Board has made clear in its 1987 'Statement' and 1990 'Guide' that where an applicant is known to be a member of a violent gang it is unlikely that he would receive an award even if his injury is not shown to be connected with his criminal activities or those of his associates. Likewise the Board would not make an award to any person convicted of terrorist activities whether or not the injury is in any way connected with that activity. It is likely that the Authority and the Appeals Panel will take the same view.

As the action of the applicant to constitute 'conduct' under para 6(c) (1990 Scheme), para 13(d) (1996 Scheme) has to be 'bad' conduct and not merely ill-judged, the negligence or contributory negligence of the applicant which may have contributed to the situation in which he was injured is not 'conduct' which would cause the reduction or withholding of an award. The 1996 Scheme makes no reference to this principle (unlike the abortive 1994 Tariff Scheme which expressly incorporated it) but it is assumed that the Authority and Appeals Panel will not regard contributory negligence which is not 'bad' conduct as warranting refusal or reduction of an award.

If a man drops a glass of beer in someone else's lap in a crowded pub, and his action is genuinely accidental or even the result of carelessness or negligence on his part, he would not be outside the Scheme in relation to injuries caused by the response to the accident on the part of the man with the wet trousers. One false remark, however, by the spiller in exacerbation of the accidental spillage could reduce considerably the spiller's prospects of a full award if he was then assaulted and injured.

A type of conduct on the part of the applicant which the Board has been required to consider in a number of cases is what might be called 'rescuing' a friend or relative who is being attacked. The criminal law permits the defence of self-defence, the principle briefly being that a person who is attacked where it is not possible in the circumstances to retreat to avoid the attack, may use such minimum force as is reasonably necessary to repel the attack. The level of force and the means used must be limited to what is reasonable having regard to the method and manner of the attack. Such reasonable and appropriate level of physical response may also be justifiable in defence of a relative or friend who is under attack from a third party.

The sort of incident in respect of which this type of self-defence argument may be put forward by the applicant to justify his own violent actions in the course of the incident might be as follows: the applicant and his companion are attacked by a group of youths who punch and kick them. The applicant and his companion, being unable to run away having been cornered, fight back with their fists to get free of their attackers. The applicant breaks free and could then have run from his assailants. At that moment he sees his companion on the ground being kicked by two or three youths and at risk of serious injury. He decides therefore to go into the fray to attempt to prevent injury to his companion. In doing so he is injured.

The above description puts the applicant's case in its most favourable light. If he used no more force than was appropriate and necessary to bring to an end the attack on his fallen companion, he would not be excluded by his conduct from receiving an award. It need hardly be said, however, that in most cases where defence of himself, his wife, child or companion is an actual or potential argument on behalf of the applicant, the evidence gives the Board a confused picture of fighting between a number of young men which, for whatever reason, starts as an attack by one group upon another, and then continues as a series of separate fights and skirmishes between individuals. Each witness's statement might contradict the statements made by the others. The Board or Authority must pick its way towards the probable truth of such situations by using its experience to overcome the shortcomings and contradictions in the evidence.

Before leaving the subject of the applicant's conduct as a factor for consideration, it is appropriate to comment on one further category of cases – those in which the crime of violence occurred in the course of a pattern of violence or a series of acts of violence involving the applicant and his assailant or their respective associates, in which the evidence shows the applicant to have been a voluntary participant. The Board has made clear that it will not make an award where it is satisfied that the injury suffered by the applicant is a consequence of a series or pattern of actions in which the applicant has probably on other occasions engaged in violence or threats of violence and given as good as he got. Just as the Scheme is not for the benefit of the loser in a fight in which he is a voluntary participant, equally it has no application to persons injured in a series of such fights. It is probable that the Authority and the Appeals Panel will take the same view.

3. Children playing dangerous games

Under para 4 of the 1990 Scheme and para 10 of the 1996 Scheme the immunity of the offender from prosecution by reason of age does not negate the crime of violence. If one boy of, say, nine years of age deliberately throws a stone at another and causes injury, the injured party may claim under the Scheme, provided that the Board is satisfied that the crime of violence has been made out. The playing of a dangerous game is not in itself sufficient to constitute a crime. Both the Board's 1990 Guide, 'Victims of Crimes of Violence', and the Authority's 'Guide to the Criminal Injuries Compensation Scheme' (1996) make the further point in respect of dangerous games that where two children are both of roughly similar age, and the applicant and the child whose action caused the injury were equal participants in the dangerous game, for example each throwing stones at the other so that there is nothing to choose betwen them, the Board and the Authority do not award compensation to the injured participant. The reason given is that the applicant's participation and 'conduct' have to be considered, and to give money to the applicant where the activity was common to assailant and victim, with nothing to choose between them, would be simply to compensate the loser. The Guide goes on to say, however, that this exclusion of any claim by mutually dangerous play would not apply where the children are of disparate ages and levels of participation and blameworthiness, and the injured participant is the younger and less likely to have understood the risks involved in the dangerous game in which he is the junior and lesser participant.

It may be arguable that just as criminality is not very readily imputed to the actions of a young child, say under ten years, so the burden of responsibility for his own wrongful conduct in participating in a game likely to cause injury should not be too readily placed upon him.

Chapter 7

Further constraints on compensation awards

Both the 1990 and 1996 Schemes provide that there should be no award if the offender who caused the injury is likely to benefit.

1. The possibility of benefiting the offender

Paragraph 7 of the 1990 Scheme is short and simple and states a fundamental principle:

> Compensation will not be payable unless the Board are satisfied that there is no possibility that a person responsible for causing the injury will benefit from an award.

The wording is slightly altered in the 1996 Scheme. Paragraph 15(a) reads:

> A claims officer will make an award only where he is satisfied that there is no likelihood that an assailant would benefit if an award were made.

Under both Schemes the onus is on the applicant to satisfy the Board or Authority that there will be no 'possibility' (1990 Scheme) or 'likelihood' (1996 Scheme) of the offender benefiting.

The 1990 Scheme provision could not be couched in more positive or absolute terms; the words 'will not be payable' and 'satisfied that there is no possibility' leave no room for argument as to what the Scheme means. The possibility of the offender benefiting is enough to preclude an award. The equivalent wording of the 1996 Scheme reduces 'no possibility' to 'no likelihood', but in practice the effect is essentially the same as, unless the offender is dead, the possibility of benefit could never be absolutely excluded. The change of words to 'no likelihood' is therefore more realistic.

The principle contained in para 7 (1990) and para 15 (1996) – in this chapter referred to together as para 7/15 – is a useful protection against fraudulent claims; although its usefulness can apply to any case where the Board or Authority considers that the offender might benefit if an award is made, its main usefulness is in cases where the assailant and victim are or were husband and wife or are or were cohabitees or the offender is the father or stepfather of the applicant. For convenience the use of the term 'Board' in this chapter includes the Authority and the Appeals Panel unless there is a need to make a distinction.

The Board has to be watchful for any fraudulent arrangement between victim and assailant whereby the benefits of a successful application to the Board might be shared. The prompt investigation of the incident by the police and evidence from the police in relation to the incident are the Board's best protection against the possibility of fraud. The importance which the Board has always placed upon prompt reporting of the incident by the applicant to the police, and upon the co-operation of the applicant in the prosecution of the offender, has already been considered and cannot be overstated.

The provisions of para 7/15 supplement the requirements relating to reporting to the police and co-operating in the prosecution of the offender. Paragraph 7 (1990) requires the Board to make no award (it has no discretion under this paragraph) if it is not satisfied that there is 'no possibility' (or 'no likelihood' in the case of the Authority or the Appeals Panel) that the assailant may benefit. The situation which carries the greatest risk of an offender benefiting is where the victim and assailant are members of the same household. In many cases the violence between assailant and victim, whatever the relationship between them, results in their leading totally separate lives by the time the application of the victim comes before the Board or Authority, so that para 7/15 do not apply. The Board receives many applications from battered wives and a large proportion of them have divorced their assailant husband or have permanently separated from him. In a number of cases, however, the victim and assailant are still together when the application comes to be considered. In such cases an award may be precluded by the provisions of para 7 and 8 of the 1990 Scheme (paras 15 and 16(b) 1996).

In a 1990 decision the Board awarded substantial compensation to a youth aged 17 who had been seriously affected psychologically by sexual abuse some years earlier by a male neighbour. The youth had subsequently also been abused by his stepfather. After strenuous efforts by various social and medical agencies, the family was reunited and became reconciled so that the applicant and the stepfather were again members of the same household. Mindful of the requirements of para 7 (1990), the Board gave specific directions for the control and investment of the award so as to prevent the possibility of the offender/stepfather obtaining a benefit from the award. Power to give such directions regarding an award is contained in para 9 of the 1990 Scheme and para 50 of the 1996 Scheme.

As the risk of an offender benefiting from an award is greatest in the context of the offender and the victim being members of the same family, or members of the same household, consideration of the provisions of para 8 of the 1990 Scheme and para 16 of the 1996 Scheme will take the matter a stage further.

2. Members of the same household

As applications received before 1 April 1996 will continue to be governed by the terms of the 1990 or earlier Schemes it is necessary once more to deal with the parallel provisions of both the 1990 and the 1996 Schemes. Paragraph 8 of the 1990 Scheme provides:

> Where the victim and any person responsible for the injuries which are the subject of the application (whether that person actually inflicted them or not) were living in the same household at the time of the injuries as members of the same family, compensation will be paid only where:
>
> (a) the person responsible has been prosecuted in connection with the offence, except where the Board consider that there are practical, technical or other good reasons why a prosecution has not been brought; and
>
> (b) in the case of violence between adults in the family, the Board are satisfied that the person responsible and the applicant stopped living in the same household before the application was made and seem unlikely to live together again; and
>
> (c) in the case of an application under this paragraph by or on behalf of a minor, ie a person under 18 years of age, the Board are satisfied that it would not be against the minor's interest to make a full or reduced award.
>
> For the purposes of this paragraph, a man and a woman living together as husband and wife shall be treated as members of the same family.

The parallel provisions in the 1996 Scheme are paras 15 and 16 which read:

> 15. A claims officer will make an award only where he is satisfied:
>
> (a) that there is no likelihood that an assailant would benefit if an award were made; or
>
> (b) where the applicant is under 18 years of age when the application is determined, that it would not be against his interest for an award to be made.
>
> 16. Where a case is not ruled out under paragraph 7(b) (injury sustained before 1 October 1979) but at the time when the injury was sustained, the victim and any assailant (whether or not that assailant actually inflicted the injury) were living in the same household as members of the same family, an award will be withheld unless:
>
> (a) the assailant has been prosecuted in connection with the offence, except where a claims officer considers that there are practical, technical or other good reasons why a prosecution has not been brought; and
>
> (b) in the case of violence between adults in the family, a claims officer is satisfied that the applicant and the assailant stopped living in the same household before the application was made and are unlikely to share the same household again.
>
> For the purposes of this paragraph, a man and woman living together as husband and wife will be treated as members of the same family.

The provisions in the 1990 and 1996 Schemes are thus essentially similar. These provisions are in effect a toughening of the requirements regarding reporting to and co-operating with the police in the prosecution of the offender. In cases other than those where the assailant and victim were living in same household, the victim's compensation is not conditional upon the assailant having been prosecuted. To have co-operated fully with the police to that end is a sufficient fulfilment of the victim's duties.

Where the victim and assailant were living in the same household as members of the same family at the time of the injuries, however, compensation will be paid only where the person responsible has been prosecuted in connection with the offence.

To some extent the strictness of this provision can be explained historically. The earlier Scheme (before 1979) expressly excluded compensation in cases of family violence. When it was decided that 'domestic' victims should not be excluded from compensation, the practical difficulties of proof did not disappear with the extension of compensation to include such cases within the Scheme, and it was deemed appropriate therefore to meet these difficulties by making external proof of the violence, by prosecution of the offender, a condition of compensation in such cases. The requirement in para 8 (1990) and 16 (1996) that the assailant has been prosecuted is coupled with the requirement, where the violence is between adults, that they have ceased to cohabit before the application was made and seem unlikely to live together (or 'share the same household' – 1996 wording) again. These provisions in combination are intended to help overcome the problems of proof of the offence, and to reduce both the risk of collusion and the chances of the offender benefiting from the award.

The requirement of prosecution in para 8/16 is not absolute, but the Scheme waives the requirement only where the Board or Authority considers that there are 'practical, technical or other good reasons why a prosecution has not been brought'.

The withdrawal of her complaint of assault by a wife against her assailant husband is not a 'good reason' and is the reason for the refusal of many applications by injured wives. If a woman is injured by her husband and reports the incident to the police, who investigate the matter and prosecute for, say, an assault occasioning actual bodily harm under section 47 of the Offences Against the Person Act 1861, and the applicant either changes her mind and makes a retraction statement, or fails or refuses to attend court, or attends court and declines to give evidence, her application will usually fail even if she did so through fear of reprisal rather than through reconciliation. If the parties are still living together as man and wife when the application is lodged, the application will fail.

It is not uncommon for the application to be the result of an assault by the husband upon the wife which proved to be the last straw in the relationship. The applicant then meets all the requirements of the Scheme, including sticking to her guns and co-operating in the prosecution of the husband for the assault, ceasing to cohabit as soon as possible after the assault – and in any event before the application for compensation is made – and achieving a final parting of the ways with separate addresses and a decree of divorce.

Divorce itself is not a requirement of the Scheme but it is the best means of establishing that the parties 'seem unlikely to live together again' (1990 Scheme) or 'share the same household again' (1996 Scheme).

Where there has been no prosecution, the Board or Authority must be satisfied that there were 'practical, technical or other good reasons' for this. Examples include the assailant living abroad, or being committed under the Mental Health Act and unfit to stand trial, or a decision by the Crown Prosecution Service not to prosecute for technical reasons, where the investigation by police nevertheless establishes the truth of the allegation of assault, so that the Board or Authority is satisfied as to the genuineness of the case by police evidence to that effect. Paragraph 8(c) of the 1990 Scheme provides a further condition on which the Board must be satisfied, where both victim and assailant were living as members of the same family in the same household at the time of the injuries, if an award is to be made:

> ... in the case of an application under this paragraph by or on behalf of a minor, i.e. a person under 18 years of age, the Board [must be] satisfied that it would not be against the minor's interest to make a full or reduced award.

Paragraph 15(b) of the 1996 Scheme contains a similar provision but, unlike the 1990 Scheme, does not restrict that consideration to situations in which the victim and the assailant were living in the same household. Paragraph 15(b) of the 1996 Scheme therefore applies to every application by a minor, so that in every case the Authority must be satisfied that making an award would not be against the minor's interest. Some assistance in understanding the purpose of this provision and its intended manner of application can be derived from consideration of the reasoning of the 1978 working party, whose report and recommendations led to the introduction of awards in cases involving family violence, subject to the safeguards which were later contained in para 8(a), (b) and (c) of the 1990 Scheme.

The working party reviewed fully the real practical difficulties of making awards at all to minors in such circumstances. These difficulties can be summarised as:

(a) the difficulties of proof where the offender is, for example, the father or stepfather of the victim with both parties still living in the same household;

(b) the problem of excluding the offender from any possible benefit, having regard to the usual pooling of domestic finances within a family household; and

(c) the question whether an award is appropriate at all and even possibly harmful.

Of these the question of possible benefit to the offender has been discussed above. The Board or Authority or Appeals Panel may also give directions on the administration and investment of an award to a minor under para 9 of the 1996 Scheme or para 50 of the 1996 Scheme. The difficulties of proof were substantially met by the terms of para 8 of the 1990 Scheme, considered above, that the person responsible must have been prosecuted unless there were practical or technical reasons why this could not be done.

The problem that an award to a minor might do a child little good and may even do positive harm, was the subject of comment in the 1978 working party report in the following terms:

> An even more serious problem is that an award may do a child little good and may even do harm. Young children are less troubled by injuries of a temporary nature than adults and in general have a better capacity for recovery ... A child who suffers non-permanent injury may well be consoled with a present or a holiday, but cannot be expected to appreciate, or make use of, a large sum of money. All that can be done is to place the money in trust until the child is of age, when he may have little recollection of the injury or the circumstances which gave rise to it, the money may well not be required for any pressing current need, and the explanation of its source may prove a source of distress or renewed family upheaval ...

Despite these understandable misgivings and anxieties as to the practical effects of bringing cases of child abuse within the family within the scope of the Scheme, the 1979 Scheme included for the first time compensation for violence within the family, including child victims. The 1990 and 1996 Schemes continue to do so.

The 1990 and 1996 Schemes continue in substantially similar terms, subject to the application of para 15(b) of the 1996 Scheme to all applications by minors, and not restricted to those circumstances in which the minor and the offender were members of the same household at the time the injuries were suffered. If the Board decides in a particular case that an award should be made to a minor, the Board makes such arrangements for payment as are deemed to be in the minor's best interests and to ensure so far as possible that the award is in responsible hands for use exclusively for the minor applicant's benefit. It is probable that the Authority and Appeals Panel will make similar arrangements under para 50 of the 1996 Scheme. The treatment of awards to minors and persons under disability is discussed in Chapter 8.

Chapter 8

Awards to minors and to persons under disability – special arrangements – structured settlements

The Board under the terms of the 1990 Scheme, and the Authority and Appeals Panel under the 1996 Scheme, may make special arrangements for payment and administration of an award where they consider it appropriate to do so.

The prime function of the Board and the Authority is to decide eligibility under the respective Schemes and to make the appropriate award. In the case of the Board under the 1990 Scheme, the assessment is on the basis of common law damages. Under the 1996 Scheme, compensation is made in accordance with the fixed tariff together with the provisions relating to loss of earnings and special expenses (as defined in paras 30 to 34 and 35 to 36 of the 1996 Scheme) in appropriate cases. In the great majority of cases the award is paid directly to the applicant and the business of the Board or Authority is entirely concluded on payment being made and a suitable discharge being signed by the successful applicant. However, in the case of awards to minors and other persons under disability, such as the mentally ill, the Board or Authority or Appeals Panel may give directions on the manner of payment and also on the initial investment of the award, so that the interests of the applicant under disability are safeguarded against misappropriation.

This chapter looks first at the powers of the Board and how the Board exercises those powers in practice, and then comments on the equivalent powers of the Authority's claims officer under the 1996 Scheme.

1. The powers of the Board under the 1990 Scheme

The powers of the Board in this regard are set out in para 9 of the 1990 Scheme:

> If in the opinion of the Board it is in the interests of the applicant (whether or not a minor or a person under an incapacity) so to do, the Board may pay the amount of any award to any trustee or trustees to hold on such trusts for the benefit of all or any of the following persons, namely the applicant and any spouse, widow or widower, relatives and dependants of the applicant and with such provisions for their respective maintenance, education and benefit and with such powers and provisions for the investment and management of the fund and for the remuneration of the trustee or trustees as the Board shall

think fit. Subject to this the Board will have a general discretion in any case in which they have awarded compensation to make special arrangements for its administration. In this paragraph 'relatives' means all persons claiming descent from the applicant's grandparents and 'dependants' means all persons who in the opinion of the Board are dependent on him wholly or partially for the provision of the ordinary necessities of life.

Where the applicant is aged under 18 at the time of the award, the Board must have regard not only to the minority as such but also to the applicant's personal and family circumstances. The papers may contain no indication of any particular difficulty as between applicant and parent, and in most cases the award will be paid to the parent as guardian, the parent being required to sign an undertaking to apply the award exclusively for the benefit of the minor applicant. In most cases this procedure, with the parent as legal guardian giving a receipt to the Board on the minor applicant's behalf, is entirely appropriate. A child over 14 years may be asked to countersign the acceptance.

The Board is not in a position to undertake research into the social background of the minor applicant. Where there are no circumstances disclosed in the papers to put the Board on enquiry, and where the award is a relatively small one, the Board simply makes payment to the parent.

In cases where the Board considers it not to be in the applicant's interest to make immediate payment to parent or guardian as trustee for that applicant under disability, the Board will hold the award in an interest-bearing account until the applicant attains majority and can give a receipt for the award. This procedure is straightforward in terms of administration, the Board retaining control of the account until the applicant's majority. The parent or guardian may apply to the Board at any time for payments out for the advancement, benefit and education of the applicant during the period of minority. The retention of these accounts is the only direct administration of awards undertaken by the Board's staff. At 31 March 1996 the Board held on behalf of applicants, a total of £31,000,000 in interest-bearing accounts.

If the applicant is approaching his or her majority, and the award is, say, £3,000 or less, the Board will occasionally ask the guardian to consent to the payment of the award direct to the applicant. This avoids the administrative process of opening an account with a bank for a matter of a few months only and gives the almost-adult applicant the satisfaction of taking charge of his or her own award.

One of the advantages of an investment account is that the cost of administration is relatively low; the cost to the applicant is nil as the arrangements to open and administer the fund until the applicant attains eighteen are carried out by the Board's staff, for which the applicant cannot be charged. The 1986 working party report commented:

> The arrangements for the administration of awards to minors and others make considerable demands on the time of the Board's staff, both in setting up arrangements for the administration of awards by other persons when this is practicable, and retaining responsibility for administering awards which cannot

> properly in the best interests of the applicant be lodged elsewhere. This work is clearly peripheral to the main function of the Board, which is to determine applications for compensation, and the increasing burden of administering awards for which the Board retains responsibility is a matter of concern ...

Where the capital sum is deemed too large to pay to the parent or to invest in a savings account, which yields a modest income but has no possibility of capital growth, and the period of the investment (up to majority) is long enough to justify a more sophisticated approach to the management of the fund (for example where the applicant is very young and there may be ten years or more before majority), the award is paid to the Official Solicitor, who is asked to accept an appointment by the High Court as guardian for the purpose only of receiving and managing the award during the applicant's minority.

In relation to awards made to victims of child abuse, where the child has already been the subject of a care order in favour of the local authority by a magistrates' court, the Board may pay the award to the Director of Social Services of the local authority to administer the award for the child's benefit.

Applicants suffering from such mental incapacity that they are unable to manage their own financial affairs require the appointment of a receiver by the Court of Protection to accept the award on their behalf. In cases of severe mental illness, there is no alternative to seeking the appointment of a receiver by the court. Many cases, however, are borderline, and the applicant may be able to function in society in a straightforward way, with help from family and friends, including running a bank account and paying domestic bills. Sensible management of a lump sum involving many thousands of pounds is a different matter, and the Board endeavours to safeguard the position so far as possible by informal arrangements, for example with the help of the applicant's solicitor, where the degree of mental incapacity of the applicant or the size of the award renders receivership inappropriate in terms of cost.

The Board may direct that a trust be established to protect the award for the applicant's benefit, but the Board does not have the powers of a court to control the actions of trustees or call them to account; the Board cannot require that any individual, professional or otherwise, should take on the required trusteeship – thus achieving the first stage of appointing trustees can prove difficult. The Criminal Injuries Compensation Act 1995 empowers the Board under the 1990 Scheme to pay awards in the form of structured settlements. These arrangements are considered further below.

2. The powers of the Authority's claims officer under the 1996 Scheme

Paragraph 50 of the 1996 Scheme is the equivalent provision to para 9 in the 1990 Scheme. It provides:

> An application for compensation under this Scheme will be determined by a claims officer, and written notification of the decision will be sent to the applicant or his representative. The claims officer may make such directions

> and arrangements, including the imposition of conditions, in connection with the acceptance, settlement, payment, repayment and/or administration of an award as he considers appropriate in all the circumstances. Subject to any such arrangements, including the special procedures in paragraph 52 (purchase of annuities), and to paragraphs 53 to 55 (reconsideration of decisions), title to an award offered will be vested in the applicant when the Authority has received notification in writing that he accepts the award.

This is a much wider provision than para 9 of the 1990 Scheme. The latter deals only with the power of the Board to make 'special arrangements' for the administration of an award once the decision to make the award has been taken. Paragraph 50, on the other hand, empowers the Authority's claims officer to 'make such directions and arrangements ... as he considers appropriate ... including the imposition of conditions, in connection with the acceptance, settlement, payment, repayment and/or administration of an award'. Paragraph 50 should be read in conjunction with para 19 of the 1996 Scheme, the first sentence of which reads:

> A claims officer may make such directions and arrangements for the conduct of an application, including the imposition of conditions, as he considers appropriate in all the circumstances.

The power to make special arrangements therefore commences with the application being first lodged with the Authority and not only after the award has been made. It is to be expected that the Authority will consider all the options with regard to payment of the award under such arrangements as are presently considered appropriate by the Board in the interest of the applicant under the 1990 Scheme. The Authority, however, may step in earlier and set up arrangements for the appropriate 'conduct of an application' which enables the Authority to require conduct of the application of an applicant under disability to be undertaken by the appropriate party, such as the parent or the person or body with parental authority under the terms of the Children Act 1989, or receiver appointed by the Court of Protection or otherwise as the case may require. The provisions of paras 19 and 50 of the 1996 Scheme are not expressly limited to cases of minors or persons under disabilities but these will be the areas of main use of these powers by the claims officers of the Authority in ensuring the proper conduct of an application throughout its passage through the Authority's procedures and the proper discharge of the Authority at the conclusion of the case.

An important new provision is the authority contained in the Criminal Injuries Compensation Act 1995 and para 52 of the 1996 Scheme which authorises the Board (1990) and the Authority (1996) to make an award in whole or in part by way of an annuity purchased for the benefit of the applicant. The Board has already made a number of awards by way of structured settlement, as these annuity-purchase arrangements are termed in the courts. The purchase by the Board or the Authority of an annuity from a life assurance company for the benefit of the applicant enables the applicant to receive his award partly or wholly in the form of a tax-free annuity. This arrangement can only be made 'where prior agreement is reached between the Authority and the applicant or his representative'. It is particularly tax efficient in the case of very substantial awards.

Chapter 9

Rape and other sexual offences

1. Victims of rape or other sexual assaults

Neither the 1990 nor the 1996 Scheme defines 'crimes of violence' or attempts to list crimes which are regarded as crimes of violence for the purposes of the Scheme. It is established that sexual assaults including rape are crimes of violence – victims of such offences are therefore within the terms of para 4 of the 1990 Scheme and para 8(a) of the 1996 Scheme. Victims of sexual offences, like any other applicants, must fulfil all the criteria of the Scheme (such as informing and co-operating with the police) if they are to be entitled to an award.

Although the victim of rape or other sexual assault may still apply for compensation under the 1996 Scheme, the change from 'common law damages' as the basis of assessment to a fixed 'tariff' system means that the detailed provisions relating to the method of assessment in para 10 of the 1990 Scheme in relation to the particular offence of rape are not necessary and are not repeated in the 1996 Scheme save in relation to the fixed sum of £5,000 (Level 10) in respect of a child conceived as a result of the rape, which provision is common to both Schemes (para 27 of the 1996 Scheme).

Paragraph 27 of the 1996 Scheme refers to the inclusion of rape as a crime of violence and reads as follows:

> Where a woman has become pregnant as a result of rape and an award is made to her in respect of non-consensual vaginal intercourse, an additional amount will be payable equal to Level 10 of the Tariff in respect of each child born alive which she intends to keep.

As the 1990 Scheme is still in operation and governs all applications lodged before 1 April 1996, this chapter deals first with relevant provisions of the 1990 Scheme. The differences created by the 1996 Scheme are referred to and explained. Paragraph 10 of the 1990 Scheme provides that:

> ... the Board will consider applications for compensation arising out of acts of rape and other sexual offences ...

This chapter first deals with applications to the Board based upon allegations of rape or other sexual assault, other than sexual offences against minors which are considered later in this chapter.

Payments of compensation by the Board to victims of rape pre-date the first cases in the High Court in which damages were awarded for this offence against the perpetrators. There being no High Court decisions to refer to as guidelines for the size of awards which might be appropriate, the Board at one time set its own guideline figure. Subsequently it decided that rape as an offence contained such widely disparate sets of circumstances that one guideline figure was inappropriate. As each individual case is considered on the basis of its own circumstances with regard to assessment of compensation, it became apparent that to publish one guideline figure was of no real assistance to applicants and their advisers, however appropriate guideline figures may be for other types of injury.

Where rape or other sexual assault forms the basis of the applicant's case, the Board faces the same difficulties which face a criminal court in terms of proof of the offence. The Board's procedure is not geared to conducting a quasi-criminal trial in respect of an offence which has not been investigated by the police. It cannot compel witnesses – nor is it the Board's responsibility, through its staff, to undertake investigations of alleged criminal offences in order to establish an applicant's case. For these reasons the prompt reporting of a rape to the police and full co-operation with the police by the victim/applicant in the investigation and prosecution of the case are of the greatest importance.

The Board looks for evidence of immediate complaint of rape by the applicant, corroboration of the circumstances by witnesses (such as the first person to see and speak to the applicant after the attack) as well as prompt reporting to the police. Evidence of medical examination as soon as possible after the attack is also very important in establishing whether the offence has been proved, even on the lower standard of proof, the civil standard of balance of probabilities rather than beyond reasonable doubt.

The Board sometimes receives applications in which the applicant has not promptly reported an alleged rape to the police or, indeed, to anyone. In cases where a victim finds herself unable to face going to the police and likewise unable to tell her mother or other close relative what has occurred until days or even months later, the Board is in no position to consider itself satisfied as to what happened and whether injury attributable to a crime of violence has been made out (para 4(a) of the 1990 Scheme, para 8(a) of the 1996 Scheme), or that the requirements of para 6(a) of the 1990 Scheme (para 13(a), (b) of the 1996 Scheme) as to informing the police and co-operating with them in bringing the alleged offender to justice have been fulfilled.

Organisations which give support and advice to victims of rape should establish as soon as possible whether the victim has informed the police and, if not, encourage her as much as possible to do so without delay. Where advisers are consulted by a client who alleges that she has been raped but has taken some time, perhaps weeks or even months, to reach a stage where she has felt able to seek advice and help, and has at that time still not reported it to the police, the advice to do so must be the same. The same considerations apply whether the victim is male or female, and whether the offence is rape or buggery or other serious sexual assault.

Although advisers should bear in mind that the likelihood of the Board or Authority making an award in such circumstances is slim, applicants should not necessarily be discouraged from making an application; it is important, however, that no false hopes should be attached to such applications where none of the basic requirements of the Scheme has been fulfilled.

In cases where the assailant's identity is known but there has been no conviction for the alleged assault or rape, and the application proceeds to a hearing, the Board (or Appeals Panel under the 1996 Scheme) is obliged to invite the alleged assailant to give evidence at the hearing. This is not expressly a requirement of the Scheme. It is a requirement of the principles of natural justice with which bodies exercising judicial functions, such as hearings under the Scheme, must comply. Although in many cases the alleged assailant does not accept the invitation to attend, the applicant who has had her application refused by the Board or Authority on the papers and is considering whether to request a hearing should be aware (and any adviser should see that he or she is aware) of the requirement to invite the alleged assailant, who may therefore attend the hearing and give evidence.

Where the offender has been convicted of a lesser offence, say indecent assault, but acquitted of rape, and the applicant seeks compensation for rape, the alleged offender has to be invited to the hearing as he has not been convicted of the offence in respect of which compensation is sought.

There are cases in which the possibility of facing the alleged assailant at a hearing was the aspect of criminal proceedings which deterred the applicant from reporting the attack to the police in the first instance, and may therefore be a factor which the applicant needs to take into consideration when deciding whether or not to request a hearing of her case before the Board or Appeals Panel. Section 1(1) Sexual Offences (Amendment) Act 1976 provides that:

> A man commits rape if –
>
> (a) he has unlawful sexual intercourse with a woman who at the time of the intercourse does not consent to it; and
>
> (b) at that time he knows that she does not consent to the intercourse or he is reckless as to whether she consents to it.

It is one of the most serious offences in the criminal law. Its statutory definition is based upon the earlier common law offence, which for the offence to be made out required that there had to be some penetration of the female organ by the male, and which provided that the consent of the woman was a complete defence to a charge of rape.

The circumstances in which rape may occur vary from the extremely brutal attack by a complete stranger, accompanied by extreme violence and threats of other injury, to the act of sexual intercourse being imposed upon the woman by the man against her will where the parties are known to each other and have, on other occasions, had sexual intercourse willingly. They might be cohabitees or former cohabitees or even husband and wife. Whatever the circumstances, rape is a crime for which compensation is payable under the Scheme. Under the 1990 Scheme, which applies the principles of common law damages, the amount of compensation depends upon the circumstances of the attack and the degree of injury suffered. Rape is often accompanied by a violent physical attack which causes injuries additional to the sexual violation. Compensation for these injuries will be paid together with the compensation appropriate to the rape itself. Under the 1996 Scheme, compensation will be awarded according to which 'Level' of the Tariff is applicable in the particular case. The Tariff of Injuries under the 1996 Scheme sets out different levels of sexual assault which attract levels of compensation varying from Level 1 to Level 16, (£1,000 to £17,500).

The Board and the Authority not only need medical evidence of any physical injury but also evidence of the psychological and emotional injury which almost invariably results from such assaults. The emotional injury is often far more serious than any physical injuries which may result and is generally far longer lasting in its effect.

Cases involving rape are matters of the greatest complexity and sensitivity. Being such an emotive subject, the validity of almost any generalised statement with regard to it is dangerous and must be qualified with exceptions and reservations to make allowance for widely differing circumstances between one case and another and also for differing perceptions of those circumstances by the victim.

The applicant who applies to the Board or the Authority for compensation in respect of rape is in the same position as other victims of crimes of violence in terms of the requirements of the Scheme. Like other applicants (excluding those cases where victim and assailant are living in the same household, which are subject to the particular requirements of para 8 of the 1990 Scheme or para 16 of the 1996 Scheme already considered), prompt reporting and co-operation with the police are of paramount importance, although conviction of the assailant is not essential.

If the police have had prompt complaint and full co-operation from the applicant and have carried out an investigation which, although not resulting in the identification and conviction of the assailant, has resulted in the police officers in the case being satisfied that a case of rape has been made out, this will go a long way in the applicant's favour in the Board's or Authority's consideration of the claim for compensation.

Where the alleged rapist is identified, charged and tried for the offence, and acquitted at the Crown Court, his acquittal will not necessarily prevent the applicant from receiving compensation. There can be many different reasons which cause a jury to return a not guilty verdict. Uncertainty of identification of the assailant may be the reason for an acquittal even though the evidence of the applicant having been raped may be unassailable. Even if identification is not in doubt, but the jury was not satisfied beyond reasonable doubt that the defendant before it was guilty of rape, the Board or Authority can still make an award if it considers that on the balance of probabilities the applicant was raped.

In such a case, if it proceeded to a hearing before the Board or Appeals Panel, much would depend upon the credibility of the applicant's evidence and the evidence of the investigating police officer. The Board or Appeals Panel would also invite the alleged assailant to give oral evidence at the hearing for reasons already explained. To assist in its deliberations, the Board or Appeals Panel would have before it the statements of witnesses interviewed by police in the course of their investigations, including the applicant's statement and usually the police record of interview or statement under caution of the alleged assailant. It would also have the benefit of any forensic and medical evidence which was before the Crown Court. If, on the evidence before it, the Board or Appeals Panel is satisfied on the balance of probabilities that the applicant was raped, an award will be made notwithstanding the acquittal at the Crown Court.

Much of the commentary in this chapter, in considering the treatment of allegations of rape or other serious sexual assault in establishing eligibility, applies equally to 1990 and 1996 Scheme cases. However, having stated that compensation will be payable for the offence of rape or other sexual assault, para 10 of the 1990 Scheme continues with the words:

> ... both in respect of pain, suffering and shock and in respect of loss of earnings due to consequent pregnancy ...

These last words, referring to loss of earnings, do not mean that in 1990 Scheme cases, the applicant may recover only loss of earnings attributable to consequent pregnancy. The applicant under the 1990 Scheme may recover any loss of earnings attributable to the attack, like any other victim of a crime of violence under the Scheme. These words simply add the loss of earnings attributable to pregnancy to the loss which would be recoverable in any other case.

Paragraph 10 (1990) concludes that the Board will consider applications for compensation:

> ... where the victim is ineligible for a maternity grant under the National Insurance Scheme, in respect of the expenses of childbirth. Compensation will not be payable for the maintenance of any child born as a result of a sexual offence, except that where a woman is awarded compensation for rape the Board shall award the additional sum of £5,000 in respect of each child born alive having been conceived as a result of the rape which the applicant intends to keep.

With the exception of the £5,000 lump sum, para 27 of the 1996 Scheme repeats none of these additional provisions so that in most cases the appropriate level of the Tariff will be the only compensation payable. There may, however, in some cases be an entitlement to loss of earnings where the requirements of para 30 of the 1996 Scheme are made out (i.e. loss of earning capacity for longer than 28 weeks). Maintenance of any child born as a result of a sexual offence is outside the terms of either Scheme.

Before making this additional award of £5,000, the Board or the Authority will need such evidence as is appropriate to satisfy it on the balance of probabilities that a child born to the applicant was conceived as a result of the rape. The Board or the Authority can only make the additional award of the fixed sum of £5,000 where it has also made an award for rape to the mother of that child. The Board or the Authority must also be satisfied on the evidence that the applicant intends to keep the child.

2. Sexual offences against minors

Earlier chapters have examined the provisions of paras 7 (1990) and 15 (1996) against any possible benefit to the offender, paras 8 (1990) and 16 (1996) regarding violence, including sexual assault, within the same household, paras 10 (1990) and 27 (1996) regarding rape and other sexual offences, and paras 9 (1990) and 50 (1996) regarding administration of awards.

It is appropriate to look at these provisions collectively in relation to sexual abuse of minors. These applications have increased in number in recent years. The publicity given to investigations, and the efforts by the media to reach children who have been abused and to provide such children with encouragement and the means to communicate their problems and obtain help, have coincided with a greater awareness on the part of social services and caring organisations that sexual assaults within the family are included in the Scheme and that compensation may therefore be claimed on behalf of such children. Where the child victim is very young, thus excluding any possibility of consent to the assault, the application based on sexual abuse of the child will be regarded in 1990 Scheme cases as falling within the Scheme either under para 4(a) as a 'crime of violence' or under para 10 as 'arising out of acts of rape and other sexual offences'. Under the 1996 Scheme these cases are crimes of violence (para 8(a) 1996) and come under the headings 'Sexual Assault' and 'Sexual Abuse of Children' in the Tariff attached to that Scheme.

The Schemes do not specify any age categories of applicants as requiring different treatment, but the Board and the Authority must have regard to the principles of the criminal law in relation to sexual offences involving children under age. The Sexual Offences Act 1956 (as amended) makes it a criminal offence to have sexual intercourse with a girl under the age of 16 and provides for certain possible defences in the case of intercourse with a girl aged between 13 and 16 years.

Although the Board and the Authority are primarily concerned with eligibility under the Scheme rather than with the criminal law, they have to be satisfied that the evidence establishes that a criminal offence has been committed against the young victim before an award can be made. A crime of violence is required for the applicant to be eligible for an award, and not all crimes involving sexual activity are self-evidently crimes of violence. It is at least arguable whether intercourse with consent by, say, a 15 year old girl with her boyfriend is a crime of violence, even though it is a criminal offence by the boyfriend. Reference should be made to para 9(c) (1996) which provides that a claim under the 1996 Scheme for 'mental injury alone' in such cases is available only to a *non-consenting* victim of a sexual offence, 'consent' for that purpose being consent *in fact*, even if the victim was deemed in law not to have consented'.

The majority of applications based upon sexual offences against minors relate to sexual abuse within the family household, often perpetrated by the child's father or stepfather. Where the offender has been convicted of the offence, the Board's or Authority's task is one of assessment only, as eligibility is not in issue.

Where the offender has not been convicted, usually because the offender has consistently denied the offence and the decision is taken by the police or the Crown Prosecution Service not to prosecute on the grounds that the child is of too tender an age to give evidence, or there is no corroborative evidence and the prospects of a conviction are not such as to justify prosecution, the Authority or the Board may still make an award. These cases often prove to be the most difficult to decide.

Before changes were made in 1990, the earlier (1979) Scheme had contained a specific reference to the problems of proving offences 'which arose out of a sexual relationship or where the relationship between the victim and the offender is such that there may be difficulty in establishing the facts or it seems possible that the offender might benefit from any award'. The Scheme, as it stood before 1990, linked the provision against any benefit to the offender to those cases where the relationship of offender to victim made proof of the offence particularly difficult.

As has been mentioned in the previous chapter, the decision to bring 'family violence' within the terms of the Scheme was made only after much anxious deliberation because of the difficulties of proof, the problems of avoiding a benefit to the offender and, above all, the concern that the inclusion of such cases might even do more harm than good to the injured applicant.

The most prompt possible reporting of the offence and the thorough and timely investigation of the offence by the police are invaluable to the Board or Authority in its efforts to do justice in such cases. The circumstances of such cases, however, are precisely those where complaint is often delayed, frequently for years, and, when made, the complaint will in the first instance usually be to a friend or close relative or a teacher or social worker, and subsequently by them on the child's behalf to the police.

In more serious cases, the Board or Authority will have the help of reports from the social services departments of local authorities, family doctors, police surgeons, psychiatrists and so on, the child often having been placed in the care of the local authority by an order in the magistrates' court, or in some cases made a ward of court, with the Official Solicitor or another party appointed as guardian. Proceedings under the Children Act 1989 will likewise produce documentary evidence and experts' reports which assist in making decisions on applications for compensation under the Scheme.

For the remainder of this chapter references to the Board include, as appropriate, references to the Authority and the Appeals Panel, and references to assessment of compensation include deciding the appropriate Level and Tariff payment under the 1996 scheme.

In the more serious cases where the emotional damage to the child is severe, the medical evidence, combined with the report of the police investigation, including where possible the police interview of the alleged offender with regard to the offences, may leave no doubt as to the genuineness of the case and the cause of the damage to the child. The Board in those circumstances is able to decide that an award should be made and proceeds to assess the appropriate sum by way of compensation.

If the decision of the Board on the papers, which is based upon the evidence shown in the papers before it, is that there will be no award, particularly where the reason for refusal of an award is that the Board is not satisfied that the offence has been made out, the applicant's advisers or representatives have to make a decision whether to request a hearing on the applicant's behalf. This is not an easy decision and it is of the greatest importance that advisers, when placed in this position, are aware of the practical implications of requesting a hearing as they may involve and affect the young applicant.

Where the alleged assailant is identified, but there has either been no prosecution or a prosecution has resulted in acquittal by the court, and the Board's decision on the papers is to make no award - partly or wholly because it is not satisfied on the papers that the offence is made out - and the applicant through his or her representative requests a hearing, the alleged assailant must be invited to give evidence at the hearing. This is a requirement of the rules of natural justice and the Board has no option but to invite. If the alleged assailant attends the hearing, the Board is for the same reason required to hear his evidence if he wishes to give evidence. Alleged assailants do not, on the whole, have a very good record of attendance at hearings but the prospect that he may do so should be taken into account. In recent years there has been a greater tendency for the unconvicted alleged offender in such cases to attend and repeat his denials at the hearing.

In these circumstances the Board would need to hear the applicant's oral evidence to enable it to assess the applicant's credibility, with the alleged assailant's denials being put similarly to the test. In dealing with such cases the Board endeavours to approach them with the interests and welfare of the minor applicant very much in mind. Where eligibility is not in issue and the applicant is of tender years, there will be no question of seeking to obtain oral evidence from the applicant; in most cases where the Board is only assessing compensation in a case of sexual abuse of a child, the applicant will not be required to attend a hearing. It is to be expected that the Appeals Panel will approach these difficult issues in a similar way; certainly the rules of natural justice will apply to its hearings, as with the Board, and the same rules of inviting the alleged offender will certainly continue to apply.

Where the applicant is, say, 15 or 16 years of age, and the hearing is for assessment only, eligibility having already been decided in the applicant's favour, he or she may attend at the Board's hearing centre on the day of the hearing but would not be called to give evidence unless the legal or other representative acting on the applicant's behalf wished the Board to hear evidence from the applicant. This is usually confined to comments on the applicant's present situation, to give the Board some first-hand impression of the extent to which the applicant has or has not recovered from the effects of the offences. The offences themselves are not rehearsed by the Board where the hearing is for assessment only.

Having given evidence, the minor applicant may, if he or she wishes, leave the hearing room while the Board hears representations regarding the emotional and psychological injury suffered by the applicant from his or her representative and considers the details of the medical and other evidence in order to assess the appropriate compensation.

The minor applicant whose application proceeds to a hearing is thus protected so far as possible by the Board's informal procedures.

Regarding the allegedly sexually abused minor whose alleged assailant is identified but denies the offences and has not been convicted, and a hearing is requested on the minor's behalf to establish eligibility, what may be required of the minor applicant at the hearing?

It has already been explained that if the alleged assailant attends, and intends to give evidence denying the allegations, the applicant's options, as in any other case, are either to give evidence so that the credibility of the allegations as well as the denials can be tested, or abandon the application. There remains one other possibility which may spare the minor applicant having to give evidence and yet succeed in achieving an award. If the sitting Board takes the view on the papers that the application is within the Scheme and the alleged assailant, having been invited, does not attend the hearing to give evidence, the applicant would not need to give evidence to establish entitlement and the Board would proceed to assess compensation. It is likely that the Appeals Panel will adopt a similar approach in these cases.

Persons advising minors, or deciding on behalf of minors, whether to request a hearing on eligibility, must have regard to what is in the minor's best interests. Their deliberations should include consideration of the practical repercussions of proceeding with a hearing and their possible effects upon the individual applicant. These observations should not be regarded as discouraging the decision to request a hearing, but are set out with a view to assisting in such a decision being made realistically in the applicant's best interests.

Chapter 10

Personal injury attributable to 'traffic offences' (1990 Scheme) or 'to the use of a vehicle' (1996 Scheme)

1. Introduction

Although there are material differences between the 1990 and 1996 Schemes in respect of their provisions relating to injuries caused by vehicles, the spirit of both provisions is similar: the exclusion from the Scheme of injuries caused by vehicles unless the vehicle is used as a weapon for that purpose. The 1990 Scheme wording is examined first – this will apply to all applications lodged with the Board before 1 April 1996.

2. Paragraph 11 of the 1990 Scheme

Paragraph 11 of the 1990 Scheme provides:

> Applications for compensation for personal injury attributable to traffic offences will be excluded from the Scheme, except where such injury is due to a deliberate attempt to run the victim down.

The question which arises under the 1990 Scheme in applications where the injuries are caused by a vehicle being driven at the applicant is: was this a deliberate attempt to run the victim down? Although the word 'attempt' is used, para 11 clearly intends a deliberate running down to be within the Scheme.

What situations amount to a deliberate running down? Is a reckless running down within the Scheme? It is sometimes argued that to establish recklessness is enough to bring the injury within the Scheme, but as the Scheme uses the word 'deliberate', which has a different meaning from 'reckless' according to both the ordinary usage of these words and the legal meaning of 'reckless', the latter cannot, it is submitted, be sufficient to bring a case within the Scheme unless the reckless act could properly also be described as deliberate.

The driving of a motor vehicle in a manner which satisfies the legal requirements for reckless driving under section 2 of the Road Traffic Act 1972 – driving in such a manner as to create an obvious and serious risk of causing physical injury to some other person who might happen to be using the road, or of doing substantial damage to property – is not the same as deliberately running down another person using the road. Recklessness can be either the failure to give thought to that obvious risk or recognising the risk and taking it none the less.

It would seem logical to conclude from this definition of recklessness that, whilst the recklessness of the second category – adverting to the obvious risk and proceeding to take that risk – might be described as 'deliberate' recklessness to distinguish it from the first category, which may be called 'inadvertent' recklessness, both kinds fall short of the requirement of the Scheme that the action of the assailant must be a 'deliberate attempt to run the victim down'. Deliberately to take the risk of running another person down is not the same as deliberately attempting to run someone down, or deliberately running them down.

It is perhaps appropriate in considering the language used in para 11 to take into account the fact that the law relating to traffic offences was already closely regulated by statute when the Scheme was first drafted and brought into effect, with specific terms established to define different levels of culpability, such as 'careless', 'without consideration', 'dangerous', 'furious', 'reckless'. It was open to the draftsman of the 1990 Scheme, if one of these terms fitted the purpose of para 11, to use it. But the term chosen was none of these existing measures of blameworthiness; instead the layman's word 'deliberate' is used.

It is reasonable to argue that the word 'deliberate' was chosen because none of the other terms accorded with the Scheme's purpose in this respect; thus only a deliberate running down is within the Scheme.

If the applicant can satisfy the Board that on the evidence before it and on the balance of probabilities the vehicle was deliberately used as a weapon to cause him injury, the application is not excluded by para 11. It is respectfully submitted that nothing less than deliberate running down, according to the ordinary meaning of these words, will do.

It is appropriate to consider the comments of the Inter-departmental Working Party in its 1978 report with regard to para 11 of the 1990 Scheme (which was then para 8 of the 1969 Scheme). At page 40 of that report, it states:

> The effect of paragraph 8 of the Scheme is to exclude from its scope those cases where the victim has been run down by a motor vehicle in circumstances where the driver of the vehicle has been guilty of an offence, except where it can be shown that the driver intended to kill or injure the victim. There are very many incidents in which injury is violently inflicted by drivers whose actions are reckless and, but for paragraph 8, such injuries would be within the scope of the Scheme. There is little need for the Scheme to apply in such cases because there are arrangements for compulsory third party insurance by motorists, backed up by the agreements with the Motor Insurers' Bureau which provide personal injury compensation where the driver was not insured or could not be identified. In the limited number of cases where there has been a deliberate attempt to run the victim down the victim (or his dependants) should be able to look to the Scheme; and where there is double benefit, the Board should be able to take account of any

compensation or damages from other sources under paragraph 24 of the Scheme.

(Paragraph 24 of the 1969 Scheme provided for repayment of compensation to the Board where the applicant obtained damages or compensation for the same injury from some other source, as does para 21 of the 1990 Scheme.)

Argument regarding the meaning of 'reckless' and 'deliberate' is not relevant where the action of the motorist is so clearly a deliberate running down that the offence is caught by the provisions of the criminal law as an offence of wounding or manslaughter. In those circumstances one is no longer considering a 'traffic offence' but a 'crime of violence' which is not excluded by para 11.

The Board's 'Guide' to the Scheme, published in 1990, comments that motor insurance, or the Motor Insurers' Bureau, is the appropriate source of redress in relation to injuries sustained as a result of traffic offences. It goes on to say that the exception to the para 11 exclusion of traffic injuries from the Scheme assists the injured party whose claim cannot be covered by motor insurance or the Motor Insurers' Bureau, where the victim was deliberately run down by a driver who cannot be traced and whose identity is unknown. Although it is not particularly helpful to attempt to clarify the meaning of a provision in the Board's Scheme by reference to the non-availability of a remedy under the quite different provisions of the Motor Insurers' Bureau, it does indicate one of the purposes of para 11, namely to provide compensation for the victim who is deliberately run down by a driver who cannot be traced and whose identity is unknown.

Paragraph 11 is not confined to such cases; very often the driver is known and identified and charged with an offence in relation to the incident. If his running down of the applicant was 'deliberate', the application is within the Scheme.

Most such cases involve the applicant as pedestrian. There may be no authority defining the precise scope of the term 'running down' but, as the term 'running down action' or 'running down claim' has been widely used for many years to describe an action for damages against the driver of a vehicle for colliding with another vehicle or a person, it is suggested that, where a person who is either the driver or a passenger in vehicle A is injured by the driver of vehicle B deliberately ramming or running into vehicle A, that injury would be attributable to a deliberate running down and would therefore be within the terms of the Scheme.

The exclusion of applications attributable to 'traffic offences' has led to the argument that since a traffic offence can only be committed on a highway or 'other road to which the public have access', where injury is due to the use of a vehicle on a private road, or a car-park or on land which does not constitute a highway or road, then the usual rule that reckless assault is a crime of violence permits the injured person to recover.

Each case depends on its own facts, both as to the nature of the place where the collision occurred, and as to the nature of the driving, but a number of awards have been made on this basis. At the time of writing, cases which have turned on these issues are due to be heard in judicial review proceedings.

3. Paragraph 11 of the 1996 Scheme

The equivalent to para 11 of the 1990 Scheme is para 11 of the 1996 Scheme which provides:

> A personal injury is not a criminal injury for the purposes of this Scheme where the injury is attributable to the use of a vehicle, except where the vehicle was used so as deliberately to inflict, or attempt to inflict, injury on any person.

One effect of the change of wording is to clarify the purpose of this paragraph. Excluding personal injury 'attributable to the use of a vehicle' is a far clearer exclusion than the earlier Scheme's reference to 'traffic offences'. Similarly the limit of that exclusion is more clearly stated by the words 'except where the vehicle was used so as deliberately to inflict, or attempt to inflict, injury on any person'.

The 1996 Scheme thus makes clear what has been thought to be the meaning of the equivalent provision in the 1990 Scheme. The word 'deliberate' is retained and the whole paragraph makes the simple and clear point that only when a vehicle is used as a weapon does it come within the Scheme. It is for the applicant to prove on the balance of probabilities that this is the case.

The Authority's 'Guide' published with the 1996 Scheme confirms this view at para 7.21 of the Guide.

The 1996 wording removes from cases under that Scheme the need for legal argument as to what is or is not a 'traffic offence', the words used in the 1990 Scheme, and the relevance or otherwise of the actions of the driver resulting in injury to the applicant having occurred on a highway or on private land.

Chapter 11

Assessment of compensation - 1990 Scheme

1. Introduction

This chapter applies only to applications received by the Board before 1 April 1996. Although it has been clear from the preceding chapters that the 1996 Scheme and earlier schemes have substantially similar principles in deciding questions of eligibility and entitlement to an award, in the matter of assessment of compensation the 1996 Scheme differs fundamentally from all the previous versions of the Scheme published in 1964, 1969, 1979 and 1990. All those Schemes based assessment of compensation entirely upon the common law principles of damages for personal injury and consequential financial loss. The 1996 Scheme fixes a tariff level for each injury.

The 1993 White Paper and the abortive 1994 Tariff Scheme had earlier made clear that the tariff payment for the injury would be the only compensation payable under the 1994 Tariff Scheme, which would thus have swept away all other heads of claim, such as past or future loss of earnings and costs of care in the case of serious injury causing permanent disablement. The manner of implementation of the 1994 Tariff Scheme was declared unlawful by the House of Lords in early 1995 and the 1996 Scheme has, with modifications, brought back into the Scheme entitlement to loss of earnings and costs of care, but only to the extent defined by the terms of that Scheme. Although no longer swept away in their entirety, as would have been the case had the 1994 Tariff Scheme survived the challenge to its validity in the courts, these heads of claim - which are recognised as additional to the fixed tariff award for the injury itself - are, for the first time, expressly set out in the Scheme itself. They are recognisably an attempt to codify in a few paragraphs of the 1996 Scheme the main common law principles by which a court would make such assessment, and at the same time make express modifications to those principles with two main objectives.

The first is to place a limit on the unlimited nature of damages, which are recoverable by a plaintiff in the court, to an extent which is considered more appropriate to a scheme funded by taxpayers' money. The second main objective is to make the running of the Scheme an administrative rather than a legal exercise, so that the Authority's claims officers have, in the Scheme itself and its attached Tariff, all that is needed to decide both eligibility under the Scheme and the appropriate level of compensation in every case.

It is necessary therefore to deal separately with the rules of assessment applicable to 1990 Scheme and 1996 Scheme cases respectively.

The present chapter sets out the rules of assessment which apply to all applications presented before 1 April 1996, and therefore all references in this chapter to the Board are references to the Board only, and do not include the Authority or Appeals Panel which came into operation on 1 April 1996.

2. General principles of assessment

Paragraph 12 of the 1990 Scheme begins:

> Subject to the other provisions of this Scheme, compensation will be assessed on the basis of common law damages and will normally take the form of a lump sum payment . . .

The jurisdiction of the Board is unlimited, and compensation is assessed according to the same principles which apply to the assessment of damages by the High Court. Where serious injuries are sustained, such as severe brain damage or paraplegia resulting in total loss of quality of life and earning capacity, and it is necessary to meet the costs of lifetime care, awards of hundreds of thousands of pounds are made by the Board as by the High Court.

Whereas the civil court determines liability and then assesses quantum (the total of general and special damages payable to the plaintiff), the Board decides eligibility under the Scheme and then makes the appropriate assessment of compensation. Although the terminology differs, the same principles by which the computation of general and special damages proceeds in the court are applied by the Board in assessing compensation, subject to certain provisions in the Scheme which differ from those of the common law or statute.

Paragraph 12 begins with the words: 'Subject to the other provisions of this Scheme . . . ', the effect of which is to allow certain provisions in the Scheme to override equivalent provisions in the common law or statute where the two conflict.

An example of such a difference is the extent to which Department of Social Security benefits are deductible from an award made under the Scheme (para 19(a)) on the one hand, and in the civil courts on the other hand. Other examples are the condition of a minimum assessment of compensation below which figure no compensation at all will be paid (para 5 of the Scheme), and a ceiling figure for loss of earnings, which under the 1979 Scheme was limited to twice the gross average industrial wage and under the 1990 Scheme is fixed at a maximum of one and a half times that figure.

This upper limit to loss of earnings affects only a very small minority of applicants and is fixed at a level which is deemed to constitute reasonable compensation out of public funds where the injured person is an exceptionally high earner.

The minimum award fixed under para 5 of the Scheme is much more important in its effect upon applicants, as there are many cases of relatively minor injuries which fall outside the Scheme altogether - simply because the injury does not merit an award of at least the specified minimum sum.

The adherence to 'common law damages' as stated in para 12 is illustrated by the wording of the decision of the Board where no award is made under para 5, which may read:

> The applicant suffered painful and unpleasant injuries in the assault. However, these injuries were of a minor nature and would not justify an award of damages in the court of at least the minimum award required by para 5 of the Scheme. Accordingly no award can be made.

The Scheme requires the Board in its assessment of compensation to award the applicant that sum which the High Court or county court would have awarded in a similar case. Awards made in the courts are therefore the guidelines to the Board's assessments under the Scheme, and submissions made to the Board on behalf of applicants frequently refer to High Court or county court decisions which give support to a particular level of damages or compensation.

It is an acknowledged difficulty in the assessment of damages that no two cases will be precisely similar. The law of precedent, the principle of the common law that a decision made by one court will in certain circumstances be an authority for the legal principle by which it was decided and binding on another court in deciding a similar case, does not apply to the assessment of damages. The courts, however, and also the Board, have what might be called a consensus with regard to the appropriate level of damages for particular injuries which are frequently before the courts and the Board. This remains necessarily flexible to take account of the considerable variations in the level of 'pain, suffering and loss of amenity' which may arise between cases.

Dealing as it does with many thousands of applications every year, the Board's collective experience is very considerable. The Board's own reported decisions are not infrequently cited to the Board by applicants and their representatives. Whilst the principle of precedent has no application to the Board's decisions with regard to either eligibility under the Scheme or assessment of compensation, such referrals can sometimes be helpful as guidelines on 'quantum', the amount to be awarded.

Reference has been made to the two main aspects of compensation, the award for the injury itself, for the pain, suffering and loss of amenity resulting from that injury, which the law refers to as the general damages, and the special damages which consist of the financial losses incurred by the injured party up to the date on which the assessment is made by the Board. The calculation of expected future financial loss is legally part of the assessment of general damages.

'Pain and suffering' take into account, for example, a number of operations to rectify the injury. 'Loss of amenity' includes those aspects of day-to-day life which the applicant would normally be able to perform or enjoy, including minor domestic and personal tasks such as washing and dressing and holding a knife and fork, and activities like running, gardening, playing golf, decorating, listening to music, playing with the children or smelling the Sunday roast; for the loss of any of these or their like has its value in damages.

As the Board is assessing compensation under the Scheme and not damages at common law, it does not always use the same legal labels as a court would use for the various heads of claim in a particular case. The Board does, however, include within the final total figure for compensation every head of claim which would have been available to the applicant had he been making a claim for those same injuries and losses in a court rather than before the Board, save where the Scheme expressly provides to the contrary.

The two heads of claim, general damages and special damages, will often be straightforward. A man suffers, for example, facial bruising and lacerations and a broken wrist. His wrist is plastered and, as he works with his hands, he is off work for ten weeks. He receives only statutory sick pay while he is off work. He makes a full recovery apart from some minor scarring and is able to resume work with no continuing problems after the period off work. For the injuries themselves the applicant would be awarded the equivalent sum which a court would award as general damages. The Board would require in such a case, as it does in every case – however straightforward – a medical report which confirms the details of the injuries, the treatment, the effects upon the applicant and the prognosis, whether the applicant has fully or partly recovered or will have symptoms such as aches and pains or scarring for the rest of his life.

For the loss of earnings, after deduction therefrom of the full value of statutory sick pay received as well as income tax and national insurance, he would receive a sum equal to that loss by way of special damages. The latter would also include other out of pocket expenses, such as fares to and from hospital for treatment, which may have been incurred. Damage to clothing is not covered by the Scheme as damage to any property is excluded unless it is relied upon as a physical aid (para 17 of the 1990 Scheme).

Let us suppose that the applicant in the above example was a bricklayer who at the date of the assessment of his claim, say 18 months or two years after the incident in which he was injured, still suffered considerable pain in his injured wrist towards the end of the day's work, and that a report from an orthopaedic surgeon indicated that the condition of his wrist would not improve any further, with some risk in the foreseeable future that he may no longer be able to work as a bricklayer which was his livelihood and only skill in terms of employment. He may perhaps be able only to work a shorter working day than normal, but as he had worked for the same employer for many years his present employer was prepared still to employ him on the basis of reduced hours. Suppose also that the evidence indicated that if he lost that job he would have great difficulty in getting another because of the continuing effects of the injury.

The applicant would in these circumstances be entitled to ask the Board (as he would be entitled to ask a court in a civil claim) to include a sum for the quite separate head of claim of having suffered prejudice in the labour market, being the risk of further loss at some future time. This would be in addition to compensation for the injury itself, for the loss of earnings while he was off work immediately after the incident, and for reduced earnings since.

Prejudice in the labour market as a head of claim is usually referred to as the 'Smith and Manchester element' in the damages or compensation, as the authority for this type of loss as a recoverable head of damage is the decision of the Court of Appeal in *Smith v Manchester City Council* (1974) 118 SJ 597.

3. Cases of serious injury

The Board frequently has cause to deal with cases of serious injury. Where a severe blow to the head or a bullet wound or other penetrating injury causes brain damage or other severe disablement such as paraplegia, the Board is called upon to assess compensation under the same numerous heads of claim as would be available to the applicant were he the plaintiff in the High Court seeking damages at common law against a defendant on the grounds of negligence.

Although many applications to the Board are lodged and conducted personally by the applicant, in cases of serious injury it is important that the applicant has competent professional advice. The Scheme requires the applicant to make out his case in all respects, and if a head of claim is not prepared and presented to the Board by an applicant it is not possible for the Board or the Board's staff to prepare the claim on the applicant's behalf. In cases of serious injury the possible heads of claim are not only wide ranging but are also complex, both in terms of the legal principles on which they are based and in terms of the evidence needed to substantiate them.

If the case is not fully and competently prepared and presented to the Board, the applicant may lose some part of his claim which may have been recoverable. The amounts involved can be considerable.

Although it is not within the power of the Board to make any award or payment in respect of legal costs, the Board will usually be prepared to make an interim award at an early stage in the conduct of the application, once the Board is satisfied that the applicant is eligible for an award. Although an interim payment is by way of a payment on account of the applicant's entitlement to compensation, an interim award paid at an early stage will put the applicant in funds and make possible the payment of legal or other professional costs incurred in further preparing his claim.

To enable the Board to do justice in cases of severe injury, it will often be necessary to have consultants' reports from several different medical disciplines. Psychiatric and psychological assessments may be necessary as well as orthopaedic and neurological reports. In cases of permanent severe disability the Board is frequently helped by specialist reports dealing with the cost of such matters as domestic equipment and the adaptation of the applicant's home to facilitate day-to-day living, and the detailed costing of the applicant's future care where care services are needed and will continue to be needed for the rest of the applicant's lifetime. In cases involving lifetime assessments the Board will need medical evidence as to the applicant's life expectancy, as such evidence is essential in deciding the period for which future care or loss will be likely to continue; it will affect the multiplier – the number of years – by which the annual rate of loss or annual cost, as the case may be – the multiplicand – is to be multiplied.

Cases coming before the Board include various degrees of paralysis such as hemiplegia and paraplegia, and the fullest medical evidence is necessary to enable the Board to assess the appropriate award for the injury itself and the general damages.

The special damages and future loss, which are quite separate from and additional to the compensation for the injury, may include some or all of the following heads of claim:

(a) Special damages in relation to the applicant's net loss of earnings, from the date of the injury to the date of assessment by the Board, less all DSS benefits received up to that date.

(b) Loss of future earnings, based upon an assessment of the applicant's 'annual rate of continuing net loss' (the multiplicand) at the date of assessment by the Board, to which the Board applies the appropriate multiplier (number of years) to arrive at the value of the loss.

(c) Prejudice on the labour market – if the applicant still has a job but his injury is such that should he lose that job, it would be harder to obtain fresh employment because of the injury, that 'prejudice' is a compensatable loss.

(d) Loss of future pension entitlement if appropriate. (If the applicant is under 30 years of age this item may be regarded as incapable of calculation, as it involves a benefit which is so far in the future as to be conjectural.)

(e) Loss of an interesting and satisfying career or loss of 'congenial employment'. This is apart from the financial loss and is sometimes regarded as part of the general damages as it is a loss of amenity, a loss of enjoyment of life. However it is recognised as an item of loss in itself which the compensation should reflect.

(f) Expenses incurred in providing special food where a special diet has been prescribed by medical advisers.

(g) The provision of special equipment to enable the applicant to perform day-to-day personal and domestic tasks.

(h) Conversion or adaptation of the applicant's home, such as a specially equipped kitchen or bathroom or ramps and widened doorways for a wheelchair. Decisions of the High Court have given guidance on how far such claims may go. Although necessary adaptation may be allowed as a claim, the capital cost of a house purchased especially to meet the applicant's needs would generally not be allowed, although a percentage of such cost may be awarded (see *Roberts v Johnstone* [1988] 3 WLR 1247).

(i) Cost of future care; this may take the form of fees for care in a home where necessary full-time care can be provided, or it may be a sum to recompense the applicant's wife or mother, or other relative, who may have given up such employment wholly or partly in order to provide home care for the applicant. The rate of net loss of earnings of a wife who gives up paid employment to care for the applicant may be the appropriate measure of the cost of care (see *Hunt v Severs* [1994] 2 AC 350).

Item (i) alone can amount to a very substantial sum in cases of severe or total disablement and should be prepared with particular care where it forms part of the applicant's claim. All necessary documentary evidence should be provided, such as evidence of earnings from the employer of the carer whose job has been given up, as well as a calculation of the cost in the form of lost wages or salary of the carer, so that if the Board is satisfied that this head of claim is appropriate, there is sufficient evidence to enable the Board to quantify it.

Where a paid carer has been engaged or it is expected, such expectation being supported by medical evidence, that in say five or ten years the applicant's condition will have deteriorated to such an extent that a part-time or full-time carer will be necessary to meet the applicant's needs, the cost of that element of future care should be established by documentary evidence.

A line of High Court decisions, including *Donnelly v Joyce* (1973), *Croke v Wiseman* (1981) and *Housecroft v Burnett* (1986), has established this head of claim (for recompense for the carer), and applicants and their advisers should refer to the authorities and to the standard text books on personal injury damages for guidance on this aspect of any claim made under the Scheme.

The above heads of claim are by no means exhaustive. The law of damages for personal injuries is complex and continually developing, and there are weighty legal tomes on the subject to which the legal practitioner needs to refer if he or she is to ensure that the applicant/client's net has been cast sufficiently widely to catch all possible heads of claim and to ensure that the applicant's case to the Board is fully presented. This book can do no more than provide some pointers on this complex area of the law.

The High Court has in recent years awarded very substantial damages in cases of severe disability and loss of career. The layman may not be aware that of these very substantial awards, approaching or even exceeding a million pounds in some cases, the heads of claim mentioned above - and other heads of claim which may be appropriate to the particular case - go to make up the greater part of such awards. The general damages for the injury itself, even in cases of total paralysis or very severe brain damage, may constitute less than a quarter of the total award. The future losses, such as future loss of earnings and the cost of lifetime care, usually represent the bulk of the award.

4. Future loss of earnings

Again it must be emphasised that this chapter has no application to 1996 Scheme cases and applies only to pre-1 April 1996 applications, as these remain regulated by the 1990 or whichever earlier Scheme was in force when the application was initially made to the Board. The rules relating to the assessment of 'loss of earnings' or 'special expenses' under the 1996 Scheme are dealt with in Chapter 13.

Where the applicant has been unable to continue in the job he had before the injury, or even in the same kind of work, and the incapacity rendering him unable to do that job is directly attributable to the crime of violence for which compensation is being sought, he will be able to claim compensation for future loss of earnings, and also, where appropriate, for loss of future pension rights.

The task of the Board in such cases is to establish the appropriate sum to compensate for that future loss. It must take into account all the known factors regarding current rates of pay and the income tax and national insurance payments which would have been deductible from that pay had the applicant been able to continue in his career.

Paragraph 19(a) of the 1990 Scheme requires the Board to deduct from the loss of net pay all social security benefits payable to the applicant, if these will continue to be payable after the lump sum from the Board has been paid. Paragraph 20 (1990) requires deduction of 'any pension' arising from the injury, so long as the pension rights have not accrued solely as a result of payments made by the victim or a dependant.

The applicant's net earnings from any alternative employment which he has been able to obtain despite the injury are also deducted.

This calculation will give the Board the figure which represents the level of the applicant's continuing loss of income resulting from the injury on a net annual basis. The rate of any continuing net loss of income is usually calculated as an annual sum, as the Board multiplies that figure by the appropriate 'number of years' to achieve the lump sum to be paid in compensation.

The net pay is taken as the basis for this calculation rather than the gross, because it is the net pay which the claimant actually received before the injury, and the deprivation of that net pay is the appropriate measure of the loss which he has suffered. In *British Transport Commission v Gourley* (1956), the Court of Appeal stated that the injured person should be placed in the same financial position, so far as can be done by an award of money, as he would have been in had the injury not been suffered.

It will be appreciated that a future loss of earnings calculation can be complex. It is for the applicant to make out his case in all respects under the Scheme. The very considerable volume of applications already in the system makes it impracticable for the Board's staff to undertake complex investigations and calculations of the applicant's financial position or potential earnings where an item such as future earnings loss might be claimed. The Board's staff will endeavour to do so, however, where the applicant for some reason cannot or will not avail himself of union or legal or other representation and advice.

In the majority of such cases where future loss is claimed it is capable of proof because the applicant was in an occupation with an established career structure and salary scale, with clearly defined pension entitlements based upon the number of years' service. Most such claims arise in cases where police officers, firefighters, public transport employees, prison officers, staff in mental hospitals or local authority employees have been injured and have been prevented by those injuries from continuing with their career until the normal retirement age.

Once eligibility has been decided in the applicant's favour, all possible heads of claim should be carefully considered by the applicant and any adviser who may be assisting him or her. Where future loss of earnings is one of those heads of claim the calculation must be made and, if possible, agreed with the Board's staff, so that the Board has an agreed set of figures for loss to date, the special damages, and a set of figures indicating the claimed future loss, which is part of the general damages.

The calculation of future loss is usually based upon the up-to-date net pay levels of persons doing the same job or the equivalent job within the pay structure applicable to that occupation at the applicant's last rank or grade. In some cases there is persuasive evidence that the applicant would have been promoted and, if this is accepted by the Board, the calculation of future loss may reflect the salary at the higher grade which the injury prevented the applicant from attaining. It is advisable to have both sets of figures (i.e. with and without promotion) calculated and available, as the Board may not be persuaded that there was any reasonable chance of securing promotion, and only compensate at the lower rate.

Having established the total net loss of earnings to date of assessment by the Board and the annual rate at which that net loss will continue from the date of assessment – usually referred to as the 'continuing loss' or the 'rate of continuing loss' – the Board will decide what is the appropriate 'number of years' to apply to that continuing annual loss in order to arrive at a lump sum which represents the appropriate compensation for that expected future loss.

In calculating future loss it is not simply a matter of multiplying the current annual rate of loss by the number of years during which that loss is expected to continue. Like the court, the Board has to make some reduction to offset the advantage of the accelerated payment of lost future earnings by way of an immediate lump sum in compensation.

It may be possible to demonstrate by producing pay scales that, for example, a police officer who was medically retired at 45 years of age instead of the usual age of 55 because of injury directly attributable to a crime of violence, has a continuing loss, at the date on which the Board assesses his claim, at the rate of £8,000 per annum, after making the appropriate deductions which the Scheme requires from the gross salary that he would have been receiving had he not been injured. Suppose the assessment is made when he is 47. His loss for two years from the date of medical retirement to the date of assessment is his 'special damage' and is calculable. His future loss from his present age, 47, to his normal retirement age, 55, runs at £8,000 per annum for a further eight years.

The rate of annual loss is called in law the 'multiplicand', and the number of years by which it is multiplied is called the 'multiplier'.

In the above example the Board would be likely to multiply the multiplicand of £8,000 by a multiplier of, say, five years rather than eight years to allow for the benefit of early payment of future earnings, and also to make some allowance for all the other contingencies of life which have to be allowed for in cases where future entitlements are being evaluated.

Such a calculation can be made only where the necessary evidence of earnings is available. The total period of loss, which in all cases commences with the date of injury and in some cases will continue for the rest of the applicant's life, is divided up into separate 'slices'. The reason for this is that the method of calculation for each slice of time varies as different considerations apply.

The separate slices of time into which the total period of loss is divided, in a case where the injury has caused the applicant to retire on medical grounds from his occupation, will include some or all of the following:

(a) from the date of incident (injury) to the date of his return to work after initial recovery;
(b) from the date of his return to work to the date of medical retirement by reason of the injuries received;
(c) from the date of his medical retirement to the date of assessment by the Board;
(d) from the date of assessment by the Board to what would have been the normal date of retirement from the applicant's pre-incident occupation (at age 55 or 60 in many occupations);
(e) from the date of normal retirement to the date of commencement of the applicant's state pension;
(f) from the date at which the applicant qualifies for the state pension until the end of his life.

Each of these periods will be the subject of a separate calculation. It will be clear that not all of these slices of the potential periods of loss will be relevant in all cases, but in those applications involving loss of career where figures are available to establish what the applicant would have received by way of salary and pension in each of these periods had he not been prevented from so doing by the injuries, the calculation must be made.

From (c) onwards - the period starting with the date of medical retirement and ending with the date on which the Board makes its assessment of compensation for past and future losses - pension becomes a factor in the calculation. At this stage the applicant will perhaps have begun to draw a reduced pension (because it has been taken prematurely) and the amount of the reduced pension received will be a deduction from the loss of earnings calculation.

This level of loss will continue through period (d) - commencing with the date on which the Board makes its assessment and ending with the date on which the applicant would have retired had he not been injured.

In period (e) the level of loss will be based upon the extent to which the full pension at, say, 55 would have exceeded the reduced pension which was taken at an earlier age on medical retirement.

Reference should be made to the decisions of the Court of Appeal in *Auty and others v National Coal Board* [1985] 1 All ER 930 and *Wells v Wells*, Court of Appeal, 23 October 1996, which establish the method of computation and in particular the method of discounting capital awards for future loss and loss of pension. The Board applies a 4½ per cent interest rate for the purpose of establishing the appropriate multiplier, making such adjustments as are appropriate to the circumstances of the case.

Where the applicant's employment is not such that a salary scale and pension figures can be produced for the Board, the applicant may produce in support of his submission on pay levels during his period off work the pay tables published in the Department of Education and Employment's Gazette for various trades and occupations.

By using these tables an applicant, who has been forced to give up his occupation because of the injury, may be able to satisfy the Board as to the net earnings he could expect to have received up to the date on which the Board assesses the loss of earnings. He may also in this way be able to establish the rate of his 'continuing loss' at the date of the Board's decision as the basis for calculating his future loss of earnings.

In the more straightforward cases the Board will rely upon the evidence from the applicant's employer for details of the applicant's period off work, rate of pay at the time of the injury, and any pay such as statutory sick pay which the applicant received during his period off work which would reduce the measure of loss. The Board's staff make enquiry of the employer (except in small claims) where loss of earnings may form part of the claim, so that the Board will always have this basic information regarding loss of earnings before it when assessing the applicant's loss.

5. Medical evidence and interim awards

The Board will require medical evidence in every case to enable an assessment to be made of the injury suffered. In those cases where the injuries are minor and the applicant did not seek any medical attention from his doctor or from the hospital, the probability is that the application will fail under para 5 of the 1990 Scheme, as there is no corroboration of the applicant's account of his injuries by medical evidence. Moreover the injuries, even if established to the Board's satisfaction as having been suffered as the applicant says, may not justify at least the minimum award required by para 5. Although medical evidence is not expressly required by the terms of the Scheme, it is in practical terms regarded as virtually indispensable to enable the Board to be satisfied as to the precise injury suffered. However, in some cases the Board may make an award without medical evidence if, for example, there is a reliable witness of the nature and extent of the injury. Contemporaneous photographs of the injury may also assist.

The application form, on which every application to the Board for compensation must have commenced, requests from the applicant details of the doctor or hospital by whom the injuries were treated, both initially and by way of any continuing treatment.

The Board's staff request a report from the doctor or hospital so named as one of the initial enquiries made in preparing the file for decision by the Board.

These initial enquiries also include the obtaining of a report from the police. Where the information contained in the application form and in the police report shows that the application is likely to be outside the Scheme, if for example the applicant did not report the incident to the police or refused to co-operate in bringing the assailant to justice, the Board does not pursue medical enquiries beyond an initial report from the doctor or the hospital, as such evidence would be necessary only where the application is within the Scheme and the Board would be required to assess the appropriate compensation.

Medical evidence will deal in most cases with the physical injuries suffered, the treatment of those injuries, the extent of recovery and of any continuing symptoms or disability. As the Scheme also covers cases where the injury is nervous shock and emotional trauma amounting to a psychiatric illness, medical evidence will be particularly required in those cases to establish injury beyond the normal level of shock and distress which physical injury inevitably brings in its wake. The common law principles governing 'nervous shock' cases involving psychological injury are considered in more detail in Chapter 2. It is important to distinguish these rules from the new rules applying to cases alleging 'mental injury' under the 1996 Scheme. These are set out in para 9 of the 1996 Scheme (see page 40).

In cases of minor injury with full recovery in a matter of weeks, the medical situation will be fully ascertainable by the time the application is considered by the Board. With more serious injuries a final prognosis may not be possible for months or even years. Where this is the case, and the Board is able to decide that the application is within the Scheme, the Board may make an interim award, leaving a final assessment until such time as the final medical picture can be made clear. This situation is expressly dealt with in para 12 of the 1990 Scheme which states:

> More than one payment may be made where an applicant's eligibility for compensation has been established but a final award cannot be calculated in the first instance - for example where only a provisional medical assessment can be given.

In a case of serious facial scarring there may be a plastic surgeon's report which suggests that the cosmetic disfigurement may be capable of improvement by surgery. An interim award may be appropriate in such a case, first because the final cosmetic effect is not yet known and will not be known until after surgery has taken place, and secondly because the Board may consider in the particular case that it would be reasonable to compensate the applicant for the cost of private medical treatment, and an interim award could be used to cover the fees for the intended operation.

This latter point is covered by para 18 of the 1990 Scheme, which states in relation to private medical fees:

> The cost of private medical treatment will be payable by the Board only if the Board consider that, in all the circumstances, both the private treatment and the cost of it are reasonable.

In a case where, say, a young person has a seriously disfiguring facial scar and suffers serious emotional effects and there is a waiting list of some years for plastic surgery on the National Health Service then, if the fees quoted for having plastic surgery carried out privately are reasonable, the Board may make an interim award which includes those fees as well as being a payment on account of the total compensation, the balance of which will in due course be paid by the Board when a final assessment can be made.

Where the Board in making the interim award has expressly approved the specific fees quoted for the operation, the applicant should produce receipts when the Board is making a final award, as the applicant is seeking as part of the total award the costs of the operation in addition to the full compensation for the injury. From this total figure the Board then deducts the amount of the interim award already made.

In cases involving physical injury and psychological injury, an interim award will sometimes be appropriate where the application is within the Scheme and a full psychological assessment of the emotional damage done cannot be made for some time. Many other types of injury render an interim award appropriate, including broken limbs requiring further surgery and medical assessment by an orthopaedic surgeon, eye injuries which can sometimes take a long time to resolve before a final ophthalmological report can give the Board the final picture, and burns requiring numerous skin-grafting operations over a period of years.

Unlike membership of the Appeals Panel, the Board members are all lawyers. In medical matters they are guided by the reports from doctors and consultants which are placed before them. The reports may be those obtained on the Board's behalf by the Board's staff or provided by the applicant or his advisers. Doctors, like lawyers, sometimes disagree, and the Board may find that, for example in a difficult case involving a back injury, there are, on the Board's papers, reports from consultant orthopaedic surgeons which conflict. One report may conclude that on the balance of probabilities the injury which is the subject of the application to the Board was the cause of the continuing pain and disability from which the applicant suffers, leading perhaps to retirement from his job on medical grounds. Another report may come to a different conclusion, ascribing the disability to another cause, such as a medical condition from which the applicant suffers and which is quite separate from the injury arising from the incident before the Board, or to a quite different incident which also resulted in an injury to the applicant's back.

The Board does not embark upon a choice between reports which are in conflict in this way. The Board's procedure does not involving calling medical experts to give oral evidence so that they may be cross-examined on their conclusions as would commonly be the case in a High Court action. The Board's practice in the event of conflicting medical reports is to request an independent joint medical report by two consultants, usually new to the case, in the appropriate medical discipline or disciplines, with a view to the Board accepting the conclusions of that joint medical report in making its assessment.

In cases where the medical report discloses that, before the incident resulting in injury, the applicant was already suffering from a medical condition which would in due course have brought about the same problems and symptoms as arose after the injury, the Board will take into account in assessing the amount of compensation the extent to which an injury has accelerated those problems and symptoms.

This situation is frequently disclosed in orthopaedic reports revealing that the applicant already had an orthopaedic disorder, such as spondylosis of the back which was asymptomatic before the incident, but since the incident the applicant has suffered back pain. The orthopaedic surgeon's report may indicate in such a case that the disorder would have remained asymptomatic for another five years or so, had the injury not been suffered. The Board will compensate for the degree of acceleration of the condition by the incident in such a case, rather than the condition itself, as the applicant would, even without the injury, have suffered those disabilities in due course, but would have had a further five years without symptoms had he not been injured.

Paragraph 12 of the 1990 Scheme states that compensation 'will normally take the form of a lump sum payment'. The 'normally' is scarcely necessary in this sentence as the form of compensation is a lump sum in every case. The slight qualification is to accommodate those relatively few cases in which the Board 'may make alternative arrangements in accordance with paragraph 9 above' of the 1990 Scheme by which it directs that the award should be paid subject to the terms of a trust, usually in cases where the applicant is a minor. Even so the Board awards a lump sum which is directed to be held subject to those trust provisions. The equivalent provisions in the 1996 Scheme are contained in paras 50 (arrangements for payment) and 51 (interim awards).

The last part of para 12 of the 1990 Scheme states:

> In a case in which an interim award has been made, the Board may decide to make a reduced award, increase any reduction already made or refuse to make any further payment at any stage before receiving notification of acceptance of a final award.

Although commencing with the words 'In a case in which an interim award has been made...' and thus apparently limiting the application of the principle which follows to such cases, the substance of this principle applies in all cases whether or not an interim award has been made.

Regardless of whether or not an interim award has been made, it is equally true to state – and it is of much greater significance as it applies in all cases – that until the Board has received notification of acceptance of a final award (which is the point at which an applicant becomes entitled to an award, as provided in the last sentence of para 22 of the 1990 Scheme) the Board may at any time reduce or further reduce an award or refuse to make an award altogether.

Cases which are most often subject to this important general principle are those in which the applicant has a record of convictions, and the initial decision of the Board was to make a reduction in the light of those convictions rather than to make no award at all. If, at any time before the Board receives notification of acceptance of the reduced award, the Board receives notice of additional convictions, the Board may, if the convictions are serious enough to be material, further reduce the award or refuse to make an award at all.

Similarly, if the Board receives new information of sums deductible under paras 19, 20 or 21 of the 1990 Scheme, an award may be reduced or extinguished altogether.

These provisions of para 12 and the last sentence of para 22 in the 1990 Scheme are substantially re-enacted in paras 50 and 51 of the 1996 Scheme.

Where the applicant is offered an award in the first instance but is not satisfied with the award offered and requests, and is granted, a hearing, it may sometimes happen that between the time of the original offer and the hearing taking place, the Board receives details of criminal convictions recorded against the applicant or of convictions additional to those before the Board at the time of the initial decision. When such a situation arose before 1 February 1990 and the coming into operation of the 1990 Scheme on that date, there was no provision (as there is under para 23 of the 1990

Scheme) for the case to be referred back for reconsideration by a member of the Board; it had accordingly to proceed to a hearing unless the applicant decided to abandon the application. At the hearing the Board would be free to consider any additional convictions or other material evidence arising up to the date of the hearing. It would be entitled to reduce or further reduce any award originally offered or refuse an award altogether if those convictions or other evidence made an award inappropriate.

Since the coming into operation of the 1990 Scheme and the 'reconsideration' provision in para 23 of that Scheme, a single member of the Board may reconsider any award offered earlier in the light of convictions or additional convictions or other evidence becoming known to the Board, and reduce or refuse an award (such reconsideration by the Authority or Appeals Panel is also permitted under para 55 of the 1996 Scheme).

This is so in relation to 1990 Scheme cases because the award under that Scheme is neither a statutory right nor a contractual entitlement. It is an *ex gratia* payment out of public funds, and the approach to questions of entitlement is not essentially legalistic. The Board under the 1990 Scheme and the Authority or the Appeals Panel under the 1996 Scheme must consider the sense of the words in the Scheme and the principles of natural justice to which those procedures and decisions must conform.

Where an applicant requests a hearing, by so doing he rejects any offer which has been made of either a full or reduced award. There is, as a result, no offer open to the applicant to accept at a later stage should he change his mind. Where the applicant changes his mind and seeks to accept the rejected offer, the Board or the Authority may consider such request on its merits and, where it is appropriate to do so, agree, as a concession entirely in its discretion, to make the original award (see *R v Criminal Injuries Compensation Board, ex parte Earls* (1982) in Appendix 1).

Neither the 1990 nor the 1996 Scheme permits payment of interest on awards. An award under the 1990 Scheme is an *ex gratia* payment, unlike an award of damages in the court which is based upon proof of a prior legal entitlement to the sum awarded. The Board, in making an award, is merely stating that an *ex gratia* award will be made of that amount.

The Authority or the Appeals panel, in making an award under the 1996 Scheme, is doing so under a Scheme which 'is made by the Secretary of State under the Criminal Injuries Compensation Act 1995' (Para 1 of the 1996 Scheme).

Paragraph 50 of the 1996 Scheme ends with the words:

> ... title to an award offered will be vested in the applicant when the Authority has received notification in writing that he accepts the award.

This provision is similar to the final sentence of Para 22 of the 1990 Scheme:

> An applicant will have no title to an award offered until the Board have received notification in writing that he accepts it.

Thus, according to the express terms of both the 1990 and 1996 Schemes, there is no 'title' to an award until the Board or Authority has received the applicant's signed acceptance. In relation to 'title' to an award under the 1996 Scheme reference should also be made to para 53 which provides, under the heading 'Reconsideration of decisions', 'A decision made by a claims officer ... may be reconsidered at any time before actual payment of a final award'. Reconsideration under paras 53, 54 and 55 is considered in Chapter 18.

The 1996 Scheme, like the 1990 Scheme, is silent on the subject of interest being payable on awards. It departs from the common law as the basis for assessment of compensation and defines fully the terms of entitlement within the scheme itself. As there is no provision in the Scheme entitling an applicant to claim interest on the award, then no such right exists. The 1996 Scheme is self-contained; it does not, unlike its predecessors, expressly incorporate by reference any other body of law to flesh out its terms.

Chapter 12

Limitations on assessment of compensation – 1990 Scheme

Like all its predecessors, the 1996 Scheme allows a claim to be made for lost earnings or earning capacity. The abortive 1994 Tariff Scheme would have abolished all heads of claim other than the standard amount of compensation for the injury itself. The changes to the 1994 Tariff Scheme which were accepted by the government and incorporated into the 1996 Scheme substantially reinstated the heads of claim which had been claimable under all earlier Schemes and which, with some important modifications, had simply followed the common law relating to personal injury claims in the courts. In reinstating these heads of claim, however, the 1996 Scheme removed altogether the provision incorporating the common law as the basis for assessment of compensation and instead defined expressly both the heads of claim which were allowed and the detailed rules by which those heads of claim were to be defined and calculated.

Paragraph 22 of the 1996 Scheme states under the heading 'Types and limits of compensation' that the compensation payable under an award will be:

(a) a standard amount of compensation for the injury by reference to the Tariff incorporated in the Scheme (paras 25 to 29);

(b) loss of earnings or earning capacity for longer than 28 weeks (paras 30 to 34);

(c) an additional amount in respect of any special expenses (defined in paras 35 and 36);

and awards in fatal cases (paras 37 to 44).

This chapter deals with the claim for loss of earnings and loss of earning capacity, defined in paras 30 to 34 of the 1996 Scheme, and with similar claims under the 1990 Scheme. As the rules differ between the two current schemes, it is necessary to examine them separately.

The rules of the 1990 and earlier Schemes in relation to a claim for loss of earnings will be looked at first.

1. Lost earnings or earning capacity (para 14)

Paragraph 14 (1990) provides:

Compensation will be limited as follows –

(a) the rate of net loss of earnings or earning capacity to be taken into account shall not exceed one and a half times the gross average industrial earnings at the date of assessment (as published in the Department of Employment Gazette and adjusted as considered appropriate by the Board);
(b) there shall be no element comparable to exemplary or punitive damages.

Where an applicant has lost earnings or earning capacity as a result of the injury, he may be required by the Board to produce evidence thereof in such manner and form as the Board may specify.

Paragraph 14(a) in the 1990 Scheme was not a new provision, in that the Scheme had always placed a maximum limit on the amount of loss of earnings recoverable. However, it contains a variation of the 1979 Scheme which allowed a maximum of twice the gross average industrial earnings. The 1990 Scheme reduced the maximum allowed to one and a half times the gross average industrial earnings. The policy behind this provision is to place a reasonable limit on the recovery of earnings by someone whose earnings are exceptionally high, having regard to the fact that the reimbursement of that loss is being made from public funds.

Paragraph 29 of the 1990 Scheme, which regulates implementation of the provisions of the 1990 Scheme, states in relation to the maximum earnings limit contained in para 14(a) of that Scheme that applications received by the Board before 1 February 1990 will continue to be dealt with in accordance with the terms of the earlier Schemes to which they were previously subject. Reference here to earlier Schemes is plural – in addition to the applications currently with the Board for adjudication under the terms of the 1979 Scheme (which applies to applications lodged before 1 February 1990), there are still some cases in which the provisions of the 1969 Scheme need to be considered, usually where a case has been reopened under para 13 (1990). A reopened case is governed by the maximum earnings rule which applied when the original application was made. The differences between the 1979 and 1969 Schemes with regard to maximum recoverable earnings will be considered in more detail below.

With a limit of twice the gross average industrial wage the very high earner found his or her claim to be limited by this provision. The reduction of this maximum limit to one and a half times catches a larger number of applications than was the case under the 1979 or earlier Schemes. The relevant average earnings by which the maximum claim is defined are not the average national wage in all occupations, but the average of industrial earnings. The limit of one and a half times the national average wage still affects only a minority of cases, however.

It is the applicant's *net* loss of earnings which may not exceed one and a half times the *gross* average industrial earnings. An applicant's gross income but for the injury may well be shown to be at a level well above one and a half times the gross average industrial earnings, but his recoverable loss may still not be limited by para 14(a) (1990) if his net loss is below that level and is therefore recoverable in full.

This is best explained by an example. Suppose the applicant is injured on 1 March 1990. He puts in an application to the Board. He is eligible for an award and his loss of earnings is being assessed by the Board on 30 November 1990. His application is 'received by the Board ... after 1st February 1990' and in accordance with para 28 (implementation) it is dealt with under the terms of the 1990 Scheme. The 'one and a half times' rule therefore applies to limit his recoverable loss of earnings. His earnings before the incident were approximately £30,000 gross per annum or £575 gross per week. After the incident he received half pay for three months and then no pay. He is, at the time of the assessment of his claim by the Board, still unable to work.

Paragraph 14(a) (1990) provides for a maximum 'rate of net loss of earnings'. Having received half pay from 1 March to 31 May 1990 his 'rate of net loss of earnings' during that three-month period may look like this:

(A)	Pre-injury weekly salary (gross)	£575.00	(£30,000 per annum)
	less tax and national insurance, say	£185.00	
	Net weekly salary	£390.00	
(B)	Weekly salary received from 1.3.90 to 31.5.90 (gross)	£290.00	
	less tax and national insurance, say	£ 80.00	
	Weekly net salary received during this period	£210.00	

(C) 'Rate of net loss of earnings' (£390 less £210) = £180 per week

(D) Assuming 'gross average industrial earnings at the date of assessment' (30.11.90) to be £250 per week, 'one and a half times the gross average industrial earnings' at that date will be £375 per week.

The applicant's 'rate of net loss of earnings' during this period is £180 per week – as this is less than the maximum at (D) above, his loss of earnings during this period is recoverable in full.

It should be noted in particular that the 'gross average industrial earnings' is a fixed ascertainable sum. It is not reduced to a net figure for the purpose of this calculation. The applicant's rate of loss, however, is his loss of net earnings. For the period 1.3.90 to 31.5.90 the applicant has lost £180 per week for 13 weeks, a total of £2,340 which is not subject to any reduction under para 14(a) (1990).

We must now examine the applicant's 'rate of net loss of earnings' for the period 1.6.90 to 30.11.90, the latter being the date on which the Board is making its assessment of the applicant's recoverable loss. It must be remembered that under the 1990 Scheme and also the 1979 Scheme the date on which the Board makes its assessment (in this example 30.11.90) is the date on which the 'gross average industrial wage' is taken. For practical purposes the most recent figure published by the Department of Employment Gazette before the date of assessment is used by the Board as the appropriate figure when making this calculation.

The applicant has received no salary during this period. His 'net rate of loss' is therefore calculated as follows:

Pre-injury weekly salary (gross)	£575.00
less tax and national insurance, say	£185.00
Net weekly salary	£390.00

As the applicant receives no salary from 1.6.90, the 'rate of net loss of earnings' from 1.6.90 to the date of assessment, 30.11.90, is £390 per week. This is therefore subject to the 'cut off' at £375, and the latter is substituted as the rate of loss during this period.

This rate would also be the rate of his continuing loss for the purpose of calculating any claim for future loss of earnings.

If in the example the applicant had been earning £50,000 per annum gross, about £35,000 net, and had found alternative part-time employment at £10,000 per annum gross, about £8,000 per annum net, the net salary before the injury would likewise be reduced by the amount of the net salary received from the new job, in order to arrive at the 'rate of net loss'. The calculation for the purpose of para 14(a) (1990) would be as follows:

Pre-injury gross salary (weekly)	£960.00	(£50,000 p.a.)
less tax and national insurance, say	£360.00	
Net weekly salary (loss)	£600.00	
Gross salary from part-time employment (weekly)	£192.00	(£10,000 p.a.)
less tax and national insurance, say	£ 38.00	
Net weekly salary (received)	£154.00	
Pre-injury net weekly salary	£600.00	
deduct net weekly salary now received	£154.00	
Thus 'rate of net loss of earnings' for purpose of para 14(a) is	£446.00	per week.

As £446 per week as a 'rate of net loss of earnings' exceeds the illustrative maximum of £375 per week, the 'maximum' figure of £375 would be substituted for the actual rate of loss as the basis for calculating the applicant's loss of earnings.

We have referred above to the maximum loss of earnings recoverable under earlier Schemes. The 1979 and 1990 Schemes have similar rules except that 'twice' under the 1979 Scheme was reduced to 'one and a half times' by the 1990 Scheme. The 1969 provision had a fundamental difference, however, in that the figure for the average industrial earnings was taken on the date on which the injury was sustained, instead of the date on which the Board made its assessment of the loss. In times of rapid inflation, and wage inflation in particular, this provision was found to operate unfairly, as the 'cut off' figure for maximum recoverable earnings was fixed to a date in the past, in many cases years past, when wages were much lower. This unfairness in the application of the rule limiting recovery of loss of earnings prompted the amendment in the 1979 Scheme to take the current industrial earnings rate as the basis for fixing the ceiling figure for the recoverable loss.

1969 Scheme calculations need only occasionally to be made, but are necessary with regard to reopened cases where the incident preceded the commencement of the 1979 Scheme.

In 1973 the Divisional Court had cause to consider the method of this calculation in *R v Criminal Injuries Compensation Board ex parte Richardson* – see Appendix 1 page 271.

Although differences between the calculation under the 1969 Scheme and the later Schemes are not confined to the different dates on which the average of industrial earnings is fixed, this is the most significant difference because of the impact of inflation.

Paragraph 11(a) of the 1969 Scheme provided:

> The rate of loss of earnings (and, where appropriate, of earning capacity) to be taken into account will not exceed twice the average of industrial earnings at the time that the injury was sustained.

A footnote to the Scheme explained that 'average industrial earnings' means 'average weekly earnings for men (21 years and over) as published in the Department of Education and Employment Gazette'.

Two further differences in wording, small but important, are that the 1969 Scheme referred to 'rate of loss of earnings', not 'rate of *net* loss of earnings' as do the later Schemes, and 'average of industrial earnings', not 'the *gross* average industrial earnings' as in the later Schemes.

The case of *Richardson* involved a fatal claim under para 12 of the 1969 Scheme, but the maximum earnings rule applied and in calculating the award the court sanctioned the method of calculation to be applied in cases caught by para 11(a) of that Scheme. Put briefly, the method applied in *Richardson* was to compare the applicant's gross income with twice the gross average industrial earnings figure at the date of the incident. The lower of those two gross figures was thus the maximum loss of earnings rate recoverable and, in accordance with *British Transport Commission v Gourley* (1956) that gross figure was then reduced to a net figure by deducting income tax and national insurance. This net figure would be the measure of loss recoverable. The need to apply the 1969 Scheme method of calculation arises less frequently as the number of cases to which it applies diminishes with the passage of time.

Before leaving the subject of the 1969 Scheme, it is convenient to mention at this point that the applicant whose maximum rate of loss of earnings is fixed at the date of the incident by para 11(a) of that Scheme is compensated to some extent by the more advantageous provisions in the 1969 Scheme, compared with the 1979 and 1990 Schemes, in relation to the deduction of pensions from the assessment of compensation. The rules relating to deduction of pension payments from compensation under para 20 of the 1990 Scheme are discussed below.

Paragraph 16 of the 1969 Scheme provided:

> Where the victim is alive the Board will determine on the basis of the common law whether, and to what extent, compensation should be reduced by any pension accruing as a result of the injury.

The common law in this context is in substance the rule established by the House of Lords in *Parry v Cleaver* (1969) which reviewed the authorities on the question of whether an occupational pension accruing to the plaintiff as a result of the accident mitigated the loss and therefore the measure of damages recoverable from the defendant. Their lordships decided that in the computation of damages for loss of earning capacity, the ill-health pension to which the injured party became entitled as a consequence of the accident was not deductible in assessing damages for his loss of earnings, although it would have to be brought into account in respect of his loss of retirement pension.

The effect of this in terms of a 1969 Scheme calculation is that the occupational pension is effectively ignored and not deducted from the loss of earnings or loss of earning capacity calculation until the applicant reaches normal retirement age, when it becomes deductible. As the 1979 and 1990 versions of the Scheme, unlike the common law, require the deduction of pension in full, those applicants whose calculations have to be made under the rules of the 1969 Scheme with the disadvantage of a low maximum earnings figure have the benefit of the non-deduction of pension to offset this to some extent.

Requirement that the applicant provide evidence of loss of earnings

The last sentence of para 14 of the 1990 Scheme was a new provision which, by virtue of the implementation provisions of para 29, took immediate effect. It reads:

> Where the applicant has lost earnings or earning capacity as a result of the injury, he may be required by the Board to produce evidence thereof in such manner and form as the Board may specify.

Although this was a new provision, in practice it had always been a requirement that the applicant, in making out his case, should provide sufficient evidence of loss in respect of lost earnings to enable the Board to be satisfied that the loss has been suffered and that it has been properly calculated. It is just one aspect of the overall requirement contained in the first sentence of para 25 of the 1990 Scheme which states: 'It will be for the applicant to make out his case at the hearing ... '

The Board also requires in relation to hearings that a schedule of net loss of earnings, showing in full the calculation of the claimed loss from the date of the injury to the date of the hearing, must be lodged by the applicant or by his advisers well before the hearing. This requirement is purely practical. It should be remembered that the Board members and Board's hearings staff sit throughout a 'hearings week'. Each hearings week has a preparation cycle, usually commencing eight weeks before it is due to take place. All documentary evidence, including schedules of special damage, must be with the Board at or near the beginning of that eight-week period if the case is to be effective on the day.

The Board's or Appeals Panel's staff must have the opportunity to check and, if possible, agree the calculation arithmetically as this cannot be done at the hearing. The Board will not make calculations on the day of the hearing – nor is there any opportunity for hasty calculations in the corridor before the hearing.

This requirement is basically similar to the Practice Direction in the High Court ([1984] 3 All ER 165) which requires that schedules of special damages be prepared in proper form and agreed if possible before a High Court action is heard, so that argument on the details of special damages can be avoided if possible in the court. As the Board is required to assess compensation in much the same way as the High Court, this requirement for the early preparation of special damages calculations and prior submission to the Board for possible agreement is entirely appropriate.

Where it is expected that the special damages calculation is likely to be lengthy and complicated, for example in a case where the applicant has been prevented from following his career as a consequence of the injury, the practice is not to list the case for hearing until that schedule and calculation have been lodged and, so far as possible, agreed with the Board's legal staff.

'Exemplary damages' not payable

Paragraph 14(b) of the 1990 Scheme states:

> There shall be no element comparable to exemplary or punitive damages.

The principle of exemplary or punitive damages presupposes first a defendant whose conduct has not merely breached but outraged the principles of the relationship from which the action arises, and secondly that the defendant thus 'punished' will be required to pay those damages personally to the injured party. Such damages would therefore be wholly inappropriate in a Scheme whereby compensation is payable from public funds.

2. Duplication of payment from public funds (para 19, 1990 Scheme)

The provisions contained in para 19 of the 1990 Scheme are of major importance as they affect a large number of claims. Unlike the provisions of para 14, limiting recovery of loss of earnings to a fixed maximum, which affect only the high earners, para 19 can limit the most modest claims by requiring deductions to be made from compensation.

Paragraph 19 (1990) states:

> Compensation will be reduced by the full value of any present or future entitlement to –

(*a*) United Kingdom social security benefits . . .

Such benefits are numerous and wide ranging, and 19(a) includes all of them. The inclusion of the words 'present or future' means that in calculating compensation the Board must take into account any continuing entitlement to social security benefit. Thus in a case in which the applicant has been awarded by the Department of Social Security ('DSS') a benefit which is expressed to be 'for life', the Board must apply an appropriate multiplier (number of years) to the continuing benefit to arrive at a capital sum representing the 'full value' of that benefit, and deduct that sum from any award of compensation.

The principle behind para 19 is that there should be no duplication of payments from public funds. If, therefore, an applicant is already receiving benefits from the state which relate to and are in respect of the injury which is the subject of the claim for compensation from the Board, the assessment of compensation is reduced by the value of those benefits.

In an application which came before the Board at a hearing in 1990 the applicant, in her twenties, had suffered a savage attack at her place of work and sustained a number of stab wounds resulting in permanent scarring. She had previously received an interim award from the Board of £5,000. In respect of those injuries she had been awarded benefit by the Department of Social Security in the form of a pension amounting to about £20 per week for life. The applicant had not suffered any significant loss of earnings. In considering the case the Board concluded that the appropriate 'general damages' for the injuries, for 'pain, suffering and loss of amenity', including the scarring, was £17,500. It also concluded that taking the most favourable view it could for the applicant in evaluating the social security pension for life, its 'value' was placed at £14,000, using a multiplier of about 14 years which was close to the minimum having regard to the young age of the applicant. After deducting the value of social security benefits at £14,000 from the assessment of compensation, £17,500, this left only £3,500. The applicant had already received from the Board an interim award of £5,000 and accordingly the Board could make no further award.

There is in such a case no question of the applicant being required to repay any interim payment should the final assessment of the case by the Board come to the conclusion that the interim award contained an element of overpayment.

The above case is somewhat unusual in that only occasionally does an applicant before the Board have a DSS benefit in the form of a pension 'for life', where the applicant has also continued in employment and has every prospect of continuing to do so in the future, and has thus incurred no significant loss of earnings which might partly or even fully 'absorb' the value of the DSS benefit which must be deducted.

The case nevertheless illustrates how the principle of deduction under para 19(a) works in practice. The Board has no discretion under this provision. The paragraph states that compensation 'will be reduced by the full value...' and the deduction must therefore be made in all cases to which it applies.

In cases where the applicant has lost earnings but has received sickness benefit from the DSS, the Board's staff obtain a statement of benefits from the DSS so that the value of these can be deducted from the compensation.

A point sometimes misunderstood in relation to such deduction is the requirement that compensation, and not merely the 'special damages', is reduced by the value of such benefits; thus where the benefits exceed the loss of earnings the amount of such excess is deducted from what would be the 'general damages' part of the compensation for the injury itself. As has been illustrated by the above example the excess may diminish the general damages or even extinguish the compensation altogether. Nor can the effect of this provision be avoided by an applicant making no claim for loss of earnings and asking for compensation in respect of the injury only. Applicants and their advisers sometimes inform the Board that no claim for loss of earnings is made as the benefits exceed the loss. In such cases the necessity to disclose the benefits is explained so that the requirement of para 19(a) can be met.

The benefits most commonly deductible were sickness benefit, where the applicant is incapable of work because of the injury, invalidity benefit where the incapacity to work continues for more than 28 weeks, and industrial injuries disablement benefit where the injury was sustained as a result of an incident at work. The latter arises frequently in the cases of police officers injured in the course of their work although the principle is of course of general application. From 13 April 1995, 'incapacity benefit' replaced invalidity benefit and sickness benefit, and from that date new procedures apply for assessing incapacity for work.

The Board in practice makes a common-sense interpretation in cases where the applicant was receiving the DSS benefit before the injury which is the subject of the application was sustained, and the receipt of that benefit is not attributable to that injury. An applicant may, for example, have been receiving unemployment benefit (now jobseeker's allowance), having been unemployed and in receipt of such benefit from a date preceding the injury. He continues thereafter to receive unemployment benefit. If the latter has no relationship to the injury before the Board, it will be ignored. The provisions of the Jobseekers Act 1995 took effect on 7 October 1996, replacing unemployment benefit with jobseeker's allowance and altering certain rules relating to income support.

Benefits paid by the DSS to the dependants of a victim who has died as a consequence of a crime of violence are similarly deductible. These benefits and their treatment by the Board under the Scheme are considered in Chapter 14.

Paragraph 19(b) (1990) requires the reduction of compensation by the full value of any award made under the separate arrangements for criminal injury compensation applying in Northern Ireland.

Paragraph 19(c) requires a reduction of compensation in respect of social security benefits or compensation awards from the funds of other countries.

Paragraph 19(d) similarly requires reduction of compensation in respect of:

> payments under insurance arrangements except as excluded below which may accrue, as a result of the injury or death, to the benefit of the person to whom the award is made.

The exclusion from this catch-all provision regarding the deduction of all 'payments under insurance arrangements' is stated as follows:

> ... the Board will disregard monies paid or payable to the victim or his dependants as a result of or in consequence of insurance personally effected, paid for and maintained by the personal income of the victim or, in the case of a person under the age of 18, by his parent.

This exclusion is preceded by the words 'Subject to paragraph 18 above ...' which deals separately with the cost of private medical treatment.

The effect of 19(d) (1990) is to reduce compensation by the amount received under any insurance arrangement, save only where the arrangement is funded wholly by the applicant or, in the case of a minor, by his parent. If the arrangement is funded or partly funded by anyone other than the applicant, or his parent if the applicant is a minor, the proceeds received under that arrangement are deducted from the compensation payable by the Board.

It will be noted that para 19 requires reduction in respect of *entitlement* to any of the items covered by subparagraphs (a), (b), (c) or (d). It is not a requirement that the applicant has received those benefits – if he is entitled to them, their full value is deductible from compensation. The 1990 Scheme also provides in para 19 that the Board may refuse to make an award to someone who is eligible for such benefits until the applicant has taken reasonable steps to claim them. This is a safeguard against any person attempting to obtain duplication of payment from public funds for the same injury. It is also not practicable for the Board to assess compensation finally until the precise amount of these benefits is known. Occasionally the adjudication of an application by the Board at a hearing has to be postponed where the applicant's DSS assessment is provisional only; it can only be listed for hearing for final assessment by the Board after the final assessment by the DSS has been made and the Board informed of the outcome.

In the majority of cases where the Board has to deduct DSS benefits, such as incapacity benefit received by an applicant who is off work because of the injury, the income of the applicant is not such that income tax is payable in relation to those benefits. Where liability to income tax will reduce the value of those benefits, however, the Board takes account of that liability and only the value of those benefits thus reduced is deducted from the compensation.

3. Pension payments (para 20, 1990 Scheme)

Paragraph 20 of the 1990 Scheme is also concerned with reductions in the amount of compensation payable under the Scheme. It states:

> Where the victim is alive compensation will be reduced to take account of any pension accruing as a result of the injury. Where the victim has died in consequence of the injury, and any pension is payable for the benefit of the person to whom the award is made as a result of the death of the victim, the compensation will similarly be reduced to take account of the value of that pension. Where such pensions are taxable, one-half of their value will be deducted; where they are not taxable, eg where a lump sum payment not subject to income tax is made, they will be deducted in full. For the purposes of this paragraph, 'pension' means any payment payable as a result of the injury or death, in pursuance of pension or other rights whatsoever connected with the victim's employment, and includes any gratuity of that kind and similar benefits payable under insurance policies paid for by employers. Pension rights accruing solely as a result of payments by the victim or a dependant will be disregarded.

Some background to this paragraph in the 1990 Scheme may make its purpose clearer. Under the 1969 Scheme, as has already been mentioned, pension payments to which the applicant became entitled as a consequence of the injury were for the most part not deductible, as the Scheme then followed the common law, and the House of Lords had decided in *Parry v Cleaver* (1969) that it was inappropriate, as between an injured plaintiff and a defendant whose negligence had caused the injury, that the benefit of the plaintiff's prudence or contractual arrangements in providing an occupational pension should accrue to the defendant and reduce his liability. It was thus quite possible at common law for the applicant to be financially better off after the injury than before if his loss of earnings was recoverable in full from the defendant in addition to his receiving pension or insurance payments accruing as a result. It was felt that the Scheme should be amended in this regard, as the basis of the Scheme was the restoring of the applicant's financial loss, and compensation was payable from public funds. A fundamental departure was therefore made from the common law principle and para 20 of the 1990 Scheme was the result.

It is sometimes argued that the deduction of pension entitlement is unfair, and even that it is not caught by the wording of para 20 as the applicant was entitled to the benefit of his pension in any event, and that the injury had merely accelerated receipt of that benefit. The background to the current Scheme and the practical operation of this provision by the Board, however, make clear that, subject only to the qualifications upon its comprehensive effect contained within its terms, para 20 requires the deduction of 'any pension accruing as a result of the injury'. A lump sum gratuity paid by the employer, for example, is caught by para 20 and is deductible. This may seem inappropriate and unfair, especially when the injury arises only a few years before normal retirement age, and the applicant would have received a lump sum gratuity of a slightly greater amount had he been able to work until his expected retirement age. It might be argued that the applicant's true loss is being reduced by benefits not 'accruing as a result of the injury', as the payment by his employer was something which he would have received regardless of the injury, the latter having merely triggered or accelerated its receipt by the applicant. The perceived purpose and effect of the provision, however, and its application by the Board in practice, run contrary to such an argument, and the deduction is made. The effect is not however unfair as the greater lump sum which he has lost has been lost as a result of the injury and an award for that loss (discounted for accelerated receipt) often restores the deduction.

The distinction is made between pensions which are taxable, of which half the value is deducted, and pensions - including any lump sums - which are not taxable, the value of which is deducted in full.

The background to this distinction is once more to be found in the deliberations of the interdepartmental working party which reported in 1978. As the working party's recommendations proposed that pensions should be deducted from compensation, it was felt necessary to make some allowance in the applicant's favour for the liability to tax on the pension in his hands and also for the extent to which he had contributed to the pension before his injury. To avoid extremely complex calculations having to be made on the precise impact of tax and contributions respectively on the net pension in the applicant's hands, it was considered that to deduct only half of the value of the pension would be broadly fair to the applicant. The 1979 Scheme (and thereafter the 1990 Scheme) provided accordingly:

> For the purpose of this paragraph, 'pension' means any payment payable as a result of the injury or death, in pursuance of pension or other rights whatsoever connected with the victim's employment, and includes any gratuity of that kind and similar benefits payable under insurance policies paid for by employers.

These words cast the net very widely, and have the effect in practice of being a catch-all provision. However, the principle that benefits which are provided solely by the applicant for his own benefit should not be deducted is fully preserved by the words 'paid for by employers'. It is also underlined by the last sentence of para 20 which reads:

> Pension rights accruing solely as a result of payments by the victim or a dependant will be disregarded.

These words preserve the benefit of pensions provided entirely by the applicant from his own resources, which are not deducted; they apply usually to a self-employed applicant and to any pension or insurance provision paid for entirely by the applicant to supplement any occupational pension provided by his employer.

Paragraph 12 of the 1990 Scheme requires the Board to assess compensation on the basis of common law damages, subject to those provisions in the Scheme which specify a different principle of assessment, such as maximum recoverable earnings under para 14(a) and the provision for deducting pension entitlement under para 20. In relation to pension deductions there is accordingly little authority by way of decision in the High Court as to the method by which the computation of the required deduction should be made.

Until about two years before the 1990 Scheme came into effect the Board had adopted a literal interpretation of para 20 so that when calculating the total deductions to be made from the assessment of compensation, including the loss of earnings or loss of future earnings calculation, the Board deducted in full any lump sum which the applicant had received upon commutation of part of his pension entitlement. This was legally correct as it was in accordance with the wording of the Scheme requiring such deduction to be made, including deduction of a 'lump sum payment' in respect of pension entitlement.

The Board was aware that one of the practical effects of such a method of calculating the total deductions was to achieve a different impact upon two categories of applicants who were in receipt of a pension, those who had chosen to commute part of their pension, and thus receive that part in the form of a lump sum immediately upon retirement and a reduced pension thereafter, and others who had decided against commutation of part and accordingly received the full annual pension.

Two pensioners who might retire at the same time and with identical pension entitlements, one commuting part and the other not, would thus incur different deductions from compensation under the Scheme in respect of that pension entitlement.

The Board considered that this was not equitable as between one applicant and another. It concluded that as the purpose of the provision in the Scheme was to deduct the value of the pension entitlement, and that it was reasonable to assume that the trustees of a particular pension fund would intend to treat pensioners with similar entitlement equally whether they commuted part of it or not, the value of the total pension entitlement on retirement would be the same in both cases. The Board decided that it should adopt a method of calculating the deduction which treated the value of the pension in both forms in the same way.

The Board will take account of the circumstances of each case. It is important to make a clear distinction, however, between the lump sum representing commutation of pension, and any other lump sum such as terminal gratuity, the latter will always be deducted.

Having ignored the commuted lump sum, the Board then treats the applicant who has commuted part of his pension as if he had not done so and as if he is in receipt of the full amount of his pension. The calculation proceeds on exactly the same basis as the calculation of the uncommuted pension and the deduction is therefore the same in both cases.

In practical terms this means that in cases where the applicant has commuted part of his pension, he or his advisers must provide the Board with a calculation based upon the full pension; to provide only the figures relating to the commuted lump sum and the reduced pension will not enable the Board's staff to check and agree the calculation submitted on the applicant's behalf.

4. Damages and other court orders (para 21, 1990 Scheme)

When the Board makes an award, the applicant is required to sign a form of receipt and acceptance that the payment is in full and final settlement of his claim for compensation under the Scheme. The document which the applicant signs also contains an undertaking by the applicant to repay the Board in the event of his receiving any payment of damages or compensation in respect of the same injury from any other source.

Paragraph 21 (1990) provides that compensation by the Board will be reduced by the amount of any such payment.

The penultimate sentence of para 21 reads:

> ... a person who is compensated by the Board will be required to undertake to repay them from any damages, settlement or compensation he may subsequently obtain in respect of his injuries.

This sentence is the most important part of para 21 in the working of the Scheme, as it is incorporated into every form of acceptance which the Board requires to be signed by all applicants receiving awards.

The other provision contained in this paragraph of the 1990 Scheme which is most often of direct relevance to applications is that part which provides:

> ... when payment of compensation has been ordered by a criminal court, in respect of personal injuries, compensation by the Board in respect of the same injuries will be reduced by the amount of any payment received under such an order ...

This clear and simple principle applies to many cases before the Board. The key word is 'received'. The Board will not reduce an award by the amount 'ordered' by the court, but by the amount actually received by the applicant. The Board's staff check with the clerk of the court how much of the sum ordered to be paid by the assailant has actually been paid at the date on which the Board is considering the application, and this sum is actually deducted from the Board's assessment. Any sums received thereafter by the clerk of the court from the assailant are payable to the Board.

The Board will not deduct from its award compensation ordered by the criminal court in respect of items for which the Board will not pay compensation. The compensation order in the criminal court may include damage to property, where for example the assailant is convicted of criminal damage as well as assault. Further enquiry has to be made of the clerk of the court to ensure that the two aspects are distinguished in order to avoid an over-deduction or under-deduction from the Board's award.

Compensation awards in magistrates' courts are usually in the lower hundreds of pounds and are subject to a maximum of £5,000. In the Crown Court, however, there is no limit. In an application involving very serious injuries the Board had notice of a Crown Court compensation order which amounted to a substantial five-figure sum and which had been paid in full, and was therefore deductible in full from the award by the Board.

The Criminal Justice Act 1988 contains provisions to encourage magistrates' courts, which readily make compensation orders in cases of damage to property, to make compensation orders in cases of personal injury. Section 104 requires the magistrates' court to give its reasons for not making a compensation order in a case where it is empowered to do so but makes no award. It is entirely appropriate that the assailant rather than the tax payer should pay for the damage.

The compensatory function of the criminal court is of greatest importance in cases where the injury is not sufficiently serious to enable the victim to claim compensation from the Board as it would not justify an award of at least the minimum award which the Board may make, which is currently £1,000 (this minimum award figure applies to applications made before and after 1 April 1996, as the 1996 Scheme – which came into force on that date – adopted the same figure as the 1990 Scheme figure). Awards for all injuries other than the more serious cases are thus entirely in the hands of the criminal courts, which are the victim's only hope of receiving compensation. Few injured parties embark on civil litigation; most victims not unreasonably dismiss it as an impractical alternative. The powers of magistrates to award compensation should make such duplication of process unnecessary.

The first part of para 21 of the 1990 Scheme has been left till last for consideration because it has relevance to fewer cases than the other parts. It provides that compensation by the Board will be reduced by the amount received by the applicant in respect of the same personal injury under the terms of a judgment for damages in the civil court, or where a claim in the civil court has been settled on terms providing for payment of money.

The Board was unable to make any award to an applicant whose injury was assessed by the Board at £25,000, as the applicant had accepted a sum paid into court by the assailant which was in excess of that sum; this was still the position even though the payment in was fully absorbed in meeting the applicant's legal costs.

It is also specified that where a civil court (not a magistrates' court or a Crown Court exercising criminal jurisdiction) has actually assessed damages for the relevant injuries, as opposed to giving judgment for damages agreed by the parties (where the figure would be the sum agreed by the parties and not a figure which results from the court making the assessment), 'but the person entitled to such damages has not yet received the full sum awarded, he will not be precluded from applying to the Board, but the Board's assessment of compensation will not exceed the sum assessed by the court'.

The applicant's obligation to hand over to the Board any payment by way of damages received by him after compensation has been paid by the Board has already been discussed.

Chapter 13

Assessment of compensation – 1996 Scheme

1. Types and limits of compensation

Paragraphs 22 to 24 define the scope of, as the Scheme puts it, the 'types and limits of compensation'. Paragraph 22 of the 1996 Scheme defines the heads of compensation payable under the Scheme. The abortive 1994 Tariff Scheme had fixed one set figure for each injury and no additions were to be made to that fixed award.

The 1996 Scheme, on the other hand, has brought back much of the substance of 'common law damages' which form the basis of claims under the 1990 and earlier Schemes. In so doing, however, the 1996 Scheme defines and limits the heads of claim, so that although they have a familiar identity to advisers and practitioners acquainted with the law of common law damages, the basis of assessment is no longer to be found in principles of common law. Instead, the terms of the Scheme itself, much more detailed than before, regulate the process of assessment more or less entirely. In assessing compensation, therefore, one looks not at the law of damages but at the Scheme itself.

Paragraph 22 begins this defining process by briefly setting out the five possible heads of claim for compensation. The first, in para 22(a), is 'a standard amount of compensation determined by reference to the nature of the injury in accordance with paras 25 to 29'. Paragraphs 25 to 29 in turn define the amount of compensation by reference to the 'Tariff of Injuries' which is printed at the end of the Scheme itself. The Tariff has three headings: 'Description of Injury', 'Levels' and 'Standard Amount'. Each injury has a level and a standard amount set against it and, so far as compensation for the injury goes, that is that. There are 25 levels and therefore 25 standard amounts. The abortive 1994 Scheme would have ended assessment of compensation at that point. However, para 22 continues its definition of how an overall award may be made up. Paragraph 22(b) provides that an applicant may claim, in addition to the standard amount for the injury under para 22(a), an additional amount if he or she has 'lost earnings or earning capacity for longer than 28 weeks'. It is estimated that less than one quarter of all applicants come within this category of lost earnings – it will clearly only be claimable by more seriously injured claimants whose injury prevents them working for more than six and a half months. This provision should therefore cut the cost both in terms of administration – under the previous Schemes much staff time was spent in calculating all periods of lost earnings, however short – and the total cost of awards, which will exclude all loss of earnings claims for periods of 28 weeks or less. The rules of calculating loss of earnings which do qualify under para 22(b) are set out in paras 30 to 34 of the 1996 Scheme. These are examined in detail later in this chapter.

Paragraph 22 continues its definition of heads of claim by providing in para 22(c) that an applicant who qualifies for an award under para 22(b) for loss of earnings or earning capacity for longer than 28 weeks will be entitled to 'an additional amount in respect of any special expenses, calculated in accordance with paragraphs 35 to 36'. These are looked at in detail later in this chapter and consist of such items as physical aids, medical expenses, special equipment and so on, and also costs of care in cases of severe injury. Paragraphs 35 and 36 contain the rules and limits for such claims.

In defining heads of claim for the purposes of the 1996 Scheme, para 22(d) allows a claim for compensation in certain circumstances 'where the victim has died in consequence of the injury (to be calculated in accordance with paras 37 to 43), and para 22(e) allows 'a supplementary amount' in certain cases 'where the victim has died otherwise than in consequence of the injury', such compensation being calculated in accordance with para 44.

Paragraph 23 states that 'the total maximum amount payable in respect of the same injury will not exceed £500,000'. Thus the top limit is fixed. Therefore the total claims of the victim in his lifetime and by any qualifying claimants on his death under para 22(d) may not exceed this ceiling figure.

Paragraph 24 defines the minimum award which can be made under the Scheme which, like its predecessors, is not intended to compensate for minor injury. The minimum award payable under the Scheme is 'Level 1' which is currently £1,000. Any injury not qualifying for at least this Level 1 figure is therefore not entitled to an award at all.

Having discussed the 'types and limits of compensation', we need now to examine in more detail how the Scheme provides the rules for calculating these heads of claim or 'types of compensation'.

2. Compensation for loss of earnings

Paragraph 30 states: 'The period of loss for which compensation may be payable will begin 28 weeks after the date of commencement of the applicant's incapacity for work and continue for such period as a claims officer may determine'. It also states expressly that: 'no compensation in respect of loss of earnings or earning capacity will be payable for the first 28 weeks of loss'.

Paragraph 31 states the method by which the loss of earnings to the date of assessment by the claims officer is calculated.

Paragraph 32 does the same in respect of any continuing or future loss which the claims officer considers the applicant will continue to incur after the date of the assessment; such loss is based upon the calculation of 'an annual rate of net loss' multiplied by the appropriate number of years. Note 3 to the 1996 Scheme gives the claims officer a table of illustrative 'multipliers', or number of years, by which the annual rate of net loss should be multiplied to arrive at the appropriate lump sum by which that future loss is compensated.

Paragraph 33 authorises the claims officer to award 'such other lump sum as he may determine' as compensation for future loss of earnings where he 'considers that the approach in the preceding paragraph [para 32] is impracticable'.

Paragraph 34 repeats from the 1990 Scheme the maximum compensatable rate of net loss as being 'one and a half times the gross average industrial earnings at the time of assessment according to the latest figures published by the Department of Education and Employment'.

The above paragraphs state only the basic provisions for calculating compensation for loss of earnings under the 1996 Scheme. An examination of these rules of calculation of loss, and the more detailed provisions of paras 31 (loss of earnings to date of assessment) and 32 (future or continuing loss) which regulate the method of calculation, will lead one to the conclusion that in this respect, comparing the 1990 and 1996 Schemes, the similarities are more marked than the changes.

In these paragraphs, what is new in particular is the setting out in detailed terms of rules which are based upon the common law rules by which loss of earnings, past and future, are calculated by the courts, and by the Board under the 1990 Scheme. The 1990 Scheme incorporated the detailed rules of common law which regulate the calculation of recoverable losses by simply stating in para 12 of that scheme:

> Subject to the other provisions of this Scheme, compensation will be assessed on the basis of common law damages...

This simple incorporation by reference rendered unnecessary the inclusion of those rules in the Scheme itself. Indeed, the textbooks and law reports which contain the detailed common law principles are volumes of considerable length and substance.

The 1996 Scheme breaks away from the common law for the first time and in doing so attempts a succinct distillation of the main principles of the common law, as amended by the express terms of the Scheme. These are based essentially on the practical rules applied by the Board under the 1990 and earlier Schemes to arrive at the fair and proper figure for loss of earnings, past and future.

Having arrived at the appropriate figure for loss of earnings under the terms of paras 30 to 34, the claims officer must make the deductions which are set out in paras 45 to 48, all of which are very familiar in principle to those who have a working knowledge of the 1990 Scheme. There is, however, one very important change in the rules relating to deductions from awards and this appears in the first sentence of para 45:

> All awards payable under this Scheme, except those payable under paragraphs 25, 27, 39 and 42(a) (Tariff-based amounts of compensation) will be subject to a reduction to take account of social security benefits or insurance payments made by way of compensation for the same contingency.

This 'protection' of the award for the injury, the Tariff award, from such deductions is totally new. It is looked at in detail later in this chapter.

Paragraph 45 goes on to say that the amount of the reduction will be the full value of any relevant payment which the applicant has received.

Paragraph 46 enables the claims officer (the Board having similar power under the 1990 Scheme) to withhold an award where he considers that the applicant 'may be eligible' for any of the benefits and payments referred to in para 45, 'until the applicant has taken such steps as the claims officer considers reasonable to claim them'.

Paragraph 47 directs reduction of a loss of earnings award (payable under paras 30 to 34) 'to take account of any pension accruing as a result of the injury', and likewise, where the victim has died in consequence of the injury, a reduction of an award for dependency payable under paras 40 to 41 to take account of any 'pension payable, as a result of the victim's death, for the benefit of the applicant'. The definition of pension and the treatment of income tax are essentially similar to the parallel provisions in the 1990 Scheme (see page 148 above).

Paragraph 48, in requiring that awards 'payable under this Scheme will be reduced by the full value of any payment which the applicant has received by way of an award under the Northern Ireland Compensation Scheme or 'from the funds of other countries' or as a result of an order of a civil court 'for the payment of damages', or 'compensation ... ordered by a criminal court', is also essentially similar to equivalent provision (para 19) in the 1990 Scheme (see page 144 above).

An applicant who receives any 'para 48' payments in respect of the same injury, after receiving an award from the Authority or Panel under the 1996 Scheme, 'will be required to repay the Authority in full up to the amount of the other payment' (para 49).

Paragraphs 45 to 49 of the 1996 Scheme provide as follows:

> **Effect on awards of other payments**
>
> 45. All awards payable under this Scheme, except those payable under paragraphs 25, 27, 39 and 42(a) (Tariff-based amounts of compensation), will be subject to a reduction to take account of social security benefits or insurance payments made by way of compensation for the same contingency. The reduction will be applied to those categories or periods of loss or need for which additional or supplementary compensation is payable, including compensation calculated on the basis of a multiplicand or annual cost. The amount of the reduction will be the full value of any relevant payment which the applicant has received, or to which he has any present or future entitlement, by way of:

(a) United Kingdom social security benefits;

(b) social security benefits or similar payments from the funds of other countries;

(c) payments under insurance arrangements, including, where a claim is made under paragraphs 35(c) and (d) and 36 (special expenses), insurance personally effected, paid for and maintained by the personal income of the victim or, in the case of a person under 18 years of age, by his parent. Insurance so personally effected will otherwise be disregarded.

In assessing the value of any such benefits and payments, account may be taken of any income tax liability likely to reduce their value.

46. Where, in the opinion of a claims officer, an applicant may be eligible for any of the benefits and payments mentioned in the preceding paragraph, an award may be withheld until the applicant has taken such steps as the claims officer considers reasonable to claim them.

47. Where the victim is alive, any compensation payable under paragraphs 30–34 (loss of earnings) will be reduced to take account of any pension accruing as a result of the injury. Where the victim has died in consequence of the injury, any compensation payable under paragraphs 40–41 (dependency) will similarly be reduced to take account of any pension payable, as a result of the victim's death, for the benefit of the applicant. Where such pensions are taxable, one half of their value will be deducted, but they will otherwise be deducted in full (where, for example, a lump sum payment not subject to income tax is made). For the purposes of this paragraph, 'pension' means any payment payable as a result of the injury or death in pursuance of pension or any other rights connected with the victim's employment, and includes any gratuity of that kind and similar benefits payable under insurance policies paid for by the victim's employers. Pension rights accruing solely as a result of payments by the victim or a dependant will be disregarded.

48. An award payable under this Scheme will be reduced by the full value of any payment in respect of the same injury which the applicant has received by way of:

(a) any criminal injury compensation award made under or pursuant to arrangements in force at the relevant time in Northern Ireland;

(b) any compensation award or similar payment from the funds of other countries;

(c) any award where:

(i) a civil court has made an order for the payment of damages;

(ii) a claim for damages and/or compensation has been settled on terms providing for the payment of money;

(iii) payment of compensation has been ordered by a criminal court in respect of personal injuries.

In the case of (a) or (b), the reduction will also include the full value of any payment to which the applicant has any present or future entitlement.

49. Where a person in whose favour an award under this Scheme is made subsequently receives any other payment in respect of the same injury

> in any of the circumstances mentioned in the preceding paragraph, but the award made under this Scheme was not reduced accordingly, he will be required to repay the Authority in full up to the amount of the other payment.

Paragraphs 19 to 21 of the 1990 Scheme contain that Scheme's equivalent provisions to paras 45 to 49 of the 1996 Scheme. As the former are discussed at pages 144 to 152, it is necessary in this chapter only to highlight the changes which the 1996 Scheme makes to those 1990 Scheme provisions.

There are two major changes. Paragraphs 19, 20 and 21 (1990) all provide that where the applicant has received defined financial benefits (social security, pension, etc), *compensation* will be reduced by the full value or full amount of those other financial benefits. Thus it is not only the special damages element, i.e. the financial loss, which is reduced by such deductions – the 'general damages', i.e. for the injury itself, may also be reduced where the special damages element has been wholly extinguished. The 1996 Scheme, however, largely 'protects' the standard amount of compensation, the fixed tariff award for the injury. The first sentence of para 45 (1996) makes this perfectly clear: paragraph 25 introduces into the 1996 Scheme the principle of a standard amount of compensation – it provides for the tariff award for each injury, the 'scale of fixed levels of compensation'. Paragraph 27 provides for the fixed award in respect of a child conceived as a result of rape. Paragraph 39 provides for the fixed single payment where there is only one qualifying claimant to a fatal award, and para 42(a) provides for the fixed annual rate for a minor claiming loss of parental services in a fatal case.

These four express categories are thus the exception to the rule that the *whole* of an award is liable to be reduced by 'other payments' to which the applicant is entitled. In these four categories the fixed tariff amount cannot be reduced by the value of 'social security benefits or insurance payments made by way of compensation for the same contingency'.

This represents a substantial change from the 1990 Scheme, under which no part of an award was protected from deductions. It remains the case in 1990 Scheme applications (i.e., all those received by the Board before 1 April 1996) that the whole of an assessed award, both general damages (for the injury) and special damages (for financial loss), may be reduced – and even extinguished altogether where the total deductions come to a higher figure than the total award.

The second of the two main differences between 1990 Scheme deductions and 1996 Scheme deductions is in the treatment of payments received under certain insurance arrangements. Whereas the 'protection' of the fixed tariff award from reduction to take account of social security or insurance benefits in para 45 (1996) works more favourably for the applicant than the 1990 Scheme which has no such protected awards, the treatment of some (though not all) insurance payments under the 1996 Scheme as deductible, even though 'paid for and maintained by the personal income of the victim', works more harshly than under the 1990

Scheme, as the latter does not deduct insurance benefits paid for wholly by the applicant. Paragraph 45 requires that, in addition to the deduction of UK social security benefits, the following will be deducted from the non-tariff part of the award (e.g. 'special expenses' or 'loss of earnings'):

- social security benefits or similar payments from the funds of other countries;
- payments under insurance arrangements, including, where a claim is made under paragraphs 35(c) and (d) and 36 (special expenses), insurance personally effected, paid for and maintained by the personal income of the victim or, in the case of a person under 18 years of age, by his parent. Insurance so personally effected will otherwise be disregarded.

Thus in the important areas of private health insurance the full value of benefits received under such policies, even though wholly paid for by the victim, will be deducted from an award, save that the 'tariff-based amounts of compensation' will not be liable to be reduced or extinguished by such a deduction. Subject to that element of protection, a wide range of private insurance benefits will be deducted from compensation for private health treatment, cost of special equipment and cost of care, whether in a residential establishment or at home. The practical working of these rules providing for reduction of awards may be illustrated by the following example.

Applicant X was a self-employed plumber before the injury was sustained. His average net profit per annum in the three years before he sustained his injury was £20,000 and his net income, after deducting income tax and National Insurance, was £14,000 per annum. His injury results in partial loss of sight in one eye. Under para 25 of the 1996 Scheme he is entitled to a standard amount of compensation. His injury entitles him to a Level 13 award, £10,000, under the Tariff of injuries. He is off work for 40 weeks. He is therefore entitled to compensation for loss of earnings from week 29 to week 40 inclusive, a total of 12 weeks (paras 30 and 31), as no compensation is payable for the first 28 weeks of loss of earnings.

As his average net annual income prior to the injury was £14,000, this makes a weekly figure of, say, £292 – the figure of £14,000 per annum being divided by 48 rather than 52 by virtue of the fact that, the applicant being self employed, this equates to the number of weeks actually worked to achieve that income. Twelve weeks' loss at £292 per week is £3,504 loss of income for which compensation is payable under paras 30 and 31. The entitlement to compensation from week 29 onwards is granted by para 30. The method of calculation is governed by para 31.

Paragraph 31(a) states that the calculation of loss is based on 'the applicant's emoluments ... at the time of the injury'. If an applicant is generally in work but is 'between jobs' at the time of the incident, the Authority and the Panel will probably take account of his usual rate of earnings as a basis of calculation, rather than disallow the claim for lost earnings altogether. Paragraph 31(b) requires deduction of emoluments received in respect of the period of loss.

Calculation of the claim should be adjusted to take account of changes in pension rights (para 31(c)) and of any pension becoming payable during the period of loss 'whether or not as a result of the injury' (para 31(e)). Perhaps the most important part of para 31, however, is para 31(d) which requires reductions to be made 'in accordance with paragraphs 45 to 47' which will include deduction of social security benefits and insurance payments.

Applying these examples to applicant X, the injured plumber, he has received, let us suppose, social security benefits during the first 28 weeks of non-compensatable loss and continuing from week 29 to week 40, the latter being the compensatable period of loss. His total social security benefits in the first 28 weeks after the injury came to £1,300. The social security benefits received between weeks 29 and 40 total £780.

He has received no para 31(b) 'emoluments' since his injury, nor any insurance payments under para 31(d) and paras 45 to 47, nor any 'pension' payments under para 31(e). His compensation is therefore calculated as follows:

- Standard amount of compensation under para 25 for the relevant description of injury in the Tariff appended to this Scheme:

  'Head: eye: partial loss of vision – 6/12 – Level 13' £10,000

- Loss of earnings 'for longer than 28 weeks as a direct consequence of the injury' under para 30:

  Weeks 29 to 40 (12 weeks) @ £292 per week net rate of loss £3,504

- Less deduction of social security benefits 'during the period of loss'.

  N.B. The 'period of loss' in this context is also limited to the period of compensatable loss, because para 45 provides 'The reduction will be applied to those categories or periods of loss or need for which additional or supplementary compensation is payable'. As the first 28 weeks of loss of earnings are not compensated, the benefits received during that earlier period of loss amounting to £1,300 are likewise not deductible.

  Thus the only deduction is the total of benefits received for the period between week 29 and week 40, i.e. £780.

  The calculation of compensation can therefore be set out as follows:

1. Injury		£10,000
2. Loss of earnings (12 weeks)	£3,504	
Less social security benefits (12 weeks)	£780	
Net loss of earnings		£2,724
Total compensation		£12,724

Let us modify this illustration and suppose that the circumstances are entirely the same, but plumber X has, in addition to social security benefits, received certain insurance payments 'made by way of compensation for the same contingency' (para 45). He paid the premiums for sickness insurance to cover the contingency of his loss of earnings through injury or illness and also to provide private health treatment entirely from his own income. He received payment under the policy for loss of earnings after week 12, the commencement date specified in the policy. The amount he received was £100 per week, the amount provided for in the policy. Up to week 40 he therefore received 28 payments of £100, a total of £2,800.

Paragraph 45(c) requires 'payments under insurance arrangements' to be deducted from all awards.

However, the last sentence of para 45(c) saves plumber X in our example from suffering deduction of any of that total of £2,800 from his award as it is only claims for 'special expenses' under para 35(c) and (d) and para 36, not loss of earnings claims, which are subject to reduction by the value of 'payments under insurance arrangements' where the insurance was personally effected and paid for by the victim.

If plumber X had private hospital treatment at a cost of, say, £2,500 and included that cost in his claim under the Scheme, and had received £1,500 from his insurers for that private treatment expense, the latter would be deducted as, although he had paid all the premiums himself, this would, unlike the loss of earnings claim, be a claim for 'special expenses' under para 35(c) in respect of which para 45 requires insurance payments received by the applicant to be deducted from the award.

He could thus only claim £1,000 (£2,500–£1,500) under para 35(c) for the cost of private health treatment in respect of the injury.

If plumber X will bear with us for one further variation of his circumstances, let us suppose that under the terms of the insurance policy 'personally effected, paid for and maintained by the personal income' of plumber X, he receives £5,000 as a lump sum from the insurers for the injury to his eye or alternatively he receives a similar lump sum by way of industrial injury benefit from the Department of Social Security.

The opening sentence of para 45 provides that all awards payable under the 1996 Scheme, except tariff-based amounts of compensation:

> will be subject to a reduction to take account of social security benefits or insurance payments made by way of compensation for the same contingency.

By the terms of para 45(a), all United Kingdom social security benefits are deductible in full and without exception, save that they cannot be deducted from the tariff award itself, but against all other heads of claim including loss of earnings *and* special expenses. The total of social security benefits (£5,000) received by plumber X would exceed and therefore extinguish his loss of earnings (£2,724) as well as his claim for special expenses (£1,000) in the worked example above.

If, on the other hand, the lump sum of £5,000 was under his personal insurance policy this would exceed and therefore extinguish his special expenses claim under para 35(c) but would not affect his loss of earnings claim as, by para 45(c), 'insurance so personally effected will otherwise [i.e. other than for special expenses] be disregarded'.

(a) Continuing loss of earnings – para 32 (1996)

Paragraphs 30 and 31 regulate what claim may be made under the 1996 Scheme for lost earnings or earning capacity up to the time the claim is assessed.

Paragraph 32 provides that 'where, at the time the claim is assessed, a claims officer considers that the applicant is likely to suffer continuing loss of earnings or earning capacity', a calculation will be made of an 'annual rate of net loss'. The compensation for continuing or future loss of earnings will be a lump sum which is arrived at by multiplying that annual rate of net loss (called the multiplicand) by the appropriate number of years (called the multiplier). This principle is essentially similar to the common law method of calculating future losses – its application to cases under the 1990 Scheme has already been explained at pages 126 and 130.

As the 1996 Scheme does not incorporate the common law but defines its own procedures and rules within the terms of the Scheme itself, para 32 continues by specifying precisely the method of choosing the appropriate multipliers 'applicable to various periods of future loss to allow for the accelerated receipt of compensation'.

This rule, and 'the summary table given in Note 3' to the 1996 Scheme, incorporates the familiar principle that calculations of present payments for expected future loss will be discounted to allow for the fact that the applicant is being paid now in respect of losses which will not be incurred until some time in the future. He has money in hand for that future loss and therefore, in order to allow for the early payment of that loss, he must receive less than the total expected future loss. The multiplier table in Note 3 incorporates that principle. Thus if the applicant can satisfy the claims officer that he will continue in the future to suffer an annual loss, which may be only a reduction of earnings from pre-injury levels and is not necessarily a total loss of earning capacity, the claims officer must calculate that annual rate of net loss and multiply that annual figure, by the multiplier (number of years) shown in Note 3 of the Scheme to arrive at the lump sum payable as compensation for continuing loss of earnings after the date on which the award is assessed.

If we take as an example railwayman Y who has suffered a severe head injury and brain damage which results in 'serious impairment of social/intellectual functions', his injury is classified as Level 20, for which the standard amount of compensation is £40,000 (para 25). He suffers loss of earnings, having been medically retired before the date of assessment by the claims officer. In order to arrive at his loss of earnings award, these losses are calculated, with the appropriate deductions, in accordance with paras 30 and 31. He will suffer continuing loss of earnings as he is unable to work at all, at any kind of employment. The claims officer must therefore calculate his continuing 'annual rate of loss' (para 32), making such deductions as are required by para 32(d), i.e. social security benefits, insurance payments and pension under paras 45 to 47, similar to those deductions applicable to the calculation of loss of earnings up to the date of assessment by the claims officer and considered earlier in this chapter.

Railwayman Y also receives a pension from his employers, having been retired on medical grounds attributable to the injury from which the compensation claim arises. This therefore is deductible under para 32(e) and para 47 of the 1996 Scheme. Calculations of future loss are subject to the same rules regarding deductions under para 32 and paras 45 to 49 as are the calculations of loss of earnings up to the date of assessment. The main difference is that rather than calculating a finite total net loss for the fixed period starting 28 weeks after the incident itself and ending with the date on which the claims officer makes the assessment, the calculation of future loss is made first by calculating the 'annual rate of net loss' by applying the rules in para 32 and multiplying that annual figure by the multiplier laid down in Note 3 to the Scheme.

There may be several such calculations necessary before future loss is finally calculated as a total figure. The reason for this is that separate 'slices of time' may suffer different rates of net loss.

Railwayman Y has lost his full earning capacity from the date of the injury. The first calculation, prescribed by paras 30 and 31, will be of his net loss of earnings from week 29 up to the date of medical retirement, if this precedes the date of assessment by the claims officer. The second calculation will cover the period between the date of medical retirement and the date of assessment. The third will be for the period from the date of assessment to the date of normal retirement from that particular occupation, e.g. to 60 years of age. The fourth will be from the date of normal retirement, taking into account loss of pension – that is to say, the amount by which his pension was reduced by early retirement resulting from the incident. This will be a different multiplicand (the annual rate of loss) and a different multiplier (the number of years by which that annual loss has to be multiplied) from the multiplier and multiplicand applying to earlier periods.

That is why para 32 specifies that 'an annual rate of net loss (the multiplicand) or, where appropriate, more than one such rate, will be calculated on the basis of . . . ' and then proceeds to set out (a) to (e), the ground rules for arriving at the appropriate figure for 'continuing loss of earnings'.

Paragraph 32(c) requires the claims officer to bring into the calculation 'the applicant's future earning capacity'. If the applicant would have continued to earn £300 per week net had the injury not been suffered, but is assessed as capable of undertaking different work which would earn, say, £100 net per week, his continuing rate of loss is only £200 net per week, even if he is not working at the date of the assessment. Although there are differences, these rules largely encapsulate the main principles by which the common law, and therefore the 1990 and earlier Schemes, arrive at the figure for future loss of earnings. The two sets of rules are not identical, however, and therefore should not be regarded as interchangeable. In cases where the 1996 Scheme is applicable, it is important to follow precisely the rules of that Scheme in order to achieve the correct calculation. In respect of the calculation of continuing or future loss of earnings, the last sentence of para 32 provides that, in selecting the multiplier:

> the claims officer may refer to the Actuarial Tables for use in Personal Injury and Fatal Accidents Cases published by the Government Actuary's Department, and take account of any factors and contingencies which appear to him to be relevant.

It should be stated at once that the 1996 Scheme attempts so far as possible to be self contained, so that the claims officer in deciding issues of eligibility and also of assessment of compensation, needs only to refer to the terms of the Scheme itself to ascertain how these issues are to be decided. At the same time, however, the terms of the 1996 Scheme have brought back into consideration a number of heads of claim (as the general law would describe them) or 'types of compensation' (as the heading to para 22 describes them). In so doing, the Scheme attempts to define exactly what those types of compensation are and to set out the precise rules by which they are to be calculated. The 'types of compensation' contain strong resemblances to their common law counterparts. Indeed the types of compensation in the 1996 Scheme are not new – they are adaptations of the common law heads of claim upon which they are undoubtedly based. It bears repeating that the rules of the Scheme govern entirely the calculation of compensation but with regard to one particular aspect – the multiplier to be applied to figures relevant to assessing future loss – the claims officer may, like his common law practitioner cousin, look outside the Scheme itself 'and take account of any factors and contingencies which appear to him to be relevant'. Thus, like the common law practitioner he may (one is tempted to say 'should', in the interests of justice) draw guidance from those tables and rules which the High Court will apply to do justice to claims comprising future loss, where such considerations as interest rates and life expectancy have to be weighed in the balance in order to achieve some level of realism in the necessarily imprecise calculation of a future loss; the imponderables, the contingencies of life, have to be placed against figures which are capable of precise calculation in order to strike the right balance.

In so providing in para 32, the Scheme rightly avoids too great a simplification or rigidity of approach which would have led to the balance needed between the interests of the injured party and the provider of the fund not always being maintained.

(b) Loss of earnings where a para 32 calculation is 'impracticable' – para 33

Paragraph 33 is a very short but very important provision. It reads:

> Where a claims officer considers that the approach in the preceding paragraph is impracticable, the compensation payable in respect of continuing loss of earnings or earning capacity will be such other lump sum as he may determine.

This gives no guide as to:

(a) the criteria by which the claims officer may reach the conclusion that, even though the loss cannot be calculated according to the rules of para 32, there is nevertheless a loss which can and should be compensated; or

(b) the method to apply in respect of a loss which cannot be precisely calculated.

Here, it is suggested, the claims officer can only look to the one available example of how this type of loss may be recognised and quantified, namely the common law principle of compensation for prejudice in the labour market.

An example of such a situation is an applicant who was sporadically employed up to the time of the incident but unemployed at the time of the incident, who has been employed erratically since the injury in a different type of work with generally lower pay than before the incident as a result of the injury, but is unemployed at the date of assessment.

The claims officer thus has no clear path to follow in making a para 32 calculation of:

(a) loss from date of injury to date of assessment, as the applicant was unemployed at the time he was injured, or

(b) continuing loss, as the applicant was erratically employed before the incident and has a broken work pattern since the incident.

What is clear, however, is that his earning capacity since the incident has been reduced as a result of the injury. That diminution is a compensatable loss although not a precisely calculable one.

It may also be the case that the type of work which the applicant was capable of before the injury was a more secure type of employment than the type of work of which he is capable after the injury.

In another case the applicant may, at the date of assessment by the claims officer, be working for a sympathetic employer who is prepared to tolerate the applicant's limitations in work capacity arising from the injury. Were the applicant for any reason to lose that job in the future, the incapacity caused by the injury may jeopardise his prospects of finding a similar job at similar rates of pay. This again is not a calculable loss but is a compensatable one. It is cases like these which, it is believed, the Scheme was intended to include in the scope of compensation under para 33. The claims officer has somehow to arrive at an appropriate lump sum to compensate for such losses. The Scheme merely tells him to award 'such ... lump sum as he may determine'.

Clearly this determination is not intended to be arbitrary. Equally clearly, the common law awards in such situations to compensate for prejudice in the labour market are the only guidelines whereby a suitable figure may be arrived at, rather than snatched from the air. This is an established principle of the common law – where it is called a *Smith v Manchester* claim – so that in addition to actual loss of earnings which are calculable, the real risk of loss arising at some future date also attracts a, usually modest, lump sum in its own right.

It should be added, however, that a forced change of job, from one kind of job which the applicant found fulfilling and enjoyable, to another, which is less congenial or satisfying, or simply from working to not working, will not, under this or any other paragraph of the 1996 Scheme, permit an award for loss of congenial employment, which is recoverable at common law and therefore recoverable under the 1990 Scheme.

3. Compensation for special expenses

The rules regarding 'special expenses', both in terms of definition of which losses or expenses are special expenses for the purpose of the 1996 Scheme and also how these special expenses are calculated, are contained in paras 35 and 36 of the Scheme.

It is worth putting this 'group' of claims in the context of the Scheme as a whole. As has already been stated at page 153, para 22 defines types and limits of compensation. This is not a necessary definition under the 1990 Scheme, as para 12 (1990) states that compensation under that Scheme 'will be assessed on the basis of common law', subject to those provisions of the 1990 Scheme which are expressly at variance with the common law. The common law of damages is a complex and comprehensive 'package' of rules providing for many different heads of claim including damages for the injury and its effects on the injured party's quality of life and work capacity, loss of earnings, future loss of earnings, costs of care in the case of serious injury, and costs of providing special equipment.

The 1996 Scheme makes no such reference to the common law as the basis for either defining or evaluating the type or amount of compensation which the applicant under the Scheme should receive; it is necessary, therefore, for the 1996 Scheme to set out its own rules for defining and evaluating such heads of claim as may be recovered by an applicant. Any heads of claim which may be found in the common law but which are not expressly included in the Scheme are not recoverable.

As has already been noted, para 22 is the paragraph that indicates which types and limits of compensation are payable in accordance with the relevant paragraphs of the Scheme.

Paragraph 22(c) provides that where the applicant has lost earnings or earning capacity for longer than 28 weeks as a direct consequence of the injury, an amount additional to the Tariff award for the injury may be calculated in accordance with paras 35 and 36 in respect of any special expenses.

Paragraphs 35 and 36 provide as follows:

Compensation for special expenses

35. Where the applicant has lost earnings or earning capacity for longer than 28 weeks as a direct consequence of the injury (other than injury leading to his death), or, if not normally employed, is incapacitated to a similar extent, additional compensation may be payable in respect of any special expenses incurred by the applicant from the date of the injury for:

 (a) loss of or damage to property or equipment belonging to the applicant on which he relied as a physical aid, where the loss or damage was a direct consequence of the injury;
 (b) costs (other than by way of loss of earnings or earning capacity) associated with National Health Service treatment for the injury;
 (c) the cost of private health treatment for the injury, but only where a claims officer considers that, in all the circumstances, both the private treatment and its cost are reasonable;
 (d) the reasonable cost, to the extent that it falls to the applicant, of
  (i) special equipment, and/or
  (ii) adaptations to the applicant's accommodation, and/or
  (iii) care, whether in a residential establishment or at home, which are not provided or available free of charge from the National Health Service, local authorities or any other agency, provided that a claims officer considers such expense to be necessary as a direct consequence of the injury.

 In the case of (d)(iii), the expense of unpaid care provided at home by a relative or friend of the victim will be compensated by assessing the carer's loss of earnings or earning capacity and/or additional personal and living expenses, as calculated on such basis as a claims officer considers appropriate in all the circumstances. Where the foregoing method of assessment is considered by the claims officer not to be relevant in all the circumstances, the compensation payable will be such sum as he may determine having regard to the level of care provided.

36. Where, at the time the claim is assessed, a claims officer is satisfied that the need for any of the special expenses mentioned in the preceding paragraph is likely to continue, he will determine the annual cost and select an appropriate multiplier in accordance with paragraph 32 (future loss of earnings), taking account of any other factors and contingencies which appear to him to be relevant.

The opening words of para 35 are largely a repetition of para 22(c). Paragraph 35 does not apply to cases where the victim has died – as these are separately provided for at paras 37 to 44 (see pages 201 to 214). It is a condition of any award of compensation for 'special expenses' incurred by the applicant from the date of the injury that the injury must have caused the applicant to lose earnings or earning capacity for longer than 28 weeks 'or, if not normally employed, is incapacitated to a similar extent'. It will be noted at once that the 'longer than 28 weeks' rule applies to claims for 'special expenses' – the same as to claims for lost earnings. However, whereas compensation for lost earnings is only recoverable if the applicant can prove his 'emoluments at the time of the injury' (para 31(a)), the applicant who claims special expenses does not have to have been in receipt of 'emoluments' from his work at the time of the injury. Paragraph 35 makes clear that, even if the applicant is 'not normally employed', he may still claim special expenses, provided that he is 'incapacitated to a similar extent'. Thus, an applicant who was unemployed at the time of the injury, but whose injury would have prevented him from working for 'longer than 28 weeks', can claim special expenses even if he has no claim for loss of earnings. The Scheme does not enlarge upon the phrase 'incapacitated to a similar extent' – these words will need to be considered in their context, and interpreted and applied by the claims officers of the Authority, and by the Appeals Panel. A common-sense interpretation suggests that if the injury would have incapacitated the unemployed applicant from engaging in what was his usual employment when he was employed, or is such as to prevent him from following any kind of employment, his special expenses may be included in his claim for compensation. It will also be noted that, once the applicant has met the criterion of incapacity for work for more than 28 weeks or, if not normally employed has been 'incapacitated to a similar extent', he is entitled to claim any 'special expenses [but not loss of earnings] incurred ... from the *date of the injury*'.

To take a different situation where, for example, the applicant was a skilled worker who was unemployed at the time of the injury, whose work, when he was employed, was well remunerated. If his injury has prevented him from permanently engaging in his usual skilled work, but after, say, 20 weeks he was able to resume work in a job that does not require the skills which his injury has prevented him from exercising, it seems that such an applicant would still be entitled to claim special expenses under para 35 as he has 'lost ... earning capacity for longer than 28 weeks', i.e. the loss, being the difference between his previous skilled earning capacity and his present unskilled earning capacity, continues indefinitely and thus exceeds 28 weeks.

Paras 30 to 32 governing claims for loss of earnings as opposed to special expenses, do not expressly deal with the situation where an applicant was unemployed at the time of the incident but who has provided acceptable evidence that he would have obtained paid work between the date of the incident and the date of assessment. It is submitted that such an applicant is entitled to loss of earnings (after the 28 week initial period) since para 22(b) expressly refers to an additional amount in respect of lost earnings for longer than 28 weeks, and para 31 sets out the 'basis' of calculation rather than strict rules from which departure is not permitted. In any event, para 33 expressly allows the award of a lump sum in such cases where the loss continues after the date of assessment, and an interpretation of the Scheme which denied identical compensation for the period before an arbitrary date of assessment would not be logical or justifiable.

The words in para 35, 'or, if not normally employed, is incapacitated to a similar extent', are not precise. It seems, however, from the *Guide to Applicants for Loss of Earnings and Special Expenses* issued by the Criminal Injuries Compensation Authority, that this could include a child or pensioner or indeed anyone who has been incapacitated for longer than 28 weeks as a direct result of the injury.

What classes of victims fall within the intended meaning of persons 'not normally employed'? Children under 16 and women over 60 and men over 65 would presumably come within this description (as would the disabled who cannot work), unless they were actually in employment at the time they were injured, as they would not be regarded *prima facie* as members of society's workforce. In relation to these groups, 'not normally employed' means that one would not generally expect them to be employed.

Is a man, say, in his forties who has been unemployed for several years immediately before his injury 'not normally employed' for the purpose of para 35? Is the same man who has been unemployed for three months at the date of his injury 'not normally employed' for this purpose?

As it is highly likely that it is intended that any man, woman or child who otherwise qualifies for an award under the rules of the Scheme should be entitled to compensation for special expenses where these have been properly incurred as a result of the injury, the probable interpretation of this first part of para 35 will be such that the applicant is in the first category if he was employed at the date of the injury or was unemployed but seeking re-employment at that date (i.e. has lost earnings or earning capacity), or in the second category of persons 'not normally employed' in all other cases.

Paragraph 35 then proceeds to define what is included in the phrase 'special expenses' in sub-paras (a) to (d).

Items defined in sub-paras (a) and (c) are similar to expenses recoverable under paras 17 and 18 of the 1990 Scheme, being items relied upon as a physical aid (para 35(a)) and the cost of private health treatment, (para 35(c)).

It is likely that claims officers and the Appeals Panel will include in the applicant's compensation the cost of hearing aids and spectacles or false teeth, where these are lost or damaged, where such loss or damage 'was a direct consequence of the injury' (para 35(a)).

Similarly, where an applicant has plastic surgery to improve the appearance of a scar resulting from the injury, the claims officer may allow the cost of private treatment but probably only if such treatment was not readily available under the National Health Service and the charges for such private health treatment are reasonable.

Special expenses under para 35(b) can be dealt with quite briefly: 'costs . . . associated with National Health Service treatment for the injury' may be included in the compensation payment to the injured applicant. Again this is similar to the position under the 1990 Scheme, although the latter does not expressly refer to this category of expense. A victim who suffers dental damage and has to pay a contribution towards the cost of dental treatment under the National Health Service can therefore include such expenses in his claim under the Scheme. If, however, he pays £1,000 in dental fees for private treatment, for example bridge work, he can only claim this sum if he satisfies the claims officer that the bridge work could not be done under the National Health Service and also that the charge for such work was in itself reasonable (para 35(c)). Prescription charges for medication made necessary by the injury and prescribed under the National Health Service are also claimable under para 35(b), as they have always been under the earlier Schemes. The words of para 35(b) 'costs ... associated with National Health Service treatment for the injury' will probably include, again similarly to earlier Schemes, travel costs necessarily incurred in getting to and from hospital for treatment or for medical examination relating to the injury on which the claim under the Scheme is based.

This leaves to be considered para 35(d), which includes potentially the most substantial category of special expenses recoverable under the Scheme. Paragraph 35(d) expenses are themselves divided into three categories;

(i) 'special equipment';
(ii) 'adaptations to the applicant's accommodation'; and
(iii) 'care, whether in a residential establishment or at home ...'.

All these categories of special expenses permitted under para 35(d) are heads of claim recognised by the common law and have therefore been allowed under previous Schemes. There are, however, important differences between the common law rules and the rules of the 1996 Scheme as they apply in detail. The provisions of the 1996 Scheme are in this particular an adaptation of the common law relating to personal injury claims. Such adaptations appear to have two main objectives.

The first of these is to create a set of rules and limitations appropriate to a Scheme, funded by the taxpayer, that is intended to regulate the payment of compensation to victims of violent crime. This distinguishes the purpose of the Scheme from the purpose of common law which regulates what is properly recoverable as damages by an innocent victim against the party whose wrongdoing caused the injury.

The second main purpose is to achieve a self-contained Scheme which does not expressly incorporate a separate body of laws or regulations to which reference has to be made in order to give effect to the Scheme. It is the intention that the operation of the 1996 Scheme should be conducted by administrators rather than lawyers. This objective is most readily achievable by setting out expressly in the Scheme itself what those rules are. The 1996 Scheme is, for this reason, a longer and more detailed document than any of its predecessors, which was unavoidable if the objective of self-containment was to be achieved.

The concluding paragraph of para 35 elaborates on the method of calculating compensation in the case of d(iii), i.e. for 'the reasonable cost of care', where it is 'unpaid care provided at home by a relative or friend of the victim'. In such cases the Scheme states that the expense of such unpaid care 'will be compensated by assessing the carer's loss of earnings or earning capacity and/or additional personal and living expenses, as calculated on such basis as a claims officer considers appropriate in all the circumstances'.

Thus, where the wife of the incapacitated victim gives up her job to care full time for her husband, her net loss of earnings would be the starting point, but not the sole criterion, for calculating 'the expense of unpaid care provided at home'. The claims officer will examine all the circumstances and will calculate the cost 'on such basis as [he] considers appropriate'. It may be that the victim is very severely handicapped, both physically and mentally, as a result of brain damage and needs physical assistance in all personal and domestic routines and round-the-clock care. In such a case the claims officer may consider that the victim's wife had no real alternative but to give up work entirely to care for her husband and that in all the circumstances of the case her net loss of earnings was the appropriate basis for calculating 'the expense of unpaid care'.

In another case, the injury may be less severe but sufficiently serious to prevent the victim from engaging in any form of employment. He is able to cope physically about the house but is depressed and spends most of the day watching television. His wife decides to give up full-time work entirely, not out of necessity in relation to the victim's needs, but because she considers that her being at home will add considerably to the victim's quality of life. In such a case the claims officer may feel that to allow part of the carer's loss of earnings would be 'appropriate in all the circumstances'. The criterion will be not what is best for the victim but what is reasonable as a payment from public funds by way of compensation.

Individual cases will of course be far more complex than the simple illustrations mentioned above, and the claims officer will be required to exercise the discretion given to him in making this assessment by weighing all the circumstances of the individual case.

The final sentence of para 35 states that where there is no readily available figure to start from, such as the carer's loss of earnings or earning capacity as in the examples given above, 'the compensation payable will be such sum as he may determine having regard to the level of care provided'.

It may be the case, for example, that the victim is cared for by a relative who was not employed and has not given up an opportunity to earn in order to care for the victim. In such a case it is likely that the claims officer will award some amount in recognition of that care. The amount awarded will vary greatly in order to recognise the difference between, say, two hours daily in providing modest domestic services for the victim in one case, and in another case the provision of substantial nursing care for many hours per week for which, if the unpaid relative had not been willing and able to provide, a professional nurse or carer would have had to be engaged by the victim and paid at the appropriate hourly rate. The hourly rate allowed would be less than the commercial rate.

The common law approach is to reimburse such a carer at about 60% of the commercial rate (see *Housecroft v Burnett* [1986] 1 All ER 332) and it may be that claims officers and the Panel will adopt a broadly similar percentage approach.

Paragraph 36 requires the claims officer to consider whether the 'need for any of the special expenses [in para 35] is likely to continue'. If so satisfied, 'he will determine the annual cost and select an appropriate multiplier in accordance with paragraph 32 (future loss of earnings), taking account of any other factors and contingencies which appear to him to be relevant'. He must also be satisfied in relation to para 35(d)(iii) costs of care, that they cannot be provided free of charge by the National Health Service or local authorities.

Where special equipment under para 35(d)(i) will have to be replaced periodically, or where nursing care or family care in respect of which a financial value has been assessed is provided (para 35(d) (iii)), the claims officer will decide upon an annual sum to meet the periodical cost of replacement of special equipment, or the annual cost of care (in each case called the multiplicand) and select a multiplier, according to the same rules contained in para 32 which apply to future loss of earnings (see Note 3 to the Scheme) and which have already been discussed at pages 126 and 130. He will then multiply the annual figure (multiplicand) by the appropriate number of years (the multiplier) to give the lump sum to be awarded for that particular head of claim.

In making that para 36 calculation, the claims officer must take account of 'any other factors and contingencies which appear to him to be relevant'. In other words the claims officer is accorded a degree of flexibility in making his calculation.

One important factor to be taken into account in all future loss or expense calculations is life expectancy. Where the injured person's life expectancy is stated by medical reports to be unaffected by the relevant injury, and his expectation of life is not impaired by any other unrelated medical condition, para 32 and Note 3 to the Scheme indicate the normal multiplier to be used for multiplying the annual cost by the appropriate number of years. It may be, however, that in another case the expectation of life is substantially reduced, in which case the multiplier will be reduced appropriately to reflect the fact that the annual cost is likely to continue in the future for a period which is less than the 'normal'.

There may be other highly individual 'factors and contingencies' arising from the circumstances of the case. For example, a man may be cared for by his fit but elderly mother; she may be able to provide such care for another two or three years at most. The victim will thereafter have to pay for caring services. The calculation should take account of this.

The *Guide to Applicants for Loss of Earnings and Special Expenses* published by the Authority comments helpfully on the scope of these heads of claim, or 'types of compensation' as the heading to para 22 puts it, and provides one or two calculations to illustrate how compensation is assessed where it involves the annual loss or cost (multiplicand) and the number of years by which that figure is multiplied (multiplier).

The Guide reminds applicants that the 1996 Scheme, like its predecessors, does not allow double benefit from the state and, in relation to care costs or other special expenses, the claims officer will need to be satisfied that all other possible sources of funding have been exhausted in providing, for example, for adaptation of the applicant's accommodation, or the provision of nursing or other appropriate levels of care, or provision of special equipment such as electric wheelchairs or computers to assist the severely handicapped victim to communicate. Such alternative public sources of funding will include the local health authority providing services under the National Health Service and the local authority social services department or housing department or Housing Association. Where the cost of services is met by such public authority, it will not be included in an award under the Scheme. Where such items are claimed under the Scheme and the claims officer considers it likely that such a public body will provide them either without payment by the victim or on a subsidised basis, by way of a grant for example, he may postpone assessment of compensation until that possibility has been fully explored.

4. Standard amount of compensation

Paragraph 22 is a key paragraph in indicating to the applicant or his adviser what types of compensation may be claimed and where to find the rules applying to that head of claim.

In the great majority of applications to the Authority under the 1996 Scheme, only para 22(a), the 'standard amount of compensation', will be relevant – this is the compensation for the injury itself according to the Tariff of injuries at the back of the Scheme. The minimum award payable under the 1996 Scheme is £1,000 – this figure is Level 1 of the Tariff. There are 27 Level 1 injuries included in the Tariff; 26 specific injuries and one called 'Minor injuries: multiple (see notes)'. Note 1 to the Tariff specifies seven types of minor injury and reads as follows:

> Minor multiple injuries will only qualify for compensation where the applicant has sustained at least three separate injuries of the type illustrated below, at least one of which must still have had significant residual effects six weeks after the incident. The injuries must also have necessitated at least two visits to or by a medical practitioner within that six-week period. Examples of qualifying injuries are:
>
> (a) grazing, cuts, lacerations (no permanent scarring)
>
> (b) severe and widespread bruising
>
> (c) severe soft tissue injury (no permanent disability)
>
> (d) black eye(s)
>
> (e) bloody nose
>
> (f) hair pulled from scalp
>
> (g) loss of fingernail.

If a cut or laceration leaves the applicant with a scarred head, he should look elsewhere in the Tariff under 'Head: scarring', where there are three levels of compensation for three levels of disfigurement: 'visible, minor' disfigurement (£1,500) 'significant' disfigurement (£3,000) or 'serious' disfigurement (£5,000). If there is no scarring resulting from the cuts or lacerations, the applicant must show three separate injuries of the minor types (a) to (g) above, and he will only qualify if at least one of the minor injuries still had 'significant residual effects six weeks after the incident'. And that is not all – the injuries 'must also have necessitated at least two visits to or by a medical practitioner within that six-week period'. Therefore, if an applicant has three minor injuries of the type stated in (a) to (g), one of which, for example a laceration, lingers for more than six weeks because it has turned septic, and having been to the doctor the day after the assault, the applicant makes his second visit seven weeks after the incident, he is not entitled to compensation (unless the laceration has left a scar, when he can look elsewhere in the Tariff). He meets all the criteria of Note 1 except two visits to or by the doctor 'within that six-week period'.

It should be remembered that the list of minor injuries is not exclusive; (a) to (g) are given as examples of qualifying injuries in cases of minor multiple injuries. It is to be assumed, therefore, that any minor injury not in that list (a) to (g) will count towards the three required to come within this provision.

One of the purposes of changing the Scheme from the previous common law basis to a tariff basis was to simplify its administration. The Tariff figures for injuries were worked out by reference to the level of award generally made by the Board on a common law basis of assessment. By describing each injury briefly in the Tariff and ranking it from 'Level 1' for minor injuries up to 'Level 25' for the most serious permanent disabling injuries, the 1996 Scheme enables the claims officer to 'read off' the appropriate award from the Tariff table given at the back of the 1996 Scheme; it also enables an applicant or his advisers to do the same. The challenge to both claims officer and the applicant in carrying this seemingly simple task into effect will be to extract the kernel from the medical reports which may be lengthy, or couched in medical terminology or medical shorthand (or illegible!), or a combination of these characteristics.

Medical reports received by the Authority, drawing on the experience of the Board, will vary from a few handwritten lines from the applicant's general practitioner or from the hospital where he received emergency treatment immediately after sustaining the injury, to perhaps a ten-page typed report from an orthopaedic surgeon, or consultant psychiatrist or other medical specialist. In every case the claims officer will have to reduce that report or, in many cases, batch of reports, to a formula of words which can be found in the Tariff.

Practitioners or advisers who regularly assist applicants in applications under the Scheme should familiarise themselves with the terminology of the Tariff. It is alphabetical but injuries are grouped according to the main part of the body which has suffered the injury. The main part of the body is used as a heading under which one then looks for the individual injury suffered in the particular case.

The most important 'part of the body' headings, in alphabetical order, are: 'Head' (103 classifications of injury), 'Lower limbs' (58), 'Neck' (14), 'Torso' (46), and 'Upper Limbs' (66).

After the main 'part of the body' key word there is in most cases a second word giving more precisely the part of the body injured, and thirdly the actual injury suffered. There is also a further indication given in respect of many injuries with regard to the degree of severity of the injury, to distinguish three or four different 'levels' of compensation. Thus:

> Lower limbs: fractured ankle (full recovery)
> Lower limbs: fractured ankle (with continuing disability)
> Lower limbs: fractured ankles (full recovery)
> Lower limbs: fractured ankles (with continuing disability)

and

> Head: eye: loss of one eye
> Head: eye: loss of both eyes

Not all injuries are to be found under a main 'part of the body' key word. Epilepsy, brain damage and sexual abuse of children, for example, each appear alphabetically under their own headings.

Mental injury is to be found under the word 'Shock' in the alphabetical Tariff, which then enlarges upon the types of injury covered in Note 2 to the Tariff.

Rape is not as a term to be found in the Tariff. Under 'Sexual Assault' there is a category described as non-consensual vaginal and/or anal intercourse, which is a Level 12 injury. It thus attracts an award of £7,500. As this single injury in the Tariff includes both rape and buggery the victim who is raped and the victim who is buggered without consent receive the same award as does the victim who is both raped and buggered. The victim who suffers both rape and buggery only receives more (Level 13 – £10,000) if the two assaults are perpetrated by two or more attackers.

In sexual assault cases there is no entitlement to an additional award for shock since that is not a separate injury but one which is part and parcel of the assault itself. Similarly with other types of injury there is an element within the Tariff award to cover the aspect of shock and distress. Paragraph 4.9 of the Guide states:

> The Tariff includes an element of compensation for the degree of shock which an applicant in normal circumstances would experience as a result of an incident resulting in injury. If the shock (as defined in Note 2 in the Tariff of Awards) is such that it would attract an award from a higher Tariff level than the injury itself, then the award for shock will be paid rather than the award for injury.

The Tariff is for the most part written in layman's terms with medical terminology kept to a minimum. As the medical reports upon which claims for compensation are based will not spare the reader the use of medical terms in describing the part of the body injured and the nature and severity of the injuries, the claims officer of the Authority and the applicant or his representative will have to translate these medical terms into the appropriate headings and lay terminology of the Tariff in order to identify the injury in the Tariff, read off the level of award and the standard amount of compensation for the injury.

The rule in para 26 where there is more than one serious injury, referred to in that paragraph as 'more serious but separate multiple injuries' (to distinguish from 'minor multiple injuries' which are compensated collectively under the rules of Note 1 to the Tariff), is that the applicant receives the Tariff amount for the 'highest-rated description of injury' plus 10 per cent of the Tariff amount for the second highest-rated and, if there are three or more such injuries, 5 per cent of the Tariff amount for the third highest-rated.

The full text of para 26 reads:

> Minor multiple injuries will be compensated in accordance with Note 1 to the Tariff. The standard amount of compensation for more serious but separate multiple injuries will be calculated as:
>
> (a) the Tariff amount for the highest-rated description of injury; plus
>
> (b) 10 per cent of the Tariff amount for the second highest-rated description of injury; plus, where there are three or more injuries,
>
> (c) 5 per cent of the Tariff amount for the third highest-rated description of injury.

The victim who sustains:

(i) an undisplaced fracture of the nasal bones (see 'Head: nose: . . .')

(ii) a fractured mandible (see 'Head: facial: . . .'); and

(iii) a detached retina (see 'Head: eye: . . .'),

is entitled to compensation for each of these 'more serious but separate multiple injuries' which will be calculated as follows under para 26:

The highest-rated is:

- detached retina – Level 10 – £5,000;

The second highest-rated is:

- fractured mandible – Level 7 – £3,000;

The third highest-rated is:

- undisplaced fracture of nasal bones – Level 1 – £1,000.

If he has sustained other injuries which are either 'minor' or Level 1 these make no difference and cannot be added to the three listed injuries.

The calculation of compensation under para 26 will be:

– Tariff amount for detached retina	£5,000
– 10% of the Tariff amount for fractured mandible (10% of £3,000)	£300
– 5% of the Tariff amount for undisplaced fracture of nasal bones (5% of £1,000)	£50
Total award	£5,350

Multiple injuries are extremely common and the rules of para 26 will be very important in the calculation of awards in such cases. Cases of serious head injury will have to be considered with particular care. For example, a builder who is involved in a fight with a work colleague and sustains serious head injury with brain damage, as a result of a blow to the head with a shovel, may suffer (Tariff terms used):

(a) 'Brain damage: serious impairment of social/intellectual functions'. If established by medical evidence, this warrants a Level 20 award of £40,000.
(b) 'Epilepsy: fully controlled'. This is a Level 12 injury – £7,500.
(c) A scar on the crown of his head. Because of partial baldness it is visible. It is not a 'serious' or 'significant' disfigurement and is therefore a 'Level 3' injury – £1,500.
(d) 'Head: skull: balance impaired – permanent'. This is a Level 12 injury – £7,500.
(e) 'Permanently disabling mental disorder confirmed by psychiatric prognosis'. This is a Level 17 injury – £20,000.

Looking at this combination of injuries, which is by no means uncommon where serious head injuries leave the applicant with permanent physical and psychological problems and assuming that each of these separate injuries is proved by written medical reports, we can say that, under para 26, the injured builder will receive:

(a) Full award for the highest level of injury, 'Brain damage: serious impairment' – Level 20	£40,000
(b) 10% of Level 17 – £20,000 – for 'permanently disabling mental disorder' – (10% of £20,000)	£2,000
(c) 5% of Level 12 – £7,500 – for 'epilepsy: fully controlled' – (5% of £7,500)	£375
Total award	£42,375

It will be seen from this illustration that, after the highest tariff injury has been compensated in full, other injuries, even if very serious in themselves, will add no significant amount to the main award, and once the second and third highest-rated injuries have made some modest addition to the award for the most serious of these multiple injuries, all other injuries count for nothing towards the final total award.

This fairly simple 'para 26' exercise assumes the successful accomplishment of the far more difficult exercise which must necessarily precede it: the identification of the conclusions arrived at by the doctors in the medical reports and translating them correctly into the appropriate somewhat cryptic definitions of injuries used by the Tariff.

Advisers who are experienced at reading detailed medical reports will be aware that reports will often be lengthy and will cover a great deal of ground and will describe numerous symptoms resulting from the injury. Many injuries included in the Tariff simply make the one distinction between, for example, 'Lower limbs: fractured tibia – shin bone (full recovery), Level 7 – £3,000' and 'Lower limbs: fractured tibia (with continuing disability), Level 10 – £5,000'.

The orthopaedic report will often go into considerable detail which will indicate degrees of recovery which might reasonably be broadly simplified as full recovery in some aspects of the injury, but not in others. For example the bone injury may have made a full recovery in that the fracture has fully recovered, but the victim has some pains which are not disabling, and has lost confidence in participating in physical sports which he previously enjoyed, or the leg aches in cold weather or on walking more than half a mile, or the removal of a plate or the orthopaedic repair has left a scar. Do these amount to 'continuing disability' or has there been a 'full recovery'? The permutations of partial recovery are endless. Claims officers will have to arrive at a settled common approach to achieve a fair solution to this process of simplification.

They and applicants must also be watchful of the Tariff table to ensure that they are looking in the right place in the Tariff. Take 'scarring' for example. The Tariff lists the following descriptions of injuries:

'Head: face: scarring: minor disfigurement';

'Head: face: scarring: significant disfigurement';

'Head: face: scarring: serious disfigurement'.

What is the difference between 'serious' and 'significant' scarring? 'Serious' is deemed worse than 'significant' as the first is Level 12 – £7,500, whereas the second is Level 8 – £3,500, a substantial variation in the award with what may be a borderline (or even subjective) difference. This group is also to be distinguished from other groups elsewhere in the Tariff including:

'Head: scarring: visible, minor disfigurement';

'Head: scarring: significant disfigurement';

'Head: scarring: serious disfigurement'.

This clearly must be 'Head' other than face.

Where a scar is, for example, across the cheek, the jawline and the neck, the claims officer and the applicant must look in the Tariff under 'Head: face: scarring' and also 'Neck: scarring' as there are the three levels 'Minor', 'Significant' and 'Serious' in the 'Neck: scarring' category as well as the 'Head: face: scarring' category. As it is 'disfigurement' which is being compensated 'Head: face' has a higher maximum award (£7,500), than 'Head: scarring' (£5,000) or 'Neck; scarring' (£4,000).

'Scarring' also appears elsewhere in the Tariff. There are three categories of 'Lower limbs: scarring', three categories of 'Torso: scarring' and three categories of 'Upper Limbs: scarring'.

One must be watchful not to regard these as necessarily the whole answer for all scarring, as burns, which will frequently leave scarring as a permanent disfigurement after the other effects of the burns injury have disappeared, are a separate category.

'Upper limbs: burns: minor'

'Upper limbs: burns: moderate'

'Upper limbs: burns: severe'.

Likewise for 'Torso: burns', there are three grades of seriousness, and also for 'Lower limbs: burns'.

Many serious burns cases come to the Authority and the Board. There will be the need to assess 'Burns' and 'Scarring' as separate heads of claim. The need to 'shop around' the Tariff tables can be further illustrated from serious burns cases as these will often result in severe psychological problems. Where the medical reports indicate mental injury, the applicant or his adviser and also the claims officer will need to consider para 9 of the 1996 Scheme. For a 'mental injury' to be made out under para 9, it must amount to 'a medically recognised psychiatric or psychological illness' – this reflects the terminology of the common law, and the 1990 Scheme.

Paragraph 9 helpfully defines in clear terms what needs to be established by medical evidence to claim compensation for 'mental injury'. The Tariff itself – the table which is intended to work on the basis of (a) naming the injury, (b) finding it in the Tariff under 'Description of Injury', and (c) reading off the level of compensation for that injury – presents 'mental injury' in quite different terms.

One will not find under 'Description of Injury' the term 'mental injury' even though this is the term the Scheme itself uses in para 9, nor will one find 'psychiatric illness' or 'psychological illness' in the Tariff. The Tariff uses the word 'Shock' as the heading for mental injury cases, and this is briefly expanded by 'Note 2' to the Tariff. The Tariff itself uses two more terms which do not appear in the definition in para 9 of the Scheme, namely 'mental anxiety' and 'mental disorder'. Although in the Tariff mental injury is headed by the single word 'Shock', it must be borne in mind that 'shock' is only one of several possible causes of compensatable mental illness. Mental illness is commonly caused by such matters as the lasting effects of disfigurement or inability to work resulting from the injury. Thus, for example, the burns victim or his adviser, and the claims officer, must look under 'Shock' for the victim's depressive illness, fit it into the appropriate category of 'mental anxiety' or 'mental disorder', and read off the level of award. (See the discussion of para 9 of the Scheme at page 40 and 'nervous shock' from page 26.)

These practical problems of using the Tariff table will be overcome as the Authority's staff and the Panel grow accustomed to using the Tariff. The transition from the established common law method of assessment with which everyone working on cases under the old Scheme had become familiar to the new Tariff method will no doubt be achieved successfully. The Authority and the Panel will soon be under the same pressure of cases as the

Board has always been, and a *modus operandi* will emerge with regard to the application of the provisions of the new Scheme and of the Tariff.

Should any aspect of Scheme or Tariff prove problematical and capable of improvement by amendment, this can be considered under para 29 of the 1996 Scheme in respect of a particular injury for which 'no provision is made in the Tariff', or more generally under para 4 of the 1996 Scheme: 'The general working of this Scheme will be kept under review by the Secretary of State.'

Chapter 14

Death of the victim - 1990 Scheme

Both the 1990 and 1996 Schemes provide for compensation to be paid to qualifying claimants where a victim has died in consequence of the criminal injury. When the change from a common law basis of assessment to a fixed tariff was first included in the abortive 1994 Tariff Scheme, the provision in that Scheme in respect of fatal cases was one of the most heavily criticised of the new provisions. After the manner of the introduction of the 1994 Scheme was ruled unlawful by the House of Lords, further consideration was given to a number of provisions in the 1994 Scheme, including fatal cases, and as a result the provisions of the 1996 Scheme in respect of fatal cases, contained in paras 37 to 44 of that Scheme, bear little resemblance to the terms of the 1994 Scheme and indeed contain a number of important similarities to the 1990 Scheme in defining the persons who may be entitled to an award, the heads of claim which may be considered and, so far as a tariff basis allows, the method of computation of the award to fit many differing situations.

It is worth repeating, however, that the 1996 Scheme contains its own rules and all applications made on or after 1 April 1996 must be considered under the express terms of the 1996 Scheme. Unlike the 1990 Scheme and all earlier Schemes it does not expressly incorporate any body of rules, statutory or common law, to help decide issues of entitlement or eligibility or in fixing the amount of compensation. As a document the 1996 Scheme is longer and more detailed than any previous Scheme. It needs to be. All previous Schemes have incorporated the common law or particular statutes to decide matters of assessment and some of its rules of entitlement. The 1996 Scheme attempts to define its own rules of eligibility and assessment. Where there is no wish to depart from what the common law provides, the Scheme to some extent codifies the common law. Although there are clear similarities between the rules applying to fatal cases in the 1990 and 1996 Schemes, there are numerous important differences and it is necessary to look at the Schemes quite separately.

This chapter looks first at the rules applying to all cases lodged before 1 April 1996 – these are governed by the 1990 or earlier Schemes.

1. Death in consequence of the injury (para 15, 1990 Scheme)

The following provisions apply only to applications received by the Board *before* 1 April 1996.

(a) Claims for financial support

Paragraph 15 of the 1990 Scheme provides that where the victim has died 'in consequence of the injury', the victim's dependants may make a claim. In England and Wales the class of persons regarded as dependants for the purpose of the Scheme are the same as those who could make a claim in the court under the Fatal Accidents Act 1976, as amended by the Administration of Justice Act 1982. The relationships which come within the statutory definition are summarised below. It is important, however, to bear in mind that the statutory relationship is not in itself sufficient to entitle the claimant to an award. It is essential to establish an actual financial dependency on the deceased. If a man who has a wife and children is killed by a crime of violence and he and the family were living entirely upon income support from the Department of Social Security at the time of his death, the family will probably continue to be so supported after the death. There is no loss suffered by the deceased's wife and children upon which to found a claim under the Scheme. The fact of dependency will be examined later in this chapter.

In Scotland a different statute, the Damages (Scotland) Act 1976, as amended by the Administration of Justice Act 1982 and the Damages (Scotland) Act 1993 for deaths on or after 18 April 1993, defines 'relatives' rather than 'dependants', and there are some differences in the Scottish definition of 'relatives' when compared with the definition of 'dependants' in England and Wales. In both cases the class is widely drawn, so that most family relationships which have any likelihood of being affected financially by the death of a breadwinner are legally included, provided that they can establish some level of financial dependency on the deceased.

In England and Wales the claim for loss of financial support by the deceased is referred to as the 'dependency' claim. In Scotland the claim is for 'loss of support'.

The categories of 'dependants' and 'relatives' include, of course, the spouse of the deceased. In the case of injuries incurred before 1 February 1990 the Scheme excluded a cohabitee and the person who is generally called a common law spouse, but in respect of injuries on or after 1 February 1990 the Scheme included such persons provided that they come within the definition stated below.

To come within the statutory definition, which the 1990 Scheme adopted in the case of injuries on or after 1 February 1990, the cohabitee must be a person who:

- (i) was living with the deceased in the same household immediately before the date of the death; and
- (ii) had been living with the deceased in the same household for at least two years before that date; and
- (iii) was living during the whole of that period as the husband or wife of the deceased.

Although difficulties can arise on the practical application of this definition, the definition itself is clear.

The definition of 'dependants' goes on to include the deceased's parent, grandparent, a person who was treated by the deceased as his parent, any child, including an illegitimate child, or other descendant, and any child who was treated by the deceased as a child of the family in the context of any marriage of the deceased, even though not an actual child of the deceased. It also includes brother or sister or uncle or aunt of the deceased, or the issue of such a person. In England and Wales the former spouse may claim even if the marriage was dissolved by divorce or annulled. In Scotland, only the former spouse whose marriage was dissolved by divorce may claim.

In all cases actual financial dependency must be established before an award may be made.

The commencing words of para 15 make clear that, save for funeral expenses, no compensation is payable for the benefit of the estate of the deceased. The provision under the Scheme arising from the death of the victim is for the benefit of the dependants of the deceased, not the estate. Thus where the deceased survived for some months before his death and the crime of violence was the cause of his death, his estate cannot claim the general damages for 'pain, suffering and loss of amenity' suffered by the deceased during the period between the incident and his death; nor does his claim for loss of earnings in that period survive his death.

Financial dependency is the test which decides whether the applicant has a claim, and the level of such dependency governs the level of compensation.

After the initial statements to the effect that the applicant's claim dies with him and regarding the right of dependants to make a claim in the event of the death of the victim of a crime of violence, para 15 (1990) goes on to state:

> Compensation will be payable in accordance with the other provisions of this Scheme to any such dependant or relative.

The discretions which the Board must exercise under para 6 (1990) of the Scheme in deciding whether an application is or is not within the Scheme apply also to a claim by a dependant of the deceased victim. The effect of this is that the Board looks initially at the victim's situation, to ascertain whether he would have been able to satisfy the Scheme's requirements under para 6 (1990) had he survived.

Where the victim dies immediately as a consequence of the fatal attack upon him, questions of prompt reporting of the incident and co-operation with the police under para 6(a) (1990) do not of course arise, although these can be material where the applicant survives the assault initially, fails to realise the seriousness of his injuries and fails also to take steps which would amount to compliance with the requirements of para 6(a) (1990).

Where the death follows immediately after the attack, the discretion which most frequently falls to be considered is that given to the Board under para

6(c) (1990). Both parts of para 6(c) may be material in a 'fatal' application, as the 'conduct' of the deceased may have been provocative or aggressive, or he may have voluntarily taken part in a violent situation which ended in his death. The deceased's conduct leading up to the fatal event is closely examined by the Board as in any other case.

If the deceased's conduct in relation to the incident which resulted in his death was such that, had the consequences been a non-fatal injury to him and he had himself made a claim, his claim would have been refused or reduced, that conduct will have the same effect upon any claim by his dependants.

The same principle will apply to the consideration by the Board of any convictions recorded against the deceased, or his unlawful conduct. If his criminal record is such that, had he survived and made a claim, it would have been withheld or reduced on account of his criminal convictions, those convictions will have the same impact upon a claim by his dependants. This principle has been reaffirmed by a decision of the Court of Appeal, *R v Criminal Injuries Compensation Board, ex parte Cook* [1996] 2 All ER 144 (see Appendix 1), in which an applicant whose application had been dismissed on the grounds of the deceased's convictions, and an oral hearing refused, had her application for judicial review of that decision dismissed by the court. This case is considered in more detail in Chapter 6 at page 86.

Paragraph 6(c) of the 1990 Scheme, in requiring the Board to have regard to the 'conduct' and 'character' of the applicant, also requires the Board 'in applications under paragraphs 15' (1990) (arising from death attributable to the incident) 'and 16' (1990) (where death occurs otherwise than in consequence of the incident) to have regard 'to the conduct or character as shown by the criminal convictions or unlawful conduct, of the deceased *and of the applicant*' (author's italics).

The widow making a claim under para 15 (1990) on the death of her husband may find that the Board considers an award 'inappropriate' by reason of her 'conduct' or 'character' even if there is nothing against the deceased in respect of either of those two considerations. If the applicant/widow herself has convictions or if, for example, her conduct provoked the violence which ended in her husband's death, she may receive a reduced or nil award.

Where an application includes minors as applicants, although the conduct or convictions of the deceased may make an award to them inappropriate – as one of those considerations in relation to the deceased may negate the whole application under para 6(c) (1990) – the character or conduct of the person making the application on the children's behalf (for example the widow who is their mother) would not affect the application of the children as dependants of the deceased. Unlike the character or conduct of the deceased, which may defeat the claim for all claimants, the applicant's own character or conduct may defeat only her own claim.

The Board must also be satisfied in these cases, as in any other, that death was attributable to a crime of violence. A violent death at the hand of another is not in itself enough to bring a case within the Scheme.

The Board considered an application for funeral expenses by the deceased's mother; the deceased had spent the evening, on which he was fatally injured, with his friends. They were all teenagers and had wandered the streets together. The deceased was regarded as the leader of the group but one young man contested this, and he and the deceased had exchanged hostile remarks during the evening. Later, when the group was making its way home, the two of them became separated from the rest. When out of view of any witnesses the deceased received a fatal stab wound. His rival was charged with his murder, was tried and acquitted, the defence being self-defence. There was other evidence that the deceased had been willing to 'see off' his rival by fighting him, and the only evidence of the fatal confrontation was that of the young man whose plea of self-defence had been accepted by the jury. The Board made no award.

It has already been stated that the Board is not fettered by the acquittal of the assailant; it frequently makes awards in cases where the Board has before it evidence which enables it to be satisfied that the applicant's injuries were attributable to a crime of violence notwithstanding the acquittal of the assailant. In a fatal claim, however, the applicant may be faced with the problem that there were no witnesses to the fatal confrontation, and the Board, like the jury, has only the assailant's version of those final moments. Much depends in such cases upon the evidence of the conduct of the protagonists leading up to the fatal violence. This will frequently give a strong indication of the intention and demeanour of the deceased and his assailant respectively in the moments immediately before the infliction of the fatal injury.

Because a death caused by violence will generally be the subject of a very thorough investigation by the police, the evidence of the investigating police officer is of great assistance to the Board in such cases.

The loss for which compensation is payable under the 1990 Scheme is the loss of financial support of the applicant/dependant by the deceased. The application form, by which an application to the Board is commenced with regard to a fatal case, requires information from the applicant on the earnings of the deceased and any other income which may go towards supporting the dependants who are claiming compensation. It also requires in full detail the outgoings of the household to which the deceased had given financial support until his death. In cases involving the death of the husband and father of the dependants, this will necessitate a statement of his employment and net earnings, the amount he provided each week for the support of the household and the family, together with details of any contribution to family expenses from the wife's earnings if she was also working. In English law the claim for financial support is called 'dependency', and in Scotland the claim is for 'loss of support'.

The sum of money which the Board decides is the level of financial support provided annually by the deceased for the dependants who are claiming compensation is the 'multiplicand'; it is multiplied by the appropriate number of years, the 'multiplier', to arrive at the capital sum which will be the amount of the Board's award to compensate for that loss.

Taking the example of the husband/father who is killed and whose earnings were the only support for his wife and children, the Board would perhaps regard 75 per cent of his income as being applied for the support of the family, leaving 25 per cent which he would have spent on himself (see *Harris v Empress Motors* [1983] 3 All ER 561). If his gross wage had been, say, £240 per week or £12,480 per annum, and his net annual wage had been £10,000, the Board may value the annual dependency of the wife and children at 75 per cent of £10,000 which is £7,500. The sum of £7,500 would thus be the multiplicand.

To arrive at the appropriate multiplier, or number of years, the Board would consider the age of the deceased and the ages of his wife and children, the dependants. The multiplier is greater where the parties, and particularly the children, are younger, to reflect the fact that the period during which the dependency would have been likely to continue is greater.

If there was medical or other evidence which indicated that the applicant had an illness which would have shortened his life, or that his career was precarious or unlikely to last more than a few years, these factors would be material in the Board's assessment of the appropriate multiplier.

If the wife was earning and was also contributing to the household expenses, the measure of the dependency would be lower than if the husband's earnings had been the only income. (Child benefit received before and after the death is not taken into account.) (See *Coward v Comex Houlder Diving Ltd*, Court of Appeal, 18 July 1988 and *Malyon v Plummer* [1963] 2 All ER 344.)

The proportion of the deceased husband's income to be regarded as the measure of the wife's dependency is less where there are no children. A surviving fully dependent wife with no children may be entitled to a sum based upon about two-thirds of her husband's net income immediately before his death, rather than approximately three-quarters where there are dependent children.

Dependency is a matter of money. Its purpose is solely to measure the financial loss. Its assessment must therefore take account of the financial realities for better or for worse. Where the deceased breadwinner has been unemployed for a long time, perhaps years, immediately before his death, with the family income consisting solely of social security benefits such as jobseeker's allowance, and the dependants continue to be entitled to social security benefits for their support following the death, there is generally no dependency award which the Board can make.

Where, however, the deceased was earning a living and providing for his dependants from his earnings up to the time of his death, and since the death the family has been in receipt of DSS benefits, the value of those benefits must be deducted in accordance with para 19(a) of the 1990 Scheme. The principle is to compensate for the loss, and the level of compensation required to make good the loss is reduced by the value of the other benefits resulting from the death.

As with non-fatal cases, the value of pensions and other benefits accruing as a result of the death will be deductible from the dependency calculation in accordance with para 20 of the 1990 Scheme.

Where the deceased was a high earner, the dependency calculation will be subject not only to the same scrutiny of the evidence to establish the financial realities of the deceased and his dependants, but also to those provisions of the 1990 Scheme which apply in all cases.

The Board examines the evidence to establish the true picture of the deceased's finances and the proper expectations of his dependants.

The Board considered an application arising from the murder of a professional man in his early thirties, who was married with two very young children. He had shortly before his death become a partner in a successful practice, and the firm's annual accounts showed his share of the profit as his income at the time of death. Accounts for the following two or three years since the death showed what that share would have produced had he been able simply to continue as a partner in the firm entitled to that share. The Board also had evidence from the deceased's partners and the firm's accountants that specific arrangements had been agreed between the deceased and his partners whereby the deceased would have been entitled to acquire additional shares in the partnership over the next few years.

Although his death occurred before the acquisition of additional shares was effected, there was clear evidence that this would have happened had the deceased not been killed. The applicants were entitled to ask the Board to take all these factors into account in assessing the measure of their loss. As the rate of loss was high, the Board had to compare this with the maximum rate of loss of earnings permitted by para 14(a) of the 1990 Scheme. The maximum rate of loss under para 14(a) being lower, this was substituted for the true rate of loss as the multiplicand.

The flexibility with which the Board must approach each individual case is further illustrated by the decision of the Board in a case in which the deceased had been a lorry driver, but was unemployed at the date of his death. He had been fatally stabbed by intruders whom he disturbed when he had investigated a noise at the rear of his home. Evidence of the deceased's work history indicated that he had earned his living mainly as an HGV driver for many years, although he had had various periods of unemployment, and the Board accepted that there was every prospect that he would have earned a living as a lorry driver in the future and would probably have done so for many years, as he would have had the prospect of fifteen or more working years ahead of him. Dependency was calculated to take into account his probable net earnings as a lorry driver (the multiplicand) and the number of years his widow would have enjoyed support at that level (the multiplier).

Lawyers are sometimes heard to say that 'every case is different'. This is true, of course, and indeed is admirably exemplified in the above case where two twists of fact illustrate two further principles which must be kept in mind when considering the kaleidoscopic possibilities which can arise under the heading of dependency in 1990 Scheme cases.

The 'widow' of the deceased was in fact his ex-wife – they had divorced about five years before his death but had nevertheless continued living together as man and wife and were still together when the deceased had been killed. The Scheme which then applied (the 1979 Scheme) excluded the common law spouse, which the 1990 Scheme includes, but included the former spouse, provided she was in fact financially dependent upon the deceased. The Board accepted that the applicant was a dependent former spouse and made a full award.

The Board also received applications from the daughters of the deceased by a previous marriage (the 'widow' thus proving to have been his second wife), in whose favour a maintenance order had been made against the deceased, their father, many years previously. The evidence as to the level of financial support actually provided by the deceased to the daughters of his first marriage indicated that this had been very irregular and very modest. The Board made a small award commensurate with the modest level of support which the daughters would probably have received between the date of the deceased's death and their attaining majority at eighteen years of age.

A widow's prospects of remarriage or even her actual remarriage are ignored when calculating her dependency in respect of the death of her husband.

Prospects of marriage are taken into account where the dependent claimants are the parents of the deceased, and the deceased upon whom they were financially dependent was their unmarried child. This accords with the common-sense possibility that on the child's marriage that support or level of support may well have ceased.

Dependency – claim by husband and children on death of wife and mother – 1990 Scheme

As the basic test to establish the amount of the dependency is to ascertain what part of the deceased's income was actually allocated for the benefit of the dependants, this test applies to the income of the deceased wife or mother in just the same way as to a deceased husband and father, where she was working and providing support for her husband and children or, where she was a single parent, for her children.

Husband and children may claim dependency in respect of the death of their wife and mother if the latter provided part or all of their financial support.

When a claim is based upon the death of a mother, however, the law and the 1990 Scheme allow certain other heads of claim to be considered in addition to the element of dependency based solely upon lost income which up to now has been considered in this chapter.

The Board assesses compensation on the basis of common law damages (para 12 of the 1990 Scheme). Accordingly, decisions of the High Court constitute the appropriate guidelines for the Board in deciding how compensation to widowers and children should be assessed on the death of the wife and mother.

In addition to any element of financial dependency arising on the death of the wife and mother who provided part or all of the family's income, the courts have acknowledged for some time that children are entitled to damages (and thus compensation under the 1990 Scheme) for their 'loss of mother's services'.

Moreover the husband may be entitled to claim compensation for the cost of providing a housekeeper. This could be a substantial item and may even be assessed by reference to the husband's loss of wages where it can be considered reasonable in the circumstances for him to have given up his job to provide those services himself, even though this results in a higher figure than the cost of paying a housekeeper.

The cases on 'loss of mother's services' which have established these principles, and which should be referred to by anyone seeking to present a claim under this heading include *Regan v Williamson* (1976), *Hay v Hughes* (1975), *Mehmet v Perry* (1977), *Spittle v Bunney* (1988), *Stanley v Saddique* (1991), *Corbett v Barking, Havering and Brentwood Health Authority* (1990), *Hayden v Hayden* (1992) and *Cresswell v Eaton* (1991).

In *Regan v Williamson* the court decided that the children were entitled to recover a sum for the loss of their mother's personal services as a mother, quite distinct from her services as a housekeeper. This is intended to cover the loss of the mother's personal care and involvement in the upbringing of a child, hour by hour, day and night, and in the case of a young child, the tender loving care that only a mother can give. The Board would not allow the full commercial rate of providing a carer where the reality is that the family is providing care on a non-commercial basis.

The value of this head of claim will vary according to the age of the child, as the very young child needs and generally receives more maternal involvement than the older child. Once a child reaches, say, eleven or twelve years of age the level of maternal involvement lessens, and the award will reflect this. If the evidence indicates that the deceased mother seriously neglected her maternal role, this may materially affect the level of compensation awarded.

The Board has considered a figure in the region of £2,500 per annum to be an appropriate guiding figure for a young child under this head of claim, subject to considerable variation according to the individual circumstances of the case, including the age of the child at the mother's death.

Hay v Hughes established that this head of claim is no less a financial claim because a grandmother has taken over that role without payment. A value is placed upon it and compensation will include a sum to represent the loss.

In England and Wales case law is continuing to develop the entitlement of a husband to damages in respect of the loss of personal and domestic services previously carried out gratuitously by his deceased wife, but in Scotland 'loss of support' is wide enough to include the cost to a widower of employing a housekeeper after his wife's death. The cost of employing a housekeeper can be established by evidence of rates of pay for providing such a service.

Where a member of the family, such as a husband or grandmother, has given up a job in order to look after young children whose mother has been killed, this can sometimes be measured by reference to the carer's loss of wages.

In *Spittle v Bunney* the court decided that the appropriate measure to value a mother's services was not the cost of fostering. However, evidence as to the cost of providing a nanny will be considered by the court which will apply a common-sense 'jury' approach. The 'nanny' yardstick would grow less as the child grew older and went to school and became more independent. As already stated, the Board would not allow the commercial rate.

In making awards in any of these circumstances the Board arrives at a total figure which then has to be apportioned between the surviving parent and the children individually. Where the award includes an element of financial dependency, part of the award is in respect of the children whose mother's earnings supplemented the family income. As the father of the children will have the continuing responsibility for meeting the family's financial commitments, the bulk of that part of the award will be paid to the father. (See also pages 199 to 200 on apportionment.)

The award to the children for loss of mother's services, the *Regan v Williamson* award, belongs to them personally, but again the practicality of the situation suggests that, if it is to be available for their benefit during their minority, it should be paid to the surviving parent to be used for that purpose. In the case of children who have been placed with foster parents after the bereavement, a loss of mother's services award might be paid to the foster parents by the Board where circumstances permit, as this award is for the children's benefit during childhood.

A substantial award under this head would, however, be protected by payment into an interest-bearing account, with only part being released initially and the remainder being available for expenditure during the child's minority. The latter is important because the award is intended to compensate the child's loss during that period. A younger child will receive more than the elder because the loss to the younger child is deemed greater as well as being of longer duration.

In practice, where the father is the parent who is killed and was the main provider financially, the apportionment to the children will be modest because the mother will be managing the finances of the family for the benefit of the children as well as herself and needs to be in funds to do this.

Where the mother is killed, the father, who may have been the main financial provider, will often continue to work. In those cases, the *Regan v Williamson* payment for the loss of mother's services may be the main part of the award and, being the children's money, should be protected by keeping its identity as a separate fund, although it will remain available for spending for the children's benefit during their respective minorities.

In cases involving the death of a mother who was the sole parent, where social security payments were the only financial support for the family, loss of mother's services may be the only head of claim, there being no financial loss in terms of dependency. The children may then be cared for by grandparents or other relatives. Although the award for loss of mother's services is the children's money, it is appropriate for such cases to release the award or most of it to the relatives who are caring for them so that the award can be expended for the children's benefit.

The common law and the 1990 Scheme allow claims for the cost of services which the deceased would generally have performed for the family. This head of claim, which might be called the 'DIY' claim, may include such items as decorating, gardening, minor domestic repairs and car maintenance. Where a husband is killed, a widow's claim will often include, as supporting documents, bills from builders, plumbers, garages and the like, together with a statement that the deceased husband had always carried out these domestic tasks which now had to be paid for. It cannot be said that these items are added arithmetically to an award, but they are taken into account in arriving at the total award.

In Scotland this aspect is covered by statute. Section 9(2) of the Administration of Justice Act 1982 provides that in a fatal claim any relative who is entitled to damages for loss of support under section 1(3) of the Damages (Scotland) Act 1976 may include as a head of claim a reasonable sum in respect of the loss to that relative of the personal services mentioned in subsection (3). This subsection then defines personal services as those which the deceased would have performed personally without cost but which would involve payment if performed by someone other than a relative. The law applying in Scotland where death has occurred on or after 18 April 1993 is now covered by the provisions of the Damages (Scotland) Act 1993.

(b) Bereavement award (England and Wales) – 1990 Scheme

After dependency, the other possible head of claim in an application based upon a fatal injury in England and Wales in applications submitted before 1 April 1996 is the bereavement award. (The position in Scotland is different and is dealt with on page 192.)

The bereavement award came into existence as an amendment in 1982 to the Fatal Accidents Act 1976, and applies to incidents occurring only on or after 1 January 1983.

It is an uncomplicated provision. The statute states clearly who is entitled to such an award. It also states the amount of the award, initially the fixed sum of £3,500. However, the Lord Chancellor exercised his power to vary the sum specified in the Act, and for deaths occurring after 1 April 1991 the statutory bereavement award is £7,500.

Before the Administration of Justice Act 1982, the law recognised no award for bereavement – the emotional loss and distress resulting from the death of a near relative.

The Act states that a Fatal Accidents Act claim may include a claim for damages for bereavement if:

(i) the claimant is the wife or husband of the deceased; or

(ii) the deceased was a minor who was never married and the claimant is the parent of the deceased if the latter was legitimate, or the mother of the deceased if he was illegitimate.

The statute goes on to state that the amount of such damages is £7,500 for deaths after 1 April 1991, and that where a claim for damages under this provision is made by both parents of the deceased, the sum awarded must be divided equally between them.

In relation to the bereavement award, 'wife' or 'husband' of the deceased does not include a former spouse, nor does it include a cohabitee or 'common law' spouse.

'Parent' means natural parent but includes an adoptive parent. It does not include a step-parent. If, for example, a mother and stepfather make a joint application, the whole award is payable to the mother.

Where one parent of a legitimate child under 18 makes an application, for example where the parents are separated or divorced, the Board must take into account the possible claim by the other parent and the fact that only one sum of £7,500 is payable. Where appropriate, the Board may make an interim award of £3,750 – half the full award – pending clarification of the position regarding the prospective claim by the other parent, and pay the balance only when that difficulty has been resolved. Where enquiries of the other parent draw a blank, the Board may wait until three years from the death (the time limit under the 1990 Scheme for making a claim) before making an award of the balance to the claimant parent.

Loss of society (Scotland) under the 1990 Scheme

Bereavement awards apply to claims in England and Wales only. In Scotland the equivalent is the claim for loss of society. In addition to the claim for loss of support which has already been considered, the Scottish claimant may claim for loss of society. The class of persons who may make such a claim is more widely drawn than the class of persons who may claim a bereavement award in England. Also, the amount of a loss of society award is not fixed but is in the discretion of the Board. Loss of society awards in Scotland are governed by the Damages (Scotland) Act 1976, as amended by the Damages (Scotland) Act 1993. The amendments in the 1993 Act apply only to cases where the death occurred on or after 18 April 1993.

The members of the deceased's family who may claim a loss of society award are defined in the Damages (Scotland) Act 1976 as:

(i) any person who immediately before the deceased's death was the spouse of the deceased; or

(ii) any person who was a parent or child of the deceased; or

(iii) any person not falling within (ii) who was accepted by the deceased as a child of his family.

The persons entitled to make the claim for loss of society include the child of the deceased in Scotland, whereas only the spouse or the parent of an unmarried minor child may claim the bereavement award in England and Wales.

The two awards are also different in the loss which each purports to compensate. The loss of society and guidance of the deceased is not compensated at all in English law, save that the claim of a child for the loss of mother's services in English law is a somewhat similar area of loss but is available only to the child who has lost his or her mother.

Applicants in Scotland claiming loss of society (as widened by the Damages (Scotland) Act 1993) are required to provide the Board with sufficient information regarding the family background to enable the Board to make an assessment of the loss of the society and guidance of the deceased.

In cases of deaths before 18 April 1993 this head of claim in Scotland is for the 'loss of society' award. This term is no longer applied to cases of deaths in Scotland on or after 18 April 1993 as the scope of the claim is widened under section 1(1) of the Damages (Scotland) Act 1993 to include the following:

(a) distress and anxiety endured by the relative in contemplation of the suffering of the deceased before his death;

(b) grief and sorrow of the relative caused by the deceased's death; and

(c) the loss of such non-patrimonial benefit as the relative might have been expected to derive from the deceased's society and guidance if the deceased had not died.

The loss in (c) above reflects the old 'loss of society' award, while (a) and (b) are the additional heads of claim created by section 1(1) of the 1993 Act. The other amendment to claims under the Scheme in Scotland in cases of deaths on or after 18 April 1993 is the provision of section 5 of the 1993 Act which adds section 9A to the 1976 Act in the following terms:

> (1) In assessing, in an action for damages in respect of personal injuries, the amount of the damages by way of solatium, the court shall, if –
>
> (a) the injured person's expectation of life has been reduced by the injuries; and
>
> (b) the injured person is, was at any time or is likely to become,

aware of that reduction, have regard to the extent that, in consequence of that awareness, he has suffered or is likely to suffer.

(2) Subject to sub-section 1 above, no damages by way of solatium shall be recoverable in respect of loss of expectation of life.

(3) The Court in making an award of damages by way of solatium shall not be required to ascribe specifically any part of the award to loss of expectation of life.

In England and Wales there is no claim under the 1990 Scheme for the equivalent of solatium or loss of expectation of life. Although the above statutory provision applies to applications in Scotland in cases of deaths on or after 18 April 1993, it is likely to apply to relatively few cases as the legislation is aimed more at the lingering illness and death arising from industrial diseases than to deaths arising from crimes of violence.

(c) Funeral expenses – 1990 Scheme

The final head of claim remaining to be considered with regard to an application in relation to a dead victim is the claim for funeral expenses. Paragraph 15 (1990) states:

> Funeral expenses to an amount considered reasonable by the Board will be paid in appropriate cases, even where the person bearing the cost of the funeral is otherwise ineligible to claim under this Scheme.

In many cases the funeral expenses are in fact paid by persons not eligible for an award in any other respect. Most common of these is the parent of the young adult victim where there is no question of entitlement to a dependency or bereavement claim. Anyone who actually met the cost of the funeral may claim.

Paragraph 15 (1990) begins with the negative statement that no compensation other than funeral expenses will be payable for the benefit of the estate of the deceased. The consequence of this is that in England and Wales no award can be made for loss of expectation of life on behalf of the deceased victim. Similarly, any loss of earnings claim which the deceased may have had for the period between the incident and his death will not be recoverable where the death is in consequence of the injury in respect of which the claim is made. Such claim as the deceased might have had on his own behalf in his lifetime and which has not been paid to him in his lifetime dies with him.

It will be noted that the position under para 16 (1990) is different. Under the provisions of that paragraph, which apply where the deceased has died otherwise than in consequence of the injury, a dependant who might otherwise have been able to claim under the terms of para 15 (1990) may claim under para 16 (1990):

> ... in respect of loss of wages, expenses and liabilities incurred by the victim before death as a result of the injury whether or not the application for compensation in respect of the injury has been made before the death.

Funeral expenses are thus recoverable only where the death is a consequence of the injury which is the basis of the claim. They are payable only to the extent that the Board considers them to be 'reasonable'.

In the 1987 Statement which was intended as a guide to the interpretation of the Scheme, the Board states that in England and Wales the reasonable cost of a tombstone will be met but no award will be made in respect of a memorial. The distinction leads to difficulties in practice. The Board adopts a sympathetic approach to the problem but when the distinction between tombstone and memorial can be made, the Board allows the one but not the other. The reasonable cost of a tombstone is likewise recoverable in Scotland.

Until recently, in England and Wales no award could be made in respect of newspaper notices, wreaths or funeral breakfasts. In Scotland these could be included in the award, provided that the cost was reasonable. Now these items, provided that they are reasonable, are payable in applications in England and Wales as well as Scotland, as are the reasonable costs of conveying family mourners to the funeral.

The Board will not generally meet the cost of transporting the body of the deceased for burial overseas where the deceased was resident in this country.

The claim for funeral expenses is not for the benefit of the 'dependant' or 'relative'. It is payable to the person who actually met the cost of the funeral who must produce evidence of such payment. Funeral expenses are not subject to the minimum award provision contained in para 5 (1990) which states:

> The application of the minimum level shall not, however, affect the payment of funeral expenses under paragraph 15 below.

Thus funeral expenses may be paid even if the total award is less than the minimum award, presently fixed at £1,000.

Where the victim has died in consequence of the injury and the case falls to be considered under para 15 (1990), an application may be made even though the victim applied for an award and received an award in his lifetime. He may, for example, have obtained compensation for the injury and for loss of earnings up to the time the award was made. The 1990 Scheme provides that any compensation payable to dependants who make application after his death will be reduced by the amount paid to the victim in his lifetime.

Funeral expenses are not subject to reduction where the value of benefits received in consequence of the death and deductible under para 19(a) of the 1990 Scheme exceeds the value of any entitlement to dependency and bereavement award under para 15 (1990). They may be reduced or disallowed, however, on the grounds of the deceased's 'conduct' or 'convictions' under para 6(c) (1990). If the Department of Social Security meets funeral expenses, these are not recoverable as part of the dependant's or relative's claim – nor can any other party claim funeral expenses, as no person has borne the cost, as required by para 15.

2. Death otherwise than in consequence of the injury (para 16, 1990 Scheme)

Reference has already been made to the very limited scope of any claim which may be made where the victim has died otherwise than in consequence of the injury. In such a case the Board 'may make an award to such dependant or relative as is mentioned in paragraph 15 in respect of loss of wages, expenses and liabilities incurred by the victim before death as a result of the injury whether or not the application for compensation in respect of the injury has been made before the death'.

It is to be noted that this is again not for the benefit of the estate. It is a claim open only to the same class of persons who could have made a claim under para 15 of the 1990 Scheme had the death been 'in consequence of the injury' – the 'dependant' in England and Wales or the 'relative' in Scotland. It does not cover funeral expenses, nor does it give the 'dependant' or 'relative' any claim for losses attributable to the death – such as the claim for loss of the breadwinner granted by para 15 (1990). It simply allows the claim for loss of wages and other expenses incurred by the victim to be paid. Such claim may be made whether or not the application for compensation in respect of the injury has been made before the death. Thus where death is attributable to the injury, a para 15 (1990) case, the dependant has no claim for the victim's loss of earnings between injury and death. His claim in those circumstances is for dependency since the death. Where death is not attributable to the injury, however, a para 16 (1990) case, the dependant may claim and recover such loss of earnings up to date of death, but for nothing else thereafter.

Paragraph 16 (1990) claims are not subject to para 5 (1990) and may not therefore be disallowed on the grounds that they do not merit an award of at least the minimum award, fixed at £1,000.

3. Deductible benefits (para 19, 1990 Scheme)

The requirements of paras 19 and 20 of the 1990 Scheme, that social security benefits and any pension or other payments accruing to the applicant as a result of the injury be deducted from compensation, apply to benefits resulting from death of the victim as well as to benefits resulting from injury. The principle is that there should be no duplication of benefit from public funds.

With regard to deduction of DSS benefits, only benefits received as a consequence of the death are deductible. The example has been given of child benefit received in respect of the children of the victim. This would have been payable before the death and continues to be payable thereafter. This benefit is not deductible.

The method of calculation is first to total the value of the award from which deductions may have to be made. In a para 15 (1990) case, the Board considers the value of each part: the net annual rate of dependency (or loss of support in Scotland), plus the bereavement award if appropriate (or loss of society or 'Damages (Scotland) Act 1993' claims in Scotland), plus funeral expenses.

The net annual rate of dependency (or loss of support) – the extent to which the applicant is financially worse off as a result of the death expressed as an annual sum – is multiplied by a suitable multiplier or 'number of years' to arrive at a lump sum. This lump sum is added to the bereavement award (or loss of society award) if payable, together with the reasonable funeral expenses, to arrive at the total value of the award.

Deductible benefits which have been paid up to the date of assessment are totalled and deducted. Those which will continue to be payable must be calculated as an annual rate of deductible benefit, and multiplied by a suitable multiplier (number of years), to arrive at the deductible lump sum.

The total value of the award, minus all deductible benefits, is the amount of the award actually paid to the applicant, apportioned as appropriate between the respective persons entitled.

The multiplier (number of years) by which the annual rate of dependency is multiplied will frequently differ from the multiplier applied to the annual value of benefits received. This is because the first is based upon the answer to the question: for how many years would the deceased have been likely to continue to work and provide at the rate he was providing at the time of his death? The second is based upon the answer to the question: for how many years will the applicant be entitled to receive the benefits now being received as a result of the death?

Even if the deceased was a young man in his twenties, the multiplier applied to his earnings would probably not exceed 18 years and could well be less. However, his dependants might receive benefits which are for life, and would therefore be based upon life expectancy.

The annual value of benefits may thus be subject to a multiplier which is considerably greater than the multiplier applied to the annual rate of loss.

If this calculation results in the value of the deductible benefits exceeding the total value of the award, the dependency and the bereavement award will be extinguished. Funeral expenses, however, are not affected by the calculation of deductions and would not be reduced by a 'benefits excess' (although, as has been seen, they may be reduced or disallowed under para 6(c) of the 1990 Scheme on the grounds of the deceased's 'conduct' or 'convictions').

The social security benefits which most commonly need to be considered in relation to fatal applications include widow's payment (a lump sum for widows under 60), widow's pension, widowed mother's allowance and income support (formerly supplementary benefit). Death grant was deductible but was abolished in 1987. Industrial death benefit is payable only in cases where death occurred before 11 April 1988.

The widowed mother's allowance has supplements in respect of dependent children.

Care must be taken where benefits are taxable, which includes widowed mother's allowance, widow's pension and income support, to establish whether the benefit will be taxed in the applicant's hands. If so, only the net benefit should be deducted from the Board's award.

Child benefit is not deducted, and the child benefit element in any of the benefit received after the death is ignored, provided the child benefit was being received before the death.

Income support as a benefit will be payable in those cases where the widow and any dependent children are not entitled to widow's pension or widowed mother's allowance. As income support is 'means tested', a lump sum award by the Board may reduce or extinguish entitlement to continued income support. If the Board's award would take the applicant's savings to a total between £3,000 and £8,000, income support will be reduced, and will disentitle the applicant to this benefit altogether if total savings exceed £8,000 as a result of the Board's award.

Deductions under 19(b) and 19(c) (1990) (criminal injury awards in Northern Ireland and foreign social security benefits) rarely arise. In a 1990 case, however, the Board was asked to make an award to the illegitimate posthumous child of a young man who had been unlawfully killed in England. The child's mother was a foreign national who had since married and continued to live in her country of origin. The child came within the Fatal Accidents Act, and the Board made an award, reduced by the full value of social security benefits paid by the state in which the child lived for the benefit of the child (para 19(c) of the 1990 Scheme).

Subparagraph 19(d) is frequently relevant to the Board's calculation. A payment to the applicant under any insurance arrangement, unless paid for entirely by the victim, will be deductible.

4. The effect of pensions on the amount of compensation awarded (para 20, 1990 Scheme)

The general application of deductions under this paragraph has already been considered in Chapter 12 (page 148). It provides that where the victim has died as a consequence of the injury, compensation will be reduced to take account of the value of any pension 'payable for the benefit of the person to whom the award is made as a result of the death of the victim'. The breadth of the meaning of 'pension' is the same as in non-fatal cases already considered; it includes:

> ... any payment payable as a result of the ... death, in pursuance of pension or other rights whatsoever connected with the victim's employment, and includes any gratuity of that kind and similar benefits payable under insurance policies paid for by employers. Pension rights accruing solely as a result of payments by the victim or a dependant will be disregarded.

As the death of a victim of a crime of violence may give rise to several separate applications, and there is no rule within the 1990 Scheme requiring the consolidation of such applications into one covering all possible claimants, this provision has need to state, as it does, the seemingly obvious that the pension and the award must be for the benefit of the same person for the award to be reduced by the value of that pension.

A widow applicant may be solely entitled to the benefit of a pension on her husband's death. Her award will be reduced by the value of the pension. The Board may receive a separate application from, for example, the deceased's elderly dependent mother. The latter's award, if she succeeded in establishing dependency, would not be affected by the occupational pension payable solely for the widow's benefit.

If a pension is taxable, half the value is deducted. If it is tax free, the full value is deducted.

A gratuity payable by the employer or the pension fund trustees will often be tax free. This is deductible in full.

The effect of the last sentence of para 20 of the 1990 Scheme is that pensions which result entirely from payments by the deceased or a dependant are the only pensions not deducted. These will usually be pensions provided for themselves by self-employed persons. A pension created by mixed employer/employee payments is deducted in full, although only half will be deducted if it is taxable.

5. Apportionment of awards and deductions under the 1990 Scheme

Although several dependants might make their application on one form under the 1990 Scheme and this is usually the case with a widow and dependent children, each is legally a separate applicant with an individual entitlement. The Board's practice, however, is to arrive at a total value for the entire award and a total figure for the social security and pension deductions.

It is necessary, having arrived at the total figures, to apportion the award between the respective dependants, at the same time apportioning the deductions. There may also be para 6(c) (1990) (conduct and convictions) deductions.

Where the deductions relate to the deceased victim's conduct or convictions, the total award, including the award to all dependants, will be reduced by the proportion specified by the Board.

Other deductions, such as pensions or proceeds of life policies, will be deducted from that part of the total award which is apportioned to the person entitled to receive the pension or policy proceeds.

Regarding apportionment between the surviving spouse and the dependent children, it has been observed that when the children are young the greater part of the award will usually be paid to the surviving parent, as the latter will have to carry the financial responsibility, and the dependency award to the children is largely to fulfil that purpose. However, the apportionment will vary from one case to another according to the individual circumstances of the case.

In one case in which the children were very young, under five years old, and the evidence proved immediate and longer term prospects of financial security and prosperity, plus the firm intention of the applicant and the deceased to educate their children on a private fee-paying basis, the Board allocated £50,000 to the two young children out of an award totalling approximately £200,000, so that the children's award would provide substantially towards the expected cost of the education that their parents would have provided had their father not been killed.

Decisions of the High Court in relation to the apportionment of the award between the surviving spouse and the dependent children, and the treatment of deductions under the Scheme, include *R v CICB, ex parte McGuffie and Smith* (13 October 1977) and *R v CICB, ex parte Barrett* (19 November 1993), both of which are referred to in Appendix 1. These cases confirm the principle that the children's awards in respect of loss of mother's services belong legally to the children. Deductions under the Scheme which may be deductible from the award to the surviving spouse, such as proceeds of a life policy, do not affect the children's award if they have no claim on the proceeds of the policy.

Chapter 15

Compensation in fatal cases – 1996 Scheme

1. Introduction

As has been shown in Chapter 14, the 1990 Scheme enables dependants and relatives to claim for financial loss (dependency), and for certain other heads of claim where the victim has died in consequence of a crime of violence. Although entitlement to an award on the part of such dependants is governed by the rules of that Scheme, so that for example the deceased's 'conduct' and 'character' as shown by his criminal convictions can result in the claim by his dependants being withheld or reduced under para 6(c) of the 1990 Scheme, the assessment of awards in fatal cases largely followed the provisions of the Fatal Accidents Acts and the common law.

The 1996 Scheme does not incorporate these statutory provisions or the common law. All the rules governing entitlement to an award are set out in the body of the Scheme, with the Tariff, which is appended to the Scheme, setting out the standard amount of compensation, with the claims officer, where appropriate, authorised to award such sum as he 'considers reasonable' or 'considers appropriate' according to the criteria laid down by the Scheme.

Paragraph 22(d) of the 1996 Scheme provides that where the victim has 'died in consequence of the injury', entitlement to an award will be regulated by paras 37 to 43.

Paragraph 22(e) states that where the victim has 'died otherwise than in consequence of the injury', para 44 regulates the terms of any award.

These paragraphs must be examined to obtain an understanding of the classes of persons who are entitled to claim in a fatal case, the conditions applying to such claims and how much they may expect to receive by way of compensation.

Paragraph 37 reads:

> Where the victim has died in consequence of the injury, no compensation other than funeral expenses will be payable for the benefit of his estate. Such expenses will, subject to the application of paragraph 13 in relation to the actions, conduct and character of the deceased, be payable up to an amount considered reasonable by a claims officer, even where the person bearing the cost of the funeral is otherwise ineligible to claim under this Scheme.

The sense of this provision is clear and is also familiar to anyone who has a working knowledge of the 1990 Scheme. The basic principle is that an applicant's claim dies with him, and only the claim for funeral expenses may be paid for the 'benefit of his estate'. This last phrase is a little misleading as in reality the recipient of compensation by way of reimbursement of 'reasonable' funeral expenses is the person who has personally paid them. That person may claim them under the Scheme, even if he or she is not a 'qualifying claimant' in any other respect under the Scheme. He or she need not therefore be a spouse or parent or child of the deceased (all defined in para 38) in order to claim for funeral expenses actually incurred. Such a claim is, however, like all other 'fatal' claims, subject to the provisions regarding the 'actions, conduct and character' of the deceased and of any applicant (paras 13 and 14). Thus a claim for funeral expenses, as with any other claim in a fatal case, may be withheld or reduced if the deceased's conduct or criminal convictions made a full award, or any award at all, inappropriate.

In these respects the 1990 and 1996 Schemes are similar with regard to claims for funeral expenses. Whereas the 1990 Scheme speaks of 'a dependant' (in England and Wales) and 'a relative' (in Scotland) by reference to the statutes which define those terms in fatal cases, the 1996 Scheme provides its own express definitions of those persons who may claim. Paragraph 38 is the defining paragraph and reads as follows:

> Where the victim has died since sustaining the injury, compensation may be payable, subject to paragraph 14 (actions, conduct and character), to any claimant (a 'qualifying claimant') who at the time of the deceased's death was:
>
> (a) the spouse of the deceased, being only, for these purposes:
>
> (i) a person who was living with the deceased as husband and wife in the same household immediately before the date of death and who, if not formally married to him, had been so living throughout the two years before that date; or
>
> (ii) a spouse or former spouse of the deceased who was financially supported by him immediately before the date of death; or
>
> (b) a parent of the deceased, whether or not the natural parent, provided that he was accepted by the deceased as a parent of his family; or
>
> (c) a child of the deceased, whether or not the natural child, provided that he was accepted by the deceased as a child of his family or was dependent on him.
>
> Where the victim has died in consequence of the injury, compensation may be payable to a qualifying claimant under paragraphs 39 to 42 (standard amount of compensation, dependency, and loss of parent). Where the victim has died otherwise than in consequence of the injury, compensation may be payable to a qualifying claimant only under paragraph 44 (supplementary compensation).

The definitions of 'qualifying claimant' differ substantially from the classes of 'dependants' or 'relatives' who may qualify for an award under previous Schemes. Previous classes of claimant are therefore best disregarded rather than examined for helpful parallels between the old Scheme and the new.

2. The spouse of the deceased

The first category of qualifying claimant is 'the spouse of the deceased'.

Paragraph 38(a)(i) and (ii) provide that, in order to qualify, the spouse of the deceased must be one of the following:

(a) *formally married* to the deceased *and* living with him as husband and wife in the same household *immediately before* the date of death; or

(b) *formally married* to the deceased *and, if not* living with him as husband and wife in the same household *immediately before* the date of death, was *financially supported* by the deceased immediately before the date of death; or

(c) *formerly* formally married to the deceased – (which presumably is the meaning of the words 'former spouse' in para 38(a)(ii) even though this gives the word 'spouse' a different meaning in para 38(a)(i) from that in para 38(a)(ii) as the former includes the two-year cohabitee up to the date of death) – and was *financially supported* by him immediately before the date of death. This would therefore include *financially dependent former wives* who were divorced from the deceased; or

(d) *not* formally married to *but living with* the deceased as husband and wife in the same household *immediately before* the date of death and had been so living *throughout the two years before* that date.

Partners or former partners of the deceased who are not 'qualifying claimants' under para 38 include:

(i) a divorced ex-wife of the deceased who was not financially supported by the deceased immediately before the date of death;

(ii) a former long-term cohabitee (i.e. separated before the deceased's death) who was never married to the deceased, even if she was financially supported by him up to the date of his death, as she is not a 'spouse' or 'former spouse' within para 38(a)(ii) and was not 'living with the deceased as husband and wife in the same household immediately before the date of death' within para 38(a)(i);

(iii) a former long-term cohabitee (i.e. separated before the death) who has never been married to the deceased and who was not financially supported by him at the date of death;

(iv) a long-term partner or ex-partner who is not of the opposite sex to the deceased (see 4.17 of the *Guide to the Criminal Injuries Compensation Scheme 1996* published by the Criminal Injuries Compensation Authority);

(v) a cohabitee (i.e. not married to the deceased) for less than two years at the date of death, even though financially supported by the deceased.

3. The parent of the deceased

The next category of qualifying claimant, where the victim has died, is a claimant who at the time of the deceased's death was 'a parent of the deceased, whether or not the natural parent, provided that he was accepted by the deceased as a parent of his family' (para 38(b)).

Thus the Scheme takes account of the day-to-day reality of the family relationship of the claimant to the deceased rather than regulating the position exclusively on the basis of blood relationship or legal relationship. There may be some evidential difficulty arising from the fact that it is the attitude of the deceased to the claimant and to their relationship which governs, rather than the other way round. Thus a stepfather (one who has married the deceased's mother but is not the deceased's natural father) may have little difficulty in satisfying the claims officer or Appeals Panel that he was established as the *de facto* parent of the deceased, whom the applicant cared for and provided for materially within the same household together with the natural children of the claimant and the mother of the deceased; likewise if the claimant was a long-term cohabitee with the deceased's mother and had brought up the deceased from childhood with their other children as one family.

More difficult to establish may be the stepfather's claim where the deceased was already largely independent – say 17 or 18 years old and working away from home much of the time – before the stepfather began cohabiting with the deceased's mother and by whom he had other younger children. Whether the applicant was 'accepted by the deceased as a parent of his family' is an issue of fact for the claims officer to decide.

Many children after the divorce of their parents are brought up by and in the household of their stepfather as their mother's second husband, but are financially supported by, and in regular contact with, their natural father, their mother's first husband.

Which of these two fathers would the deceased be deemed to have 'accepted . . . as a parent of his family'? The claims officer will require detailed evidence of the situation to make this choice between two fathers. This might be a difficult one where the child has died as a consequence of a crime of violence. The claims officer would have to examine the closeness of the tie between the deceased and the claimant and the likely or proven impact of the death on the claimant. The clear purpose of this provision is to compensate for the reality of the claimant's loss resulting from the death – it focuses on the everyday relationship within the family between the deceased and the claimant, rather than on their legal or blood ties.

Thus an adoptive parent would be likely to succeed; likewise a step-parent who actually brought up the deceased as a member of his family, or a long-term foster parent whom the deceased is shown to have regarded in his lifetime as his parent.

The natural parent who put the deceased up for adoption as a child would not *prima facie* come within para 38(b) unless, exceptionally, the adoptive relationship had failed and the natural parent had resumed the parental role.

4. A child of the deceased

Paragraph 38(c) includes in the definition of a qualifying claimant a person who at the time of the deceased's death was:

> a child of the deceased, whether or not the natural child, provided that he was accepted by the deceased as a child of his family or was dependent on him.

Again the phrase 'accepted by the deceased' is used – therefore, with regard to this provision, it is the proved or assumed attitude of the deceased which forms the basis of 'acceptance'.

In many cases the straightforward relationship of parent and child, both legal and natural, will be obvious and sufficient to establish that the applicant is the child of the deceased and a qualifying claimant. It will, however, be necessary to satisfy the claims officer that this was the *de facto* position, and that this relationship was the 'everyday' reality for the deceased parent and the claimant child.

The comments made above in relation to para 38(b) as regards step-parents, foster parents, adoptive parents, natural parents, and parents outside the family but providing financial support (sometimes creating a situation where there might be said to be two 'fathers' or two 'mothers' competing for the description of 'parent' under para 38(b)) apply to para 38(c); save that in para 38(c), in the definition of a child of the deceased who may be a qualifying claimant, there are, after the words 'accepted by the deceased as a child of his family', the additional words '*or* was dependent on him'. These last words strengthen the claim of the child who, for example, is financially supported by his natural father who dies as a result of a crime of violence, even though his parents have divorced and his mother remarried, giving the child, in everyday terms, a new father who takes on the everyday tasks of father of the family within the household, in addition to his natural but 'absent' father on whom he is financially dependent up to the latter's death.

It is even possible, although decisions by claims officers of the Authority or by the Appeals Panel will, in due course, make clear whether this is so, that such a 'child' would be a qualifying claimant on the death by crime of violence of either of his 'fathers', i.e. his natural but absent father who financially supports him, or his mother's second husband who conducts himself in all respects as the child's father in the context of daily life within the family home.

It must also be borne in mind that there is no age limit upon a child of the deceased. Thus, for example, a man of 50 may claim as a 'child of the deceased' if his father aged 80 is murdered.

5. The amount of compensation payable

Paragraph 38 concludes with an indication of the appropriate paragraphs of the Scheme to consider next, having defined who is or is not a 'qualifying claimant'.

We are told that paras 39 to 42 deal with claims for 'standard amount of compensation, dependency, and loss of parent' where the victim has died in consequence of the injury, and that para 44, where the victim has died otherwise than in consequence of the injury, deals with cases where 'supplementary compensation' may be claimed.

(a) The standard amount of compensation

Paragraph 39 provides as follows:

> In cases where there is only one qualifying claimant, the standard amount of compensation will be Level 13 of the Tariff. Where there is more than one qualifying claimant, the standard amount of compensation for each claimant will be Level 10 of the Tariff. A former spouse of the deceased is not a qualifying claimant for the purposes of this paragraph.

This is an interesting provision as it defines two situations – one claimant only and more than one claimant – and states the standard amount of compensation payable to each claimant in those two different cases; it also excludes from the application of para 39 one particular category of 'qualifying claimant', namely a former spouse of the deceased.

The effect of this is two-fold. One is to save diluting the *standard* award to another qualifying claimant in respect of the same deceased where there is a former spouse of the deceased who also qualifies for an award. Thus, where a murdered man is survived by his widow, who is his second wife, and also by his dependent former wife, there being no other qualifying claimants, the widow receives a Level 13 award, as there is 'only one qualifying claimant' for the purposes of para 39.

The second effect of the former spouse not being a qualifying claimant (for the purpose of para 39 only) is that she does not receive the '*standard* amount of compensation' at all (author's italics). She may, however, qualify for a payment in respect of dependency which is regulated by para 41 of the Scheme.

(b) The amount of compensation payable in respect of dependency

Having defined in para 39 entitlement to the *standard* award of compensation where the victim has died as a consequence of a crime of violence, the Scheme deals with the next head of compensation payable in fatal cases, namely the amount of compensation payable in respect of *dependency*.

Paragraph 40 reads:

> Additional compensation calculated in accordance with the following paragraph may be payable to a qualifying claimant where a claims officer is satisfied that the claimant was financially dependent on the deceased. A dependency will not be established where the deceased's only normal income was from:
>
> (a) United Kingdom social security benefits; or
>
> (b) social security benefits or similar payments from the funds of other countries.

In brief, this defines dependency as *financial* dependency. It applies therefore to compensate only *financial* loss resulting from the death of the victim. There can be no financial dependency where the deceased's only normal income was from UK social security benefits or similar payments from the funds of other countries.

Claims officers and members of the Appeals Panel will have to interpret the phrase 'only normal income'. In cases where the deceased was long-term unemployed or had received invalidity benefits or the like continuously for several years before his death, this definition presents no difficulty. There will no doubt be cases where the deceased was in and out of work periodically before his death, for example a self-employed worker in the building industry who had regular work in the summer months but drew jobseeker's allowance most of the winter. As it would be something of an injustice to do otherwise, it is to be hoped that the Authority will base their decision on the deceased's regular annual income, where this can be proved by annual accounts and tax assessments. Where this averaged, say, £18,000 net per annum over the three years prior to his death, it is to be hoped that his dependants will not be denied a dependency payment under the Scheme where that annual income was made up of, say, £14,000 from work as a builder and £4,000 from social security benefits, were his death to occur during a period when the deceased was receiving social security benefits as his only current income, rather than weekly wages from his building work. It is possible, however, that the words 'only normal income' will be construed strictly and narrowly, in which case the entitlement to a dependency award in this example might be governed entirely by the deceased's status as employed or unemployed at the date of death.

Paragraph 41 reads as follows:

> The amount of compensation payable in respect of dependency will be calculated on a basis similar to paragraphs 31 to 34 (loss of earnings). The period of loss will begin from the date of the deceased's death and continue for such period as a claims officer may determine, with no account being taken, where the qualifying claimant was formally married to the deceased, of remarriage or prospects of remarriage. In assessing the dependency, the claims officer will take account of the qualifying claimant's income and emoluments (being any profit or gain accruing from an office or employment), if any. Where the deceased had been living in the same household as the qualifying claimant before his death, the claims officer will, in calculating the multiplicand, make such proportional reduction as he considers

> appropriate to take account of the deceased's own personal and living expenses.

The claims officer will therefore examine the deceased's income as if he were assessing an injured applicant's loss of earnings claim. One major difference, however, will be that the loss will commence with the date of the deceased's death (unlike the injured victim's loss which is only allowed from the 29th week onwards of such loss). The claims officer will require evidence of the deceased's 'emoluments' at the time of the fatal injury, whether self employed or employed, and will decide what those emoluments would have been during the period of loss. He will then deduct from the deceased's income an appropriate sum to take account of the deceased's own personal and living expenses. Again, as is the case with the calculation of an injured person's claim for financial loss resulting from the injury, a dependant's claim will be subject to deduction of various payments received such as 'social security benefits or insurance payments made by way of compensation for the same contingency' (para 45) and 'pension accruing as a result of the injury' (para 47). Paragraph 47 expressly provides:

> Where the victim has died in consequence of the injury, any compensation payable under paragraphs 40 to 41 (dependency) will similarly be reduced to take account of any pension payable, as a result of the victim's death, for the benefit of the applicant.

The claims officer will take no account of remarriage or prospects of remarriage if the dependant is the lawful widow or widower of the deceased (described in the Scheme as having been 'formally married to the deceased'). This will mean that a 'qualifying claimant' who is the lawful widow of the deceased victim who has, since the death, remarried or who may have every prospect of remarriage in the future, may nevertheless claim compensation in respect of dependency based upon loss of the deceased's earnings up to what would have been his normal date of retirement, together with loss of pension resulting from the 'breadwinner's' premature death, but will have deducted from that calculated loss all the deductions required by the Scheme in relation to claims for loss of earnings or dependency based on the loss of the deceased's earnings, such as social security benefits and pension entitlements arising from the death and any damages or payment in settlement of any civil claim arising from the death (para 48(c), which applies to all awards payable under the Scheme). The assessment of the dependency will also take into account the qualifying claimant's own 'income and emoluments', as these will represent a measure of financial independence on the part of the qualifying claimant and a dependency award is based upon the level of the qualifying claimant's financial dependency on the deceased.

The final sentence of para 41 reads:

> Where the deceased had been living in the same household as the qualifying claimant before his death, the claims officer will, in calculating the multiplicand, make such proportional reduction as he considers appropriate to take account of the deceased's own personal and living expenses.

This is the principle which has applied under earlier Schemes and under the common law which requires the proportion of the deceased breadwinner's income which was necessarily expended in meeting his own personal and living expenses to be deducted in assessing the dependant's measure of loss. Paragraph 41 limits the application of this principle, however, to cases where the deceased and the qualifying claimant were living in the same household before his death.

With regard to the appropriate 'proportional reduction' to take account of the deceased's 'own personal and living expenses', previous Schemes and the common law which have the same rule in principle will usually start with a reduction of one-quarter where there is a fully dependent wife and children, and a reduction of one-third where the dependent family household consisted of only the deceased and his surviving spouse, the qualifying claimant. These proportions are calculated under the old Scheme with great flexibility to allow for varying family and financial circumstances, and will in all likelihood be applied under the Tariff Scheme. (See page 186 and the Authority's 'Guide to Applicants for Compensation in Fatal Cases'.)

As para 41 incorporates in its rules for calculating dependency in fatal cases the rules which apply to the calculation of loss of earnings contained in paras 31 to 34, and states that 'the period of loss will begin from the date of the deceased's death and continue for such period as a claims officer may determine', the calculation will, as with calculations of loss of future earnings (or 'continuing loss of earnings' as the Scheme terms this type of loss) under para 32, consist of a 'multiplicand' (the amount of money calculated by the claims officer as the annual rate of compensatable net loss suffered by the qualifying claimant, as a consequence of the death) which will then be multiplied by the 'multiplier' (the number of years appropriate to the particular case). As has already been seen in the discussion of para 32 in cases of loss of earnings in non-fatal cases, the claims officer is assisted in fixing the multiplier (or number of years by which to multiply the annual loss) by the table given in Note 3 of the Scheme.

Applying Note 3, headed 'Illustrative Multipliers', to an example suggests that where the deceased had a net annual wage of £9,000 and was murdered at the age of 45, with a normal retirement age from his job at age 60, the dependent widow of the deceased has suffered 15 years of loss in respect of her husband's continuing support up to his retirement at 60. If the claims officer decides that the deceased's annual emoluments under para 31 and para 41 should be reduced by one-third to allow for the deceased's own personal and living expenses under para 41, and assuming no other factors under the Scheme affect the claims officer's determination of the amount of the *multiplicand* (the annual loss suffered by the dependant) and the period of the *multiplier* (the number of years by which the multiplicand should be multiplied to calculate the dependent spouse's total financial loss as a result of the death), the multiplicand in the example will be £6,000 (£9,000 less one-third for the deceased's own living expenses) multiplied by 10.5 (the illustrative multiplier given for a loss of 15 years in Note 3 to the Scheme). The widow's dependency award under para 41 will thus be:

(multiplicand) £6,000 × (multiplier) 10.5 (for 15 years of loss) = £63,000

It has to be kept in mind that the claims officer of the Authority, or the Appeals Panel, will take into account all the factors which may affect the calculation, such as social security benefits (para 40) or pension received by the qualifying claimant, both of which have to be deducted (paras 31 and 47) in arriving at the appropriate multiplicand and the appropriate multiplier. If, in the example above, the widow receives social security benefits or an employer's pension as widow of the late employee, these must be deducted from the 'annual loss' figure, the multiplicand. If there is medical evidence that the deceased was seriously ill and likely to have retired anyway within say, five years, at age 50, the multiplier (the number of years by which the annual loss is multiplied) would be reduced appropriately.

(c) Loss of parental services – claimants under 18

Paragraph 42 of the 1996 Scheme reads as follows:

> Where a qualifying claimant was under 18 years of age at the time of the deceased's death and was dependent on him for parental services, the following additional compensation may also be payable:
>
> (a) a payment for loss of that parent's services at an annual rate of Level 5 of the Tariff; and
>
> (b) such other payments as a claims officer considers reasonable to meet other resultant losses.
>
> Each of these payments will be multiplied by an appropriate multiplier selected by a claims officer in accordance with paragraph 32 (future loss of earnings), taking account of the period remaining before the qualifying claimant reaches age 18 and of any other factors and contingencies which appear to the claims officer to be relevant.

The claims officer must, where dependent 'children' have lost the 'parental services' of the deceased, calculate the compensation for that head of loss. The 'annual rate' of loss is fixed – Level 5 of the Tariff – £2,000. This must be multiplied by the appropriate multiplier, again by reference to the illustrative multipliers contained in Note 3. Thus a ten-year-old schoolboy who suffers, as the result of a crime of violence, the loss of the parent upon whom he was dependent 'for parental services' is entitled to compensation under para 42 based on an annual 'loss' of £2,000 – the multiplicand – and an appropriate multiplier. He will attain the age of 18 eight years after the death of his parent – the table in Note 3 indicates that eight years of loss warrant a multiplier of 7: £2,000 × 7 = £14,000.

There is little guidance as to the meaning and scope of 'parental services'. The minor applicant must in any event be a qualifying claimant within the definition given in para 38(c), which specifies who is or is not a 'child of the deceased' and thus a 'qualifying claimant'. Once the claimant has passed this hurdle he may claim, as has been seen, a 'standard amount of compensation' at either Level 13 or Level 10 depending on whether there is only one or more than one qualifying claimant (paras 38 and 39). He may also claim 'dependency' under para 41.

As has been described above, para 42 adds to these heads of claim 'parental services' at £2,000 per annum (Level 5) with the appropriate multiplier. This claim is therefore additional to the 'standard amount of compensation' and 'dependency' and is intended to cover some other aspect of the child's loss. The 1990 Scheme (under common law principles) compensates 'loss of mother's services' which are the day-to-day services provided by a mother for her children, especially young children. They are a mixture of domestic services and moral support and guidance and are quite separate from any aspect of financial support.

It is likely that in a case where the father is killed and was the main or sole financial provider, leaving a dependent wife with one or more dependent children (under 18), the children, as qualifying claimants, would be entitled to the standard award and the dependency award and also, it would seem, the para 42 award for loss of parental services as the 1996 Scheme includes the death of either parent, even though parental services will continue to be provided by the surviving parent. Where the deceased was the mother or father and a 'single parent' who was the sole parent caring for the children day by day, as well as supporting them financially by his or her earnings, the child would be entitled under all three heads: standard, dependency and loss of parental services.

These comments on the 'loss of parent's services' in para 42 are subject to decisions yet to be made by claims officers and by the Appeals Panel as to the scope of para 42. This paragraph also has a 'sweeper' provision in para 42(b) which allows the claims officer an apparently wide discretion to make such additional payments of compensation as he 'considers reasonable to meet other resultant losses'. Paragraph 42 allows the claims officer to take account of 'any other factors and contingencies which appear to the claims officer to be relevant'. It will be interesting to see what scope is given to these seemingly open-ended phrases.

(d) 'Fatal' applications where the victim received an award before his death

Paragraph 43 reads:

> Application may be made under paragraphs 37 to 42 (compensation in fatal cases) even where an award had been made to the victim in respect of the same injury before his death. Any such application will be subject to the conditions set out in paragraphs 56 to 57 for the re-opening of cases, and any compensation payable to the qualifying claimant or claimants, except payments made under paragraphs 37 and 39 (funeral expenses and standard amount of compensation), will be reduced by the amount paid to the victim. The amounts payable to the victim and the qualifying claimant or claimants will not in total exceed £500,000.

Not infrequently, the victim of a crime of violence will have made an application for compensation in respect of the injury suffered, received an award and subsequently died as a consequence of that injury. In such cases persons who are 'qualifying claimants' – who will usually be members of the victim's immediate family – may, under para 43, make a claim under paras 37 to 42 (for funeral expenses, standard amount of compensation, dependency and loss of parental services, as the case may be).

Such applications are, however, subject to the rules relating to the reopening of cases in paras 56 and 57 of the Scheme. These enable the Authority to reopen applications after a decision has been accepted by the applicant, either where the applicant is alive but has suffered such 'a material change' in his medical condition that it would be an injustice if the original assessment of compensation were allowed to stand, 'or where [the victim] has since died in consequence of the injury'.

On practical grounds, however, in the case of an application to reopen more than two years after the date of the final decision, the Authority will not be required to agree to reopen the case on either of the grounds of (i) a 'material change' in the victim's medical condition where the victim is still alive, or (ii) where the victim has 'since died in consequence of the injury', 'unless the claims officer is satisfied, on the basis of evidence presented in support of the application to re-open the case, that the renewed application can be considered without a need for further extensive enquiries'.

It is important that the fullest possible supporting case is submitted with the application to reopen. The claimant's personal belief that the medical deterioration or the subsequent death of the victim was attributable to the original injury will not be sufficient. There must be medical evidence, which in a fatal case would often be a pathologist's report, or the decision of a coroner's court on cause of death based upon an autopsy, to justify reopening by the claims officer. The burden is on the applicant to provide evidence that there are factors which would justify reopening, and it is important that such evidence accompanies the application. It is not for the claims officer to undertake such research.

In cases where an award has been made to the victim in his lifetime, an award to a qualifying claimant 'will be reduced by the amount paid to the victim', save that 'funeral expenses' and the award of the 'standard amount' of compensation – the fixed Tariff award defined in para 39 – will not be subject to such deduction.

In no circumstances will the total of the awards payable to the victim and to the qualifying claimant(s) exceed £500,000, the ceiling figure which applies to all awards under the Scheme.

(e) Where a victim has died 'otherwise than in consequence of the injury'

Paragraph 44 provides as follows:

> Where a victim who would have qualified for additional compensation under paragraph 22(b) (loss of earnings) and/or paragraph 22(c) (special expenses) has died, otherwise than in consequence of the injury, before such compensation was awarded, supplementary compensation under this paragraph may be payable to a qualifying claimant who was financially dependent on the deceased within the terms of paragraph 40 (dependency), whether or not a relevant application was made by the victim before his death. Payment may be made in accordance with paragraph 31 in respect of the victim's loss of earnings (except for the first 28 weeks of such loss) and in accordance with paragraph 35 in respect of any special expenses incurred by the victim before his death. The amounts payable to the victim and the qualifying claimant or claimants will not in total exceed £500,000.

The 1996 Scheme is in many respects the 'child' of its predecessors; its structure is often similar even if the detailed provisions are dissimilar to previous Schemes. This is so with fatal awards.

The 1996 Scheme, like the 1990 Scheme, makes the initial division of 'fatal' applications into those where the death of the victim is caused by the crime of violence on which the application is based (paras 37 to 43) and those where the death is not attributable to the injury (para 44). In 1990 Scheme shorthand these were either 'para 15' (death attributable) cases or 'para 16' (death not attributable) cases.

Paragraph 44 of the 1996 Scheme is the equivalent of the para 16 – death not attributable – category in the 1990 Scheme. Where death of the victim is simply a supervening event and is not attributable to the injury resulting from the crime of violence, compensation under para 44 (1996) is very limited, as was the case under earlier Schemes. It can, however, be a very valuable head of claim to the qualifying claimant. In such cases the only person who is entitled to make a para 44 claim is 'a qualifying claimant who was financially dependent on the deceased within the terms of paragraph 40 (dependency)'. Such person may make a para 44 claim 'whether or not a relevant application was made by the victim before his death'.

Financial dependency is a question of fact for the claims officer to decide on the evidence provided by the claimant with the application. As has been seen, the definition of financial dependency excludes applications where the deceased's 'only normal income' was from social security benefits.

It must also be remembered that 'qualifying claimant' is a status defined by para 38. No one who is not within the definition prescribed by para 38 may make a para 44 claim.

The only award which may be made under para 44 is for 'loss of earnings' and/or 'special expenses'. These, as we have seen, are carefully defined in paras 30 and 35 of the Scheme.

Any loss of earnings suffered by the late victim will only qualify for an award under para 44, as in a claim by the victim himself, if the loss has run for more than 28 weeks and 'will begin 28 weeks after the date of commencement of the [victim's] incapacity for work.'

Under para 35 (special expenses), where the victim had lost earnings for 'longer than 28 weeks' and had incurred one or more of the 'special expenses' defined in para 35, a qualifying claimant who was financially dependent on the deceased may make a para 44 claim for those special expenses.

At all times it should be borne in mind that the amounts payable to the victim and the qualifying claimant or claimants will not in total exceed £500,000.

Chapter 16

Procedure for determining applications

1. Introduction

Paragraph 83 of the 1996 Scheme provides that 'this Scheme', both its rules on entitlement and rules of procedure, apply to all applications received by the Board or the Authority on or after 1 April 1996.

Paragraph 84 of the 1996 Scheme states:

> . . . applications for compensation received by the Board before 1 April 1996 will be dealt with according to the provisions of the non-statutory Scheme which came into operation on 1 February 1990 ('the old Scheme'), which includes the earlier Schemes mentioned therein insofar as they continue to have effect immediately before 1 April 1996 by virtue of the old Scheme or corresponding provisions in an earlier Scheme.

With the commencement of the new Scheme from 1 April 1996, and at the same time the express preservation of the 1990 and earlier Schemes in respect of all pre-1 April 1996 applications, there are established from that date two quite separate systems and rules for the consideration and decision of all cases, divided according to the date on which the applications were received.

The rules governing eligibility for an award, under both the 1996 Scheme and the 'old' 1990 Scheme, have been dealt with in previous chapters. It is now necessary to consider the rules of procedure under both Schemes.

In the first edition of this book, this chapter began with the following paragraph: 'There is always the risk that the provisions of the Scheme, or indeed any body of regulations, which are described collectively as "procedural" will be regarded as the poor relation of other provisions which may be described as "substantive". If procedural matters are neglected as a result, important points in the conduct of an application may be missed. A proper appreciation of the regulations governing the process of an application and the machinery by which it progresses through the system is as important as an understanding of the substantive provisions which regulate matters of principle. One reason for this is that the regulations which govern the process contain within them a number of substantive provisions. Only by understanding the whole process in some detail will the applicant, either personally or through his adviser, know what he is entitled to expect from the Scheme.'

Although the 1996 rules will govern all applications received on or after

1 April 1996, there were at that date about 100,000 applications in the system which will continue to be governed by the terms of the 'old' Scheme. Only in 1998 or 1999 can the greater part of those cases be expected to have completed their passage through the system to final decision. For practitioners and advisers dealing with applications lodged before 1 April 1996 there will therefore continue to be a need to know the rules of the 'old' Scheme.

Although para 85 provides for the abolition of the Board on a 'transfer date' yet to be fixed by the Secretary of State, paras 84 and 86 preserve the basic 'old' Scheme rights of 'old' Scheme applicants; in practical terms it is unlikely that the Board will be abolished whilst there are tens of thousands of cases still with the Board for decision, as this would have the effect of swamping the Appeals Panel, two of whose legally qualified members would be required to hear all outstanding 'old' Scheme hearings (para 86(b)).

It was a criticism of the 1990 and earlier Schemes that some of the paragraphs contained a number of important but unrelated items of principle (for example paras 22 and 25 of the 1990 Scheme). The 1996 Scheme has reordered the drafting of the rules of the Scheme, and has substantially changed a number of them, so that the 1996 Scheme is in some respects a more straightforward document than its predecessors.

However, although certain similarities remain, there are a number of differences between the procedures contained in the 1990 and 1996 Schemes. The 1996 Scheme has replaced the 'common law damages' awarded under earlier Schemes with a fixed tariff figure, 'the standard amount of compensation' (para 25, 1996), for the injury suffered, together with any 'loss of earnings' (paras 30 to 34) and 'special expenses' (paras 35 and 36). The 1996 Scheme also provides for the new 'Authority' and 'Appeals Panel' to replace the Board in deciding all cases received on or after 1 April 1996.

The Board, which under the 1990 Scheme decided all applications for compensation for criminal injury, continues to exist and, until 'the transfer date' explained below, has exclusive jurisdiction to decide applications received before 1 April 1996, applying the rules of the 1990 Scheme (or earlier Schemes if appropriate) to those cases. The Authority and the Panel decide all applications received after 31 March 1996. Subject as below, they do not have jurisdiction to decide any applications received before 1 April 1996.

Paragraph 85 of the 1996 Scheme provides that 'The Board will cease to exist on such date ("the transfer date") as the Secretary of State may direct' and at that time the Board will 'transfer to the Authority all its records of current and past applications'. The 1993 White Paper referred to a likely transition period of two years. The 1996 Scheme thus provides for the cessation of the Criminal Injuries Compensation Board, at which point the only bodies with responsibility for dealing with applications for compensation will be the Authority and the Panel.

It is apparent from these rules postponing the 'transfer date' that applicants whose applications were received before 1 April 1996 will need to know the rules and procedures of the 1990 Scheme (or earlier Schemes as appropriate) as the Board will continue to decide those applications on all issues of eligibility and assessment and will apply 'old' Scheme rules in so doing.

Paragraph 86 of the 1996 Scheme contains an express safeguard entitling all 'old' Scheme cases to continue to be decided under the 'old' rules even after the transfer date on which the Board will cease to exist.

Part A of this chapter contains a discussion of the provisions of the 1996 Scheme which preserve the existence and jurisdiction of the Board up to the transfer date, and which preserve the right of 'old' Scheme applicants to have their cases decided in accordance with the 'old' rules.

Part B considers in detail the procedure for determining applications under the 1990 Scheme.

Part C deals with the entirely new procedures of the 1996 Scheme.

Part A

Rules preserving applicant's rights in 'old' Scheme cases

The paragraphs of the 1996 Scheme which preserve the right of pre- 1 April 1996 applications to be considered under the 'old' rules are paras 84 to 87. The full text of these four paragraphs reads as follows:

> 84. Subject to paragraphs 85 to 87, applications for compensation received by the Board before 1 April 1996 will be dealt with according to the provisions of the non-statutory Scheme which came into operation on 1 February 1990 ('the old Scheme'), which includes the earlier Schemes mentioned therein insofar as they continue to have effect immediately before 1 April 1996 by virtue of the old Scheme or corresponding provisions in an earlier Scheme.
>
> 85. The Board will cease to exist on such date ('the transfer date') as the Secretary of State may direct. Immediately before the transfer date, the Board will transfer to the Authority all its records of current and past applications.
>
> 86. On and after the transfer date, applications required by paragraph 84 to be dealt with according to the provisions of the old Scheme will be so dealt with by the Authority, and:
>
>   (a) any decision authorised under the old Scheme to be made by a Single Member of the Board may be made by a single legally qualified member of the Panel appointed for the purposes of this Scheme;
>
>   (b) any decision authorised under the old Scheme to be made by at least two Members of the Board may be made by at least two legally qualified members of the Panel;

(c) any decision authorised under the old Scheme to be made by the Chairman of the Board may be made by the Chairman of the Panel.

In this paragraph 'legally qualified' means qualified to practise as a solicitor in any part of Great Britain, or as a barrister in England and Wales, or as an advocate in Scotland.

87. On and after the transfer date, any application to re-open a case under paragraph 13 of the old Scheme (or any corresponding provision in any of the earlier Schemes) must be addressed to the Authority, which will deal with it according to the provisions of the old Scheme, applying paragraphs 84 and 86 above as appropriate.

Paragraph 84 preserves the jurisdiction of previous Schemes (i.e. 1969, 1979 as well as 1990) where appropriate, although the overwhelming majority of cases outstanding at 31 March 1996 are subject to the rules of the 1990 Scheme.

In cases where the injury was sustained before 1 October 1979, the text of para 7(b) of the 1996 Scheme precludes compensation if, at the time of the injury, the victim and assailant were living together as members of the same family. This reflects the provisions of the 1969 Scheme. On 1 October 1979, the 1979 Scheme came into force – this enabled the Board to entertain such cases subject to certain conditions.

The Board and the Authority still receive applications, usually involving childhood sexual abuse, which are partly or wholly based on incidents which occurred before 1 October 1979. Although cases concerning pre- 1 October 1979 abuse which involved members of the same household cannot be entertained by the Board, many such cases are based also on post- 1 October 1979 abuse, and this can be considered for compensation.

The most significant changes made by the 1996 Scheme are:

(i) to change the basis of compensation for the injury from the 'common law damages' system, which applied under previous Schemes, to a fixed tariff figure described by para 25 as the 'standard amount';

(ii) to make a separate award for loss of earnings only if the period of such loss continues for longer than 28 weeks;

(iii) to allow 'compensation for special expenses' only so far as such expenses come within the scope of paras 35 and 36 of the 1996 Scheme;

(iv) to provide an absolute ceiling figure of £500,000 in any one claim which will not in any circumstances be exceeded, even if the total of all 'heads' of claim calculated according to all other rules in the Scheme would otherwise have exceeded that figure;

(v) to create entirely new rules of entitlement in fatal cases;

(vi) to define express rules regarding entitlement to compensation for mental injury;

(vii) to create an entirely new decision-making hierarchy, comprising claims officers of the Authority, and adjudicators, members of the newly created Appeals Panel; and

(viii) to create for a temporary period a dual system for deciding old Scheme and 1996 Scheme cases; and

(ix) to provide for the abolition of the Criminal Injuries Compensation Board which, up to its abolition on the 'transfer date' yet to be fixed by the Secretary of State, will have administered and adjudicated all applications for compensation for criminal injury lodged from the Scheme's commencement in 1964 up to 31 March 1996.

Provisions for reopening cases, which have been included in the 1979, 1990 and 1996 Schemes, bring before the Board many cases which are regulated by earlier Schemes, including some 1969 Scheme cases. The rules of assessment of 1969 cases differ in a number of important respects from those in the 1979 and 1990 Schemes, but those apparently obsolete rules nevertheless apply to any reconsideration of the assessment.

Until the Secretary of State exercises his powers under para 85 of the 1996 Scheme to abolish the Board, it will continue to decide old Scheme cases. The Board members will continue to exercise their powers under the 1990 and earlier Schemes in deciding eligibility and in assessing awards of compensation on common law principles (para 12, 1990 Scheme). This is likely to continue at least into 1999 on the basis of the two-year period suggested in the White Paper as the time needed by the Board to deal with most, if not all of the cases already lodged before 1 April 1996.

When the Secretary of State decides that it is appropriate to do so, he will specify 'the transfer date' referred to in para 85 at which time 'the Board will cease to exist' and 'all its records of current and past applications' will be transferred to the Authority. From 'the transfer date' the Authority and the Panel will exercise all the powers of the then defunct Board in respect of all unfinished old Scheme cases, in addition to the 1996 Scheme cases. The Authority and the Panel must, however, apply old Scheme rules to all old Scheme cases which they take over after the transfer date.

It has to be remembered that one of the differences between the Board and the 'claims officers' of the Authority and the Panel is that all Board members are legally qualified whereas the Authority is made up of civil servants employed by the Home Office and the Scottish Office; the Panel membership contains a number of lawyers and also members of other professions.

The 1990 Scheme and earlier Schemes are stated to be 'administered by the Criminal Injuries Compensation Board, which will be assisted by appropriate staff' (para 1, 1990 Scheme). Shortly after the 1990 Scheme came into operation the Board used its powers of delegation under para 3 of that Scheme to authorise certain members of the Board's staff, who are civil servants, to decide some issues of eligibility and assessment. Although this was a delegation of Board members' powers under the Scheme, responsibility for the Scheme remained vested in the Board.

Continuity of experience will be assisted by the fact that since 1 April

1996, civil servants, who for some time exercised delegated authority to make decisions for the Board under the 1990 Scheme, became 'claims officers' making decisions in their own right under the 1996 Scheme.

Important decisions which must be decided by one or more Board members and which have not been delegated include:

(a) reconsideration of a case under para 23 (1990) on a hearing being requested with additional evidence (one Board Member);

(b) the decision whether or not to grant a hearing under para 24 (1990) (two Board Members);

(c) the decision whether to reopen a case after it has already been decided by the Board under para 13 (1990) (one Board Member); and, perhaps most important of all;

(d) the decision of all matters of eligibility and assessment at a hearing 'which, if granted, will be held before at least two members of the Board . . .' (para 22 (1990)).

In order to give the 1990 Scheme applicant whose case has not been decided by the Board before the transfer date the same right to have his case decided by a legally qualified Panel member, or members, as would have been the case had the Board continued in existence, para 86(a) and 86(b) expressly preserve the 1990 Scheme decision-making hierarchy by either one or two legally qualified members of the Panel in those specific cases where the 1990 Scheme would have required one or two Board members to make that decision.

On the same basis, para 86(c) provides that any decision which under the 1990 Scheme would have been made by the Chairman of the Criminal Injuries Compensation Board may be made by the Chairman of the Panel. This covers such 'chairman' decisions as refusal to waive the time limit for making the original application (para 4, 1990), refusal to reinstate a hearings cases dismissed for failure to attend without reasonable excuse (para 25, 1990), refusal to waive the time limit for requesting a hearing (para 22, 1990), or refusal to reopen a case on medical grounds (para 13, 1990).

Where an applicant wishes after the transfer date to have his or her old Scheme application reopened under the provisions for reopening contained in para 13 of the 1990 Scheme, para 87 of the 1996 Scheme provides that the Authority 'will deal with it according to the provisions of the old Scheme'.

In this way the 1996 Scheme ensures the principle: once a 1990 scheme case, always a 1990 Scheme case. Despite the changes introduced by the 1996 Scheme and even the provision that 'the Board will cease to exist' on the transfer date, pre- 1 April 1996 applications will, like a piece of Blackpool rock, say '1990' right the way through to the end.

Part B

Applications under the 1990 Scheme

This part deals with the procedure for determining applications under the 1990 Scheme. The requirements of para 22 of the 1990 Scheme are considered in the paragraphs which follow, starting with the commencement of the application to the Board, although it will be appreciated that the last originating applications under the 1990 Scheme would be those which were received by the Board on 31 March 1996. It is desirable for continuity, however, to explain the 1990 Scheme procedures from commencement through to final decision, as the 1996 Scheme expressly provides that all pre- 1 April 1996 applications will be governed by the 1990 Scheme.

1. Commencement of application

References to individual paragraphs or to 'the Scheme' in this part refer to the 1990 Scheme only.

Paragraph 22 of the 1990 Scheme requires that 'every application will be made to the Board in writing as soon as possible after the event on a form obtainable from the Board's offices'. The reason why the Board's form of application must be used, and there is no exception to this, is that it contains all the questions to which the Board needs answers with regard to the incident, reporting to the police and medical treatment and gives authority to the Board to make enquiries of employers, hospitals, doctors and police authorities. Only when the Board has the application form fully completed and signed by the applicant can the Board's staff make their own enquiries and thus begin the process of gathering all the information needed before the application can be adjudicated.

When the latter stage is reached, the Board will decide eligibility and, if this is decided in the applicant's favour, the Board will also assess compensation. If the decision on eligibility is that the application is outside the Scheme, for example on the grounds that the applicant did not report the incident to the police, or that the award should be reduced rather than refused altogether, the applicant will be notified of that decision and the reason for it.

> Where an award is made the applicant will be given a breakdown of the assessment of compensation, except where the Board consider this inappropriate.

Where there are special damages, such as loss of earnings and out-of-pocket expenses, these will generally be expressed as a separate figure within the total assessment of compensation. Occasionally, however, the Board allows an unspecified sum for the loss of earnings factor, where this is not capable of precise calculation, and makes an inclusive award which is one figure, without breakdown, for both the general and the special damages.

A provision in the 1990 Scheme enables the Board to give 'authority to determine applications on the Board's behalf' to members of the Board's staff. The extent of such delegation is a matter for the Board to decide.

When an applicant has been offered an award by the Board with which he is not satisfied, or has been refused an award or had an award reduced, 'he may apply for an oral hearing which, if granted, will be held before at least two members of the Board excluding any member who made the original decision'.

The provisions referred to in this last sentence contain several important variations of the Scheme as it stood before 1 February 1990, on which date the 1990 Scheme came into operation. The most important of these amendments is contained in the words 'if granted'.

Until 1 February 1990 the granting of a hearing was, in effect, as of right in all cases, but there was no provision in the earlier Schemes for reconsideration of the decision by the single member of the Board which the applicant sought to have reviewed.

The related provisions to the conditional granting of an oral hearing are contained in paras 23 and 24. These will be considered in detail but, put briefly, the provision in para 23 enables the single Board member to reconsider the initial decision if this appears to have been 'based on information ... which was incomplete or erroneous'. Thus in a number of cases such reconsideration will produce a decision which the applicant accepts, and the cost and delay of proceeding to a hearing are avoided.

The specific reference of the words 'if granted' in para 22 is to the provision in para 24, which sets out the precise criteria for granting or refusing a request for an oral hearing after the initial decision on the papers.

Returning to the details of para 22, it will be noted that a hearing will be 'held before at least two members of the Board excluding any member who made the original decision'. The 1979 and earlier Schemes provided for a hearing to be before three members of the Board, although the applicant could agree to adjudication by a two-member Board. If he did not agree, the application would be adjourned to the next available date with a view to its being heard by a three-member Board. After 1 February 1990 the applicant is required to accept adjudication by a two-member Board. The Board still convenes a three-member Board when it is practicable to do so, but with the pressure of cases awaiting a final hearing, the two-member Board arises more frequently than before.

The member of the Board who made the original decision (other than a referral) is disqualified from sitting as a member of the Board which adjudicates at the oral hearing.

Paragraph 22 (1990) continues:

> The application for a hearing must be made within three months of notification of the initial decision; however the Board may waive this time limit where an extension is requested with good reason within the three month

period, or where it is otherwise in the interests of justice to do so. A decision by the Chairman not to waive the time limit will be final.

Regarding the time limit, advisers should be aware that the Scheme expressly anticipates the need to obtain an extension, which arises from time to time. In so doing, it provides for a waiver 'where an extension is requested with good reason within the three month period'. It is important, therefore, to take stock of the situation well within the time limit so that, if more time is needed to obtain a further medical report or legal aid for advice, or for any other proper requirement in the preparation of the applicant's case, a request for extension of the Board's time limit can be lodged within the three-month period. It is the Board's practice to agree to an extension of, say, two or three months where this is appropriate to give an opportunity for the full preparation of the applicant's case, and where the request for extension has been lodged before the original three-month limit has expired.

Where the applicant or his advisers fail either to apply for an oral hearing or to request an extension within the time limit, the applicant's opportunity to be granted a hearing may be lost. The applicant who is out of time is required to explain and justify the delay and to persuade the Board that granting a hearing out of time is 'in the interests of justice'.

Compared with time limits for giving notice of appeal in other types of proceedings, three months is regarded as a very reasonable period within which to decide whether to request a hearing and, if necessary, to obtain advice before doing so. Where solicitors act for the applicant and fail to act in time to preserve their client's position, the Board may be inclined to take a stricter view than where, perhaps, a layman has overlooked the requirement or misunderstood the position.

The Scheme is not a statute, and an application to the Board is not litigation between conflicting parties. It is arguable that, having regard to the nature and purpose of the Scheme, it is not demonstrably fair to treat differently the applicant who in good faith instructs a solicitor to represent his interests and who then lets him down, and the layman who does not take the trouble to seek advice and falls into the same trap unaided. It is sometimes said that the first applicant has his remedies 'elsewhere', that is by an action against the solicitor in negligence, but that course with all its difficulties, uncertainties and expense is often not practicable.

The 'broad justice' approach rescues many cases, if narrowly; it is a situation which applicants and their advisers should be at pains to avoid by the simple expediency of reading the Scheme and meeting its stated time limit or exercising within that period the option of requesting an extension.

The burden of decision in such matters falls upon the chairman of the Board whose decision 'not to waive the time limit will be final'.

2. Referral to an oral hearing

Almost buried in the heart of para 22 of the 1990 Scheme is the valuable provision that the Board may refer an application straight to an oral hearing without deciding it at first instance on the papers. The option to refer in this way is used only in those cases where the Board member who would otherwise make the initial decision on eligibility, and also the assessment of compensation if the application is within the Scheme, considers that, on either of those two aspects, justice cannot be done to the case without the benefit of hearing oral evidence.

This part of the Scheme states:

> It will also be open to a member of the Board, or a designated member of the Board's staff, where he considers that he cannot make a just and proper decision himself to refer the application for a hearing before at least two members of the Board, one of whom may be the member who, in such a case, decided to refer the application to a hearing.

The circumstances in which the Board member may consider that he or she cannot make a just and proper decision on the papers vary greatly. Eligibility decisions which can prove very difficult to decide to the point that a decision on the papers alone may not do justice in the case may include situations such as affray, which can involve large numbers of witnesses with much conflicting evidence and no clear picture as to the part that the applicant may have played, and situations such as neighbour disputes which become violent with no independent evidence, and cases of alleged rape where there has been no prosecution of the alleged assailant. In these and many other situations an assessment of the applicant's credibility may be of the essence in arriving at a just decision, and this can be tested only be hearing oral evidence from the applicant and from any other witnesses, and from the investigating police officer.

The procedure at the Board's hearings is considered in the next chapter. It is appropriate to make reference at this point, however, in dealing with the Board's power to refer a case to a hearing under para 22 (1990), to the evidence of the investigating police officer. As the Board is not restricted by the laws of evidence as they apply in a court, the Board may 'take into account any relevant hearsay (or) opinion' (para 25) (1990). The investigating police officer may therefore give evidence to the Board not only of details of fact established by the police investigation of the alleged offence. He may also be asked by the Board for his opinion on matters relating to the investigation, including his assessment of the credibility of the various accounts given by witnesses and in particular that of the applicant and, where he has been interviewed, the alleged assailant. The officer may have interviewed, say, four or five witnesses, whereas the Board might perhaps hear oral evidence from merely the applicant and the investigating officer.

The weight which the Board places upon such opinion in any particular case is a matter for the Board members in the light of their experience to decide. The professional view which an experienced officer formed with regard to a particular case can be of great value to the Board and to the applicant.

Questions of credibility may also arise in relation to medical evidence. A case may have a long and complex medical history, or an applicant may be claiming loss of earnings for, say, 18 months when the medical evidence suggests that the level of injury would not justify more than a few weeks off work.

Referral under para 22 (1990) is a procedure used sparingly, however, as in the majority of cases the matters to be considered under the Scheme will be apparent from the papers and the experience of the Board members, or of the designated member of the Board's staff, will enable them to make the decision on the basis of the evidence which the papers alone provide.

Where a case has been referred to a hearing, the 1990 Scheme makes clear that the Board member so referring the case may be one of the two or three Board members before whom the case is heard. It thus differs from the general rule which excludes the single member of the Board who decided the case initially from hearing the case on appeal.

3. Entitlement to an award

The final sentence of para 22 of the 1990 Scheme contains a principle which is entirely separate from the main theme of that paragraph and, short though it is, should stand on its own in the text of the Scheme. It states:

> An applicant will have no title to an award offered until the Board have received notification in writing that he accepts it.

Lawyers brought up on the law of contract, and the formation of a contract according to the principles of offer and acceptance, need to learn a different principle regarding the acceptance of an 'offer' of compensation by the Board and the effect of 'acceptance' of that offer. Entitlement to an award arises only when the Board has actually received the acceptance of the award signed by the applicant.

A defined point of time at which the applicant becomes entitled to the award has particular importance where the applicant dies after the offer of the award and before the Board has made payment. If the applicant has signed the acceptance of the award but it has not been posted before he dies there is no title to the award and the offer lapses. If the acceptance has been posted but not received by the Board when the applicant dies there is likewise no title; however, the Board may possibly consider sympathetically a case where the applicant has signed and posted the acceptance and dies before the acceptance is received by the Board, if in the ordinary course of post it could have been expected to have been received by the Board before the applicant's death. Any such consideration would, however, be *ex gratia* as there would be no title to the award.

The death of the applicant before he has become entitled to the award under this provision in the Scheme can be a double blow to the applicant's dependants: not only must they contend with the bereavement itself, but also the financial loss may be considerable as the applicant's claim dies with him. If his death is attributable to the injury, the death may bring into operation a fresh claim by dependants under para 15 (1990). One of the mischances which can arise is where the death is not attributable to the injury which is the subject of the award offered, but coincides with the offer of an award to which there is no title at the time of death. Applicants and their advisers should bear in mind this risk, which is present in every case, particularly where the applicant is elderly or in poor health, and see that, if the offer is considered acceptable, the acceptance is signed and posted forthwith.

The Board could do nothing to assist in a case in which the applicant, who was infirm, was assisted by a voluntary agency, whose representative went to the applicant's home to obtain the applicant's signature to the acceptance of the Board's offer. After the acceptance was signed there was a delay of a few days before it was posted. When it was posted on the applicant's behalf by the agent the applicant had already died, although the agent was not aware of this. The Board received the acceptance signed by the applicant, but once the facts and sequence of events had been established, the offer had unfortunately lapsed on the death of the applicant before the Board had received the acceptance. No award could be made.

This important tail-piece to para 22 (1990) regarding title must also be kept in mind in relation to the tail-piece to para 12 (1990). The latter provides that the Board may reduce or further reduce an award or refuse an award altogether 'at any stage before receiving notification of acceptance of a final award'. This provision has been considered in an earlier chapter and the point is made that, although the last sentence of para 12 begins with the words 'In a case in which an interim award has been made', the principle which follows those words is an important one and is general in its application. It is related closely to the last sentence of para 22 as the latter is the legal basis on which the principle contained in the last sentence of para 12 rests. It is precisely because the applicant has not obtained 'title' to an award that he may in certain circumstances lose his entitlement to it either partly or wholly.

This arises most commonly where the Board receives information regarding criminal convictions or additional convictions recorded against the applicant after an offer of an award has been made and before an acceptance of it has been received. The Board may reduce or further reduce or refuse altogether to make an award in such a case if the information in the Board's hands makes that decision appropriate.

The position is the same where the applicant has requested a hearing, and subsequent information received by the Board before the hearing renders the original offer inappropriate. Once the applicant has requested a hearing, there is strictly no longer any offer for him to accept. The request for a hearing is itself a rejection of the offer (*R v Criminal Injuries Compensation*

Board, ex parte Earls (1992) – see Appendix 1, page 280). The latter thus lapses and the whole matter is then entirely at large as to both eligibility and assessment. The Board is unfettered by the earlier lapsed offer, and its further consideration of the merits of the application is by way of a 'fresh start', based on all the information then before the Board.

A decision by the Board to allow an applicant who has requested a hearing and who subsequently asks that he be allowed to accept the single member's award to do so is essentially a fresh offer of an award equal to the award originally offered. The latter having been rejected by the request for hearing, there is, as a matter of law, no 'single member's award' on the table. The fresh offer of the same award is therefore a matter wholly in the discretion of the Board and is not an entitlement within the applicant's power to accept simply by deciding not to proceed after all with his hearing.

The 1996 Scheme deals with these matters in paras 53 to 55, 'Reconsideration of decisions'.

4. Hearings

Paragraphs 22 to 27 of the 1990 Scheme regulate all aspects of hearings in cases which have to be decided under the terms of that Scheme. The provisions of para 22 have already been considered.

References to paragraphs of the Scheme in this part relate to 1990 (or earlier) Scheme cases only.

(a) Application for a hearing (para 23, 1990)

Paragraph 23 commences:

> Applications for hearings must be made in writing on a form supplied by the Board and should be supported by reasons together with any additional evidence which may assist the Board to decide whether a hearing should be granted.

The fundamental change in the 1990 Scheme from its predecessors was the removal of the *right* to a hearing. The 1979 Scheme provided that if an applicant was not satisfied with the initial decision 'he will be entitled to a hearing'. Under the 1990 Scheme the applicant must establish that he meets the criteria for a hearing contained in para 24 before he is entitled to one. Under earlier Schemes the applicant was asked to give reasons for his requesting a hearing, although he was not required to do so. Since the 1990 Scheme came into effect the applicant must state his reasons and these must be sufficient to justify a hearing.

Paragraph 23 continues:

> If the reasons in support of the application suggest that the initial decision was based on information obtained by or submitted to the Board which was incomplete or erroneous, the application may be remitted for reconsideration by the member of the Board who made the initial decision,

or by another member of the Board where this is not practicable or where the initial decision was made by a member of the Board's staff.

This provision was one of the most useful and beneficial of the amendments introduced in the 1990 Scheme; it had long been apparent that there was a need to have such a provision to deal with cases where new information made reconsideration the most appropriate course. Before 1 February 1990, however, the only way in which a single member's decision could be reconsidered was to proceed to a hearing.

The applicant is still required under the 1990 Scheme either to accept the initial decision or to request a hearing. If the terms of the request for hearing suggest to the Board's staff that the case is suitable for reconsideration by the Board member, the provision in para 23 enabling this to be done will be acted upon. New information may reach the Board at any time between the date on which the initial decision is made and the date of the hearing, if a hearing is granted. The case may therefore be referred for reconsideration at any time between those two dates.

The advantages of this procedure to the applicant, to the Board and also to other applicants are considerable. A case which does not need to wait for a hearing or fill a hearing slot in due course, making the latter available to another case which does need to be heard, can achieve a more expedited reconsideration at much less cost.

The gap in the earlier Schemes which had no provision for reconsideration was most obvious in those cases where the need for correction was clear, such as where the application had been refused on the basis of a police report stating that the incident had not been reported, and further enquiry had disclosed that the incident had indeed been reported.

It is highly desirable that cases which are stood on their head by new information can be dealt with by a straightforward procedure for varying the initial decision. Not all cases, however, are so simple, having no obvious error of fact requiring correction.

The provision is widely drawn. 'If the reasons (for a hearing) ... suggest that the initial decision was based on information ... which was incomplete or erroneous', it may be remitted. The above example of 'reporting' illustrates the applicability of 'erroneous', which will often be a reasonably straightforward matter to decide. 'Incomplete', however, is a term which is much more susceptible to variation of interpretation. Again there will be simple cases of 'incomplete' information. Paragraph 23 has been used, for example, in an assessment case where the Board allowed loss of earnings from employment, but was only informed after the initial decision that there was also a loss of earnings claim from a second, part-time job. What constitutes 'incomplete' medical evidence, however, may create difficulties. In a case, for example, where the applicant appeared to have suffered minor injuries, and the application has been refused under para 5 of the Scheme as not justifying at least the minimum award, the application for a hearing may have with it a fresh medical report. This may elaborate upon the injuries and bring to light additional symptoms attributable to the injury which were not in the medical evidence when the initial decision was made. Such a case would be likely to be remitted to the single member of the Board for reconsideration under para 23. If, however, the report adds little of substance so that it could not be said that the initial decision was based upon incomplete or erroneous evidence, it would fall to be considered under para 24, which regulates the granting or refusal of a hearing, rather than 23. Paragraph 23 has proved to be a very beneficial provision, adding as it does to the flexibility of the Scheme and facilitating the appropriate treatment of cases. This paragraph is primarily a means of providing for reconsideration by the single Board member where the new and additional evidence makes it clear that such reconsideration is appropriate and where the additional evidence suggests that a reversal or variation of the initial decision, made without the benefit of that evidence, is probable.

If the criteria for referral back to the Board member under para 23 are not set fairly high, in terms of the probability of the initial decision being altered, the provision would prove more burdensome than beneficial. The reason for this is practical. If too high a proportion of cases were to have two bites at the initial decision stage, the administration of the Scheme would become increasingly overburdened with unresolved cases and the purpose of the provision would be defeated.

However, this consideration must be balanced with the need, for similar practical reasons, to avoid adding to the list of cases requiring a hearing those cases which are seen, at the point where a hearing is requested, to be capable of resolution by submission for reconsideration by a single member of the Board.

Submission for reconsideration is not a right; the applicant may not insist on it by, for example, electing for submission for reconsideration rather than requesting a hearing. He has no such choice. His choice is either to accept the original decision or to request a hearing. The application *may* be remitted for reconsideration if the additional evidence and reasons given for a hearing 'suggest' that the original decision was based on incomplete or erroneous information. The decision whether or not so to remit a case under para 23 is made by a member of the Board's staff.

The three-month limitation period for requesting a hearing after reconsideration starts from the date of notification of the reconsidered decision.

(b) Entitlement to a hearing (para 24, 1990)

Paragraph 24 is the 'partner' to para 23 which created a new discretion to remit a case back to the single Board member. Paragraph 24 specifies strict criteria for entitlement to a hearing after the initial decision, and any reconsidered decision, have been made.

Paragraph 24 begins 'An applicant will be entitled to an oral hearing only if –' and then proceeds to state the three alternative bases upon which an applicant may be entitled to a hearing. It concludes:

> An application for a hearing which appears likely to fail the foregoing criteria may be reviewed by not less than two members of the Board other than any member who made the initial or reconsidered decision. If it is considered on review that if any facts or conclusions which are disputed were resolved in the applicant's favour it would have made no difference to the initial or reconsidered decision, or that for any other reason an oral hearing would serve no useful purpose, the application for a hearing will be refused. A decision to refuse an application for a hearing will be final.

Paragraphs 23 and 24 represented a fundamental change in the rules for the administration of the Scheme. Since its inception, the Scheme had provided for an initial decision by a Board member, a right to a hearing if that decision was not accepted by the applicant, and a hearing. A case was necessarily at 'single member' stage or it was a 'hearings' case. The transition from one to the other was automatic on receipt of the request for hearing by the applicant, as the hearing was as of right. The hearings door was open to all applicants regardless of the strength or weakness of their case.

These two paragraphs created a new stage in the consideration of cases which is both administrative and substantive. This intermediate stage created by para 24 is a clearing house between 'single member' and 'hearings'. The 1990 provisions require that each request for a hearing is examined on its merits by a member of the Board's staff to consider whether it is a para 23 re-submission to a single Board member, a para 24 submission to 'not less than two members of the Board', or a clear-cut 'hearings' case. Whenever the Board receives a request for a hearing under the 1990 Scheme its merits have to be examined according to the criteria laid down in these two paragraphs and a decision made to proceed in one of these three directions.

A consideration of parts (a), (b) and (c) of para 24 makes quite clear that only those cases which have no prospect of success at a hearing will be refused at this stage.

Just as the purpose of para 23 is to make it possible for the single member to review his decision in the light of new evidence, and thus avoid the cost and delay of a hearing which may not be necessary to achieve the justice of the case, so the purpose of para 24 is to weed out hopeless cases where to proceed to a hearing would give the applicant no realistic prospect of varying the initial decision.

The purpose in both cases is to render the system more efficient while safeguarding the right to a hearing where something genuinely needs to be decided.

Category (a) allows a hearing if the application was disallowed under para 5 (on the grounds that the injury did not merit compensation of at least the minimum award) 'and it appears that ... the Board *might* make an award' (author's italics).

Category (b) allows a hearing if an award was made in the initial decision 'and it appears that ... the Board might make a *larger* award' (author's italics).

Both (a) and (b) require the Board, when considering a hearings request under para 24, to apply 'the principles set out in paragraph 26' of the Scheme in deciding whether the Board at a hearing might make an award (in a category (a) case) or a larger award (in a category (b) case).

Paragraph 26 states that the amount of compensation as assessed in the initial decision 'will not be altered' at the hearing 'except upon the same principles as the Court of Appeal in England or the Court of Session in Scotland would alter an assessment of damages made by a trial judge'. Put simply, this means that the Board at a hearing will not 'tinker' with an assessment made by the single Board member. It will alter it only if a significantly different award is appropriate in the light of the evidence then before the Board. The Court of Appeal, and therefore the Board, will not make marginal adjustments to the assessment of damages or compensation made at first instance. The reason for this is that there is no strictly correct figure for damages for a particular injury, and the court, and therefore the Board which is required to follow the common law of damages under para 12 of the 1990 Scheme, works within a range of awards, not to a specific figure. If the award made at first instance is within the accepted range, it will not on the same evidence be altered at a hearing to a different figure within that range.

Suppose that an award of £3,000 was made by the single member, and the applicant requested a hearing which was referred to two Board members to consider under para 24(b). The Board members would be required to ask themselves the question: is the original assessment, based upon the evidence now before the Board, within the range of awards made by the court in similar cases? If the answer to that question is affirmative, the request for an oral hearing will be refused.

The two Board members considering the merits of the request for a hearing will have before them whatever additional representations the applicant wishes to make, such as further medical reports, statements regarding continuing symptoms, difficulties at work or loss of earnings caused by the injury. The Board's procedure under para 24 makes clear to the applicant that his request for a hearing is to be considered under that paragraph and invites submissions to be made in support of that request. All available evidence is produced and, together with any additional written submissions by the applicant, placed before the Board members who are to consider the merits of the request for a hearing.

If the Board considering a para 24 referral decides that the range within which the award should be assessed is, say £2,750 to £3,500, the application of the para 26 principle (against 'tinkering' with the original award) would mean that the applicant who was offered £3,000 initially would not be entitled to an oral hearing.

It is most important that the applicant whose request for a hearing is referred under para 24 makes all possible representations and sends to the Board all medical or other evidence which would assist the Board in making a proper assessment.

The last sentence of para 24 states: 'A decision to refuse an application for a hearing will be final'. It is essential, therefore, that applicants and their advisers ensure that any evidence, particularly medical evidence or substantial loss of earnings schedules which may not have been before the Board at the time of the initial decision, are ready and made available to a 'para 24' Board, as the right to a hearing may otherwise be lost.

Although para 24 contains no express provision for so doing, the 'para 24' Board – where it is considered appropriate to do so – sometimes increases the single member's award which the applicant may then accept, although he may still proceed to a hearing if the increased award is not acceptable, as an increased offer by a 'para 24' Board is treated as an increased offer by a single member after reconsideration of the case under para 23.

The third category of applicants entitled to an oral hearing is described in part (c) of para 24 as those cases where:

> no award or a reduced award was made and there is a dispute as to the material facts or conclusions upon which the initial or reconsidered decision was based or it appears that the decision may have been wrong in law or principle.

These words permit hearings in a great number of cases, as there is often a dispute as to material facts. The dispute of facts may be between the applicant's version of events and the alleged assailant's version where the applicant's 'conduct' is in issue under para 6(c), or the applicant may claim that he reported the incident under para 6(a) and the police file reveals no record of the incident being reported, and so on *ad infinitum*.

There is an entitlement to a hearing if it is apparent that the initial decision 'may have been wrong in law or principle'. This would include an erroneous interpretation of the terms of the Scheme.

The paragraph qualifies the 'open door' which (c) might provide where 'there is a dispute as to the material facts or conclusions' by stating:

> If it is considered on review that if any facts or conclusions which are disputed were resolved in the applicant's favour it would have made no difference to the initial or reconsidered decision, or that for any other reason an oral hearing would serve no useful purpose, the application for a hearing will be refused.

There are many cases in which the applicant requests a hearing where the request in its terms admits certain material facts, including those which caused his application to be refused in the first instance, and protests certain others which, even if true, could not cause the Board at a hearing to alter the original decision. Examples of this situation are:

(a) 'I admit that I went round to Mr Jones' house to sort him out, but I did this only because he had hit my child. Any parent would do the same. When he came to the door I hit him. He then attacked me and injured me.'

In the above example, there would be little prospect of a Board at a hearing altering the initial decision to refuse an award on the grounds of the applicant's 'conduct' under para 6(c).

(b) 'I did not report the assault because I knew the assailant was a violent man and I thought I would get more trouble if I told the police.'

This applicant would have little prospect of an award at a hearing as he had failed to inform the police under para 6(a) – likewise the applicant who has been turned down on the grounds of his criminal convictions under para 6(c), and who requests a hearing protesting:

(c) 'I admit I have a bad criminal record but I've been punished for my crimes and my convictions have nothing to do with my being assaulted.'

It is a requirement of the 1990 Scheme that the Board considers all the applicant's convictions. If the applicant had a number of recent convictions for serious offences resulting in custodial sentences, his request for a hearing would be referred under para 24 to a two-member Board and would almost certainly be refused.

Each of the above examples focuses on only one issue, and is merely to illustrate the para 24 (1990) process. In reality the Board has before it all the circumstances of a case which it will weigh in the balance before reaching a decision as to whether or not to grant a hearing.

(c) The hearing

Paragraph 25 (1990) commences as follows:

> It will be for the applicant to make out his case at the hearing ...

The burden of proof is thus clearly stated to be upon the applicant. It is not for the Board acting through its staff to prepare and prove the case. It is for the applicant to do this,

> ... and where appropriate this will extend to satisfying the Board that compensation should not be withheld or reduced under the terms of paragraph 6 or paragraph 8.

Paragraph 25 thus requires the applicant to satisfy the Board on the evidence that his application is not caught by the provisions in the Scheme by which an award may be reduced or withheld. It is this negative requirement which has not been met by an applicant whose application is disallowed on the grounds of the applicant's conduct, with the words:

> I am not satisfied that the applicant was not the first to resort to violence ...

The applicant must establish that his application is within the terms of the Scheme in both the positive sense that he has sustained injury directly attributable to a crime of violence and in the negative sense that there is no aspect of his case which disqualifies it under those provisions which give the Board a discretion (such as para 6 (1990)) or a duty (such as para 7 (1990) – possible benefit to the assailant) to reduce or refuse an award.

It is for the applicant to satisfy the Board 'that there is no possibility that a person responsible for causing the injury will benefit from an award' under para 7 by which 'compensation will not be payable' unless the Board is so satisfied.

Reference should be made to preceding chapters for a consideration of the issues which may need to be decided by the Board at a hearing, as these can arise from almost any part of the Scheme. The principles within the Scheme which qualify, or may disqualify, an application are the same whether the application is being considered for the purpose of initial decision on the papers or is being decided by a Board after an oral hearing.

Matters most frequently in issue are whether the crime of violence has been proved (para 4(a) (1990)) and whether the injury is directly attributable to that crime, plus matters of non-reporting, delay in reporting, failure to co-operate with the police in bringing the offender to justice (para 6(a)) and the applicant's conduct or character and criminal convictions (para 6(c)).

Injuries involving motor vehicles will generally have to be considered with reference to para 11 (1990), and the main issue in applications arising from a fatal injury (para 15 (1990)) will frequently be the question of the conduct and character of the deceased.

The requirements of para 8 (1990) must be considered in cases where the injuries involve persons living in the same household; para 8 contains rules which relate only to those cases, to take account of the particular difficulties of proving violence within the context of a family, and to test the appropriateness or otherwise of an award being made in such cases.

A hearing is a fresh start. It is not an appeal from the initial decision. This principle was considered by the Court of Appeal in *R v Criminal Injuries Compensation Board ex parte Earls* (1982) – see Appendix 1, page 280 – in which the applicant had been offered an interim award of £500 by the single member, subject to a reduction of one-third by reason of the applicant's own conduct. The applicant rejected the decision of the single member and requested a hearing. The applicant then died. The Court of Appeal upheld the Board's decision at a hearing that if the applicant rejects the initial decision the whole matter is at large.

This principle should be committed to memory by anyone concerned with applications to the Board, as it is one of the most important and fundamental rules of the Scheme. Regarding the interim award offered by the single member, the Court of Appeal ruled that there was nothing to vest in the applicant unless and until a further decision was made in the applicant's favour at a hearing by the Board, as the request for a hearing was a total rejection of the single member's decision which included the offered interim award.

Having considered the terms of the Scheme and the steps by which an applicant may either accept the initial decision or reject it *in toto*, Lord Justice Waller, quoting from the judgment of Lord Parker in the earlier case of *R v Criminal Injuries Compensation Board ex parte Lain* (1967), stated: 'This is in no sense an appeal but merely a renewal of the application, and I can see nothing wrong in the three members hearing and deciding the application *de novo*'.

Paragraph 25 states:

> The Board will reach their decision solely in the light of evidence brought out at the hearing, and all the information and evidence made available to the Board members at the hearing will be made available to the applicant at, if not before, the hearing.

When a hearing has been requested and granted, the Board's procedure in preparation for a hearing is as follows:

(a) A bundle of documents is prepared and copied including the application form, the letter of notification of the initial decision, the request for a hearing, medical reports already on the Board's file, a copy of the Scheme and the Board's notes on procedure at hearings. This bundle is sent to the applicant or his solicitors, so that the applicant can see what documents the Board already has and so that he can decide what additional evidence on either eligibility (if his claim has been refused or reduced in the initial decision) or assessment he may wish to prepare and submit to the Board in readiness for hearing. This may involve the need for additional medical evidence or a calculation and supporting evidence in relation to any loss of earnings being claimed by the applicant.

(b) A summary of the issues to be decided by the Board at the hearing is prepared, usually by the Board's advocate, and sent to the appliant or his solicitors. The summary will refer to the paragraphs in the Scheme relevant to those issues, for example delay in reporting, or conduct. The summary will also state which witnesses are to be invited by the Board, it being a matter for the applicant to decide whether to invite any other witnesses whose evidence he wishes the Board to hear. The Board can only invite witnesses. It has no power to compel their attendance.

    Where the alleged assailant is identified and has not been convicted of the alleged assault upon which the applicant relies in his application for compensation, and eligibility is in issue at the hearing, the Board will invite the alleged assailant to attend the hearing and give evidence if he or she wishes to do so. The Board will generally also invite to the hearing a police officer involved in the investigation of the incident in cases where police evidence is relevant to eligibility, particularly where the points in question include delay in reporting, non-co-operation in the prosecution of the alleged offender or the applicant's own conduct in the context of the incident giving rise to the claim.

(c) When the Board's staff consider the case ready for hearing, notice of the listing of the case for hearing will be sent out, giving the applicant the time, date and venue of the hearing. At the same time any witnesses invited by the Board will be given similar notice inviting them to attend.

(d) Before the hearing the Board's staff will prepare copies of any witness statements provided to the Board by the police and particulars of any convictions where these are to be produced to the Board and to the applicant at the hearing.

The reason why police statements and copies of convictions are produced to the applicant only on the day of the hearing, and not before, is that the Board, at an early stage in the history of the Scheme, secured the co-operation of the Chief Constables in making witness statements available to the Board to assist in its adjudication of applications under the Scheme, without the police having first to obtain the consent of the witnesses to do so, by giving an undertaking that the statements of witnesses provided to the Board by the police would not be disclosed before the actual hearing. This procedure was considered and judicially approved in *R v Chief Constable of Cheshire ex parte Berry* (1985) (see Appendix 1). In that case application had been refused under para 6(c) relating to the applicant's conduct, the Board member not being 'satisfied that the applicant did not provoke the attack upon him'. The applicant requested a hearing and requested of the Chief Constable details of convictions, which the Chief Constable refused. The applicant sought an order of mandamus (a High Court procedure for compelling the performance of a public duty) requiring their production. Nolan J (as he then was) reviewed the Board's procedure and the wording of para 23 of the 1979 Scheme, the provisions of which in respect of the Board's conduct of hearings were similar to para 25 of the 1990 Scheme.

The Board members who are to hear a case have the same papers (the Board's bundle) as those sent to the applicant, with the exception of the witness statements supplied to the Board by the police, the latter not being produced to the applicant and his adviser until he arrives at the Board's hearing centre. The practice with regard to convictions is similar.

Neither the Board members hearing the case nor the applicant have copies of the police report provided at an earlier stage by the police to the Board, even though this would have been before the Board member who made the original decision on the papers. The explanation for this is that the evidence of the police is given orally at the hearing.

The substance of Mr Berry's case to the High Court was that receiving copies of the witness statements on the morning of the hearing deprived him of the right to put his case adequately before the Board. The learned judge considered the reasons behind the Board's practice in regard to statements and the need for confidentiality, which the person who had made the statement to the police would expect, and the undertaking given by the Board to the Chief Constables to preserve this confidentiality. The court accepted that the Board had a duty to protect the statements from improper use.

The learned judge observed: 'It is primarily in order to discharge this obligation that the Board retains custody and control of the statements, discloses them to applicants only on the morning of the hearing, and recovers them from the applicants before they leave.' The court noted that it was the Board's practice to agree to an adjournment if the applicant considered that he was unable to read through the statements before his case came on for hearing. In practice this rarely occurs. The Board members hearing the case usually read the police statements with the Board's papers relating to the case the evening before the hearings, together with ten or so other cases listed for the following day.

Mr Berry's complaint was that the Chief Constable was acting in breach of a public duty in placing the statements in the Board's hands on these terms, as these amounted to an unfair and improper use. The learned judge agreed that Mr Berry's common law rights included 'the right to a fair hearing before the Board'. Applying the Wednesbury principle, the learned judge did not consider that the practice of the Board, in relation to the disclosure of statements at the hearing, was in breach of the principles of natural justice, and he held that the Chief Constable was not acting perversely in limiting his disclosure of the witness statements to the Board, and denying them to Mr Berry, knowing that the Board would show them to Mr Berry only on the morning of the hearing. The application to the court seeking an order for prior disclosure therefore failed. This decision was expressly confirmed by the High Court in *R v Criminal Injuries Compensation Board ex parte Brady* (1987), in which case the Board was respondent. See Appendix 1 page 283.

Paragraph 25 continues:

> The applicant and a member of the Board's staff will be able to call, examine and cross-examine witnesses. The Board will be entitled to take into account any relevant hearsay, opinion or written evidence, whether or not the author gives oral evidence at the hearing.

The Board's summary, which is sent to the applicant some weeks before the hearing, states which if any witnesses the Board will invite to the hearing. 'It will be for the applicant to make out his case at the hearing', and this includes inviting such witnesses as he considers may be able to assist his case.

The Board will not necessarily invite all known witnesses. Where the witnesses are friends of the applicant who the applicant states were present when he alleges he was attacked, and there is no police statement provided to the Board by such witnesses, it will generally be for the applicant to invite those witnesses if he wishes to do so.

It is helpful to see the Board's rules and practices in relation to hearings in the practical context of a day's hearings. The Board's advocate will usually list about ten or twelve cases on each hearings day. In many cases the trial of the crime of violence on which the application depends lasted days or weeks in the Crown Court. In such cases as murder or affray there may be a wealth of statements and documentary evidence. The Board's advocate, having obtained the police papers, will have selected from this cornucopia those statements and documents which relate to the points which the Board must decide. It may be that three-quarters of the police file is of no assistance to the Board. If the matter before the Board is the applicant's (or the deceased's) 'conduct' under para 6(c), and the 'crime of violence' which the police file was prepared in order to prove has been proved in a Crown Court trial and the assailant convicted, the Board needs to hear only those witnesses whose evidence goes to the 'conduct' of the applicant (or the deceased, in a 'fatal' application).

It is unusual, therefore, for the applicant and his advisers to be handed more than half a dozen statements to read through on their arrival at the Board's hearings centre. In most cases there are only two or three, even where the prosecution file may have been very substantial.

Where there is no alternative but to put in numerous witness statements for consideration by the Board, and likewise for the applicant to consider and question as he sees fit in the conduct of his application before the Board, the Board's staff may, if requested to do so, make arrangements for an earlier reading of the statements by the applicant or his adviser, provided that those arrangements comply with the Board's undertaking to retain control of the statements on the basis of which they have been made available to the Board by the Chief Constable.

In cases where the statements of perhaps ten or more witnesses indicate that they are pertinent witnesses to the matters to be decided by the Board, all of those witnesses will usually be invited by the Board to attend. If the Board is to read a witness's statement as relevant to the matters for decision at the hearing, the person who made the statement will be invited. This is necessary – otherwise the applicant would be denied the opportunity to cross-examine the witness at the hearing on aspects of the witness's evidence with which the applicant may disagree.

Even though invited to attend, civilian witnesses usually do not do so where they are not connected with the applicant as a relative or friend. The alleged assailant attends the hearing in only a minority of cases. Regardless of the number of witness statements the Board and the applicant may have read before the hearing commences it is unusual for the Board to hear oral evidence from more than the applicant and the police officer and two or three other witnesses.

These factors put into context the part of para 25 which states:

> The Board will be entitled to take into account any relevant hearsay, opinion or written evidence, whether or not the author gives oral evidence at the hearing.

The Board may have before it statements of witnesses, including those of the assailant and his friends, which are completely damning of the applicant's 'conduct' in relation to the incident giving rise to the applicant's claim. The applicant may cross-examine any witnesses who attend and give evidence and he may make submissions in relation to the allegations in those statements. Where the Board has heard the oral evidence of the applicant but not the assailant or his associates, it will apply its considerable experience in weighing the evidence which it has read and heard in deciding where the truth probably lies and whether the applicant has discharged the burden placed upon him by the Scheme 'to make out his case at the hearing'.

The burden of proof, as has already been noted, is the burden of proof which rests upon a plaintiff in a civil case, that is, to prove his case on the balance of probabilities, and not the more onerous burden of proof upon a prosecutor in a criminal trial to prove the case beyond reasonable doubt. It has also been noted that the applicant must not only establish that his injury was on the balance of probabilities directly attributable to a crime of violence. He must also satisfy the Board that on the balance of probabilities his own 'conduct' (or non-co-operation with the police, or whatever negative factor may be in issue in the particular case) was not such that an award would be inappopriate. It is worth noting that the 1996 Scheme (para 64) expressly provides for the burden of proof to be on the 'balance of probabilities' – this has always been the practice of the Board, although not previously expressed in earlier Schemes.

The evidence of the police officer witness will often be of great assistance to the Board in such adjudication. As the Scheme permits opinion and hearsay evidence the police officer is able to tell the Board what was his view of factors on which the Board otherwise has no evidence or only the applicant's account of what occurred. This evidence is as often helpful to the applicant's case as adverse to it. The police officer will in many cases have interviewed the assailant and other witnesses very soon after the incident which gave rise to the applicant's injury. His assessment is therefore of value, as it is based upon more first-hand evidence than the Board has heard.

The applicant and any other person giving evidence to the Board may be examined or cross-examined by the Board's advocate and may also be questioned by the Board members to bring out the evidence material to the issues which the Board needs to decide.

In cases where the applicant recalls little or nothing of the incident giving rise to the application the facts established by the police investigation may be the only evidence the Board has.

Of the 50 or so cases which came before the Board in the course of one week's hearings in 1990, three relied almost entirely upon police evidence to establish whether or not the application was within the Scheme. Each of these three cases involved serious injury. One of the cases involved a house fire at night which caused the death of several members of the applicant's family; in the second the applicant had been left completely blind as a result of a head injury, and in the third, a severe penetrating chest injury had left the applicant in a wheelchair and with no recollection of the incident. In all three cases the results of thorough investigation by the police gave the Board an invaluable insight into the circumstances of the incident.

In two of these three cases, only one police officer gave evidence. The provision of the Scheme which permits hearsay evidence means that in this type of case one police officer with detailed knowledge of the investigation can give evidence of the results of investigation by perhaps 40 of his colleagues. This evidence can be given in half an hour or so of hearing time, resulting in the Board having had the best available evidence of the circumstances of the applicant's injury.

If this evidence plus the professional opinion of the investigating officer (which is usually sought in such difficult cases) lead to the conclusion that the applicant's injury was on the balance of probabilities directly attributable to a crime of violence, the Board is able to make an award. This is possible even if the offender is never identified or apprehended.

In cases where the injuries were fatal, the police officer as witness may give oral evidence to the Board of the result of the coroner's inquest. Where there has been a trial the police officer may give evidence not only of the outcome of the trial as a matter of record, but also of such matters as the nature of the alleged assailant's defence, for example self-defence, and whether or not the applicant co-operated with the prosecution by attending court and giving evidence.

At the conclusion of the police officer's oral evidence, the chairman of the Board will generally thank the police officer for attending and assisting the Board by giving evidence at the hearing. This is not merely a courtesy; no witness can be compelled to attend a Board hearing and this applies to police witnesses just as to any other; it is simply stating a fact when the chairman, thanking the officer for attending, states 'We could not operate the Scheme without your co-operation and we are obliged for your assistance in this case'. The blind applicant and the applicant in the wheelchair in the cases referred to above both received full awards.

Applications to the Board are confidential, and para 27 of the Scheme states:

> Procedure at hearings will be as informal as is consistent with the proper determination of applications, and hearings will in general be in private.

When a hearing commences, the only persons in the hearings room will be the Board members, the Board's advocate and hearings clerk, who are both officers of the Board, and the applicant and his or her representative. In cases where the applicant is a minor, a parent may also be present unless he or she is to give evidence. The wife or husband or friend of the applicant, provided she or he is not giving evidence, may also sit in if the applicant so requests, subject to the discretion of the chairman to permit it.

All witnesses who are to give evidence remain outside the hearings room until called in to give their evidence, and are released and leave the room as soon as their evidence is concluded. No witnesses will therefore be present and hear the decision of the Board and the award, if one is made, except those persons authorised by the chairman to be present. The privacy of the application and of the hearing, including the Board's decision, is in this way maintained. Press or other reporters are not permitted to attend a hearing, although under the terms of para 27 the Board has a discretion to permit observers. The latter who may be given permission to be present during a hearing might include staff of the Board, trainee solicitors or other legal clerks in training, barrister's pupils and trainee union representatives. The Board attaches great importance to the applicant's right of privacy given him by the Scheme and is very strict in protecting it.

If press or other representatives of the media are permitted to be present at a hearing, which is very rare, the applicant's anonymity will be safeguarded by undertakings in that respect required by the Board. Decisions by the Board are reported in legal publications but anonymously as regards the identity of the applicant (para 27), unless the applicant's representatives see fit to disclose it – reports of cases in the Board's Annual Reports never disclose the identity of the applicant.

If permission is sought to 'observe', it must be done before the case commences. Late arrivals who might have obtained the Board's permission before a hearing commences will usually not be permitted to enter after the hearing has commenced and thus interrupt it. There is no question of the free and continuous entry and exit of witnesses, lawyers and members of the public which is the norm in magistrates' courts and Crown Courts.

The terms of paras 25 and 27, whereby the laws of evidence do not apply and the procedure at hearings is 'as informal as is consistent with the proper determination of applications', have a direct relationship to the experience of the Board. It is a particular feature of the Board that at a hearing the adjudication of eligibility and the assessment of compensation are undertaken by two or, more usually, three Queen's Counsel or solicitors of equivalent experience. Most of the Board members are Queen's Counsel and sit as recorders in the Crown Court or as deputy High Court judges. When on the Board they sit as a two or three member Board. This unique weight of experience has enabled the Board from its inception to operate with the minimum of formality and procedural limitations. The experience of the Board members is the guardian of the applicant's rights under the Scheme. That combination of experience and informality also enables the Board to go straight to the heart of a case, to sort the wheat from the chaff. In reaching a decision each Board member has not only his or her own experience to draw upon but also that of his or her fellow Board members.

These factors also make possible the adjudication of numerous cases in the course of a day's hearings, which is important when one considers the volume of cases with which the Board has to deal.

At the conclusion of the oral evidence in a case where eligibility is in issue, the chairman will generally invite brief submissions on the points in question first from the Board's advocate and then from the applicant or his or her representative, so that the latter has the last word. The Board will then decide the case, usually in its retiring room which gives the Board members the opportunity to consider the evidence and reach a joint decision.

In giving the Board's decision the chairman will also make the Board's award where the applicant has succeeded in establishing his entitlement to an award; the applicant or his representative will be given the opportunity to make submissions on quantum as well as eligibility if he wishes to do so.

The informality of proceedings means that advocates and witnesses remain seated when addressing the Board or giving evidence, and witnesses do not take the oath which they would be required to take before giving evidence in court. Board members are addressed simply as 'Sir' or 'Madam'.

Although the order in which witnesses giving evidence before the Board are examined, cross-examined and re-examined will generally follow a similar order to that in a court, this is not subject to any strict rule and the taking of evidence and the conduct of argument involving the applicant's representative and the Board's advocate will be informal and subject to the direction of the chairman.

Paragraph 3 of the Scheme provides that:

> The Board, or such members of the Board's staff as the Board may designate, will be entirely responsible for deciding what compensation should be paid in individual cases and their decisions will not be subject to appeal or to Ministerial review.

The decision by a Board at a hearing is therefore final.

Reference has been made in an earlier chapter to the matter of judicial review, and the principle that an applicant may seek judicial review of a decision by the High Court, which is not an appeal, where it is considered that the Board has misdirected itself on a matter of law or in respect of the terms of the Scheme, or has reached a decision which is perverse (the Wednesbury principle) or which is in some other way contrary to the rules of natural justice.

A summary of cases which have been the subject of such a procedure is contained in Appendix 1.

The Board may adjourn a hearing for any reason. Where the only issue remaining is the assessment of compensation, it may remit the application to a single member of the Board for determination in the absence of the applicant, subject to the applicant's right to apply for a further hearing if he is not satisfied with the assessment.

Paragraph 25 also gives the Board the power to dismiss an application where the applicant fails to attend a hearing and has offered no reasonable excuse for his non-attendance. A person whose application has been so dismissed may apply in writing to the chairman of the Board for his application to be reinstated. A decision by the chairman that an application should not be reinstated will be final.

The Board cannot award costs in any circumstances but may meet the expenses of the applicant and witnesses in attending a hearing.

Part C

Procedure for determining applications under the 1996 Scheme

1. Introduction

The procedural provisions are contained in paras 17 to 20 and 50 to 71 of the 1996 Scheme. Paragraphs 72 to 82 deal with the conduct of hearings before the Criminal Injuries Compensation Appeals Panel – this is a new body created by para 2 of the 1996 Scheme to hear appeals from the decisions of the Criminal Injuries Compensation Authority.

Although there are parallels between the procedure for determining applications by the Board under the 1990 Scheme and by the Authority and the Panel under the 1996 Scheme, the 1996 Scheme does contain substantial procedural changes. The most important single change effected by the 1996 Scheme is the change in the basis of assessment of compensation for injury from common law damages to a fixed tariff sum for each injury.

2. The initial decision

Paragraph 17 of the 1996 Scheme, like para 22 of the 1990 Scheme, requires each application to be made in writing 'on a form obtainable from the Authority' as soon as possible after the incident. The time limit, however, is two years rather than the three years previously allowed. To avoid unfairly disallowing out of time applications in the first year of operation of the new Scheme up to 1 April 1997, it is likely that in that first year applications will be accepted up to the three-year period as before, although the two-year time limit will thereafter be applied. A claims officer may waive the time limit where he considers it 'reasonable and in the interests of justice to do so' (para 17 of the 1996 Scheme). Paragraph 50 (1996) provides that an application 'will be determined by a claims officer, and written notification of the decision will be sent to the applicant or his representative'. Before doing so the Authority will, generally, obtain reports of the incident from the police and of the injuries of the applicant from the hospital or medical practitioner who treated the applicant. The police reports will assist in establishing the 'crime of violence' upon which eligibility will continue to depend. The medical reports will enable the Authority to decide the extent and nature of the injury and into which 'Level' of the 'Tariff of Injuries' the injury falls.

The provision in para 20 (1996) for examination of the injury on behalf of the Authority by a medical practitioner follows the practice of inspection of injuries by Board members under the 1990 and earlier Schemes where it was felt that the nature of the injury, especially where scars were involved, could best be assessed by visual inspection of it. Unlike the inspecting Board member under the 1990 Scheme, however, the medical practitioner carrying out the examination on the Authority's behalf will not also be the person to assess the level of compensation; this assessment is made by a claims officer, a member of the Authority's staff, with the help of a written report from the medical practitioner who carried out the examination. Reasonable expenses incurred by the applicant in connection with arrangements for such examination will be met by the Authority.

3. Review of the decision

Paragraph 18 (1996) brings into the initial consideration of the application the principle that is also contained in the 1990 Scheme (para 25) in relation to hearings:

> It will be for the applicant to make out his case.

The burden of proof is on the applicant throughout to satisfy the claims officer making the first decision – and, where applicable, the officer reviewing that decision at the request of the applicant and, should the case go to appeal, the adjudicator or the Appeals Panel – that his application is within the 1996 Scheme and 'that an award should not be reconsidered, withheld or reduced under any provision of this Scheme'. This again echoes the 1990 Scheme, para 25 of which states:

> It will be for the applicant to make out his case at the hearing, and where appropriate this will extend to satisfying the Board that compensation should not be withheld or reduced under the terms of paragraph 6 or paragraph 8.

Paragraph 18 (1996) also carries into the 1996 Scheme another part of para 25 of the 1990 Scheme, that the applicant will not in any circumstances be entitled to recover the 'costs of representation'.

Paragraph 19 (1996) incorporates expressly the rule regarding the standard of proof which the Board has always applied since the inception of the Scheme:

> The standard of proof to be applied by a claims officer in all matters before him will be the balance of probabilities.

Paragraph 19 (1996) also gives a power to claims officers as follows:

> A claims officer may make such directions and arrangements for the conduct of an application, including the imposition of conditions, as he considers appropriate in all the circumstances.

This is a new and useful power which helps to ensure that the Authority obtains all necessary evidence to do justice to the application.

The full text of paras 58, 59 and 60 of the 1996 Scheme reads as follows:

> Review of decisions
>
> 58. An applicant may seek a review of any decision under this Scheme by a claims officer:
>
> (a) not to waive the time limit in paragraph 17 (application for compensation) or paragraph 59 (application for review); or
>
> (b) not to re-open a case under paragraphs 56 to 57; or
>
> (c) to withhold an award, including such decision made on reconsideration of an award under paragraphs 53 to 54; or

(d) to make an award, including a decision to make a reduced award whether or not on reconsideration of an award under paragraphs 53 to 54; or

(e) to seek repayment of an award under paragraph 49.

An applicant may not, however, seek the review of any such decision where the decision was itself made on a review under paragraph 60 and either the applicant did not appeal against it or the appeal was not referred for determination on an oral hearing, or where the decision was made in accordance with a direction by adjudicators on determining an appeal under paragraph 77.

59. An application for the review of a decision by a claims officer must be made in writing to the Authority and must be supported by reasons together with any relevant additional information. It must be received by the Authority within 90 days of the date of the decision to be reviewed, but this time limit may, in exceptional circumstances, be waived where a claims officer more senior than the one who made the original decision considers that:

(a) any extension requested by the applicant within the 90 days is based on good reasons; or

(b) it would be in the interests of justice to do so.

60. All applications for review will be considered by a claims officer more senior than any claims officer who has previously dealt with the case. The officer conducting the review will reach his decision in accordance with the provisions of this Scheme applying to the original application, and he will not be bound by any earlier decision either as to the eligibility of the applicant for an award or as to the amount of an award. The applicant will be sent written notification of the outcome of the review, giving reasons for the review decision, and the Authority will, unless it receives notice of an appeal, ensure that a determination of the original application is made in accordance with the review decision.

The provisions in para 59 for requesting an extension of the 90 day time limit for a review or waiving it where 'it would be in the interests of justice to do so', continue the rules of the 1990 Scheme (para 22) in relation to the time limit for appealing the initial decision. It is important to bear in mind the need to request the extension before the time limit of 90 days has expired and to give 'good reasons' with that request.

The 1996 Scheme provides that all initial decisions and all reviews of initial decisions on both eligibility and compensation will be made by claims officers of the Authority who are civil servants. Although this represents a substantial change from all earlier Schemes which accorded sole responsibility to the Board for the administration of the Scheme in all cases received up to 31 March 1996, the real differences after that date are fewer than may appear to be the case because of the extent to which the Board has delegated initial decisions to members of the Board's staff under its power to do so under paras 3 and 22 of the 1990 Scheme. It is worth noting that the 'members of the Board's staff' referred to in para 3 of the 1990 Scheme, who have for some time made delegated decisions under that Scheme, and the staff of the Authority are in fact the same body of persons. They are civil servants appointed by the Home Office and the Scottish Office to assist the Board under the 1990 Scheme – these same officers also constitute the Authority under the 1996 Scheme. They will continue to serve as 'members of the Board's staff' in concluding cases received before 1 April 1996, for which the Board has responsibility, as well as being the decision-making and reviewing officers of the Authority under the 1996 Scheme.

Paragraph 59 (1996) states that applications for review of a decision by a claims officer must be made in writing and must be supported by reasons together with any relevant additional information. This is substantially the same as the form of request for hearing under the 1990 Scheme. The major change, however, is that under the 1996 Scheme the next step is the review of the initial decision by an officer of the Authority more senior than the one who made the original decision, and not an oral hearing.

Paragraph 60 (1996) provides that all applications for review will be considered by an officer of the Authority more senior than the one who made the original decision, and that in conducting the review such officer will 'not be bound by any earlier decision either as to the eligibility of the applicant for an award or as to the amount of an award'.

An applicant whose application has been found initially to be within the 1996 Scheme and awarded, say, £1,500 under the appropriate level of the tariff for that injury, and who regards his injury as entitling him to a higher tariff award, could lose all on applying for a review if the reviewing officer concludes that the application is not within the Scheme. This will arise where the reviewing officer considers that the circumstances of the case do not meet the rules of eligibility set out in paras 13 to 16 of the 1996 Scheme and disagrees with the conclusions of the officer who initially decided the case. Additional information received by the Authority since the initial decision may cause the reviewing officer to take a different view on eligibility.

This risk is similar to that prevailing under the 1990 Scheme, as under that Scheme an application for an oral hearing under para 22 is a rejection of the initial decision, and the matter proceeds thereafter as a fresh application open in all respects on issues of eligibility as well as assessment. An applicant requesting review of an initial decision whereby an award was offered should bear in mind that, if there is any real doubt on eligibility, a review of the original decision by the reviewing officer may not reach the same conclusion on eligibility; the applicant would then receive no award.

The claims officer of the Authority making the initial decision and the reviewing officer will apply exactly the same rules in deciding eligibility and which level of the tariff applies in each case. The Authority regulates the decision-making process within the terms laid down by the 1996 Scheme so that the rules of the Scheme are applied fairly and uniformly in deciding the thousands of applications received by the Authority each month.

Where an applicant has applied for review, he or she will be notified in writing of the outcome of the review, giving reasons for the review decision (para 60 of the 1996 Scheme).

Before considering the machinery for appeal to the Appeals Panel reference must be made to the provisions of paras 53 to 55 under the heading 'Reconsideration of decisions'. These create the power of the Authority *at any time before actual payment of a final award* to reconsider a decision made by a claims officer where there is new evidence or a change of circumstances. (See Chapter 18.)

4. Appeals against review decisions

The opening sentence of para 61 of the 1996 Scheme reads:

> An applicant who is dissatisfied with a decision taken on a review under paragraph 60 may appeal against the decision by giving written notice of appeal to the Panel on a form obtainable from the Authority.

The Panel was brought into being by the 1996 Scheme. Paragraph 2 states:

> Appeals against decisions taken on reviews under this Scheme will be determined by adjudicators. Persons appointed as adjudicators are appointed as members of the Criminal Injuries Compensation Appeals Panel.

The function of the Appeals Panel is essentially similar to the role played by the Criminal Injuries Compensation Board in relation to hearings. The significant change is the establishment of the Appeals Panel as a wholly independent body from the Authority. This distinguishes it from the Board in relation to hearings under the earlier Schemes, as the Board by its single member would also have been the body responsible for the initial decision. The distinction is perhaps more apparent than real, however, as the single member who made the initial decision in respect of which a hearing has been granted is disqualified from being a member of the hearings Board on an appeal from that decision. In recent years it has also been the case that the Board at hearings is often deciding appeals from decisions made by members of the Board's staff under the delegated powers granted to them by the Board.

The Appeals Panel (referred to in the Scheme as 'the Panel') is totally separate from the Authority. Unlike the Board under earlier Schemes it has no say or responsibility with regard to the functions of the Authority and the Authority's staff whose officers make the initial decision on all applications under the 1996 Scheme and likewise undertake all reviews of those initial decisions. In performing its role as the final appeal body, the Panel is wholly independent.

The Authority is, by para 2 (1996), responsible for the determination of claims and for deciding what awards should be paid in individual cases. Its decisions on reviews are subject to appeal to the Panel. Thus is the total separation of function defined.

Members of the Panel ('adjudicators') are appointed by the Secretary of State – that is to say, the Home Secretary or the Secretary of State for

Scotland. Unlike the Board whose members are all lawyers (as required by para 1 of the 1990 Scheme) membership of the Panel comprises lawyers and members of other professions and occupations.

Paragraph 3 (1996) states:

> No decision, whether by a claims officer or the Panel, will be open to appeal to the Secretary of State.

The 1996 Scheme sets out in paras 61 to 71 detailed rules whereby an applicant may or may not be entitled to an oral hearing.

The 1990 Scheme had introduced for the first time a form of clearing process to decide whether an applicant was entitled to an oral hearing. All earlier Schemes had given the applicant an automatic entitlement to a hearing if a hearings request was lodged within the time limit, even if the request for hearing had no merit and no prospect of the initial decision being altered at a hearing. Paragraph 24 of the 1990 Scheme introduced a clearing procedure so that only appeals with some merit were granted a hearing.

The 1996 Scheme provides in detail the procedure whereby appeals to the Panel under para 61 (1996) are vetted and designates in detail the powers of members of staff of the Panel and of the Authority, as well as 'adjudicators' who are members of the Panel, in the initial decision whether or not the application will proceed to an oral hearing.

The whole process which follows from the refusal of the applicant to accept the decision of the reviewing officer of the Authority under para 60 and his giving written notice of appeal to the Panel under para 61 is regulated under four headings in the 1996 Scheme:

- Appeals against review decisions (paras 61 to 65);
- Appeals concerning time limits and re-opening of cases (paras 66 to 68);
- Appeals concerning awards (paras 69 to 71); and
- Oral hearing of appeals (paras 72 to 78).

The fourth heading relates to those cases which succeed in qualifying for and reaching an actual hearing before the Appeals Panel.

There is much in paras 61 to 78 which is similar in principle to the procedure under the 1990 Scheme. The rules relating to the time limit for lodging an appeal where the review decision is not accepted, including the discretionary extension or waiver of the time limit, are there, although the time limit itself is 30 days, not three months as under the 1990 Scheme. Like the Chairman of the Board in 1990 Scheme cases, the Chairman of the Panel or another Panel member (termed 'adjudicator' in the 1996 Scheme) nominated by the Chairman makes the final decision not to waive the time limit.

Under the 1990 Scheme a Board's advocate has delegated authority to waive the time limit where a request for a hearing is out of time and may also grant an extension of time for lodging an appeal where there are good reasons for so doing. Under the 1990 Scheme (para 13) only a Board member may reopen a case and only the Chairman of the Board may refuse to do so.

Under the 1996 Scheme (para 62) a member of the Panel's staff 'may, in exceptional circumstances, waive the time limit' where an extension is requested for 'good reasons' within the thirty days, or where 'it would be in the interests of justice to do so'. This is a wide discretion. It has been operated quite generously in the past by the Board. It remains to be seen how it will be exercised by the members (adjudicators) and staff of the Appeals Panel. There may be reason to regard the words 'in exceptional circumstances' as a warning that the time limits under the 1996 Scheme will be more strictly construed than under earlier *ex gratia* Schemes.

Paragraph 66 of the 1996 Scheme provides that the Chairman of the Panel or another Panel adjudicator will determine any appeal against a decision taken on review (i.e., by a reviewing officer of the Authority) not to waive the time limit in para 17 (applications for compensation) or para 59 (applications for review) or not to reopen a case under paras 56 and 57.

The rules governing the reopening of a case under paras 56 and 57 of the 1996 Scheme are very similar to the old 'para 13' rules of the 1990 Scheme. The new Scheme gives a claims officer of the Authority the power to reopen a case (i) which has been decided by a claims officer and the decision has been accepted by the applicant, or (ii) which has been decided by the Panel. Reopening is only possible 'where there has been such a material change in the victim's medical condition that injustice would occur if the original assessment of compensation were allowed to stand . . . '.

Paragraph 57 states that a case will not be reopened more than two years after the date of the final decision unless the case can be considered 'without a need for further extensive enquiries'. This is a restatement of a familiar principle.

Paragraphs 66 to 68 which deal with time limits and the reopening of cases, and paras 69 to 71 which relate to appeals concerning awards, are necessarily more detailed and complex than their equivalent provisions of the 1990 Scheme because of the creation of two separate bodies, the Authority and the Panel, to replace the unified Board, and the transition of cases from the reviewing officers of the Authority to the staff and members of a separate body, the Appeals Panel.

Under the 1996 Scheme the whole procedure is no longer conducted within the unified structure of one authority, the Board. Cases have to be 'passed up' by the Authority to the Panel, and in some cases, after a Panel decision has been made – for example to waive a time limit on an original application (para 17) or on an application for review (para 59) – they have to be 'passed back down' by the Panel to the Authority for suitable decision by a claims officer of the Authority (para 68).

The division of the overall operation of the Scheme between these two different bodies, combined with the transfer of the greater part of the decision-making process to civil servants who are the 'claims officers' of the Authority, creates the need to define the respective functions of, for example, claims officers, reviewing claims officers and adjudicators of the Panel, and to set out expressly within the Scheme the administrative machinery whereby an application completes its passage through the whole system.

The nature of the Scheme has undergone a substantial 'sea change' under the 1996 Scheme in both its legal and administrative aspects. A new and more complex hierarchy has been introduced in order to administer the Scheme, and the respective functions of the constituent parts of that administrative machine have therefore to be defined in detail. This explains why the 1996 Scheme as a document is far longer and more detailed than any of its predecessors. In broad terms, however, much of the administrative machinery is recognisable to those familiar with the administration of the 1990 and earlier Schemes.

In many ways the working rules governing the powers and functions of claims officers of the Authority and adjudicators of the Appeals Panel are largely similar to those of the 1990 Scheme under which officials of the Board, acting under their delegated powers as decision makers, and Board members have operated. Paragraph 58 of the 1996 Scheme is something of an anchor provision. It usefully subdivides applications for *review* of the initial decision by a claims officer into five different categories. In respect of *appeals* to the Panel, para 63 points to the different procedures and the relevant paragraphs of the Scheme which regulate each appeal according to its category. Therefore cases falling within categories (a) and (b) of para 58 (appeals concerning time limits and reopening of cases) are dealt with according to the procedures laid down in paras 66 to 68; cases falling within categories (c), (d) and (e) of para 58 (appeals concerning awards) are dealt with by the procedures laid down in paras 69 to 71.

Paragraph 63 tells the applicant or his adviser which part of the Scheme to look at in order to establish the rules applying to the next stage of his appeal. If, for example, an applicant has appealed against a reviewing claims officer's decision to withhold an award, say on the grounds of his 'conduct' under para 13(d) of the Scheme, para 58 will show him that it is a '58(c)' case. Paragraph 63 will then indicate that, being a '58(c)' appeal, its procedure is governed by paras 69 to 71, under the heading 'Appeals concerning awards'.

Paragraph 69 states that 'a member of the staff of the Panel may refer [the case] for an oral hearing', and that the procedure for the hearing itself is governed by paras 72 to 78. The applicant and his adviser are thus given, in relation to their particular case, a clear route through the Scheme.

The substance which lies behind this carefully stated procedure is largely familiar ground. Under previous Schemes, however, the procedures of the Board were largely matters of internal administration within the one entity, the Board. The introduction of the 1996 Scheme has led to the creation of two new and quite separate bodies, the Authority and the Panel, each of which has officers or members with clearly defined functions – this has led to the need to codify procedures within the 1996 Scheme. Whereas the 1990 Scheme has at its core a Board of senior lawyers, assisted by a staff of civil servants, operating a largely discretionary ex-gratia Scheme, the 1996 Scheme reflects a change to a body of civil servants who make essentially administrative decision under the rules of a tariff Scheme. Such a change has made more important the need for clear definition of the rules of procedure, the *modus operandi*. The detailed provisions of the 1996 Scheme perform that task. It will be helpful to give another example of the 'routing' of an application through the system.

Let us suppose that the applicant has stated that he did not report the incident to the police until seven days after it had occurred. The police report obtained by the Authority confirms this. The applicant was able to go back to work after three days. Under para 13(a) of the 1996 Scheme, therefore, the claims officer disallows the application entirely. This provision reads as follows:

> A claims officer may withhold or reduce an award where he considers that:
>
> (a) the applicant failed to take, without delay, all reasonable steps to inform the police ... of the circumstances giving rise to the injury.

The applicant does not accept this decision and wishes to challenge it. He does so, under paras 58, 59 and 60, the relevant parts of which read as follows:

> 58. An applicant may seek a review of any decision under this Scheme by a claims officer ...
>
> (c) to withhold an award ...
>
> 59. An application for the review of a decision by a claims officer must be made in writing to the Authority and must be supported by reasons together with any relevant additional information ...
>
> 60. All applications for review will be considered by a claims officer more senior than any claims officer who has previously dealt with the case...

The 'more senior' claims officer upholds the original decision and the applicant is notified in writing of that decision. The applicant wishes to appeal to the Appeals Panel. He does so under para 61, the relevant part of which reads as follows:

> An applicant who is dissatisfied with a decision taken on a review under paragraph 60 may appeal against the decision by giving written notice of appeal to the Panel on a form obtainable from the Authority. Such notice of appeal must be supported by reasons for the appeal together with any relevant additional material which the appellant wishes to submit ...

This is an appeal against a decision on review 'to withhold an award', and para 63, which follows para 58 in dividing appeals into categories, indicates which paragraphs of the Scheme apply to this particular category of appeal.

Paragraph 63 states that appeals against a decision on review 'to withhold an award' – being a '58(c)' case – are dealt with under the procedures laid down in paras 69 to 71 under the heading 'Appeals concerning awards'.

We follow this 'signpost' and then look at paras 69 to 71. After carefully reading these three paragraphs anyone familiar with the 1990 Scheme will recognise their purpose. They are the equivalent of para 24 of the 1990 Scheme which was the 'filter' through which all requests for an oral hearing must pass. Only cases with some clear merit – some real prospects of success at a hearing – would pass through the 1990 'para 24' filter and be granted an oral hearing; appeals without merit, and with no realistic prospect of reaching a decision which differs from the original decision, will be refused a hearing. This need to sort the wheat from the chaff, performed by para 24 of the 1990 Scheme, can now be identified in paras 69, 70 and 71 in the 1996 Scheme. The full text of paras 69, 70 and 71 reads as follows:

> Appeals concerning awards
>
> 69. A member of the staff of the Panel may refer for an oral hearing in accordance with paragraphs 72 to 78 any appeal against a decision taken on a review:
>
> (a) to withhold an award, including such decision made on reconsideration of an award under paragraphs 53 to 54; or
>
> (b) to make an award, including a decision to make a reduced award whether or not on reconsideration of an award under paragraphs 53 to 54; or
>
> (c) to seek repayment of an award under paragraph 49.
>
> A request for an oral hearing in such cases may also be made by the Authority.
>
> 70. Where a member of the staff of the Panel does not refer an appeal for an oral hearing under the preceding paragraph, he will refer it to an adjudicator. The adjudicator will refer the appeal for determination on an oral hearing in accordance with paragraphs 72 to 78 where, on the evidence available to him, he considers:
>
> (a) in a case where the review decision was to withhold an award on the ground that the injury was not sufficiently serious to qualify for an award equal to at least the minimum amount payable under this Scheme, that an award in accordance with this Scheme could have been made; or
>
> (b) in any other case, that there is a dispute as to the material facts or conclusions upon which the review decision was based and that a different decision in accordance with this Scheme could have been made.
>
> He may also refer the appeal for determination on an oral hearing in accordance with paragraphs 72 to 78 where he considers that the appeal cannot be determined on the basis of the material before him or that for any other reason an oral hearing would be desirable.
>
> 71. Where an appeal is not referred under paragraphs 69 or 70 for an oral hearing, the adjudicator's dismissal of the appeal will be final and the

> decision taken on the review will stand. Written notification of the dismissal of the appeal, giving reasons for the decision, will be sent to the appellant and to the Authority.

Our applicant whose application has been refused by the claims officer and on review, has lodged his appeal under para 61. As an 'appeal concerning awards', the appeal is received by the Panel. The member of staff of the Panel who considers it may decide that the appeal has merit and some prospect of success at an oral hearing and will accordingly refer it for an oral hearing (para 69(a)).

Paragraph 69 authorises 'a member of the staff of the Panel' to refer for an oral hearing 'any appeal against a decision taken on a review' (by the Authority) 'to withhold an award' or 'to make an award, including a decision to make a reduced award'. Thus if in our example the claims officer or reviewing officer had made, say, a reduction of 50 per cent on grounds of delay in reporting under para 13(a), an appeal against that decision would take the same 'route' under the Scheme as an appeal against the decision to refuse an award altogether. It may, under para 69(b), likewise be referred to an oral hearing by 'a member of the staff of the Panel'.

In addition to appeals against decisions to withhold or reduce awards, para 69 covers appeals from a decision by the Authority under para 49 requiring an applicant to make a repayment of an award in full or in part where he 'subsequently receives any other payment in respect of the same injury'. This covers cases where, under para 48, 'an award ... will be reduced by the full value of' such payments as compensation orders in a criminal court or damages in a civil court.

Paragraph 69 also entitles the Authority, where the applicant has appealed from a review decision, to request an oral hearing by the Panel in cases involving:

(a) the withholding of an award;
(b) the making of an award or a reduced award; or
(c) requiring repayment under para 49,

where it is felt that justice cannot be done on the papers alone and that the hearing of oral evidence is desirable in order to arrive at a fair decision. There is however, no power on the part of the Authority to refer an application to a hearing of its own initiative.

Paragraph 70 is the 'clearing house' provision, rather like para 24 of the 1990 Scheme. Where it is apparent to a member of the staff of the Panel that the appeal has merit and warrants an oral hearing, he will refer it for an oral hearing without any reference to a member of the Panel (an 'adjudicator') and the case will in due course be listed for hearing. Where, however, he 'does not refer an appeal for an oral hearing ... he will refer it to an adjudicator' i.e. a member of the Panel.

Paragraph 70 defines the grounds upon which the adjudicator will decide to grant or refuse a hearing. If one reads para 70(a) and 70(b) alone, the criteria appear to be narrow and restrictive – they allow appeals to proceed to an oral hearing only if:

(i) the refusal had been made in accordance with the 'minimum award' rule contained in para 24 and that on the evidence available an award could have been made (para 70(a)), or

(ii) 'there is a dispute as to the material facts or conclusions upon which the review decision was based and that a different decision ... could have been made' (para 70(b)).

These narrow criteria are greatly widened, however, by the final sentence of para 70: 'He [the adjudicator] may also refer the appeal' for an oral hearing 'where he considers that the appeal cannot be determined on the basis of the material before him or that for any other reason an oral hearing would be desirable'. Thus paras 70(a) (minimum award) and 70(b) (dispute as to material facts) speak of only two categories of appeal which may qualify for an oral hearing, but the adjudicator is seemingly given a very wide discretion where 'for any other reason' an oral hearing would be desirable.

Taking our applicant who has been refused by the Authority, by the claims officer and on review on grounds of delay in reporting, and who then appeals to the Appeals Panel, a member of staff of the Panel may refer it for an oral hearing or, alternatively, to an adjudicator, who must decide whether or not the case goes to a hearing. Paragraph 71 states that the adjudicator's decision dismissing the appeal will be final and that the decision taken on the review will stand.

The policy of the Appeals Panel and its members, who are referred to in the Scheme as the 'adjudicators' has yet to be established. It is likely that, initially at least, the adjudicators will look to the experience of the Board, in exercising its equivalent powers under para 24 of the 1990 Scheme, for guidance.

When the power to refuse a hearing was first introduced in February 1990 (under all previous Schemes an oral hearing was a right in all cases) the Board was very cautious in its exercise of the power of refusal. The Appeals Panel, like the Board, is bound by the terms of the Scheme and by the rules of natural justice which apply to any body which exercises a quasi-judicial role. It has not, however, been the case that the court, on judicial review of decisions by the Board to refuse a hearing under para 24 of the 1990 Scheme, has condemned the exercise of the power to refuse a hearing as in itself a denial of natural justice. Provided that the power is exercised reasonably and within the terms of the Scheme, it appears to be the case, therefore, that the decision refusing an oral hearing will not be quashed by the court on judicial review. If, however, the adjudicator has acted in a way which contravenes the principles of natural justice or has erred in law, the position may be different. For example, it is considered desirable that if the appeal is not referred to a hearing by a member of the Panel's staff under para 69, but is referred to an adjudicator under para 70, the applicant should be notified in writing that:

(a) his appeal has been so referred;

(b) that a decision by the adjudicator refusing a hearing would be final (para 71); and

(c) that he should therefore promptly make any further submissions that he wishes the adjudicator to take into account in addition to any evidence and submissions already made on requesting a review of the initial decision and on lodging his appeal against the decision of the reviewing officer.

It may be open to challenge in the court if, after lodging his appeal, the appellant is simply told, as the next communication from the Panel or the Authority, that his appeal has been referred to an adjudicator who has decided to refuse an oral hearing, that that decision is final, and that therefore the decision refusing an award on review stands.

Returning to our applicant who has appealed against the refusal on the grounds of seven days' delay in informing the police of the circumstances of his injury, it may well be the Panel's policy to allow such a case to proceed to an oral hearing. Circumstances giving rise to delay vary considerably between one case and another. As has been considered in Chapter 5, it is possible that an applicant may have been knocked unconscious and sustained a broken jaw, making speech difficult if not impossible in the first two or three days after the incident and he may have spent several of those seven days in hospital. In another case it may be that the applicant has undergone emergency surgery for serious internal injuries so that the police could not interview him for medical reasons for a week or so. More difficult is the not uncommon situation where the applicant could only give basic details to the police, such as his name and address, before being taken to hospital by ambulance and thereafter believing the police would contact him, delayed a week before himself going to the police to make a statement. These few examples of the dozens of variations on the theme of 'delay' are sufficient to show that dogmatic rules of policy will not be appropriate as this would not be dealing with each case on its merits.

Decisions on eligibility are arrived at by exercising the discretion which the Scheme gives to the decision makers at all levels: claims officer, reviewing claims officer, and Panel adjudicator. Under the heading 'Eligibility to receive compensation', para 13 states: 'A claims officer may withhold or reduce an award where he considers that . . . '. The word 'may' is an indication that the claims officer is given a discretion to withhold or refuse an award. The High Court has made clear that that discretion must be exercised on the merits and demerits of the individual case, and must not be fettered by a fixed policy or approach to particular categories of case (*R v CICB, ex parte Powell* – see page 87). It is considered that in cases involving some element of delay, where the applicant has a reasonable argument that in all the circumstances he took the earliest opportunity to inform the police of the circumstances of his injury, the delay in itself may not be regarded as sufficient to justify a refusal of an oral hearing by an adjudicator under para 70 of the Scheme, and the applicant may therefore be granted an oral hearing in such a case.

The other 'layer' to be considered in the process of deciding whether to allow a hearing is the fact that the choice open to the Panel at the hearing is not merely a choice between a full award and a nil award – the Panel may also decide that neither of these is appropriate and that a reduced award should be made.

It may be something of an over-simplification to say that para 70 (1996), like para 24 (1990), is essentially only a 'weeding out' provision, so that hopeless appeals do not clog the appeals system. Before 1990 it became obvious that some amendment to the Scheme was desirable to limit the right to a hearing to those cases that had some prospect of success. The applicant with a long list of convictions for serious offences was the standard example of the need for a 'weeding out' provision in the Scheme. Other examples of 'hopeless' appeals are the injury which is not the result of a crime of violence at all, but an accident; the trivial injury which would not justify the minimum award; cases of child sex abuse within the family home before October 1979; and those cases which may or may not have been crimes of violence, but the applicant admits that he never gave a report to the police (or other appropriate body where that alternative applies) and so the circumstances alleged by the applicant were never investigated and therefore never verified.

Such 'hopeless' cases apart, it remains to be seen whether the Panel decides to be less cautious than the Board has been in exercising the power to refuse a hearing. It should be remembered that caution in refusing a hearing is founded upon the experience of the Board, in hearing thousands of cases on appeal under the 1990 and earlier Schemes, that cases have a habit of taking on a very different appearance after hearing oral evidence than appeared to be the case on a reading of the papers alone.

5. Oral hearing of appeals (paras 72–78 and 79–82 (1996))

The applicant who successfully makes the step from a decision on review by the Authority which he does not accept, to a hearing by the Appeals Panel, will first have satisfied either 'a member of the staff of the Panel' that a hearing by the Panel is appropriate in his case (para 69) or an adjudicator (member of the Panel) that a hearing by the Panel should be granted under the rules contained in para 70.

As the Authority and the Panel are two distinct and separate organisations with separate powers and duties under the 1996 Scheme, the staff of the Panel take over from the staff of the Authority the arrangements for bringing the application to a hearing before the Panel. Although details of the administration of preparation for a hearing and listing by a member of staff of the Panel are not given, it is likely that this will follow a similar pattern to the practice of the Board's staff in arranging hearings under the 1990 Scheme. This will involve the gathering into the Panel's bundle, all relevant documentary evidence to assist the Panel in deciding issues of eligibility and also the amount of the award under the rules of the 1996 Scheme.

Paragraph 73 repeats the familiar 'golden rule' that the Panel sees only those documents which have also been seen by the applicant either before or at the hearing.

It can be expected that the Panel will deal with police witness statements in the same way as the Board, i.e. making copies of such statements available to the applicant and his representative only at the hearing. Subject to any new arrangements which may be made between the Appeals Panel and the constabularies to make his own statement available to the applicant at an earlier stage, the Panel will have to comply with the same rule which governs making a police statement available to the Board, namely that the Board maintains control of such statements, and that they are made available only for the purpose of the hearing and should not in any circumstances leave the Board's control. The Panel's staff will prepare a schedule and copy bundles of documents to be read by those Panel members who are hearing and deciding the case, and the staff will ensure that the applicant has copies of the same documents. Panel staff will also provide a summary of the issues to be decided by the Panel at the hearing and indicate names of witnesses to be invited by the Panel staff to attend the hearing. A copy of this will also be sent to the applicant before the hearing.

Paragraph 73 states that 'written notice of the date proposed for the oral hearing will normally be sent to the appellant and the Authority at least 21 days beforehand'. Paragraph 72 provides that 'the hearing will take place before at least two adjudicators'. One difference which this paragraph makes to the equivalent hearing by at least two members of the Board under the 1990 Scheme is that whereas a Board member who has referred a case to a hearing may sit as a Board member at the hearing of the case, a Panel adjudicator who has referred the case to an oral hearing under para 70 of the 1996 Scheme 'will not take part in the hearing'.

The 1996 Scheme provides:

- 'The procedure at hearings will be as informal as is consistent with the proper determination of appeals' (para 75).
- 'Hearings will take place in private' (para 76).
- The appellant may bring a friend or legal adviser to a hearing 'but the costs of representation will not be met by the Authority or the Panel' (para 74).
- The applicant must see all documents which are before the Panel members – the 'golden rule' mentioned above (para 73).

This is all familiar ground as these provisions are the same as the Board's rules under the 1990 Scheme.

Paragraph 77 provides that adjudicators may adjourn the hearing and in so doing may make an interim award, a payment on account of the final award, which will be deductible from the final award when that is subsequently assessed. This again is similar to the power of the Board at a hearing under the 1990 Scheme.

An entirely new provision follows the reference to interim awards in para 77:

> On determining the appeal, the adjudicators will, where necessary, make such direction as they think fit as to the decision to be made by a claims officer on the application for compensation, but any such direction must be in accordance with the relevant provisions of this Scheme.

This is, on the face of it, a utility provision so that in certain cases where 'directions' as to the disposal of the case are needed, such as setting up a trust or other administrative arrangement in the case of an award to a minor until he or she is 18, those arrangements can be carried out by the Authority in accordance with directions made by the Appeals Panel when making the final award. It is in fact a major provision which establishes the Authority as the means of giving effect to a decision of the Appeals Panel at a hearing. Where disposal of a case at a hearing is an assessment of a full award or reduced award, the Authority will give effect to that final decision and make payment of the award.

If at a hearing further directions are needed to obtain additional evidence before a decision can be made, the adjudicators (the Panel) can 'direct' the Authority's presenting officer to do so.

The decision made by a claims officer by direction of the Panel under this paragraph would be a final decision as if made by the Panel, and thus not capable of any further consideration either by the Authority or the Panel under the terms of the Scheme.

The last sentence of para 77 confirms that the appellant and the Authority:

> ... will be informed of the adjudicators' determination of the appeal and the reasons for it, normally at the end of the hearing, but otherwise by written notification as soon as is practicable thereafter.

It will be remembered that at the hearing before the Panel 'the claims officer presenting the appeal' is an officer of the Authority. When the Panel give their decision orally at the end of the hearing the appellant and/or his representative and also 'the claims officer presenting the appeal' are present to hear that oral decision. Generally, therefore, as with hearings before the Board under the 1990 Scheme, there will be no need for any written notification of the decision and none will be given.

The penultimate sentence of para 77 is a new provision. It reads as follows:

> Where they are of the opinion that the appeal was frivolous or vexatious the adjudicators may reduce the amount of compensation to be awarded by such amount as they consider appropriate.

It will be interesting to observe how this new power is used in practice. The experience of the Board and its staff is perusing many thousands of requests for hearings is that members of the public consider themselves free to express their requests for hearings in whatever terms they see fit, ranging from simple and courteous disagreement with the Board's decision to a boisterous verbal attack on the decision maker's soundness of mind. Often the request simply says something like: 'I disagree with the decision to refuse compensation' or 'the award is not high enough for the pain I suffered' or similar responses deemed appropriate by lay applicants. The view is expressed that the merits of the case, viewed according to its facts and the terms of the Scheme, should be the criterion for all decisions made under the Scheme. It is to be hoped that applications colourfully or inadequately expressed will not be deemed frivolous or vexatious if the substance of the case warrants evaluation.

For the applicant to have received a decision from the claims officer or reviewing claims officer and, having requested a hearing by the Panel, to have been allowed a hearing either by a member of the staff of the Panel (para 69) or by a member of the Panel (para 70), the application will already have been seen to have merit, otherwise the hearing would not have been granted. It is possible, however, to envisage that an applicant might secure a hearing on what turns out to be an entirely false premise. For example, an appeal against a reduced award by reason of convictions might be made on the applicant's insistence that he has no convictions which the hearing establishes is untrue.

The power granted to adjudicators under this provision to reduce an award must, like any other power under the Scheme, be exercised in accordance with the principles of natural justice and not exercised arbitrarily.

Paragraph 78 is the equivalent of the familiar 'para 25 dismissal' provision of the 1990 Scheme, where the applicant fails to attend his own hearing, having given no reasonable explanation – but with a difference. Paragraph 78 does not expressly give the Panel power to dismiss for non-attendance, but empowers the Panel to 'determine the appeal', so that the issues and the merits can be decided in the absence of the applicant if the adjudicators see fit to deal with the case in this way. Alternatively, it may be adjourned.

6. Rehearing of appeals

Paragraphs 79 to 82, which appear under the above heading in the 1996 Scheme, regulate the procedure where the appeal has been determined in the absence of the applicant under para 78, and the applicant subsequently applies 'to the Panel in writing for his appeal to be reheard, giving the reasons for his non-attendance' (para 79). Such applications for a rehearing must be 'received by the Panel within 30 days of the date of notification to the appellant of the outcome of the hearing which he failed to attend' (para 79).

Paragraph 81 provides as follows:

> Where a member of the staff of the Panel considers that there are good reasons for an appeal to be reheard, he will refer it for a rehearing. Where he does not refer it for a rehearing, he will refer the application to the Chairman of the Panel or to another adjudicator nominated by the Chairman to decide such applications, and a decision by the adjudicator concerned not to rehear the appeal will be final ...

In essence these provisions for granting or refusing a request for a rehearing of an application which has been decided in the absence of the applicant are similar to the rules and practice under para 25 of the 1990 Scheme, under which the Board delegates to the Board's advocates the power to decide to allow a rehearing, but reserves to the Chairman of the Board exclusively the power to refuse a rehearing. Thus, if the Board's advocate considered that the merits of the application for rehearing do not justify the granting of a rehearing, the application goes to the Chairman of the Board to decide whether or not to grant a rehearing.

Two important differences remain, however, between the 1990 and 1996 Scheme rules on the granting or refusal of a rehearing. One is the creation of a 30 day time limit within which to apply for a rehearing after notification of the Panel's decision arrived at in the absence of the applicant. The 1990 Scheme (para 25) has no specified time limit. This time limit may be waived by a member of the staff of the Panel, however, if it is in the interests of justice to do so (para 80). Where the time limit is not so waived, the question of waiver is decided by the Chairman of the Panel or other adjudicator nominated by the Chairman. It must be likely that the power to waive the time limit where 'it would be in the interests of justice to do so' (para 80) will make fairly marginal any differences between the treatment of applications for 'reinstatement' under para 25 of the 1990 Scheme and for 'rehearing' under para 79 of the 1996 Scheme.

The other and perhaps more important difference is that para 78 grants the Panel the power to 'determine the appeal' in the absence of the applicant; the wording of para 25 (1990) in that respect is that 'the Board at the hearing may dismiss his application'.

The Board's practice under the 1990 Scheme in these circumstances is usually simply to dismiss the application without 'determining' the appeal on those matters which would have been adjudicated had the applicant attended the hearing and the hearing proceeded, with all issues being determined on the merits. The Panel under para 78 of the 1996 Scheme 'may determine the appeal in [the appellant's] absence'. This seems to include reaching a decision on all issues for decision, such as delay in informing the police, or failing to co-operate with the police, or the applicant's 'conduct' before, during or after the incident. Even though there may be a power under para 78 to adjudicate the application entirely on all aspects where the appellant has failed to attend, it may in practice be the view of the adjudicators that hearing evidence from other witnesses or argument on the issues would be a waste of time and adjourn the application. (They may also consider whether dismissal of the application under para 13(c) – failure to give all reasonable assistance to the Authority – is appropriate.) If the appellant subsequently applies for a rehearing under para 79 and succeeds, all the evidence would have to be heard again at a subsequent hearing, on all the issues of the case.

The Panel may determine appeals on the amount of the award in the absence of the applicant as para 78 is not confined to eligibility decisions.

The Panel may however regard an adjournment of such cases a safer course, especially where the assessment is complex.

Where an appeal is to be reheard, the adjudicators who determined the appeal originally will not take part in the rehearing (para 82). Otherwise all the rules and procedures applying to an oral hearing under paras 72 to 78 will apply to the rehearing.

Chapter 17

Reconsideration of a case after a final award

Paragraph 56 of the 1996 Scheme follows the same principles as the now familiar para 13 of the 1990 Scheme in defining the circumstances in which the Authority may reopen a case after a final decision has been made by the Authority or the Panel.

Both paragraphs state that although the decision of the Board (or the Authority or Panel, as the case may be) will normally be final, the Board or Authority has a discretion to reopen and reconsider a case where change in the applicant's medical condition makes reconsideration and reassessment the proper course. The paragraphs use slightly different language to express the same basic principle. The principle is that, subject to certain safeguards with regard to the evidence required, a case will be reopened where subsequent medical evidence indicates that the seriousness of the injury would make it wrong and unjust to leave the original assessment undisturbed. A helpful change in the wording in the 1996 Scheme expressly enables the Authority to reopen a 'nil' award case as well as one in which a final award has been accepted; the Board has always found difficulty in reopening cases which have originally been refused under para 5 (1990) on the grounds that the injury did not justify the minimum award, as para 13 uses the words 'after a final award of compensation has been accepted' in describing cases capable of being reopened under this provision.

The effect of these parallel provisions in the 1990 and 1996 Schemes will now be examined.

1. Reopening cases – para 13 of the 1990 Scheme

Paragraph 13 of the 1990 Scheme states:

> Although the Board's decisions in a case will normally be final, they will have discretion to reconsider a case after a final award of compensation has been accepted where there has been such a serious change in the applicant's medical condition that injustice would occur if the original assessment of compensation were allowed to stand, or where the victim has since died as a result of his injuries. A case will not be re-opened more than three years after the date of the final award unless the Board are satisfied, on the basis of evidence presented with the application for re-opening the case, that the

> renewed application can be considered without a need for extensive enquiries. A decision by the Chairman that a case may not be re-opened will be final.

Earlier Schemes had no provision for reopening; in suitable cases the Board would make a so-called 'permanent' interim award to protect an applicant's right to come back to the Board in the event of a serious change in his medical condition.

This most valuable provision, whereby an applicant may ask the Board to reopen a case – even after a final award has been made – provided that he can show that the situation meets the conditions for reopening set out in the above paragraph, was introduced in the 1979 Scheme.

Its usefulness is twofold. At the time when the Board is making a final award it does not have to attempt to evaluate every contingency which the evidence before it suggests as a possibility in the future. The Board can expressly state when making a final award that its award does not take into account the possibility of, for example, the onset of epilepsy. The award would thus not include any sum to compensate for that possibility. Should epilepsy subsequently occur and be shown by medical evidence to be attributable to the injury, the applicant may apply for the assessment to be reopened under para 13 of the Scheme so that an award may be made to compensate for that condition.

Secondly, para 13 applications may comprise those cases where there has been a deterioration in the applicant's condition which was not anticipated at the time of the earlier decision by the Board as a specific basis for reopening. In this situation the decision whether or not the applicant is entitled to a reopening can prove far more difficult.

Paragraph 13 (1990) requires as criteria for reopening:

(i) that a change in the applicant's medical condition has occurred;
(ii) that such change is a 'serious change' and is attributable to the original injury; and
(iii) that it is 'such a serious change ... that injustice would occur if the original assessment of compensation were allowed to stand'.

The Board does not lightly reopen a case under the 1990 Scheme and these conditions are strictly applied. The success or otherwise of an application to reopen will depend almost entirely upon the medical evidence produced to support it.

A change which is both 'serious' and 'medical' will not justify reopening unless it is 'attributable'. A serious change of circumstances, such as forced retirement from employment, will not justify reopening unless the cause of the forced retirement was a serious change in the medical condition. A later decision by the employer to dismiss or prematurely retire the applicant where the medical position has remained unchanged is not a basis for reopening. The latter situation may, however, be anticipated by the Board at the date of the original decision by expressly providing that in the event of forced retirement from employment attributable to the injury the applicant may apply for reopening, on the basis that this was seen as a possibility but considered best left for evaluation at a later date should it arise – although it is doubtful whether such reopening is strictly within the terms of para 13.

What is or is not 'a serious change in the applicant's medical condition' is entirely a question of fact for the Board to decide. Occasionally the alleged serious change is the belated discovery of a condition which inadequate medical evidence at the time of the earlier final award failed to disclose, or where subsequent events have shown the medical evidence at that time to have been wrong.

It is submitted that such cases are not within para 13. Also, where the 'serious change' is proved but has a cause other than the incident causing the original injury, it is not attributable to the incident giving rise to the original claim and the application cannot be reopened.

The Board's twenty-third report in 1987 and twenty-fifth report in 1989 cite cases on each side of the line in terms of attributability. In a case where both eyes were damaged in an attack and a final award made on the basis that the right eye would remain stable although the left eye may deteriorate, the Board allowed a reopening and made a further award where medical evidence proved seven years later that the applicant's vision was deteriorating and he was also developing a squint. The Board refused a reopening, however, where the final award had been made on the basis of an injury resulting in deafness in the left ear and the request for reopening was based upon deafness in the right ear which had developed subsequently and which medical evidence indicated was not attributable to the injury.

The rule that a case will not be reopened more than three years after the date of the final award is applied only if such reopening would involve extensive enquiries. It is not uncommon for cases to be reopened more than three years later, as the new medical evidence submitted with the application for reopening will often contain a strong prima facie case of serious change attributable to the incident.

Under the 1990 Scheme the decision by the chairman that a case may not be reopened is final.

Paragraph 13 expressly includes provision for reopening cases where the applicant has died as a result of his injuries. This aspect is considered in Chapter 14. The above deals with the reopening of cases decided under para 13 of the 1990 Scheme. The equivalent provisions of paras 56 and 57 of the 1996 Scheme will now be considered.

2. Reopening cases – paras 56 and 57 of the 1996 Scheme

Paragraphs 56 and 57 of the 1996 Scheme provide for the reopening of cases in the following terms:

> 56. A decision made by a claims officer and accepted by the applicant, or

a decision made by the Panel, will normally be regarded as final. The claims officer may, however, subsequently re-open a case where there has been such a material change in the victim's medical condition that injustice would occur if the original assessment of compensation were allowed to stand, or where he has since died in consequence of the injury.

57. A case will not be re-opened more than two years after the date of the final decision unless the claims officer is satisfied, on the basis of evidence presented in support of the application to re-open the case, that the renewed application can be considered without a need for further extensive enquiries.

As with para 13 of the 1990 Scheme, this new provision for reopening is discretionary – para 56 gives the basis for reopening as being 'such a material change in the victim's medical condition that injustice would occur if the original assessment of compensation were allowed to stand'.

The significant change in wording which may make requests for reopening more likely to succeed than under para 13 of the 1990 Scheme is the use of the words 'material change' in para 56 rather than 'serious change' as in the 1990 Scheme.

The 1990 Scheme requires the 'serious change' to be such that it would be an 'injustice' to leave the original award unchanged. Paragraph 56 (1996) requires a 'material change' which suggests that a change will only be 'material' if it is sufficiently serious to result in the original assessment being 'materially' below the level of compensation appropriate to the injury currently established by new medical evidence.

It will not be 'material' unless it is also attributable to the injury which was the basis of the original application.

The decision to reopen or not to reopen is made by the claims officer of the Authority. If that decision is not accepted, it may be reviewed by a more senior claims officer than the claims officer who made the original decision under the provisions for review of decisions contained in paras 58(b), 59 and 60 of the 1996 Scheme. If the decision on review is not accepted, an appeal from that decision is made to the Chairman of the Appeals Panel or another adjudicator nominated by him (para 66, 1996 Scheme). Paragraph 67 provides that where the Chairman or other adjudicator 'dismisses the appeal, his decision will be final'.

The decision whether or not to reopen under para 13 of the 1990 Scheme is made by a Board Member but only the Chairman of the Board may refuse to reopen and his decision in that regard is final.

Paragraph 57 of the 1996 Scheme provides that applications to reopen will not be accepted more than two years after the date of the final decision unless the evidence presented in support indicates that this can be done without the need for further extensive enquiries.

Chapter 18

Reconsideration of decisions

The immediately preceding chapter, *Reconsideration of a case after a final award*, deals with the last possible stage of an application, namely a fresh consideration of an application which has, at an earlier date, been the subject of a final decision by a claims officer or by the Appeals Panel under the 1996 Scheme. Earlier chapters have considered the process of an application through the stages of decision by a claims officer, review by a more senior claims officer, decision by the Appeals Panel and the additional possible procedures involving re-hearing of appeals (paras 79 to 82, 1996) and reopening of cases (paras 56 and 57, 1996) where the conditions for re-hearing or reopening contained in those paragraphs of the Scheme are met.

This chapter deals with the provisions in the 1996 Scheme which entitle the Authority, or in certain cases the Appeals Panel, to reconsider a decision already made. It does not fit into the sequence of initial decision, review, hearing by the Appeals Panel or re-hearing of appeal or re-opening, as it is a statement of a right vested in the Authority by the Scheme to 'think again' with regard to a decision already made, whether or not that decision has already been communicated to the applicant.

In an earlier chapter under the heading 'Entitlement to an award' at page 225, the effect of paras 12 and 22 of the 1990 Scheme has been considered. These paragraphs contain, amongst other provisions, the principle that 'an applicant will have no title to an award offered until the Board have received notification in writing that he accepts it' (para 22, 1990) and in para 12, 1990 the provision that the Board may reduce or refuse an award 'at any stage before receiving notification of acceptance of a final award'.

The combined effect of these provisions in the 1990 Scheme, consistent with the nature of an *ex gratia* scheme for compensation payments out of public funds, is that the Board is free at any time in the light of the information coming before it, to make an appropriate decision on the merits of the application. This power is exercised usually where fresh information comes to hand which places a different complexion upon the case, justifying or even requiring that the original decision should not stand.

The classic example of this is where the Board has decided to make a full award on the merits of the application but subsequent information discloses to the Board that the applicant has a serious record of criminal convictions. In a recent case dealt with by the Board at a hearing, the Board refused to make any further award on the grounds of the applicant's record of convictions, even though without knowledge of the convictions, the single member had offered a substantial award for serious injuries in respect of which the applicant had requested a hearing. The applicant had already been offered and accepted an interim award which had been paid to him but, there being no title to an award until written notification of acceptance has been received by the Board, the Board was free to reach a fresh decision on eligibility at the hearing based upon all the information then before it.

Paragraphs 53 to 55 of the 1996 Scheme under the heading 'Reconsideration of decisions' incorporate similar principles to the above in the new Scheme. In the new 1996 Scheme, however, the provision for reconsideration has been more tightly drawn and should avoid difficulties which have from time to time arisen in the interpretation of the 1990 Scheme as to the point at which an applicant is entitled to an award. Paragraph 53 states that 'a decision made by a claims officer ... may be reconsidered at any time before *actual payment of a final award* where there is new evidence or a change in circumstances' (author's italics). It goes on to make clear that even if an interim payment has been made, this does not preclude reconsideration of issues of eligibility.

The most significant change in the 1996 Scheme in this regard is to give the Authority the express right to reconsider at any time before payment of a final award, so that even if the applicant has accepted an award in writing and the Authority has received that written acceptance, reconsideration is still possible 'where there is new evidence or a change in circumstances'.

Paragraph 54 is essentially a safeguard to ensure that where a claims officer proposes to reconsider a decision which has already been communicated to the applicant, the principles of natural justice (and the terms of para 54) require the Authority to give the applicant an opportunity to make further representations which he wishes the Authority to take into account in reconsidering the decision. Whether or not the applicant takes this opportunity, he will be sent written notification of the outcome of the reconsideration.

Paragraph 55 deals with the situation where the decision which is to be reconsidered has been made 'with a direction by adjudicators on determining an appeal under paragraph 77' – in other words, where it is a decision on a hearing by the Appeals Panel which is to be the subject of the reconsideration. In such a case where the claims officer considers, before the award has been paid, that there is new evidence or a change in circumstances which justifies reconsideration, the Authority 'will refer the case to the Panel for rehearing'.

It can thus be seen that this power to reconsider on new evidence or a change in circumstances is a continuing thread which runs throughout the decision-making procedures under the 1996 Scheme, up to actual payment of a final award. This principle is consistent with a scheme providing compensation from public funds and ensures, so far as possible, that payments of awards are made only where the circumstances of the case establish eligibility under the terms of the Scheme.

Appendix 1

Judicial review of the Board's decisions – summaries of selected cases

R v Criminal Injuries Compensation Board, ex parte Lain

20 April 1967 – Request for hearing – not an appeal – a fresh start

This decision of the High Court came early in the history of the operation of the Scheme and contains within the judgment of the court several important statements of principle. The decision established that in determining applications under the Scheme the Board was performing a public duty and a quasi-judicial function and that the High Court had jurisdiction to supervise the discharge of those functions even though the function of the Board was derived from the prerogative of the Crown and not by way of statute. The court accordingly had jurisdiction in relation to decisions of the Board by way of judicial review, and not by way of appeal.

With regard to the principles of the Scheme itself, the court made clear that the hearing by three members of the Board subsequent to a decision by a single member of the Board was in no sense an appeal from the decision of the single member of the Board. The hearing before three members of the Board was a hearing of the application *de novo*.

It had been submitted on behalf of the applicant that the decision of the three-member Board that no award should be made, the single member having decided that the applicant was entitled to an award, was wrong in law. It was argued on the applicant's behalf that the Board wrongfully assumed a power to reduce or set aside an original award made by the single member and that there was no such power under the Scheme which only entitled the Board at a hearing to dismiss the appeal and thus uphold the original award of the single member or to allow the appeal so as to increase the compensation payable under the Scheme. The court rejected those submissions. A hearing before three members of the Board was a renewal of the application, a fresh start, and was not therefore an appeal against the decision of the single member.

The limitations of the process of judicial review were also considered within the terms of the court's decision. The court found that the decision of the three-member Board disclosed no error of law on its face and the motion for an order of certiorari to quash the decision of the Board was dismissed.

R v Criminal Injuries Compensation Board, ex parte Townend

9 June 1970 – Not pursuing complaint of common assault – not 'conduct' (1969 Scheme)

This case concerned an application for an order of certiorari to quash a decision of the Board. The order applied for was granted by the High Court. The decision centred upon what amounted to 'conduct' for the purposes of para 17 of the 1969 Scheme in equivalent terms to para 6(c) of the 1990 Scheme. The court held that not pursuing a complaint under section 42 of the Offences Against the Person Act, a charge of common assault which can only be brought by the victim, did not amount to 'conduct' under para 17 of the 1969 Scheme. The court stated that the mere fact that the applicant does not pursue a complaint under section 42 or 43 or that he asks the police not to prosecute under those sections in order to avoid the effect of section 45, which is that other remedies would be closed to him, is not in itself 'conduct' which would make it inappropriate to make an award. The court went on to state, however, that in other cases and other situations the failure or refusal to prosecute or co-operate in a prosecution might well be matters which the Board would be entitled to take into account under para 17 of the 1969 Scheme.

R v Criminal Injuries Compensation Board, ex parte Schofield

31 March 1971 - Bystander knocked down in pursuit of suspected thief - accidental injury - directly attributable (pre 1979 Scheme)

This decision of the court, in allowing the application for certiorari quashing a decision of the Board, was a decision upon the wording in the 1969 Scheme, equivalent to para 4 of the 1990 Scheme, in relation to persons sustaining injury directly attributable to an arrest or attempted arrest of an offender or suspected offender. The applicant had suffered injury when she was knocked down when a store detective was chasing a suspected thief from a department store which the applicant was about to enter. It was not clear whether the pursuer or the pursued had knocked the applicant down, but the court held this distinction was not material to the decision. The majority decision of Lord Parker LCJ and Widgery LJ (as he then was), Bridge J (as he then was) dissenting, was that the Board had been in error in deciding that the applicant, having been knocked down accidentally, had not sustained injuries which were directly attributable to the arrest, the Board taking the view that these injuries were indirectly attributable to the arrest. The court held that the Scheme contained no such distinction, the cause of the applicant's injury being directly attributable to the attempt to arrest a suspected offender. The application was therefore within the Scheme.

In his dissenting judgment, Bridge J considered that the Board's decision should not be disturbed by the court, stating that as a document the Scheme merely enshrined the rules for the Board's conduct. It was not recognisable as a legislative document. It was not expressed in the kind of language one expects from a Parliamentary draftsman and bore all the hallmarks of a document which laid down the broad guidelines of policy. The learned judge further commented that the Scheme contained in its terms the words 'the Board will be entirely responsible for deciding what compensation should be paid in individual cases and their decisions will not be subject to appeal or ministerial review'. The working of the Scheme, however, was stated to be subject to review by Parliament, and if Parliament saw fit to alter the Scheme it could do so with a minimum of formality. The learned judge concluded his dissenting judgment by indicating that he could not resist the conclusion that the majority decision of the court widened the Scheme beyond the scope which it was intended to have.

It should be noted that this decision of the court was largely instrumental in the addition of what is now para 6(d) of the 1979 Scheme and the 1990 Scheme. This provision has meant that a person who accidentally sustains injury directly attributable to the circumstances envisaged by para 4(b) of the scheme needs to show that he had taken an exceptional risk justified in all the circumstances before being entitled to an award.

R v Criminal Injuries Compensation Board, ex parte Baptiste

30 July 1971 – Board not obliged to state separate elements of claim when making award

The applicant applied to the court for an order of certiorari to quash a decision of the Board on the grounds that the decision of the Board did not accord with the principles of natural justice. In the course of argument the court made clear that it was not incumbent upon the Board, when making an award, to indicate either an arithmetical approach to the calculation of the award or to show as separate elements within the claim the award for pain and suffering, loss of earnings and loss of future pension rights respectively. The application was allowed, however, on the grounds that the Board had misdirected itself with regard to the medical evidence, and the Board reheard the case as a result of the granting of the order in the High Court and made a further award.

R v Criminal Injuries Compensation Board, ex parte Staten

2 February 1972 – 'Members of the same family' – question of fact

The application to the court was for an order quashing a decision of the Board refusing compensation. The court considered the meaning of the words 'living together ... as members of the same family' in para 7 of the 1969 Scheme. Under that Scheme personal injury arising from such circumstances was excluded. The court ruled that the question whether the parties were living together as members of the same family was essentially a question of fact to be decided by the Board. The application was dismissed. (See *Richardson* on page 303.)

R v Criminal Injuries Compensation Board, ex parte Fox

8 February 1972 – Para 7, 1969 Scheme

This was an application to the High Court for an order of certiorari in respect of a decision of the Board refusing compensation. The case was decided largely on questions of fact as to the meaning of para 7 of the 1969 Scheme and the meaning of the word 'family' for the purposes of that Scheme.

R v Criminal Injuries Compensation Board, ex parte Lawton

22 June 1972 – Whether suspected thief escaping from restraint under Mental Health Act is a 'suspected offender' – attempted apprehension

The applicant had sustained injury when pursuing a man who had been arrested on suspicion of theft and who had remained in custody during the course of which an order requiring his admission to hospital under section 29 of the Mental Health Act 1959 had been made. Before being taken to hospital, the suspect escaped from police custody. The applicant, a police officer, was injured in giving pursuit. The court observed that although a person who escaped from restraint under a Mental Health Act order committed no offence, in these particular circumstances the person whom the officer was pursuing when he sustained injury was not escaping from restraint under the Mental Health Act but from the original arrest on suspicion of theft. Accordingly, the court held that the applicant's injury was directly attributable to his attempting to apprehend a suspected offender. The application was allowed.

R v Criminal Injuries Compensation Board, ex parte Ince

20 July 1973 (Court of Appeal) – Direct attributability – not affected by contributory negligence of applicant

The applicant was the widow of a police officer killed when his police car was in collision at a time when he was answering a call to attend at the scene of a crime or suspected crime. The Board was at that time of the view that police officers, being continuously engaged in the prevention of crime, in order to bring themselves within the Scheme had to show that they were present at the scene of the crime and were taking active steps to prevent its commission when they sustained injury.

The Court of Appeal decided that the Board had misdirected itself in this regard, and allowed the application. Moreover the negligence of the applicant would not prevent the circumstances from coming within the scope of the Scheme if the actions of the police officer were in the course of his preventing or attempting to prevent an offence or arrest a suspected offender.

The Board had concluded that the cause of the death of PC Ince was his act of folly in crossing the lights at red, and accordingly his death was not directly attributable either to the attempted arrest of a suspected offender or to the attempted prevention of an offence. The Divisional Court had felt that this was a finding with which it could not interfere, but the Court of Appeal came to a different conclusion, stating that attributability was a question of law just as causation was. The Court of Appeal stated that 'directly attributable' did not mean 'solely attributable'. It meant directly attributable, in whole or in part, to the state of affairs as PC Ince assumed them to be. If the death of PC Ince was directly attributable to his answering the call for help, it did not cease to be so attributable because he was negligent or foolish in crossing traffic lights at red in the course of doing so.

The Court of Appeal also had cause to comment upon the Board's decision that any conduct on the part of the applicant had to be taken into account. The Court of Appeal concluded that the Board could not treat such matters as contributory negligence as conduct. To be 'conduct' within the meaning of the Scheme there had to be something reprehensible or provocative, something which could fairly be described as bad conduct or misconduct, rather than failure to take reasonable care (in the particular case) for his own safety. In the particular case the Court of Appeal did not consider that the principle was altered by the fact that information upon which the late PC Ince was acting was erroneous.

The application to the Court of Appeal for certiorari was allowed and the Board was required to grant a fresh hearing.

R v Criminal Injuries Compensation Board, ex parte Richardson

26 November 1973 – Maximum loss of earnings – 1969 Scheme

The court dismissed an application for an order of certiorari to quash a decision of the Board in relation to the assessment of compensation. The applicant was the widow of a serving police officer who was murdered while on duty. The compensation was assessed in accordance with the Board's 1969 Scheme which was different in a number of material respects from the 1979 and 1990 Schemes. The judgment of this case is authority for the method of calculation of loss of earnings under para 11(a) of the 1969 Scheme. Although the application was under para 12 of the 1969 Scheme, being the application by a dependent widow, the court applied para 11(a). The judgment specifies the method by which the maximum figure of 'twice the average of industrial earnings' applied under the 1969 Scheme. These rules remain material in cases subject to the terms of the 1969 Scheme which will generally be only those cases which have been reopened under para 13 of the present Scheme.

The substantial differences between a calculation under para 11(a) of the 1969 Scheme and a calculation under para 14(a) of the 1979 or 1990 Schemes are explained in Chapter 12.

R v Criminal Injuries Compensation Board, ex parte Tong

14 June 1976 (Court of Appeal) - Death of applicant - point of time at which entitlement to award arises (prior to 1990 Scheme)

The applicant had sustained injury. The Board had decided that the application was within the terms of the Scheme and an interim award had been made. Subsequently the Board made a final award but before that final award could be communicated to the applicant he died for reasons unrelated to the incident which caused his injury. The single member had made the decision to make a final award on 25 February 1973. The applicant died on 6 March 1973, the single member's final award never having been communicated to the applicant in his lifetime. The Board decided that there was no entitlement to the award and that the award had lapsed.

The decision of the Board was under the terms of the 1969 Scheme. The situation which arose in this case was one which was not envisaged by the framers of that Scheme who had made no provision stating at what point in time entitlement to an award rose. It was not disputed that the applicant's entitlement to an award died with him as in the case of personal injuries at common law before the Law Reform Act 1934. However, argument in the case centred upon the point of time at which an award vested in the applicant. The court decided in the circumstances of the case, and having regard to the wording of the Scheme as it then stood, that the award should be regarded as vested in the applicant as soon as the single member had made his award, regardless of whether it had been communicated before the applicant's death. The court accordingly allowed the appeal.

(It should be noted that this aspect of the Scheme became expressly regulated by the last sentence of para 22 of the 1990 Scheme, and can now be found in the last sentence of para 50 of the 1996 Scheme.) (See also *Earls* on page 280.)

R v Criminal Injuries Compensation Board, ex parte Clowes

30 March 1977 - Crime of violence - interpretation of 'recklessness' for purposes of Scheme - section 1(2) of Criminal Damage Act 1971 considered

The applicant applied for an order of certiorari quashing a decision of the Board in relation to an injury suffered by Mr Clowes. The applicant had sustained injury from a gas explosion. The circumstances were that a man had committed suicide by taking a hammer and chisel and breaking off the end of a gas standpipe in the house. The Board had refused compensation, concluding that the deceased, when he broke off the top of the gas main with the hammer and chisel, intended no harm to anyone other than himself - nor did he foresee that his actions might cause physical harm to another.

The court considered in some detail the nature of crime of violence and whether or not the actions of the deceased amounted to a crime of violence. In particular the court considered section 1(2) of the Criminal Damage Act 1971 and decided that the Board had not considered this specific offence in dealing with the applicant's case. This section made it an offence without lawful excuse to destroy or damage any property intending (*inter alia*) by the destruction or damage to endanger the life of another or being reckless as to whether the life of another would be thereby endangered. The court allowed the application for an order quashing the Board's decision, the Board being required to rehear the case and to give consideration to section 1(2).

The Board, in rehearing the matter, again disallowed the application. Having applied the principles of section 1(2) of the Criminal Damage Act 1971 to the facts of the case, the Board was not satisfied on the balance of probabilities that there was present in the mind of the deceased any consideration other than his desire to take his own life. Accordingly, on the interpretation of 'reckless' as set out in *R v Parker* (1976), the application failed.

R v Criminal Injuries Compensation Board, ex parte McGuffie and Smith

13 October 1977 – Fatal application – child's award for loss of mother's services belongs to the child

The applicants applied for an order for certiorari in respect of a decision by the Board. The claim arose from the unlawful killing of the mother of young children, and the claim had been made by Mrs McGuffie and Mrs Smith in respect of their financial losses relating to their caring for those children following the death of their mother. The court decided that the Board had made its compensation award in the wrong form, in that it awarded sums to the carers whereas in law the awards belonged to the children because, in respect of loss of mother's services, the awards were similar to a claim made under the Fatal Accidents Act. The court referred to the authority of *Donnelly v Joyce*, decided in 1974 in the Queen's Bench Division, which indicated that the award may be measured by the reasonable loss of earnings of the persons providing services in respect of the mother, but that the award when so assessed was the children's money and any award should be made to the children accordingly. The judgment also indicates the approach to the assessment of an award in cases of loss of mother's services.

R v Criminal Injuries Compensation Board, ex parte RJC (An Infant)

20 January 1978 – In making its decision Board should not limit or fetter its discretion

The applicant, an infant, sought an order quashing a decision of the Board refusing compensation. The circumstances were that the applicant had become involved in a fight with a number of teenagers. Paragraph 17 of the 1969 Scheme required the Board to have regard to the applicant's conduct and also to his character and way of life. The Board's advisory statement dated June 1977, which indicated the Board's interpretation of para 17 of the Scheme as it then stood, indicated that a member of a gang who was injured in the course of a gang fight would not receive an award. In its decision the Board stated that it was its impression that the applicant had willingly entered into a fight with a member of the rival gang, and that in those circumstances it was inappropriate to make an award from public funds.

It was argued for the applicant that the Board had not fully exercised its judicial function. The Board was given a discretion and was required to exercise that discretion under para 17 of the Scheme. By making its decision on the basis of the principle contained in the Board's statement, the Board was purporting to limit its discretion. As this discretion was an essential part of the Board's powers and duties under the Scheme, the application was wrongly decided in principle. The court stated that it had power to review the decision and the Board's exercise of its quasi-judicial function. In the circumstances the court allowed the application and the matter was sent back to the Board for reconsideration.

R v Criminal Injuries Compensation Board, ex parte Westrop

18 February 1980 (Queen's Bench Division) – Reduction – award reduced by payment recovered as result of civil proceedings

The application to the court was to seek direction by the court that the Board further consider the applicant's claim for compensation. The applicant had received £25,000 on the compromise of his action against a third party for common law damages. It was not contended that such sum represented the full value of his injuries, but was the sum accepted in settlement. The applicant had also received a total of £20,000 by way of interim payments by the Board under the Scheme. The court was asked to rule on the duty of the Board under the provisions now contained in para 21 of the 1990 Scheme and para 48 of the 1996 Scheme, whereby a claim for compensation will be reduced by the amount of any sum recovered as a result of civil proceedings. It was held that an applicant or plaintiff was entitled to no more than full compensation, i.e. full satisfaction of the value of his claim, but if he has settled his civil claim for those reasons which generally apply in such matters, at a sum less than the full value, and the circumstances of the injury entitle him to full compensation under the Scheme for the equivalent of common law damages for the injury suffered, he may look to the Board for that part of the damages in full not recovered as a result of the civil proceedings.

R v Criminal Injuries Compensation Board, ex parte Comerford

19 June 1980 – Crime of violence – 'conduct' – severity of applicant's injuries not regarded in test of 'appropriateness' in making or withholding award

Application was made to the court for an order of judicial review by way of certiorari. The applicant suffered very severe injuries after being butted in the course of a fight in a public house, as a result of which he fell to the ground, hit his head and suffered severe brain damage. The court considered the detailed evidence before the Board in deciding the application, including the question of self-defence and the question of conduct. The first question went to whether there had been a crime of violence, and the second concerned the discretion of the Board to reduce or withhold compensation under para 17 of the 1969 Scheme. The Board decided on the whole of the evidence that even if a crime of violence had been committed against the applicant (and the Board was not so satisfied) his conduct, both in his actions and his words, was of so provocative a nature as to render it inappropriate to make an award of compensation. The court rejected the submission on behalf of the applicant that 'appropriateness' under para 17 (the same word as in para 6 of the 1990 Scheme) should be interpreted to have regard to the severity of the applicant's injuries. To do so would mean that the court was judging the quality of the applicant's acts and words by the accident of their result, a proposition which was not in accordance with the Scheme. The proper approach was to look at the conduct of the parties, both in their words and actions, and not to have regard to the consequences of the blow which caused the injury, although the Board should have regard to the nature of the blow. If the Board concluded on the evidence that the applicant was hit because 'he asked for it' then that is a situation which the Board is entitled to take into account by either rejecting or reducing the claim, regardless of the unforeseen and unforeseeable and appalling circumstances which in the particular case occurred.

R v Criminal Injuries Compensation Board, ex parte Lloyd

4 July 1980 – Burden of proof – conduct – reliance on hearsay evidence rather than oral evidence – principles of natural justice

The court considered a request for an order quashing a decision of the Board refusing compensation. The judgment contains the consideration of numerous principles relating to the 1969 Scheme, in particular 'conduct' under para 17 of that Scheme, the burden of proof in relation to considerations of conduct, and the consideration by the Board of written statements of witnesses who declined to give oral evidence at the Board's hearing as against the oral evidence of the applicant at the hearing. It was submitted for the applicant that it was contrary to the rules of natural justice that the Board should permit itself to rely on hearsay evidence of that sort to the exclusion of the oral evidence given by the applicant himself and the police officer.

The court considered various authorities on the rules of natural justice in relation to a person exercising a quasi-judicial function including the principle that the decision must be based on evidence. The court considered that the written statements of witnesses who declined to attend the Board's hearing to give oral evidence had some probative value. Having come to that conclusion it was not for the court to reopen the consideration which the Board then gave to such evidence as this was a matter for the Board. The application was dismissed.

R v Criminal Injuries Compensation Board, ex parte Carr

10 July 1980 – Injury attributable to 'attempting to prevent offence'

The Board had rejected an application in which the applicant had suffered an injury while giving pursuit to a motorcyclist whom the applicant wished to stop at the scene of an accident. The question was whether the applicant had suffered his injury whilst preventing or attempting to prevent an offence. The offence relied on was failing to stop after an accident under section 25 of the Road Traffic Act 1972. The Board had come to the conclusion that the motorcyclist, having started his machine with a view to departing the scene, had already committed the offence and the applicant was therefore not in a position to prevent it. The application had therefore been rejected. The court disagreed with this interpretation of the effect of the motorcyclist's actions and decided that the Board had not had sufficient evidence to come to the conclusion that it came to in the case. The application for an order quashing the Board's decision and requiring a rehearing was therefore allowed.

R v Criminal Injuries Compensation Board, ex parte W (An Infant)

18 December 1980 – 1969 Scheme – 'satisfaction' of claim by civil proceedings

The applicant had received a settlement of a civil claim in respect of the injuries which were the subject of his application to the Board. The application was made under the terms of the 1969 Scheme. The 1969 Scheme contained a provision that it was not intended that a person who had pursued a claim for damages for personal injuries should obtain compensation from the Board in respect of those injuries in addition to obtaining satisfaction from that claim. The court interpreted the word 'satisfaction' as full satisfaction. In the particular case there had merely been a settlement which could have taken into account doubts on the question of liability. Accordingly the settlement did not amount to satisfaction under what was then para 24 of the 1969 Scheme.

(It should be noted that this matter is addressed by para 21 of the 1990 Scheme and paras 48 and 49 of the 1996 Scheme.)

R v Criminal Injuries Compensation Board, ex parte Richard C

3 February 1981 – 'Material factor' not considered by the Board in exercising discretion – Board's Statement for guidance (1979 Scheme)

The applicant had what the court described as 'an appalling criminal record'. The court was asked to consider the Board's Statement. The Statement was described as having been issued for the benefit of applicants and their advisers as a guide to how the Board was likely to determine applications (the court underlining the word 'likely'). The Statement also indicated that in making its decisions the Board would exercise its discretion subject to its proper interpretation of the Scheme. The Statement indicated that it would be unlikely that an application would be rejected because the applicant's convictions where the injury had been sustained in a genuine attempt to uphold the law or when rendering assistance to someone who was being attacked.

While confirming that the discretion was entirely a matter for the Board, the court found that there was no evidence that the Board had taken this material factor, namely the injury having been sustained in a genuine attempt to uphold the law, into account in deciding to reject the application. In accordance with the *Wednesbury* case, failure to take into account a material consideration was a ground upon which the decision may be quashed. There being nothing on the face of the Board's decision to indicate that it had paid the slightest regard to those matters, the application to the court succeeded and the matter was referred back to the Board for further consideration.

R v Criminal Injuries Compensation Board, ex parte Parsons

19 May 1981 – Principle of 'direct attributability'

Application was made for an order of certiorari to quash a decision of the Board on the grounds that the injuries suffered by the applicant were not directly attributable to a crime of violence. The applicant had claimed compensation for personal injuries in the form of nervous shock and depression caused as a result of seeing the headless body of a suicide on a line next to that along which he was driving a train. The judgment of the court considered in detail questions of what constitutes a crime of violence and the law relating to nervous shock cases, including the Court of Appeal decision in *McLoughlin v O'Brian* (1981) – reversed by the House of Lords in 1983. Authorities referred to included *R v Criminal Injuries Compensation Board ex parte Ince* (1973). The principle of direct attributability was also considered in the course of the judgment.

The court held that the Board had decided the case wrongly because the court took the view that the applicant's injuries were directly attributable to a crime of violence and that the injury was not too remote.

(It should be noted that the subsequent decision of the Court of Appeal in *Warner* relating to injury attributable to a suicide on a railway line ruled out such cases for the purposes of the Scheme in England and Wales. In relation to injuries sustained after 1 February 1990, however, such cases fell within the new subpara (c) of para 4 of the 1990 Scheme. Paragraphs 8 and 9 of the 1996 Scheme apply to all applications received on or after 1 April 1996.)

R v Criminal Injuries Compensation Board, ex parte Crangle

6 November 1981 – 'Wednesbury' rule – unreasonable decision

Application to the court was for an order of certiorari in relation to a decision of the Board refusing compensation. The applicant had sustained injuries the circumstances surrounding which he was unable to recall. The applicant had been drinking with two friends. All three young men had laid down on a piece of common land with a view to sobering up. The two friends left the applicant. He was found the following morning suffering from a number of injuries including a serious injury to the head.

The Board had considered the available evidence indicating the circumstances in which the applicant might have sustained his injuries. The Board had indicated that it was for the applicant to establish on the evidence that his application came within the terms of the Scheme, that he had sustained injury attributable to a crime of violence rather than from an accident. The Board was not satisfied that the applicant had been robbed. The Board found the recollection of his friends unreliable; in the circumstances the Board did not know precisely how or why any violence arose – nor did the Board know whether any assailant may have acted in self-defence.

Having considered all the evidence before the Board, the court concluded that on that evidence the possibility of the applicant having sustained his injuries as a result of an action in self-defence by his assailant was so slight that the Board should have ignored it. Accordingly the application to the court to set aside the Board's decision was granted. The court made clear the principle that it could interfere in a Board's decision only where it came to the conclusion that no reasonable Board could have reached the conclusion that was reached on the evidence before it and the court so concluded in this particular case.

R v Criminal Injuries Compensation Board, ex parte WEB

4 February 1982 – Reduction for convictions – further convictions after Board's decision – no final award

The applicant sought judicial review of the Board's decision. The single member of the Board had made no award to the applicant, having regard to the applicant's convictions – the Scheme entitling the Board to consider the applicant's character and way of life including his criminal convictions.

The applicant requested a hearing before three members of the Board who, having considered the applicant's convictions, decided that an award would be made but subject to a reduction of two-thirds of what would have been the full award. The application was then adjourned as the Board was not in a position to make a final award, there being various calculations to be made in relation to social security benefits and also further medical evidence to be obtained in relation to the applicant's injury. Before the Board was in a position to make a final award, it received notice of further criminal proceedings against the applicant and indicated that the decision of the Board would be further adjourned until the result of those subsequent criminal proceedings was known.

It was submitted to the court on behalf of the applicant that the Board had no power to consider such further matters as the Board had, it was submitted, already made a binding determination of the appropriate reduction under para 17 of the 1969 Scheme and, having made that determination, was not entitled to reopen that matter. The court rejected that submission. Although it might be the case that the Board could not alter its decision to make a two-thirds reduction on the same evidence as was before it when that decision was made, the Board was entitled to reopen that decision if subsequent events altered the position as it was then before the Board. On the occurrence of such further event, namely further convictions, the Board was entitled to go into that new matter because there would be no unfairness in doing so, and the only limitation on the Board's power in this respect was the requirement that the Board acted fairly. The application to the court was therefore dismissed.

R v Criminal Injuries Compensation Board, ex parte Cragg

23 April 1982 – Reduction by single member – request for hearing – fresh start – hearing de novo – nil award at hearing

Application was made for judicial review of a decision of the Board. The applicant claimed compensation in respect of the loss of an eye resulting from injuries sustained when he was shot with an airgun. The case involved the consideration by the Board of circumstances in which the applicant, aged thirteen at the time of the injury, was engaged in a dangerous game with other children. The injury was caused in the course of that dangerous game. The single member had made a reduction of 50 per cent having regard to the applicant's conduct. The applicant requested a hearing. Before the commencement of the hearing, the chairman of the Board had indicated to the applicant in the presence of his solicitor that the Board would consider the matter afresh if the hearing proceeded. It would reach its decision solely in the light of the evidence which would be adduced at the hearing, and if the Board took a different view from that taken by the single member it was possible that the Board might come a different conclusion including the possibility that it might reject the application entirely.

That is what in fact happened and the Board, having heard the evidence, concluded that the applicant's behaviour was such in relation to the dangerous game in which he was taking an active part that it would be inappropriate to make any award at all.

Having heard submissions on behalf of the applicant, the court was unable to conclude that the Board had come to a wholly unreasonable decision, and accordingly the application to the court failed.

R v Criminal Injuries Compensation Board, ex parte Blood

11 May 1982 – Convictions – pre and post incident causing injury

Application for leave to apply by way of judicial review was refused by the court. The matter related to the refusal of an application for compensation by the Board on the grounds of the applicant's convictions. The applicant had a sustained pattern of assaults and violence over a period of 15 years. The applicant had then kept out of trouble after the start of a probation order but then was convicted again of a crime of violence a few months after he had himself been injured and made application to the Board. It was pleaded for the applicant that the Board had not allowed evidence as to the merits of the matter before dealing with the subsequent conviction and disallowing the application. The court concluded that the Board had heard submissions and was entitled to come to the decision it had come to in the case.

R v Criminal Injuries Compensation Board, ex parte Penny

18 November 1982 (Court of Appeal) – Crime of violence – back injury – carrying heavy prisoner – no crime of violence

This was an appeal from a decision of Hodgson J whereby he refused to allow judicial review of a decision of the Board. The applicant had sustained injury when, together with three other prison officers, he was engaged in removing from his ordinary cell to a hospital strip-cell a prisoner who was very large, weighing eighteen stone and with a history of violence. As had been expected by the applicant and his prison officer colleagues, the prisoner was reluctant to be so removed and as a consequence had to be carried some 200 yards by the four men including the applicant during the course of which journey the prisoner was obstructive. Immediately after the incident the applicant felt acute back pain. It was discovered that he had a disc lesion in his back which had been exacerbated or possibly caused during the course of the journey carrying the prisoner from one cell to the other.

The Board had concluded on the evidence that the injury was not directly attributable to a crime of violence but that on the balance of probabilities the applicant's injury was caused by the strain imposed by the weight of the prisoner and the course over which the prisoner had to be carried. The application to the Board had therefore been rejected.

There was little evidence in the view of the court to suggest that there had been even a technical assault which had resulted in the injury to the applicant, and that essentially the dead weight of carrying a very large man in these circumstances had been the cause of the injury. Nor was the court persuaded that the action, in removing the prisoner in these circumstances, was an attempt to prevent the commission of a crime of violence. The appeal was dismissed.

R v Criminal Injuries Compensation Board, ex parte Prior

19 November 1982 – Onus of proof on applicant to show that he comes within the Scheme

The applicant sought judicial review of a decision of the Board on the grounds that the Board had misdirected itself as to the proper standard of proof to apply and also that there was no proper material on which the Board could come to the decision which it did.

The applicant had been attacked at the door of his own home when he was shot in the leg.

The court considered the terms of para 17 of the 1969 Scheme – the equivalent to the present para 6 – giving the Board discretion to reduce or withhold an award having regard to the conduct or to the character and way of life of the applicant. The court also considered the effect of the provision under the Scheme whereby 'at the hearing, it will be for the applicant to make out his case ... ', and the provision in the Scheme whereby the applicant had a duty to co-operate with the police.

At the hearing the Board had heard evidence from the applicant and from a senior police officer. The application was dismissed by the Board.

In the written reasons given by the Board for its decision, which were before the court, the Board stated that the burden of proof in respect of matters arising under para 17 of the 1969 Scheme, namely conduct and character and way of life, was on the applicant, citing *R v CICB ex parte Lloyd*, a judgment of the Divisional Court on 4 July 1980.

The court disagreed with this statement of the burden of proof upon the applicant, stating that although the onus is upon the applicant to show that he comes within the Scheme and has sustained injury directly attributable to a crime of violence, the onus is not on the applicant to show that matters of conduct and character and way of life do not apply to his case, as these matters are for consideration in the Board's discretion under the Scheme. However the legal burden should not be confused with the evidential burden, the court stating that if there was *prima facie* evidence against the applicant in respect of such matters as conduct or character it was then up to the applicant to discharge the resulting evidential burden. If evidence was put before the Board which showed a *prima facie* case which would make para 17 (para 6 of the 1990 Scheme; para 13 of the 1996 Scheme) applicable, there was an onus on the applicant to show, on the balance of probabilities, that those facts were not such as to bring that paragraph into operation, giving the Board a discretion to withhold or reduce compensation.

The case turned upon whether the applicant had some knowledge of the circumstances in which he came to be shot and had not made full disclosure to the police with regard to it.

The court stated that the test was not whether the court or another tribunal might have come to another decision had it had that evidence before it, but whether there was no material before the Board to justify the decision which it reached. Although the court expressed disagreement with the Board's statement of the onus of proof, the court was satisfied that this had not affected the proper exercise of the Board's discretion with regard to the evidence which the Board had before it. The application was dismissed.

R v Criminal Injuries Compensation Board, ex parte Earls

21 December 1982 (Court of Appeal) – Request for hearing – total rejection of single member's decision – no vesting of interim award by single member

The initial decision of the Board had been to make an award to the late applicant, Michael Earls, subject to a reduction of one-third by reason of the late applicant's own conduct. Subject to the decision of the Board being accepted, i.e. the reduction, the Board also made an interim award of £500. The late applicant had, through his solicitors, requested a hearing. Before the hearing the applicant died. The solicitors for the estate of the deceased applicant requested that the hearing should take place nevertheless. The Board heard the application. The Board decided that, although before requesting the hearing the late applicant was entitled to the interim award of £500, having requested the hearing he had rejected the Board's decision *in toto* so that the whole matter was once more at large. There was accordingly nothing to vest in the applicant unless and until a further decision was made in the applicant's favour by a Board at the hearing. The claim was personal to the applicant and, the applicant having died, the application must fail. The Board made no award and the entitlement to the interim award thus lapsed, the applicant having rejected the single member's reduced award and interim award in his lifetime and the Board having no basis upon which to make an award subsequent to the applicant's death. This did not preclude an application by the deceased's widow under what were then paras 12 and 13 of the Scheme (now, in amended form, paras 15 and 16 of the 1990 Scheme).

The judgment made reference to *R v Criminal Injuries Compensation Board ex parte Lain* (1967) (see page 268) in which the court had rejected the submission that at a hearing by three members of the Board the Board could only allow the appeal and increase the award or dismiss the appeal leaving the award of the single member untouched. This submission was not correct. The hearing was not an appeal. It was a fresh start to the application. The request for a hearing was a total rejection of the single member's decision, and there was nothing that could vest in the applicant after that request had been made unless and until the Board made a subsequent decision in the applicant's favour. The offer of the interim award had been conditional upon the acceptance of the single member's decision.

In the judgment, the court also made reference to the decision of the Court of Appeal in *R v Criminal Injuries Compensation Board ex parte Tong* (1976) (see page 272), Lord Denning having stated in the course of that case that the award of compensation under the Scheme was personal to the applicant and that, like damages for personal injuries at common law before statutory reform, this personal claim on the part of the applicant died with him.

R v Criminal Injuries Compensation Board, ex parte Thompstone; R v Criminal Injuries Compensation Board, ex parte Crowe

2 October 1984 (Court of Appeal) – Convictions – test of appropriateness of compensation at public expense

Both applications to the court challenged decisions by the Board rejecting an application on the grounds of the applicants' criminal convictions under para 6(c) of the Scheme.

The judgment restated the principle that decisions by the Board acting as a servant of the Crown by executive instruction, with a duty to distribute bounty of the Crown to persons who sustained personal injury directly attributable to a crime of violence or to assisting in apprehending an offender or preventing an offence, were subject to a duty to act judicially and that the Board's decisions were subject to judicial review by the court.

In the two cases before the court, the Board had decided that on the evidence before the Board it was not appropriate that the applicant should receive any award at all from public funds.

It was submitted on behalf of the applicants that unless the applicants' conduct, character or way of life (under para 6(c)) had some ascertainable bearing on the occurrence of the injury or its aftermath, such matters should not be considered by the Board as grounds for rejecting an application. The court rejected that submission, stating that the Board's decisions could be reviewed only if the Board misconstrued its mandate or, on the basis of the *Wednesbury* principle, had reached a decision which no reasonable body could have reached.

Paragraph 6(c), in establishing a test of 'appropriateness', referred to quite distinct considerations, namely 'conduct' and 'character and way of life', including convictions. It was not necessary for the court to make a ruling on the bearing that matters of 'conduct' might have in relation to the occurrence of the injury. The court made clear that no such relationship was necessary for the Board to consider convictions, and indeed the latter would be much less likely to have any ascertainable bearing on the occurrence of the injury. The question which the Board had to ask itself in such matters was: 'Is the applicant an appropriate recipient of an *ex gratia* compensatory payment made at the public expense?'

Both appeals were dismissed.

R v Chief Constable of Cheshire and another, ex parte Berry

30 July 1985 – Police witness statements – available only at hearing

Although the Board was not respondent in this case, the court had cause to review the Board's procedure at hearings in relation to the making available to the applicant statements made by witnesses to the police. The judgment of the court made detailed reference to the evidence of Sir Michael Ogden QC, then chairman of the Board, explaining fully the Board's procedure in relation to witness statements provided to the Board by the police and the reasons for that procedure.

The matter for decision by the court in the particular case was whether the Chief Constable had acted reasonably in making statements of witnesses available to the Board without making the same statements available to the applicant and knowing that the Board's procedure in relation to those statements was subject to an undertaking given by the Board to the Chief Constable that statements provided by the police would remain under the control of the Board and would be made available to the applicant only at or immediately before the hearing.

The court decided that the Chief Constable had not acted perversely in dealing with the statements in that manner and the appeal was dismissed. The contention that the applicant in these circumstances was placed at a disadvantage at a hearing as a result of such procedure in relation to police statements was considered by the court. On the evidence before it, the court did not consider that the Board's procedure placed the applicant at such disadvantage as to amount to a denial of natural justice or a breach of the common law right of the applicant to a fair hearing.

R v Criminal Injuries Compensation Board, ex parte Warner and Others

8 May 1986 (Court of Appeal) – No crime of violence – railway suicide – (pre 1990 Scheme)

The applicants maintained that the injuries which they had sustained were directly attributable to a crime of violence within para 4(a) of the 1979 Scheme. The applicants were train drivers who had suffered nervous shock as a result of persons placing themselves on the railway line ahead of the applicants' train, those persons having committed a criminal offence under section 34 of the Offences Against the Person Act 1861. It was submitted on behalf of the applicants that such an offence was a crime of violence because the likely consequences of jumping on to a railway line in front of an oncoming train were that the train driver would suffer physical or psychiatric injury.

The court reviewed the meaning of the term 'crime of violence'. The court considered (*inter alia*) the decision of the court in *R v Criminal Injuries Compensation Board ex parte Clowes* (1977) (see page 272).

In giving the judgment of the court, Lawton LJ stated 'In my judgment the submission of counsel for the Board that what matters is the nature of the crime, not its likely consequences, is well founded. It is for the Board to decide whether unlawful conduct because of its nature, not its consequence, amounts to a crime of violence'.

The appeals were dismissed.

It should be noted that in relation to injuries sustained after 1 February 1990, applicants could have the benefit of para 4(c) which was a new provision in the 1990 Scheme whereby personal injury directly attributable to an offence of trespass on a railway came within the Scheme. Paragraphs 8 and 9 of the 1996 Scheme apply to all applications received on or after 1 April 1996.

R v Criminal Injuries Compensation Board, ex parte Whitelock

4 December 1986 – Witness statements – not referred to at hearing – meaning of evidence 'brought out' at hearing (para 23, 1979 Scheme)

The court was asked to grant an order of certiorari to quash a decision of the Board refusing compensation to the applicant Miss Whitelock, and an order of mandamus requiring that compensation be awarded by the Board. It was submitted for the applicant that the Board had taken into account witness statements which were not produced at the hearing and that the Board had acted contrary to the rules of natural justice and contrary to para 23 of its own Scheme.

The applicant, then aged 15, had sustained injury when she fell from a window, it being alleged that the fall had been caused by the unlawful act of an assailant, he either having pushed her or caused her to jump through fear. At his trial the alleged assailant had been acquitted of any offence in relation to causing bodily harm to the applicant.

Legal argument in relation to the motion to quash the Board's decision centred upon certain witness statements which were before the Board but which had not been referred to expressly in the course of the Board's hearing. It was submitted for the applicant that three witness statements had been taken into account by the Board in reaching its decision to make no award, although those statements were not produced at the hearing, and that so doing was contrary to the rules of natural justice and contrary to para 23 of the Scheme, whereby the Board will reach its decision solely in the light of the evidence 'brought out at the hearing', and all the information and evidence made available to the Board members will be made available to the applicant at, if not before, the hearing. It was not disputed that those statements had been available to the applicant at or before the hearing.

The Board considered the meaning of the words 'brought out at the hearing'. The court considered those words not to be particularly clear in their meaning and considered that they should be read in the context of the other wording in para 23, which provided that all the information and evidence made available to the Board members would be made available to the applicant at, if not before, the hearing, and it was not disputed that all the information made available to the Board members was made available to the applicant before the hearing.

Having considered the terms and contents of those witnesses' statements, the evidence of the way in which the hearing had proceeded, and the terms of the Scheme, the court concluded that there had been no miscarriage of justice by reason of those statements having been before the Board, and the application was dismissed.

R v Criminal Injuries Compensation Board, ex parte Brady

20 February 1987 – Police witness statements available only at hearing

As in the case of *Berry* (see page 281), this application to the court was based upon a consideration of the Board's procedure in relation to witness statements provided by the police to the Board before the hearing. The judgment of the court contained a detailed review of the evidence which was before the members of the Board at the hearing of the applicant's case, and the court's observations in relation to the Board's procedure with regard to statements provided by the police. The applicant contended that the Board's having knowledge of a statement made to the police by a particular witness, who had been invited by the Board to attend the hearing but who had not attended, placed the applicant at a disadvantage amounting to a denial of natural justice, as there was no opportunity for the applicant's representative to interview that witness or effectively to challenge the contents of that witness' written statement to the police if the witness did not attend the Board's hearing.

Having considered once more the evidence of Sir Michael Ogden QC, the chairman of the Board, in relation to the Board's procedure on this point, and in particular that the Board would reasonably consider any application for an adjournment so that statements may be challenged, there having been no such application for an adjournment in the particular case, the court dismissed the appeal.

R v Criminal Injuries Compensation Board, ex parte Sorrell

2 March 1987 – Court jurisdiction based only on 'Wednesbury' rule or error of law in setting aside Board's decision

The applicant sought judicial review by way of order of certiorari in respect of a decision of the Board refusing compensation. The applicant had been found injured. He had head injuries and had been drinking.

In making no award the Board stated: 'Whilst we have sympathy for the applicant's injuries, on the totality of the evidence we were just not satisfied on the balance of probabilities how the applicant came by his injuries. They might have been caused by a fall or in a fight, but at all events the onus of proving his case rested upon the applicant and we were satisfied that he had not discharged that onus and in the circumstances no award could be made.'

In giving judgment, the court stated that it could interfere with a decision of the Board in respect of an application for compensation only on the well-known *Wednesbury* principle. The court would thus interfere only if there was an error of law on the face of the record or if the decision arrived at by the tribunal was one at which no reasonable tribunal properly directing itself could have arrived. As there was no error of law contended on behalf of the applicant, the latter could succeed only if the decision was shown to be a perverse one.

The judge stated that there would be cases in which the Board on the material before it was entitled in law to say that an applicant had not discharged the onus upon him, and that it just did not know how the relevant injury was sustained. However, in the particular case the alternatives as to cause of the applicant's injuries were a fall, or that he had been in a fight in which someone hit him otherwise than in self-defence, or that he had been in a fight in which he came by his injuries through somebody hitting him in self-defence. The third of those alternatives had not been canvassed in the case. After referring to the decision of the court in *R v Criminal Injuries Compensation Board ex parte Crangle*, which came before the High Court in 1981 (see page 276) the court decided that, in the light of the clear medical evidence of a severe blow to the back of the head and injuries to the front of the face on both the left and right side, no reasonable tribunal should, in weighing a fight on the one hand against a fall on the other, have reached the conclusion that they were both equally likely. The court stated that any reasonable tribunal, faced with that choice on the material available, must have been forced to the conclusion that a fight was more likely than a fall. If that was so, then it was demonstrated that this was a decision of the Board which was perverse according to the *Wednesbury* principle and the application was allowed.

R v Criminal Injuries Compensation Board, ex parte Brown

12 November 1987 – Para 13, 1990 Scheme – refusal by chairman to reopen case – chairman's decision final – 'Wednesbury' unreasonableness only basis for court to interfere

The application to the court involved consideration of a decision by the then chairman of the Board, Sir Michael Ogden QC, refusing to reopen the applicant's case under para 13 of the Scheme. The applicant had been shot in the leg on 19 February 1977. On 3 November 1981 the Board made a final award of compensation, and in 1982 that award was accepted – the amount of compensation awarded for the injury and for the risks of future trouble, as then envisaged, was £22,500.

In 1985 the applicant had further trouble with his left leg and had further operations upon it, at one stage being advised medically that he might lose the leg. In fact the latter did not occur and the final prognosis after further surgery was good.

The applicant requested a reopening of the case under para 13 of the Scheme, a matter for decision by the chairman of the Board, his decision thereon being final. The court stated that the only basis upon which it could overturn the chairman's decision in such a case was on the *Wednesbury* principle that the decision was perverse.

The court considered the precise terms of para 13, and in particular the need for the applicant to establish that there had been not only a serious change in the medical condition but also that injustice would occur if the original assessment of compensation was allowed to stand. The court stated that it was not appropriate to conjecture how much more compensation might be appropriate having regard to the level of change which had occurred in the particular case. The problems which Mr Brown had suffered after the final award had been made by the Board had been foreseen in the earlier medical opinion, although the extent and seriousness of that further medical change had been greater than expected. However the Scheme contemplated the reopening of cases only where there was a strong smell of injustice should there not be a reopening of the case. Whether the court would have come to the same conclusion on evidence before it as the chairman had reached was not the test. Looking at the matter in the round and balancing what actually did occur against the possibility foreseen by the doctors, the court concluded that the chairman's decision was not perverse in the *Wednesbury* sense of unreasonableness, and the application was dismissed.

R v Criminal Injuries Compensation Board, ex parte Emmett

16 December 1988 – Crime of violence – deliberate or reckless act of alleged offender – 'Wednesbury' rule – Board's decision not perverse

The application was for judicial review by way of certiorari of a decision of the Board refusing compensation in relation to injuries suffered by a woman police constable. The facts briefly were that the applicant with other officers had been giving chase to a suspected stolen vehicle. The driver of the suspected stolen vehicle had partly crossed a crossroads, and when partly across had for no apparent reason stopped. The applicant driving the police car behind had also entered the crossing to follow the suspect's car. The result of the latter stopping before it had completed its crossing of the junction was to leave the applicant for some moments stuck in the path of oncoming traffic, and she sustained injury when an oncoming vehicle struck her police vehicle from the side.

Counsel for the applicant had argued before the Board that the applicant's case came within para 4(a) as she had deliberately or recklessly been stranded at the crossing which constituted a crime of violence. It was further argued for the applicant that her case came within para 4(b), as her injury was directly attributable to the attempted apprehension of an offender. Counsel further submitted that para 11, in excluding traffic offences from the Scheme, did not apply as the circumstances were not a traffic offence, the wrongdoer's action in deliberately stranding the applicant being the equivalent of trying to run somebody down.

The Board was not satisfied that the conduct of the driver of the other vehicle had been shown to be deliberate or reckless. The onus was on the applicant. The Board was not satisfied that the application came within para 4(a).

The Board was likewise not satisfied that the injury was directly attributable to the attempted apprehension of a suspect offender, it being the Board's view that the injury was sustained accidentally and that as the applicant was not taking an exceptional risk the requirements of paras 4(b) and 6(d) were not satisfied.

The court considered the terms of the Scheme and the Board's statement providing guidelines on the interpretation of the Scheme by the Board, although the latter was not binding upon it in any particular case.

The court concluded that there was no basis on which it could be said that the conclusion on the evidence before the Board was unreasonable or perverse within the *Wednesbury* principle, and accordingly the application failed.

The court made observations regarding the meaning of 'at the time' in relation to the taking of an exceptional risk and decided that these words involved taking into account not precisely what was happening when the injuries were sustained but the context in which those injuries were sustained, which in the particular case involved looking at matters which occurred some little time before, namely the chase by the police car of the suspect's car. In the case before it, the court was satisfied that the Board had taken the question of risk in its context and not in isolation at the moment of the injury being sustained. Accordingly the decision of the Board in relation to there being no exceptional risk could not be impugned. The application was dismissed.

R v Criminal Injuries Compensation Board, ex parte Letts

8 February 1989 – Para 11, 1990 Scheme – traffic offence – no crime of violence – judicial review not court of appeal from Board's decision

The applicant sought an order of certiorari to quash a decision of the Board refusing compensation. The applicant had been knocked over by a car in the car park of a public house. The court had cause to consider the meaning of para 11 of the Scheme which excluded traffic offences unless they amounted to a deliberate attempt to run the applicant down. The fact that the driver had undoubtedly driven negligently and would have been liable in a civil action was not material to a consideration of injury caused by a vehicle under the Scheme. The Board considered the terms of the Scheme itself, and the Board's Statement published for guidance of applicants and their advisers as to the interpretation of the Scheme by the Board. The court also reviewed the authorities on what constituted a crime of violence, including *R v Criminal Injuries Compensation Board ex parte Clowes* (1977) (see page 272). It was for the Board to decide whether unlawful conduct because of its nature and not its consequence amounted to a crime of violence. In the case before the court, the Board – in making its decision – had stated 'the circumstances in which the applicant was run over by a car are far from clear. What is clear is that no crime of violence was committed. Paragraph 4(a) is not satisfied'. The Board made no award.

The Board had considered the principle of recklessness in the context of driving. The Board had concluded as a fact in the particular case that the actions of the alleged assailant, the driver of the car, did not show recklessness according to the judicial interpretation of that term (*R v Lawrence* (1981)).

The Board had also considered the question of wanton driving, a consideration which applied to cases generally where a road traffic offence had not been committed because the place of the alleged offence was private and not a public road. The Board had concluded that it was not satisfied that the applicant suffered injury as the result of any crime of violence or recklessness and did not satisfy para 4(a) of the Scheme.

The court was not a court of appeal from the Criminal Injuries Compensation Board. The process in which the court was engaged was that of judicial review. The decision of the Board was not flawed as to its conclusion nor had there been any misdirection or failure to apply the law to the facts. There was no possible way in which perversity or irrationality could be alleged against the Board. The application was dismissed.

R v Criminal Injuries Compensation Board, ex parte Gould

16 February 1989 – Refusal of adjournment – natural justice

The applicant sought judicial review and an order of certiorari in respect of a decision of the Board to reduce compensation by 50 per cent because of the applicant's conduct. The applicant submitted that the decision was contrary to natural justice on the grounds that the Board's chairman had rejected an application made by the solicitor appearing for the applicant that the matter should be adjourned to another day and that the applicant had been prejudiced.

In accordance with the Board's practice, the applicant's representative had been handed certain statements on his arrival at the venue of the hearing and on his request was given further time to consider those documents during the course of the Board's hearing day. In due course the case proceeded, and the judgment of the court reviewed the evidence as to the manner in which the question of adjournment was dealt with by the Board and by the applicant's legal representative.

The material issue in relation to the reduction of 50 per cent in the Board's award was the conduct of the applicant. As there was nothing before the court which suggested that any evidence could have been obtained on adjournment which would have effectively countered the particular allegation of conduct upon which the reduction was based, there had been no prejudice of the applicant's case. The application to the court was refused.

R v Criminal Injuries Compensation Board, ex parte Parsons

17 January 1990 – Board's duty to consider evidence – no general duty on Board to make enquiries of its own initiative

The applicant sought judicial review of a decision of the Board refusing to make an award. The grounds of the application to the court were that there was important evidence which should have been, but was not, before the Board and which, had it been before the Board, might well have, or could have, led to its reaching a conclusion favourable to the applicant.

The documents to which this contention on the applicant's behalf referred were a police officer's record of an interview with the alleged assailant and the prosecutor's summary of the case outlining the prosecution case against the alleged assailant. The prosecution had never proceeded to trial as the alleged assailant had gone abroad.

The court considered para 23 of the 1979 Scheme which provided that it was for the applicant to make out his case at the hearing and, where appropriate, this will extend to satisfying the Board that compensation should not be withheld or reduced under those parts of the Scheme which gave the Board a discretion whether to withhold or reduce compensation. The court considered *R v Chief Constable of Cheshire and another ex parte Berry* and the Board's procedure whereby the police are requested to provide to the Board relevant statements and to give oral evidence at the hearing.

It was accepted in the particular case that there was never brought to the Board's attention at the hearing the terms of the police officer's interview with the alleged assailant immediately after the alleged assault.

It was argued for the applicant that the Board had an investigatory function which extended to gathering the relevant evidence, and that the Board should have appreciated that probably an interview would have taken place and should, failing the police officer's production of it at the hearing, have exerted itself to obtain it. The failure to obtain that relevant evidence before the Board, it was suggested on the applicant's behalf to the court, imported culpability on the part of the Board. It was submitted that it was incumbent upon the Board to request all material information from statements or interviews, which the Board's letter to the police before the hearing did. Secondly the Board should, on receipt of documents from the police, have given thought to their adequacy, which would have led to its asking for the interview because it should have deduced that an interview probably existed. It was submitted that the failure of the Board to do so was a material irregularity which vitiated the proceedings. In performing its functions fairly and properly, the Board was under a duty to enquire; it had failed in that duty.

For the Board it was submitted that the Board had a duty to present fairly and impartially the evidence through its representative, and that duty did not extend to evidence gathering in the sense that had been submitted on the applicant's behalf to the court. For the Board it was submitted that, provided reasonable steps were taken to obtain material and place it before the Board, and provided the material that had been obtained was fairly deployed and there was no concealment or unfair advantage taken, the Board had fulfilled its proper function.

The court stated that nowhere could it find any indication that the obligations of the Board extended to the making of full enquiries on its own initiative or the gathering of evidence in the sense in which it had been submitted on the applicant's behalf to the court, and that submission was rejected.

The court then turned to the further submission on the applicant's behalf that although the Board's conduct could not be impugned because of failure to ferret out and place before the three members of the Board the interview between the police officer and the alleged assailant, the fact that for whatever reason that information was not placed before the Board entitled the applicant to a remedy in the court.

The court found it unnecessary to deliver a judgment on the correctness or otherwise of that particular submission as, having considered in detail the substance of the documents which, it was submitted on the applicant's behalf, should have been before the Board in deciding the case, the court was of the view that there was nothing in those documents which would have supported the applicant's case and caused the Board to come to any different conclusion to the one that it had reached. The application was therefore dismissed.

R v Criminal Injuries Compensation Board, ex parte Wilson

5 February 1991 (Queen's Bench Division) – Para 4, 1990 Scheme – refusal by chairman to waive three year time limit

Application was made to the court in relation to a decision of the Chairman refusing to waive the three year time limit contained in para 4 of the Scheme. That paragraph of the Scheme stated that the Board may, in exceptional cases, waive the time limit, but that a decision by the Chairman not to do so will be final. The application was founded upon abuse by a member of the applicant's family between 1974 and 1980. The applicant attained 18 in 1982 but made no application to the Board until 1990. The applicant's submission that the Chairman's decision was wrong in law, or *Wednesbury* unreasonable, was rejected by the court. The argument that the Board had, in some cases, waived the time limit where the delay had been for a shorter period, did not make the decision refusing to waive the time limit unreasonable.

R v Criminal Injuries Compensation Board, ex parte Cummins

17 January 1992 (Queen's Bench Division) – Assessment – adequacy of reasons for decision

The judgment of Hutchison J contains a detailed consideration of the facts of this case and review of the authorities relating to the adequacy of reasons given for the decision of a Board carrying out a judicial function. The applicant challenged, in particular by way of judicial review, the adequacy of the Board's written reasons in arriving at a particular sum by way of compensation for the cost of future care. The court considered the adequacy of the reasons given by the Board and the extent of the court's powers to interfere with the assessment itself. The court, after outlining the evidence and the Board's detailed reasons for arriving at the conclusions that it did, decided that the Board had not given sufficient reasons to enable the applicant to know the basis of fact upon which the Board's assessment of the cost of future care was based. 'Nothing elaborate was necessary. All that was required was an indication whether on this issue they accepted or rejected' the specialist medical evidence and the evidence of the applicant and his mother on the applicant's future care needs; the level of care they found to be necessary and how it was to be provided; and the factors which led them to reject calculation in favour of a round figure. It was argued for the applicant that the round figure of £100,000 was neither sufficient nor appropriate in its method of assessment. Having found the reasons given to be inadequate the court allowed the application and granted the relief claimed.

R v Criminal Injuries Compensation Board, ex parte Gray

13 May 1992 (Court of Session) - Para 4(a), 1990 Scheme - bigamous marriage - sexual intercourse - no crime of violence

The applicant had made application to the Board for compensation in respect of sexual intercourse with her believed husband before discovering that the marriage was bigamous. The court rejected the application to quash the Board's refusal to make an award. The court concluded that, although the applicant may have a claim for damages against the other party under civil law, the Board's decision that there was no crime of violence was held by the court to contain no error in law, and the application was dismissed. The proper approach was to look at the nature of the crime and whether the acts of sexual intercourse were crimes of violence under the terms of the Scheme. The court, like the Board, concluded that they were not.

R v Criminal Injuries Compensation Board, ex parte Barrett

19 November 1993 (Queen's Bench Division) - Para 15, 1990 Scheme - fatal case - apportionment of award - apportionment of reductions - children's award not to be subject to reductions affecting award to surviving parent only

The applicant, the husband of the deceased, sought an order quashing the decision of the Board in so far as it applied to claims by the children of the applicant, their father, their mother having been killed. In particular the application sought a declaration that insurance monies received by the applicant as a result of the death of his wife should not be deducted from the claims of the children of the applicant and the deceased.

The court approved the manner in which the Board had calculated the various financial claims of the applicant, as husband of the deceased, and the children, but allowed the application quashing the decision of the Board in relation to the application of the deduction which had to be made under the terms of the Scheme in respect of proceeds of insurance policies received by the applicant on the death of his wife. The Board had correctly arrived at the total award for the applicant and the two children as three persons entitled to make claims under para 15 of the 1990 Scheme and under the various heads of claim permitted by the Fatal Accidents Act. Under the Fatal Accidents Act each individual dependant had his or her separate claim which he or she was entitled to have separately valued. However, in procedural terms it is one claim under the Act, usually brought by the personal representative of the estate of the deceased. That one claim when calculated and brought to a total figure for dependency under all heads is then apportioned between the dependants. The court acknowledged that over the years the practice had developed whereby the separate heads of claim were calculated and then a total figure arrived at, with the apportionment of the overall figure between the respective dependants on a pragmatic basis. The court sought to provide as much money in free cash terms for the parent who is caring for the child as is sensible in all the circumstances. The practice of the court has, therefore, been to apportion the greater part of the overall claim to the parent. The court stated however: 'That was and is a fiction, because in most cases, when analysed, it is plain that the children were in fact the parties, or the dependants, for whom the substantial proportion, where care was concerned, of the value of the claim was intended. It was for their benefit'. The court concluded that the Scheme required a similar approach in principle that each dependant had his or her own separate claim even though the application was brought by one party, the parent, on behalf of all dependants.

The court decided that the Board had wrongly reduced the overall award by the value of the proceeds of life policies payable to the father alone on the death of his wife, and the proportion of the overall award which belonged to the children had thereby been wrongly reduced by that deduction, which should apply only to the award payable to the surviving parent who was the only person entitled to the proceeds of the policies.

R v Criminal Injuries Compensation Board, ex parte Gambles

3 December 1993 (Queen's Bench Division) – Para 6(c), 1990 Scheme – conduct – Board's decision – failure to show its reasons

The Board had refused compensation under para 6(c) of the 1990 Scheme in relation to the applicant's 'conduct'. The court upheld the application for a judicial review on the basis that the facts found by the Board were 'capable of sustaining the whole spectrum of possible decisions, from a nil award to a complete award'. Sedley J concluded that the Board had not proceeded to ask itself (a) does the applicant's conduct make a full award inappropriate? (b) if so to what extent does the applicant's conduct impact on the appropriateness of an award? (c) what award, if any, should the applicant consequently receive? The court concluded that the Board had failed to show its reasons in deciding that the applicant should receive no award rather than a reduced award, and granted the relief sought.

Author's note – This decision has been disapproved by the Court of Appeal in *R v CICB, ex parte Cook* (see page 301).

RP & TG v Home Secretary and Criminal Injuries Compensation Board

4 May 1994 (Court of Appeal) – Para 7, 1969 Scheme – preclusion of award based on offences where offender and victim living together – pre 1 October 1979 – not unreasonable

The applications for judicial review were made in respect of the rejection by the Board of claims for compensation founded upon offences involving sexual abuse committed before 1 October 1979. In one of the cases the abuse was partly before and partly after that date. The judgments of the Court of Appeal contain a review of the authorities relating to the scope of the Scheme from its origins and in particular the provisions of para 7 of the 1969 Scheme which governed applications for compensation in respect of incidents which occurred before 1 October 1979. It was argued for the applicants (*inter alia*) that it was unreasonable to refuse to make an award under the provisions of para 7 of the 1969 Scheme, Parliament having subsequently decided to allow compensation in cases which had heretofore been precluded by that paragraph of the earlier Scheme, where the violence occurred on or after 1 October 1979. The court concluded that the Board was not acting unreasonably in deciding that applications founded on violence occurring prior to 1 October 1979 were caught by the terms of the 1969 Scheme which expressly precluded compensation where the victim and the offender were living together at the time as members of the same family. The remedy sought by way of judicial review was refused.

R v Criminal Injuries Compensation Board, ex parte Aston

16 June 1994 (Queen's Bench Division) – Para 6(a), 1990 Scheme – Board's decision – adequacy of reasons for decision

The applicant sought judicial review in respect of the Board's decisions refusing an award under para 6(a) of the 1990 Scheme (informing the police and co-operating in the prosecution of the offender) and a hearing under para 24(c) of the Scheme. The court reviewed the reasons given by the Board's advocate on behalf of the Board for refusing an award under para 6(a) of the Scheme, and the reasons given by the Board for refusing a hearing under para 24(c). The decision of Sedley J in *R v CICB, ex parte Gambles* was referred to. Whilst the court concluded that the Board's reasoning in refusing a hearing was in some respects technically flawed, the court exercised its discretion against the applicant and refused the remedy by way of judicial review (*inter alia*) because the Board did not, in any event, have before it sufficient information in relation to the circumstances in which the injury was sustained on which to make an award under the Scheme.

R v Criminal Injuries Compensation Board, ex parte Maxted

8 July 1994 (Queen's Bench Division) – Para 6(c), 1990 Scheme – convictions – Board's discretion – court not empowered to substitute its discretion for that of the Board

The application for judicial review sought a ruling by the court that the Board had, in reaching its decision in the case, failed to consider paragraphs in the Guide to the Scheme and had failed properly to approach their task under the Scheme in exercising their discretion under para 6(c) to withhold or reduce compensation on the grounds of the applicant's character as shown by his criminal convictions. The Board, in its written reasons for its decision for refusing an award, had regard to the convictions of the applicant and had taken account of the decision of the High Court in *R v CICB, ex parte Thompstone and Crowe* (1983) in which the court had observed: 'I am satisfed that the Scheme, as published, is intended to afford the widest possible discretion to the Board in its administration of the Scheme'. The Board also referred to the comment of the Master of the Rolls in the Court of Appeal in that case in 1984: 'As in all discretionary decisions, there will be cases where the answer is clear one way or the other and cases which are on the borderline and in which different people might reach different decisions. The Crown has left the decision to the Board ...'. The Board made clear that they had, having thus directed themselves, considered how their discretion under para 6(c) of the 1990 Scheme should be exercised in relation to the applicant's convictions. In so doing they decided that an award would be refused.

It was argued for the applicant in seeking judicial review of this decision that the Board had made no reference to para 37 to 39 of the Guide to the 1990 Scheme, which illustrated how the Board might approach in the exercise of its discretion certain specific criminal offences. It was further argued that as the particular offences for which the applicant had been convicted were not referred to in those paragraphs of the Guide, as an offence, which on its own might lead to the Board refusing an award altogether, the Board should have at least indicated why, in relation to the wording of the Guide, the Board had decided that the particular offences of the applicant were sufficient to refuse an award altogether. The court rejected this submission.

The Board was entitled in the exercise of its discretion to take the view that the indecent assault five years earlier, for which the applicant had been convicted, was a matter that should cause it to withhold compensation, and that the Board did not act illegally in so doing. The Board were under no obligation to spell out matters further in their decision letter than they did, the Board's discretion being very wide, and the width of that discretion had not been reduced by the issue of the guidance in the Guide referred to. The court concluded by stating: 'This court is not empowered to substitute its discretion for that of the Board and this application fails'.

R v Criminal Injuries Compensation Board, ex parte Johnson

20 July 1994 (Court of Appeal) – Para 4(a), 1990 Scheme – direct attributability of injury under the Scheme – reasonable foreseeability not the test to be applied by the Board

The applicant had discovered the recently murdered body of a friend lying on the floor of the friend's home. This experience caused her considerable emotional distress and since that date she had suffered from a shock induced psychiatric illness. This case raised the question whether, in such circumstances, she was entitled to compensation under the Criminal Injuries Compensation Scheme. The court referred to para 4(a) of the 1990 Scheme and to the decision of the single member of the Board rejecting the application giving his reasons as: 'I am not satisfied that the applicant's illness was directly attributable to a crime of violence (para 4(a) of the Scheme)'.

The applicant applied for an oral hearing and a report prepared by a consultant psychiatrist was submitted to the Board in support of her application for a hearing. The applicant made detailed legal submissions in her request for a hearing and these were considered by the Board which again refused the application, stating that having considered the authorities placed before them, the Board concluded that where the injury alleged is psychiatric, in order that it should be directly attributable to a crime of violence, it is necessary to consider whether the victim has a sufficiently proximate relationship with the immediate victim of the crime within the definition provided by the cases. On the evidence the Board were not so satisfied. In considering the application for judicial review the court considered the case of *R v CICB, ex parte Parsons* which was reported in *The Times*, 25 November 1982. In that case, a train driver claimed compensation under the Scheme for a shock related psychiatric condition following upon his discovery of the body of a man who had committed suicide on the railway line. The Board had refused that application giving, as one of its reasons, that the Board were not satisfied that it was reasonably foreseeable that a person who found the dead man's body, which may have been lying on the line for a considerable time, would suffer personal injuries in the form of nervous shock or depression as a result of doing so. Accordingly the Board considered that those injuries were too remote and were not directly attributable to a crime of violence. On the judicial review of that decision Glidewell J found against the Board and granted an order quashing the decision. The Board appealed and the Court of Appeal upheld the decision of Glidewell J. In upholding the decision of the judge in the court below Cumming-Bruce LJ said: 'The Criminal Injuries Compensation Scheme may involve a payment of compensation in a case where, if the person who committed the crime of violence, which almost inevitably will also be a tort in civil law, were able to say that nevertheless were he sued, the injured person would not obtain compensation in tort; and this is because the test of foreseeability plays no part in that Scheme'.

Fox LJ in agreeing with Cumming-Bruce LJ said: 'The illness in this case is the direct consequence of the crime. The crime caused the very state of affairs on the railway which constituted the condition which would lead to the shock; the shock was produced by what the applicant saw and what he saw was the direct consequence of the crime'.

The court concluded that it was bound by the decision of the Court of Appeal in *Parsons* and that it was quite impossible to distinguish the facts in the present case in anyway that would permit a different outcome. The court concluded that the Board's decision could not be allowed to stand as there had been an error on a point of law.

By way of caveat in relation to any concern there may be that the court's decision would open the floodgates to let in numerous applications not previously considered by the Board to be within the terms of the Scheme, the Court indicated as follows:

'Lest it be thought otherwise, it should be understood that it will not be in every case that a person who discovers a body, the result of a crime of violence will be entitled to compensation. It is necessary for the applicant to satisfy the Board that he/she is suffering from personal injury caused by the experience. There are thus two elements to be established. First it must be shown that the applicant suffered personal injury. Shock, distress and emotional upset cannot in themselves suffice however unpleasant the experience. There must be some sort of injurious after-effects brought on by the shock and such injurious effects must, of course, satisfy the financial limitations for claims imposed by the Scheme. Secondly, it will be necessary to establish that the nervous shock-related injury was caused by the finding of the body. Whilst foreseeability is in no way the test for entitlement to compensation, clearly the less foreseeable a consequence of an event is, the more difficult it may be to establish the necessary causal link. Thus it would not be improper for the Board to have in mind foreseeability in determining whether the evidence established causation in a case such as this'.

The psychiatric evidence in the case made clear that the personal injury was directly attributable to the crime of violence and the application was therefore allowed, the Board's decision being quashed and the Board being required to reconsider the application, taking into account the conclusions of the court on the correct legal approach to the claim.

R v Criminal Injuries Compensation Board, ex parte Cobb

26 July 1994 (Divisional Court) – Para 6(a), 1990 Scheme – delay reporting – officer with knowledge of circumstances not giving evidence – hearsay evidence by another officer – denial of opportunity to cross-examine original officer by refusing adjournment – natural justice

The application to the court to quash the decision of the Board at a hearing refusing compensation was upheld. The application to the Board had been refused after a hearing on the grounds that the applicant had unreasonably delayed reporting the matter to the police. The applicant's evidence to the Board was that he had been visited by the police in hospital and had understood that the CID would visit him later on. When he did not hear from the police he went to the police station a few days later to make a complaint. He said that he was not aware of the possibility of making a claim to the CICB. A police constable had prepared a report to the effect that he had seen the applicant at hospital and that the applicant had declined to make a complaint as he was not able to assist the police with the circumstances of his injury. That report also indicated that the applicant had said he had made the report because he believed that he was eligible for compensation. Before the Board, the particular officer who had prepared that report was not called and the Board did not hear his evidence. Another officer gave evidence to the Board from the original officer's report. The applicant had applied to the Board for an adjournment so that the original police officer could be called and questioned and this application was refused.

On application to the court for judicial review the court concluded that the evidence of the original police officer who had prepared the report was essential in dealing with the merits of the issue before the Board, whether or not the applicant had unreasonably delayed reporting the matter to the police and other circumstances in relation to the application. The court concluded that the denial of the opportunity to adjourn so that the original police officer could give oral evidence and be cross examined was unfair and accordingly the Board's decision was quashed and the applicant given the opportunity for a fresh hearing by another Board. It had been contended for the Board that it was entitled to take account of hearsay evidence as expressly provided in para 25 of the Scheme and that the Board had quite properly proceeded to hear the evidence of another officer, albeit being the evidence of the report of the original officer. The court stated that there was an overriding consideration, namely the one of fairness, and referred to the judgment of Lord Chief Justice Lane in *R v Hull Visitors, ex parte St Germain* (1979) in which the Lord Chief Justice stated: 'However it is clear that the entitlement of the Board to admit hearsay evidence is subject to the overriding obligation to provide the accused with a fair hearing.... Depending upon the nature of that evidence and the particular circumstances of the case, a sufficient opportunity to deal with the hearsay evidence may well involve the cross examination of the witness whose evidence is initially before the Board in the form of hearsay'.

The court also concluded that the Board had not given reasons for its decision and it was incumbent on the Board to explain the basis of its decision. 'This did not require an elaborate statement of reasons to give detailed justification for each finding of fact. It did however require a statement of reasons and findings of fact sufficient to enable the applicant to see how the decision was arrived at.'

Author's note – On the latter point reference should also be made to the case of *R v CICB, ex parte Cook*, Court of Appeal, December 1995 which decision (*inter alia*) ruled upon the issue of the requirement to give reasons for the Board's decision.

R v Criminal Injuries Compensation Board, ex parte Thomas

18 October 1994 (Queen's Bench Division) – Para 6(c), 1990 Scheme – convictions after interim award – delay in Board's final assessment

The court dismissed the application to quash a decision of the Board refusing to make an award having regard to the applicant's criminal convictions under para 6(c) of the 1990 Scheme. The applicant had sustained serious injury in 1985 and, in 1987, had received a substantial interim award from the Board. Subsequent to that date the applicant had become involved in criminal activities and had been convicted of a number of criminal offences. In November 1992 the Board decided that it would be inappropriate to make any further award having regard to the applicant's criminal convictions. It was contended for the applicant (*inter alia*) that the convictions were unrelated to the applicant's injury, that the applicant had no criminal convictions at the time his injury was sustained and that had there not been such delay in bringing the application to a Board for final assessment, the applicant would not have had a record of convictions when such final assessment should have been made.

The court rejected those submissions, making clear that para 6(c) required the Board to have regard to the applicant's criminal convictions as at the date on which the application fell to be considered. There was, therefore, no error in law nor was the Board's decision perverse according to the *Wednesbury* rule, paras 6(c) and 12 of the 1990 Scheme and *R v CICB, ex parte Thompstone and Crowe* [1984] 3 All ER 572 considered.

R v Criminal Injuries Compensation Board, ex parte Powell

16 July 1993 (Queen's Bench Division) - Para 6(a), 1990 Scheme - Board's discretion - refusal to co-operate with police - Board fettered its discretion

The applicant sought by way of judicial review the quashing of the Board's decision refusing an award under para 6(a) of the 1990 Scheme. The applicant had refused to disclose the name of his alleged assailant for fear of reprisals. The case was therefore one in which the Board had to exercise its discretion whether to withhold or reduce an award under para 6(a) of the Scheme. In its written reasons for the decision refusing an award, the Board stated that although they had sympathy with the applicant, his failure to inform the police of the name of the assailant, precluded him from an award under para 6(a) of the Scheme.

It was argued for the applicant that in using the word 'precluded' the Board was not exercising its discretion nor giving thought to the alternative option to withholding compensation, namely, to reduce it. It was also submitted for the applicant that that decision was unreasonable and perverse. The court accepted that if the Board had fettered its discretion in arriving at this decision, rather than properly exercising its discretion whether to make a full, or reduced, or indeed no award at all, the decision was unlawful and should therefore be quashed. For the Board it was contended that the Board had not fettered its discretion and had given acceptable reasons, and that the Board had considered all relevant matters in coming to the conclusion that it considered appropriate in the case. The indications of the Board's policy in certain types of case contained in the Guide to the 1990 Scheme and referred to in the Board's evidence to the court, indicated that the Board had considered the factual matters of the individual case as well as the policy indicated in the Board's Guide.

The court concluded that if the Board were effectively giving effect to a policy decision rather than exercising its discretion under the terms of the Scheme, the decision of the Board had been reached wrongly. The Board had every right to formulate a policy, 'provided they do not follow slavishly that policy but in each case look properly at the facts and circumstances of the instant case. They must look to see whether it is appropriate in that case to follow that policy or whether the circumstances of the case make it appropriate for the Board to adopt a different course and to arrive at an award which is appropriate'.

The court concluded that the Board had fettered its discretion in arriving at its decision to make no award and the application for the decision to be quashed was granted.

R v Criminal Injuries Compensation Board, ex parte Dickenson

22 February 1995 (Queen's Bench Division) – Para 4, 1990 Scheme – chairman's refusal to waive three year time limit – proper consideration of circumstances – chairman's decision final

The applicant sought judicial review of the Board's decision refusing the application for compensation, such refusal being the decision of the Chairman not to waive the three year time limit under para 4 of the 1990 Scheme, that paragraph also providing that such decision by the Chairman is final. The application was founded upon various sexual offences between 1976 and 1988. Offences committed by a member of the applicant's family prior to 1 October 1979 were in any event precluded by the terms of the earlier Scheme. Only offences subsequent to that date could therefore be considered. The Chairman's detailed reasons for refusing the application contained the following statement: 'In this case the complainant has made allegation of sexual abuse at the hands of her brother-in-law between 1978 and 1988 at which time she was 27 years of age. Although the complainant made a complaint to the police which resulted in a successful prosecution, this was not done until 1992 when she was 30 years old and then only after complaints were made by others against her then brother-in-law. The application was not made until July 1993 when she was almost 32'.

The decision of the Chairman indicated that he had considered the circumstances of each of the offences upon which the application was founded. The court concluded that under the terms of the Scheme 'the Chairman was invested with the widest discretion. The policy of the Scheme is clearly that stale complaints should not in general be the subject of compensation'. The Chairman had to ask himself whether or not the present was a case where an exception should be made. He decided that it was not and had given reasons for that decision. In the circumstances the court decided that it was not appropriate to quash the decision and the application was refused.

R v Criminal Injuries Compensation Board, ex parte Scott

24 March 1995 (Queen's Bench Division) – Para 6(a), 1990 Scheme – rape – delay reporting – proper consideration of reasons for delay – Board's reasons for refusal of compensation in exercise of its discretion

The applicant made application to the Board for compensation on the grounds that she had been attacked, raped and assaulted. The application was refused by a single member of the Board and at a subsequent hearing the application was again refused. The basis of the refusal was under para 6(a) of the 1990 Scheme (providing that the Board may withhold or reduce compensation if they consider that the applicant has not taken, without delay, all reasonable steps to inform the police ... of the circumstances of the injury ...). The Board had before them evidence of the applicant's circumstances following the attack and the unsuccessful attempts by friends and colleagues to get her to talk about what had happened.

The circumstances put in evidence before the Board included an account of how the applicant allowed six weeks to elapse after the rape before reporting it to the police, albeit that at that time she still had not returned to work. The applicant picked out a suspect at an identification parade and the Board heard evidence from the investigating police officer that he was satisfied that the suspect had been responsible for the rape. However, the case against him was dismissed by Justices at an old-style committal.

In dismissing the application, the Board indicated that they had considered the contention made by her representative that she was an innocent victim of a crime of violence and that due to her mental state, the Board should exercise its discretion under para 6(a) of the 1990 Scheme and make a full or partial award. The Board accepted that the applicant was an innocent victim of a crime of violence and therefore was *prima facie* entitled to damages under the Scheme. The Board indicated, however, that they had to consider the provisions of para 6 which gives the Board a discretion to withhold or reduce compensation if the applicant has not taken, without delay, all reasonable steps to inform the police of the circumstances of her injury. This paragraph also requires the Board to consider withholding or reducing compensation if the applicant has not co-operated with the police in bringing the offender to justice. The Board were satisfied that once the incident was reported, the applicant had co-operated fully with the police. There was, however, the admitted delay of six weeks in so reporting it.

Having considered all the evidence before them the Board had to decide whether, accepting that the applicant had not reported the matter without delay to the police, this was a case where the Board should exercise its discretion and withhold or reduce the compensation which should be paid to her. The Board had considered at some length whether a reduced award should be made but, bearing in mind the length of the delay and the fact that the applicant had been advised to report it to the police and had discussed it with her boss the following day, the Board decided this was a case where the Board should withhold compensation in its entirety. In his affidavit the Chairman of the Hearing Board had added to the statement of written reasons: 'Regard was paid to the obvious trauma experienced and the particular circumstances of the applicant's condition'.

The Board had also indicated its view of the effect of the delay on the possibility of bringing the offender to justice. Sedley J observed: 'Having formed its view of the effect of the delay on the possibility of bringing the offender to justice, and having assured itself that the applicant had been advised to report the offence within 24 hours, the Board failed to return to the critical question: given the significance of the delay in reporting the crime, to what extent, if any, was it fair, in the light of the reasons for the delay, to reduce her award? In my judgment simply to acknowledge that "people who are subject to rape do suffer a mental reaction thereto" and to depose that "regard was paid to the obvious trauma experienced and the particular circumstances of the applicant's condition" is not to have grappled with this issue at all. It is not a question of simply having regard to the fact and circumstances of the trauma but of reasoning out whether a woman who, on the face of the evidence, has been emotionally and mentally frozen by a terrifying and degrading experience should have the consequent delay in reporting it held against her. Instead the Board has treated as determinative the effect of the delay on the criminal process and this, in my judgment, is an error of law in the interpretation and application of paragraph 6(a) of the Scheme. I will therefore grant the order ... sought by the applicant'.

Author's Note – The decision in this case should be considered in the light of the observations of the Court of Appeal in *R v CICB, ex parte Cook* [1996] 2 All ER 144 in relation to the adequacy of reasons given for the Board's decision. It should also be noted that the Court of Appeal is to hear, in April 1997, an appeal against a decision of the court upholding the Board's decision refusing compensation in a case of rape where one of the issues is delay in reporting under para 6(a) of the Scheme. (See *Cook* on page 301.)

R v Criminal Injuries Compensation Board, ex parte Jobson

4 May 1995 (Queen's Bench Division) – Adequacy of Board's reasons for decision

The applicant had made application for compensation to the Board which application was refused by a single member of the Board on the papers. The applicant sought an oral hearing. After hearing the evidence the Board at the hearing disallowed the application under para 6(a) of the 1990 Scheme on the grounds that the Board were not satisfied that the applicant had reported the incident to the police without delay. The Board's written reasons contained the following: 'The Board were satisfied that the applicant could have made the complaint at the time that the police were on the scene, thus enabling the police to commence enquiries there and then, but the applicant had failed to do so'.

Thereafter the Board considered whether taking into account, the applicant's failure to report the matter at the earliest opportunity, they could exercise their discretion to make a full or reduced award to the applicant. The Board took the view, taking into account all the circumstances of the case, that this was not a situation in which they should exercise their discretion in favour of the applicant and that his delay in reporting the matter properly to the police rendered an award of compensation inappropriate and the application was therefore dismissed under para 6(a) of the 1990 Scheme.

On behalf of the applicant it was submitted that the Board's reasoning was inadequate, it being contended that the Board failed to follow the proper chain of reasoning or that it failed to give any or any adequate reasons for the decision to award no compensation rather than reduced compensation. Alternatively, the Board misdirected itself as to the meaning of the Scheme in that it considered the effective delay in reporting the matter to the police as determinative of the question of compensation and failed to consider whether and to what extent, in the light of the circumstances of the case, it was fair to the applicant to award reduced compensation. The applicant relied upon the decision of Sedley J in *R v CICB, ex parte Gambles* which was an application turning upon para 6(c) of the 1990 Scheme but giving a similar discretion to the Board to make a full or reduced award or a nil award.

The court considered the authorities in relation to the reasons given by an informal tribunal such as the Board and what constituted adequate reasons for the Board's decision.

The court concluded that the Board, in saying that in exercising its discretion it took into account all the circumstances of the case, did not provide any reason for that decision at all. To say that compensation is refused, taking account of all the circumstances of the case, is no different in effect, from simply saying that compensation is refused. In each case no reasons are given. The court therefore came to the conclusion that this decision was flawed on the grounds that no adequate reasons were given for the decision not to award at least some compensation.

Author's note – This decision should be considered in the light of the disapproval of the decision in *Gambles* by the Court of Appeal in the case of *R v CICB, ex parte Cook*, Court of Appeal, December 1995.

R v Criminal Injuries Compensation Board, ex parte Hopper

7 July 1995 (Queen's Bench Division) – Para 6(c), 1990 Scheme – convictions – adequacy of Board's reasons for decision

The applicant sought judicial review of the Board's decision refusing compensation under para 6(c) of the 1990 Scheme having regard to the applicant's convictions.

The Board's initial response to the request for reasons for its decision indicated that the applicant's convictions and cautions made it inappropriate that he should receive an award of compensation from public funds. The Board gave more detailed reasons in response to proceedings for judicial review stating (*inter alia*) that the Board took the view that the applicant's convictions 'were sufficiently serious and persistent to persuade (the Board) that discretion should not be exercised in favour of the applicant and a reduced award would be inappropriate for these circumstances and that no award should be made'. The court rejected the applicant's argument that these subsequently more detailed reasons should be ignored as an *ex post facto* reconstruction. It was also submitted that the principles regarding the reasoning by which the Board reached its decision contained in the judgment of Sedley J should apply, and that the reasoning of the Board in the present case was deficient. *Gambles* was a case relating to conduct. The present case related to convictions. The court did not accept that the Board had failed to show proper reasons for its decision, distinguishing *Gambles*. After reviewing the relevant authorities the court adopted as a brief summary of the implications of para 6(c) the question posed by Lord Donaldson MR in the case of *R v CICB, ex parte Thompstone* [1984] 1 WLR 1234: 'Is the applicant an appropriate recipient of an *ex gratia* compensation payment made at the public expense?' The application for judicial review was dismissed.

R v Criminal Injuries Compensation Board, ex parte Young

9 August 1995 (Court of Session) – Para 6(c), 1990 Scheme – reasons for refusal of award – convictions – reasons for refusal of hearing (para 24, 1990 Scheme)

The applicant sought judicial review of the Board's decisions refusing an award under para 6(c) of the 1990 Scheme on the grounds of the applicant's convictions, and refusing a hearing under para 24(c) of that Scheme. The court was also asked to consider paras 37 to 39 of the Guide to the Scheme published by the Board. It was argued for the applicant that the decision to refuse the request for an oral hearing contravened the Scheme, that the decision was vitiated by a failure to give reasons, and that the provision in the Scheme which enabled the Board to deny the applicant an oral hearing was contrary to natural justice. The court reviewed the facts of the particular case and rejected the first and second of these submissions and with regard to the third, that the provision for refusal of a hearing under para 24(c) was contrary to natural justice, the court stated 'if that were so, the Scheme would contravene natural justice no matter how reasonably the (Board) attempted to apply it. In my opinion the argument for the petitioner ... is flawed. It fails to distinguish between a right to a hearing and a right to be heard'. The application was refused.

R v Criminal Injuries Compensation Board, ex parte Milton

30 November 1995 (Queen's Bench Division) – Para 25, 1990 Scheme – no duty on Board to make full enquiries of its own initiative

The application was for judicial review of the decision of the Board rejecting the application. The claim was founded on allegations of abuse by the applicant's stepfather from the age of 7 to the age of 13 years which would have been in about 1956. Thereafter, for a period of about 30 years up to 1985, the applicant had been, for the most part, a patient in a psychiatric hospital. In her claim to the Board she described a history of more than 20 years of sexual and physical abuse by her stepfather who had died in 1983. The application was outside the time limit of three years and was therefore subject to the decision by the Chairman whether or not to waive the time limit. In his decision in 1993, the Chairman of the Board decided in all the circumstances to waive the time limit but in his capacity of single member stated: 'I reject the application being ineligible under the Scheme since these allegations were never reported to the police. Paragraph 6(a) under the Board's Scheme refers'. The applicant did not accept this decision and had an oral hearing before the Board in 1994. The Board heard oral evidence from the applicant and from two persons who had treated the applicant when she was undergoing psychotherapy. Their evidence, the court observed, did not include any direct evidence of any of the matters of which the applicant complained. In giving its reasons for refusing the application the Board stated that: 'The burden of proof is on the applicant. Having heard all the evidence the Board is not satisfied that the applicant was the victim of a crime of violence and accordingly this application is refused'. Reference was made to para 4(a) of the 1990 Scheme (personal injury directly attributable to a crime of violence) and to para 25 of the 1990 Scheme which states that it is for the applicant to make out her case at the hearing. The Board further stated that having heard and considered all the evidence before them they were not satisfied that the applicant had been the victim of a crime or crimes of violence.

The Board expressly stated that they had come to that conclusion 'Despite the acceptance of her account by the two counsellors called on her behalf'.

The court stated: 'In the application to this court there is therefore in issue a decision of that specialist tribunal on a question of credibility and fact after that tribunal had heard and seen witnesses deployed by the applicant in support of her case, including herself'. It was submitted on behalf of the applicant that the Board, as an inquisitorial body, had a duty corresponding to its power to obtain evidence in appropriate cases. The court accepted that the Board had the power, if it is so minded, to make its own enquiries but that it has to be remembered that the Board's Scheme provides that it is for the applicant to make out his or her own case at the hearing (para 25 of the 1990 Scheme). It was contended for the applicant that the Board could, and should, have taken steps to obtain more medical evidence which would have supported the applicant's case before the Board. The Board considered the case of *R v CICB ex parte Parsons* (7 January 1990, unreported) a judgment of Hutchison J. In that case the court concluded 'Nowhere can I find any indication that the obligations of the Board extend to the making of full enquiries on its own initiative or the gathering of evidence in the sense to which (counsel for the applicant) contends'. The court also referred to *R v The Chief Constable of Cheshire and another, ex parte John Berry* (30 July 1985, unreported) a decision of Nolan J in which it was held that it was not a duty of the Board to look for evidence but rather a duty if it has material in its possession, to make sure that the applicant was apprised of it before the Board relied on it. 'That is something quite different from the requirement to make enquiries of its own initiative.'

It was further contended for the applicant that there was no evidence called to put the applicant's credibility in question and that the Board had therefore no sufficient evidence on which it could in effect disbelieve the applicant. The court rejected this submission stating 'As ... it is for the applicant to make out her case, it is clearly open to the Board to disbelieve her without there being specific evidence in contradiction of her'. The application was dismissed.

R v Criminal Injuries Compensation Board, ex parte Avraam

15 December 1995 (Queen's Bench Division) – Allegations of rape – delay (para 6(a), 1990 Scheme) – medical report not available at hearing – whether application should have been adjourned to obtain report

The applicant made application to the Board in respect of injuries sustained at her home on 25 May 1991. On that date the applicant had reported the matter to the police as an incident of burglary. She was taken to hospital where she was examined to a limited extent arising out of an allegation that in the course of the burglary she had suffered some injury. On 28 May 1991, the applicant reported to the police that she had been raped and buggered on 25 May 1991. On 30 May the police took a written statement from her and took her to see a police surgeon. On the application to the Board the single member had referred the application to an oral hearing. The Board refused to make an award at the hearing, not being satisfied that the applicant was the victim of a crime of violence as alleged and in so doing taking into account the onus on the applicant to satisfy the Board initially that she was a victim of a crime of violence as alleged and the delay on the part of the applicant in reporting the injuries on which the application was founded, and failure to co-operate with the police in that respect. On the balance of probabilities the Board were not satisfied and the application was refused.

The applicant sought judicial review of the Board's decision. The evidence before the court indicated that it became apparent in the course of the hearing before the Board that there had been a medical examination of the applicant on 30 May 1991 and that the report of the police surgeon in respect of that examination was not before the Board. For the applicant it was submitted that the applicant was prejudiced by the absence of this report and that the Board should have adjourned the application to enable that report to be made available to the Board in considering the merits of the applicant's case.

Whilst acknowledging, by reference to the cases of *R v CICB, ex parte Parsons* (17 January 1990, unreported), and *R v The Chief Constable of Cheshire and another, ex parte Berry* (30 July 1985, unreported), that there was no duty on the Board to look for evidence, this being a matter for the applicant to take the initiative, it was for the Board to bring out all relevant evidence in the Board's possession whether it is for or against the applicant. There was, in the view of the court, a general principle which had to be applied in such cases namely the principle of fairness. Popplewell J stated: 'General principles are easy to state and much more difficult to apply. In my judgment the word "fairness" is the hallmark by which this case should be determined. It seems to me that there is a proper ground for complaint and that in fairness the Board, alerted to the fact that there had been this report, should, of their own volition, have sought it out, or at least invited the applicant's view as to whether there should be an adjournment to obtain it'.

Relief was, however, refused by the court on the grounds of delay on the part of the applicant in seeking relief by way of judicial review.

Author's note – At the time of writing, this case is the subject of an appeal to the Court of Appeal.

R v Criminal Injuries Compensation Board, ex parte Cook

18 December 1995 (Court of Appeal, Civil Division) – Para 24, 1990 Scheme – refusal of oral hearing – para 6(c) (1990) – convictions of deceased victim – character of widow of deceased as applicant (para 15, 1990 Scheme)

The Court of Appeal heard the appeal by Mrs Cook against the refusal of the court below to allow judicial review of the Board's decision refusing compensation for the murder of her husband and refusing an oral hearing.

The single member of the Board, deciding the application initially on the papers, disallowed it under paras 6(c) and 15 of the 1990 Scheme, the single member having regard to the character of the deceased as shown by his criminal convictions. It was noted by the single member in that decision that, at the time of his death, the deceased was still serving a prison sentence for serious crime and the single member accordingly decided that it would be inappropriate that any award should be made from public funds in respect of his death.

The applicant, the widow of the deceased, requested a hearing in respect of that decision refusing the application. The request for a hearing was refused by the Board under para 24 of the 1990 Scheme. In seeking judicial review of the Board's decisions the application was refused by the judge and the applicant appealed to the Court of Appeal against that refusal.

The court reviewed the relevant paragraphs of the 1990 Scheme. In particular, it was noted by the court that para 6 of the 1990 Scheme confers a discretion on the Board to withhold or reduce compensation and is enjoined to consider the conduct or character of the applicant as well as the conduct or character of the deceased. It was accepted by the applicant that even when her conduct or character was beyond reproach, the conduct or character of the deceased had to be considered and the Board's discretion exercised in relation to the character of the deceased. It was argued for the appellant that the Board had erred in not taking into account the good character of the applicant. It was submitted that the Board had not taken into account the good character of Mrs Cook and weighed that against the bad character of the deceased to arrive at a decision as to what compensation, if any, should be awarded.

The court held that the Board was entitled to decide that no award was appropriate having regard to the character of the deceased and that the reasons given were, in the view of the court, adequate even though they did not refer to the character of the applicant. There was, in that case, no need to do so. The appeal was refused.

The Court of Appeal also reviewed the decision of Sedley J in *R v CICB, ex parte Gambles* and concluded that the decision in that case as to the appropriate process of reasoning from the facts required in a decision by the Board was wrong. It was not incumbent upon the Board, as suggested in that decision, to demonstrate in their reasons that the conclusion has been reached by an appropriate process of reasoning from the facts. The reasons must, however, be adequate to indicate the basis of the Board's decision.

The court decided that the judge was right in concluding that there was nothing to suggest that the single member of the Board, in refusing the application initially, had failed to exercise his discretion correctly and it was not possible to say that his decision in so doing was *Wednesbury* unreasonable. With regard to the separate decision by the Board refusing an oral hearing to appeal the initial refusal by the single member, the court concluded that the Board had a discretion whether or not to grant an oral hearing under para 24 of the 1990 Scheme and in the present case the application for an oral hearing raised nothing new and it was, therefore, open to the members of the Board to conclude as they did that the decision of the single member was right in law and in principle and that their conclusion that there should be no oral hearing was right.

R v Ireland

14 May 1996 (Court of Appeal, Criminal Division) – Telephone calls – Offences Against the Person Act 1861, s 47 – whether telephone calls can constitute an assault

The appellant appealed against his conviction and sentence on various charges of assault occasioning actual bodily harm contrary to section 47 of the Offences

Against the Person Act 1861. The particulars of the offences were that he had assaulted a woman thereby occasioning her actual bodily harm. Other charges were in similar terms. The charges arose as a result of the appellant making a large number of unwanted telephone calls to the three women named in the charges. The telephone calls occurred very frequently and when the women answered the telephone there was silence. The calls lasted, sometimes, for a minute or so and sometimes for several minutes. On occasions there were repeated calls over a relatively short period. Each of the complainants was examined by a psychiatrist who told the court that the result of the repeated telephone calls was that each of them suffered significant psychological symptoms.

The issue for decision by the court was whether a telephone call followed by silence can constitute an assault for the purposes of section 47 of the 1861 Act.

It was argued for the appellant that telephone calls followed by silence does not constitute an assault for the purposes of section 47. It was submitted that an assault is any act by which a person intentionally or recklessly causes another to apprehend immediate and unlawful violence. (*R v Savage* [1992] 1 AC 699 at page 740.) Referring to the case *R v Chan-Fook* [1994] 1 WLR 689, it was noted that 'actual bodily harm' may include injury to any part of the body, including internal organs, the nervous system and the brain. It was capable of including psychiatric injury but not mere emotion such as fear, distress or panic.

In the present case, the court decided that there was abundant evidence that the victims had suffered psychiatric damage. It was further held by the court that as to immediacy, by using the telephone the appellant put himself in immediate contact with the victims and when the victims lifted the telephone they were placed in immediate fear and suffered the consequences to which the court had already referred. The court in its judgment referred to a number of authorities as to the law of assault. These included cases in which threats had been uttered over the telephone. In the present case the appellant had not uttered threats but had followed each telephone call with silence. However, the Court of Appeal was satisfied that the assault occasioning actual bodily harm offence was made out. The Court of Appeal approved an Australian decision which had decided that a threat made over the telephone was capable of amounting to an assault and in the circumstances of the present case were satisfied that the calls made were as capable of being terrifying to the victims as if actual threats had been made. Whether a particular act or particular acts amount to an assault is a question of fact which will depend on the circumstances.

R v Criminal Injuries Compensation Board, ex parte R

11 March 1996 (Queen's Bench Division) – Para 7. 1969 Scheme – victim and offender living together at the time as members of a family

The applicant had been seriously injured in infancy. The application for compensation to the Board was refused on the grounds that the applicant and the offender were living together at the time as members of a family. The applicant requested a hearing and the Board heard and rejected the application. The circumstances at the time of the injuries being sustained were not entirely clear but it was accepted that at the time the injuries were sustained the two adults in the household were the applicant's mother and a Mr Jenney and that the applicant's mother and Mr Jenney were, at the time, living together as husband and wife. The applicant, then living with his mother and Mr Jenney, sustained injury in infancy. Application to the Board for compensation was not made until the applicant was nearly 14 years old. The application was made by his adoptive mother. The decision of the Board, both by the single member and at the hearing, was based upon para 7 of the 1969 Scheme which provided that where the victim who suffered injuries and the offender who inflicted them were living together at the time as members of the same family no compensation will be payable. For the purposes of this paragraph where a man and woman were living together as man and wife they would be treated as if they were married to one another.

The Board had decided that the application came within the terms of para 7 of the 1969 Scheme and, therefore, no award could be made. The applicant contended that a distinction was to be made between the children of the offender and the child of one party and the offender's cohabitee. The court did not accept that argument. The court concluded that the assumption must be made in such circumstances as the present case that the two persons in the household were married to each other and that it would be wholly illogical to say that the child who was living with them in the household was not a member of the family; the child was undoubtedly a member of his mother's family and his mother was to be taken to be married to her cohabitee under the relevant paragraph of the Scheme. Any outside observer looking at the situation would, in the court's judgment, without any hesitation have said that 'there is a family living together'. The court observed that a broad look at what the situation or set-up was is the right approach in deciding as a matter of fact whether persons are living together as members of the same family. The appeal was dismissed.

R v Criminal Injuries Compensation Board, ex parte Dickson

1 July 1996 (Court of Appeal, Civil Division) – Para 24, 1990 Scheme – refusal of oral hearing – para 6(c) (1990) – convictions

The application for compensation had been dismissed by the Board on the papers and on the applicant requesting a hearing the Board had refused a hearing under para 24(c) of the 1990 Scheme, a provision which empowered the Board to refuse an oral hearing in the circumstances set out in that paragraph. The judge at first instance, Carnwath J, allowed the application for judicial review and quashed the Board's decision. That decision was appealed and decided by the Court of Appeal on 1 July 1996.

The grounds for refusing the application to the Board had been the applicant's criminal convictions which fell to be considered under para 6(c) of the 1990 Scheme.

Paragraph 24(c) of the Scheme provides:

> An applicant will be entitled to an oral hearing only if –
>
> (c) no award or a reduced award was made and there is a dispute as to the material facts or conclusions upon which the initial or reconsidered decision was based or if it appears that the decision may have been wrong in law or principle.

That paragraph of the Scheme goes on to provide:

> If it is considered on review that if any facts or conclusions which are disputed were resolved in the applicant's favour it would have made no difference to the initial or reconsidered decision, or that for any other reason an oral hearing would serve no useful purpose, the application for a hearing will be refused.

Such a decision refusing an oral hearing is final.

The case before the court turned on the construction of the phrase 'facts or conclusions' which appears twice in the text of para 24 quoted above. The court found that it was clear from the language of the Scheme itself that 'conclusion' is distinguished from the 'decision' itself.

The court concluded by a two to one majority, Ward LJ, dissenting, that there is no entitlement to a hearing simply because an applicant disputes the factual basis of the original decision or provides additional information for consideration. Any other conclusion would, effectively, permit an oral hearing on demand in virtually every case and that would be contrary to the language of para 24(c) and the intentions behind para 23 (which provided the procedure for requesting an oral hearing). The court observed in the present case that the judge who had decided the present case at first instance did not have the advantage of the decision of the Appeal Court in *R v CICB, ex parte Cook* [1996] 2 All ER 144 in which judgment had been given a few days after the hearing of the present case at first instance.

The court also referred to *R v CICB, ex parte Young*, an unreported decision dated 9 August 1995, the facts of which were very similar to the present case. The application had been refused on the grounds of the applicant's convictions. An oral hearing had been refused. It had been submitted for that applicant that the challenge of the single member's decision 'meant that there was a dispute about the conclusion on which the decision was based'. In that case Lord Gill said 'In making a decision under paragraph 24(c) (the Board) had to ask themselves two questions; namely whether there was a dispute as to the material facts or conclusions on which the decision to refuse compensation was based, and whether it appeared that the decision to refuse compensation might have been wrong in law or in principle'. Lord Gill continued 'The references in paragraph 24(c) to "material facts" and to "conclusions" are references, in my view, to the primary facts and to the conclusions of a factual nature which fall to be drawn from such primary facts ... In the present case compensation was refused by reason of the petitioner's character as shown by his previous convictions. The convictions constituted the material facts on which the decision was based. The petitioner did not dispute these material facts. He disputed the decision itself. Accordingly the requirements of paragraph 24(c) were not made out. The petitioner's argument fails to distinguish between the conclusions on which a decision is based and the decision itself'.

The court found that approach to be consistent with the views expressed by the Court of Appeal in *ex parte Cook* and were a correct analysis of the effect of the relevant part of the Scheme and the proper construction of para 24(c) in particular. The appeal by the Board was therefore allowed.

R v Criminal Injuries Compensation Board, ex parte C

6 November 1996 (Queen's Bench Division)

The applicant was a minor and sought to quash the determination by the Board awarding compensation for his injuries, which were such that a substantial part of the award was in respect of the cost of future care. The Board had before it written evidence which included two experts reports and a statement from the applicant's mother as to the applicant's care requirements and the projected cost of care. The written reasons for its decision given by the Board included the following paragraph: 'We do, when considering this or any case, have regard to the written reports before us: the nature of the Scheme is such that the evidence is not subjected to cross-examination or alternative views and reports, and in coming to our conclusions we have, therefore, to rely also on our own experience in this type of case'. The applicant's complaint was that the Board assessed the cost of future care at figures which were substantially below those set out in the experts' reports. It was contended for the applicant that whilst accepting that it was open to the Board to reach conclusions which, to a degree, diminished the quantum of the overall claim, it should not reach conclusions which went to undermine the root of certain parts of the claim without affording the applicant the prior opportunity to seek to maintain and successfully to sustain them.

The court acknowledged the propriety of the Board drawing upon its experience to reach the appropriate assessment in a particular case but, there being no right of appeal from an award by the Board at a hearing, there was an underlying need for the application of what the court described as 'scrupulous procedural fairness' when dealing with matters of this kind.

The court upheld the complaint for the applicant that the Board had not, before arriving at its decision, given the applicant's representative the opportunity to deal with, by way of evidence or submission, those matters which the Board had in mind in reaching a conclusion in the assessment of compensation which was substantially at variance with the expert evidence before them and upon which the applicant's case was founded.

Appendix 2

Criminal Injuries Compensation Scheme – 1990 Scheme

Criminal Injuries Compensation Board
Tay House
300 Bath Street
Glasgow G2 4JR
Telephone 0141 331 2726

A Scheme for compensating victims of crimes of violence was announced in both Houses of Parliament on 24 June 1964 and in its original form came into force on 1 August 1964.

The Scheme has since been modified in a number of respects. The 1990 revision below applies to all applications for compensation received by the Board on or after 1 February 1990 subject to the exceptions set out in paragraph 28. The 1990 Scheme also applies to applications received by the Board before 1 February 1990 to the extent set out in paragraph 29.

Requests for application forms and all enquiries should be directed to the above address.

THE SCHEME

Administration

1. The Compensation Scheme will be administered by the Criminal Injuries Compensation Board, which will be assisted by appropriate staff. Appointments to the Board will be made by the Secretary of State, after consultation with the Lord Chancellor and, where appropriate, the Lord Advocate. A person may only be appointed to be a member of the Board if he is a barrister practising in England and Wales, an advocate practising in Scotland, a solicitor practising in England and Wales or Scotland or a person who holds or has held judicial office in England and Wales or Scotland. The Chairman and other members of the Board will be appointed to serve for up to five years in the first instance, and their appointments will be renewable for such periods as the Secretary of State considers apppropriate. The Chairman and other members will not serve on the Board beyond the age of 72, or after ceasing to be qualified for appointment, whichever is the earlier except that, where the Secretary of State considers it to be in the interests of the Scheme to extend a particular appointment beyond the age of 72 or after retirement from legal practice, he may do so. The Secretary of State may, if he thinks fit, terminate a member's appointment on the grounds of incapacity or misbehaviour.

2. The Board will be provided with money through a Grant-in-Aid out of which payments for compensation awarded in accordance with the principles set out below will be made. Their net expenditure will fall on the Votes of the Home Office and the Scottish Home and Health Department.

3. The Board, or such members of the Board's staff as the Board may designate, will be entirely responsible for deciding what compensation should be paid in individual cases and their decisions will not be subject to appeal or to Ministerial review. The general working of the Scheme will, however, be kept under review by the Government, and the Board will submit annually to the Home Secretary and the Secretary of State for Scotland a full report on the operation of the Scheme, together with their accounts. The report and accounts will be open to debate in Parliament.

Scope of the Scheme

4. The Board will entertain applications for ex gratia payments of compensation in any case where the applicant or, in the case of an application by a spouse or dependant (see paragraphs 15 and 16 below), the deceased, sustained in Great Britain, or on a British vessel, aircraft or hovercraft or on, under or above an installation in a designated area within the meaning of section 1 subsection (7) of the Continental Shelf Act 1964 or any waters within 500 metres of such an installation, or in a lighthouse off the coast of the United Kingdom, personal injury directly attributable –

(a) to a crime of violence (including arson or poisoning); or

(b) to the apprehension or attempted apprehension of an offender or a suspected offender or the prevention or attempted prevention of an offence or to the giving of help to any constable who is engaged in any such activity; or

(c) to an offence of trespass on a railway.

Applications for compensation will be entertained only if made within three years of the incident giving rise to the injury, except that the Board may in exceptional cases waive this requirement. A decision by the Chairman not to waive the time limit will be final. In considering for the purposes of this paragraph whether any act is a criminal act a person's conduct will be treated as constituting an offence notwithstanding that he may not be convicted of the offence by reason of age, insanity or diplomatic immunity.

5. Compensation will not be payable unless the Board are satisfied that the injury was one for which the total amount of compensaiton payable after deduction of social security benefits, but before any other deductions under the Scheme, would not be less than the minimum amount of compensation. This shall be £750. The application of the minimum level shall not, however, affect the payment of funeral expenses under paragraph 15 below or, where the victim has died otherwise than in consequence of an injury for which compensation would have been payable to him under the terms of the Scheme, any sum payable to a dependant or relative of his under paragraph 16.

6. The Board may withhold or reduce compensation if they consider that –

(a) the applicant has not taken, without delay, all reasonable steps to inform the police, or any other authority considered by the Board to be appropriate for the purpose, of the circumstances of the injury and to co-operate with the police or other authority in bringing the offender to justice; or

(b) the applicant has failed to give all reasonable assistance to the Board or other authority in connection with the application; or

(c) having regard to the conduct of the applicant before, during or after the events giving rise to the claim or to his character as shown by his criminal convictions or unlawful conduct – and, in applications under paragraphs 15 and 16 below, to the conduct or character as shown by the criminal convictions or unlawful conduct, of the deceased and of the applicant – it is inappropriate that a full award, or any award at all, be granted.

Further, compensation will not be payable –

(d) in the case of an application under paragraph 4(b) above where the injury was sustained accidentally, unless the Board are satisfied that the applicant was at the time taking an exceptional risk which was justified in all the circumstances.

7. Compensation will not be payable unless the Board are satisfied that there is no possibility that a person responsible for causing the injury will benefit from an award.

8. Where the victim and any person responsible for the injuries which are the subject of the application (whether that person actually inflicted them or not) were living in the same household at the time of the injuries as members of the same family, compensation will be paid only where –

(a) the person responsible has been prosecuted in connection with the offence, except where the Board consider that there are practical, technical or other good reasons why a prosecution has not been brought; and

(b) in the case of violence between adults in the family, the Board are satisfied that the person responsible and the applicant stopped living in the same household before the application was made and seem unlikely to live together again; and

(c) in the case of an application under this paragraph by or on behalf of a minor, ie a person under 18 years of age, the Board are satisfied that it would not be against the minor's interest to make a full or reduced award.

For the purposes of this paragraph, a man and a woman living together as husband and wife shall be treated as members of the same family.

9. If in the opinion of the Board it is in the interests of the applicant (whether or not a minor or a person under an incapacity) so to do, the Board may pay the amount of any award to any trustee or trustees to hold on such trusts for the benefit of all or any of the following persons, namely the applicant and any spouse, widow or widower, relatives and dependants of the applicant and with such provisions for their respective maintenance, education and benefit and with such powers and provisions for the investment and management of the fund and for the remuneration of the trustee or trustees as the Board shall think fit. Subject to this the Board will have a general discretion in any case in which they have awarded compensation to make special arrangements for its administration. In this paragraph 'relatives' means all persons claiming descent from the applicant's grandparents and 'dependants' means all persons who in the opinion of the Board are dependent on him wholly or partially for the provision of the ordinary necessities of life.

10. The Board will consider applications for compensation arising out of acts of rape and other sexual offences both in respect of pain, suffering and shock and in respect of loss of earnings due to consequent pregnancy, and, where the victim is ineligible for a maternity grant under the National Insurance Scheme, in respect of the expenses of childbirth. Compensation will not be payable for the maintenance of any child born as a result of a sexual offence, except that where a woman is awarded compensation for rape the Board shall award the additional sum of £5,000 in respect of each child born alive having been conceived as a result of the rape which the applicant intends to keep.

11. Applications for compensation for personal injury attributable to traffic offences will be excluded from the Scheme, except where such injury is due to a deliberate attempt to run the victim down.

Basis of compensation

12. Subject to the other provisions of this Scheme, compensation will be assessed on the basis of common law damages and will normally take the form of a lump sum payment, although the Board may make alternative arrangements in accordance with paragraph 9 above. More than one payment may be made where an applicant's eligibility for compensation has been established but a final award cannot be calculated in the first instance – for example where only a provisional medical assessment can be given. In a case in which an interim award has been made, the Board may decide to make a reduced award, increase any reduction already made or refuse to make any further payment at any stage before receiving notification of acceptance of a final award.

13. Although the Board's decisions in a case will normally be final, they will have discretion to reconsider a case after a final award of compensation has been accepted where there has been such a serious change in the applicant's medical condition that injustice would occur if the original assessment of compensation were allowed to stand, or where the victim has since died as a result of his injuries. A case will not be re-opened more than three years after the date of the final award unless the Board are satisfied, on the basis of evidence presented with the application for re-opening the case, that the renewed application can be considered without a need for extensive enquiries. A decision by the Chairman that a case may not be re-opened will be final.

14. Compensation will be limited as follows –

(a) the rate of net loss of earnings or earning capacity to be taken into account shall not exceed one and a half times the gross average industrial earnings at the date of assessment (as published in the Department of Employment Gazette and adjusted as considered appropriate by the Board);

(b) there shall be no element comparable to exemplary or punitive damages.

Where an applicant has lost earnings or earning capacity as a result of the injury, he mat be required by the Board to produce evidence thereof in such manner and form as the Board may specify.

15. Where the victim has died in consequence of the injury, no compensation other than funeral expenses will be payable for the benefit of his estate, but the Board will be able to entertain applications from any person who is a dependant of the victim within the meaning of section 1(3) of the Fatal Accidents Act 1976 or who is a relative of the victim within the meaning of Schedule 1 to the Damages (Scotland) Act 1976. Compensation will be payable in accordance with the other provisions of this Scheme to any such dependant or relative. Funeral expenses to an amount considered reasonable by the Board will be paid in appropriate cases, even where the person bearing the cost of the funeral is otherwise ineligible to claim under this Scheme. Applications may be made under this paragraph where the victim has died from his injuries even if an award has been made to the victim in his lifetime. Such cases will be subject to conditions set out in paragraph 13 for the re-opening of cases and compensation payable to the applicant will be reduced by the amount paid to the victim.

16. Where the victim has died otherwise than in consequence of the injury, the Board may make an award to such dependant or relative as is mentioned in paragraph 15 in respect of loss of wages, expenses and liabilities incurred by the victim before death as a result of the injury whether or not the application for compensation in respect of the injury has been made before the death.

17. Compensation will not be payable for the loss of or damage to clothing or any property whatsoever arising from the injury unless the Board are satisfied that the property was relied upon by the victim as a physical aid.

18. The cost of private medical treatment will be payable by the Board only if the Board conisder that, in all the circumstances, both the private treatment and the cost of it are reasonable.

19. Compensation will be reduced by the full value of any present or future entitlement to –

(a) United Kingdom social security benefits;

(b) any criminal injury compensation awards made under or pursuant to statutory arrangements in force at the relevant time in Northern Ireland;

(c) social security benefits, compensation awards or similar payments whatsoever from the funds of other countries; or

(d) payments under insurance arrangements except as excluded below which may accrue, as a result of the injury or death, to the benefit of the person to whom the award is made.

In assessing this entitlement, account will be taken of any income tax liability likely to reduce the value of such benefits and, in the case of an application under paragraph 15, the value of such benefits will not be reduced to take account of prospects of remarriage. If, in the opinion of the Board, an applicant may be eligible for any such benefits the Board may refuse to make an award until the applicant has taken such steps as the Board consider reasonable to claim them. Subject to paragraph 18 above, the Board will disregard monies paid or payable to the victim or his dependants as a result of or in consequence of insurance personally effected, paid for and maintained by the personal income of the victim or, in the case of a person under the age of 18, by his parent.

20. Where the victim is alive compensation will be reduced to take account of any pension accruing as a result of the injury. Where the victim has died in consequence of the injury, and any pension is payable for the benefit of the person to whom the award is made as a result of the death of the victim, the compensation will similarly be reduced to take account of the value of that pension. Where such pensions are taxable, one-half of their value will be deducted; where they are not taxable, eg where a lump sum payment not subject to income tax is made, they will be deducted in full. For the purposes of this paragraph, 'pension' means any payment payable as a result of the injury or death, in pursuance of pension or other rights whatsoever connected with the victim's employment, and includes any gratuity of that kind and similar benefits payable under insurance policies paid for by employers. Pension rights accruing solely as a result of payments by the victim or a dependant will be disregarded.

21. When a civil court has given judgment providing for payment of damages or a claim for damages has been settled on terms providing for payment of money, or when payment of compensation has been ordered by a criminal court, in respect of personal injuries, compensation by the Board in respect of the same injuries will be reduced by the amount of any payment received under such an order or settlement. When a civil court has assessed damages, as opposed to giving judgment for damages agreed by the parties, but the person entitled to such damages has not yet received the full sum awarded, he will not be precluded from applying to the Board, but the Board's assessment of compensation will not exceed the sum assessed by the court. Furthermore, a person who is compensated by the Board will be required to undertake to repay them for any damages, settlement or compensation he may subsequently obtain in respect of his injuries. In arriving at their assessment of compensation the Board will not be bound by any finding of contributory negligence by any court, but will be entirely bound by the terms of the Scheme.

Procedure for determining applications

22. Every application will be made to the Board in writing as soon as possible after the event on a form obtainable from the Board's offices. The initial decision on an application will be taken by a single member of the Board, or by any member of the Board's staff to whom the Board has given authority to determine applications on the Board's behalf. Where an award is made the applicant will be given a breakdown of the assessment of compensation, except where the Board consider this inappropriate, and where an award is refused or reduced, reasons for the decision will be given. If the applicant is not satisfied with the decision he may apply for an oral hearing which, if granted, will be held before at least two members of the Board exluding any member who made the original decision. The application for a hearing must be made within three months of notification of the initial decision; however the Board may waive this time limit where an extension is requested with good reason within the three month period, or where it is otherwise in the interests of justice to do so. A decision by the Chairman not to waive the time limit will be final. It will also be open to a member of the Board, or a designated member of the Board's staff, where he considers that he cannot make a just and proper decision himself to refer the application for a hearing before at least two members of the Board, one of whom may be the member who, in such a case, decided to refer the application to a hearing. An applicant will have no title to an award offered until the Board have received notification in writing that he accepts it.

23. Applications for hearings must be made in writing on a form supplied by the Board and should be supported by reasons together with any additional evidence which may assist the Board to decide whether a hearing should be granted. If the reasons in support of the application suggest that the initial decision was based on information obtained by or submitted to the Board which was incomplete or erroneous, the application may be remitted for reconsideration by the member of the Board who made the initial decision or, where this is not practicable or where the initial decision was made by a member of the Board's staff, by any member of the Board. In such cases it will still be open for the applicant to apply in writing for a hearing if he remains dissatisfied after his case has been reconsidered and the three-month limitation period in paragraph 22 will start from the date of notification of the reconsidered decision.

24. An applicant will be entitled to an oral hearing only if –

(a) no award was made on the ground that any award would be less than the sum specified in paragraph 5 of the Scheme and it appears that applying the principles set out in paragraph 26 below, the Board might make an award; or

(b) an award was madc and it appears that, applying the principles set out in paragraph 26 below, the Board might make a larger award; or

(c) no award or a reduced award was made and there is a dispute as to the material facts or conclusions upon which the initial or reconsidered decision was based or it appears that the decision may have been wrong in law or principle.

An application for a hearing which appears likely to fail the foregoing criteria may be reviewed by not less than two members of the Board other than any member who made the initial or reconsidered decision. If it is considered on review that if any facts or conclusions which are disputed were resolved in the applicant's favour it would have made no difference to the initial or reconsidered decision, or that for any other reason an oral hearing would serve no useful purpose, the application for a hearing will be refused. A decision to refuse an application for a hearing will be final.

25. It will be for the applicant to make out his case at the hearing, and where appropriate this will extend to satisfying the Board that compensation should not be withheld or reduced under the terms of paragraph 6 or paragraph 8. The applicant and a member of the Board's staff will be able to call, examine and cross-examine witnesses. The Board will be entitled to take into account any relevant hearsay, opinion or written evidence, whether or not the author gives oral evidence at the hearing. The Board will reach their decision solely in the light of evidence brought out at the hearing, and all the information and evidence made available to the Board members at the hearing will be made available to the applicant at, if not before, the hearing. The Board may adjourn a hearing for any reason, and where the only issue remaining is the assessment of compensation may remit the application to a Single Member of the Board for determination in the absence of the applicant but subject to the applicant's right to apply under paragraph 22 above for a further hearing if he is not satisfied with the final assessment of compensation. While it will be open to the applicant to bring a friend or legal adviser to assist him in putting his case, the Board will not pay the cost of legal representation. They will, however, have discretion to pay the expenses of the applicant and witnesses at a hearing. If an applicant fails to attend a hearing and has offered no reasonable excuse for his non attendance the Board at the hearing may dismiss his application. A person whose application has been dismissed by the Board for failure to attend a hearing may apply in writing to the Chairman of the Board for his application to be reinstated. A decision by the Chairman that an application should not be reinstated will be final.

26. At the hearing the amount of compensation assessed by a Single Member of the Board or a designated member of the Board's staff will not be altered except upon the same principles as the Court of Appeal in England or the Court of Session in Scotland would alter an assessment of damages made by a trial judge.

27. Procedure at hearings will be as informal as is consistent with the proper determination of applications, and hearings will in general be in private. The Board will have discretion to permit observers, such as representatives of the press, radio and television, to attend hearings provided that written undertakings are given that the anonymity of the applicant and other parties will not in any way be infringed by subsequent reporting. The Board will have power to publish information about its decisions in individual cases; this power will be limited only by the need to preserve the anonymity of applicants and other parties.

Implementation

28. The provisions of this Scheme will take effect from 1 February 1990. All applications for compensation received by the Board on or after 1 February 1990 will be dealt with under the terms of this Scheme except that in relation to applications in respect of injuries incurred before that date the following provisions of the 1990 Scheme shall not apply –

(a) Paragraph 4(c);

(b) Paragraph 8, but only in respect of injuries incurred before 1 October 1979 where paragraph 7 of the 1969 Scheme will continue to apply;

(c) Paragraph 10 but only insofar as it requires the Board to award an additional sum of £5,000 in the circumstances therein prescribed;

(d) Paragraphs 15 and 16 but only insofar as they enable the Board to entertain applications from a person who is a dependant within the meaning of section 1(3)(b) of the Fatal Accidents Act 1976 or who is a relative within the meaning of paragraph 1(aa) of Schedule 1 to the Damages (Scotland) Act 1976 other than such a person who is applying only for funeral expenses.

29. Applications for compensation received by the Board before 1 February 1990 will continue to be dealt with in accordance with paragraph 25 of the Scheme which came into operation on 1 October 1979 ('the 1979 Scheme') or the Scheme which came into operation on 21 May 1969 ('the 1969 Scheme') except that the following paragraphs of this Scheme will apply in addition to or in substitution for provisions of these Schemes as specified below –

(a) Paragraph 3 of this Scheme will apply in substitution for paragraph 4 of the 1969 Scheme and paragraph 3 of the 1979 Scheme;

(b) Paragraph 6(c) of this Scheme will apply in substitution for paragraph 17 of the 1969 Scheme and paragraph 6(c) of the 1979 Scheme;

(c) Paragraph 14 of this Scheme will apply additionally to applications otherwise falling to be considered under the 1969 or 1979 Schemes but only insofar as it allows the Board to require an applicant to produce evidence of loss of earnings or earning capacity;

(d) Paragraphs 22, 23 and 25 of this Scheme will apply in substitution for paragraphs 21 and 22 of the 1969 Scheme and paragraphs 22 and 23 of the 1979 Scheme;

(e) Paragraph 26 of this Scheme will apply additionally to applications otherwise falling to be considered under the 1969 or 1979 Schemes;

(f) Paragraph 27 of this Scheme will apply in susbtitution for paragraph 23 of the 1969 Scheme and paragraph 24 of the 1979 Scheme.

30. Applications to re-open cases received before 1 February 1990 will continue to be dealt with under the terms of paragraph 25 of the 1979 Scheme. Applications to re-open cases received on or after 1 February 1990 will be considered and determined under the terms of this Scheme.

Appendix 3

Criminal Injuries Compensation Scheme – 1996 Scheme

The Secretary of State, in exercise of the powers conferred on him by sections 1 to 6 and 12 of the Criminal Injuries Compensation Act 1995 (c.53), hereby makes the attached Criminal Injuries Compensation Scheme, a draft thereof having been approved by both Houses of Parliament:

Home Office	*Michael Howard*
12 December 1995	One of Her Majesty's Principal Secretaries of State

Criminal Injuries Compensation Authority
Tay House, 300 Bath Street
Glasgow G2 4JR
Telephone: 0141 331 2726
Fax: 0141 331 2287

Table of contents

Paragraph	*Provision*
1.	Preamble.
	Administration of the Scheme
2.	Claims officers and Panel.
3.	Decisions and appeals.
4.	Annual report on Scheme.
5.	Advice by Panel.
	Eligibility to apply for compensation
6.	Criminal injury sustained since August 1964.
7.	Ineligible cases.
8.	Criminal injury.
9.	Personal injury.
10.	No criminal conviction.
11.	Use of vehicle.
12.	Accidental injury.

Eligibility to receive compensation

13. Applicant's actions, conduct and character.
14. Actions, conduct and character in fatal cases.
15. Beneficiary of award.
16. Victim and assailant living in same household.

Consideration of applications

17. Written application within time limit.
18. Onus on applicant.
19. Powers of claims officer.
20. Medical examination of injury.
21. Guide to Scheme.

Types and limits of compensation

22. Types of compensation.
23. Maximum award.
24. Minimum award.

Standard amount of compensation

25. Tariff amount for listed injuries.
26. Multiple injuries.
27. Child born of rape.
28. Unlisted injuries.
29. Interim award for unlisted injuries.

Compensation for loss of earnings

30. Period of loss.
31. Loss up to time of assessment.
32. Loss continuity at time of assessment.
33. Alternative calculation of future loss.
34. Limit on rate of loss.

Compensation for special expenses

35. Types of special expenses.
36. Special expenses continuing at time of assessment.

Compensation in fatal cases

37. Funeral expenses.
38. Qualifying claimants.
39. Standard amount of compensation.
40. Dependency.
41. Calculation of dependency compensation.
42. Compensation for loss of parent.
43. Award to victim before death.
44. Supplementary compensation.

Effect on awards of other payments

45. Social security benefits and insurance payments.
46. Refusal of award pending claim.
47. Pensions.
48. Compensation and damages from other sources.
49. Repayment of award.

Determination of applications and payment of awards

50. Notification of award.
51. Lump sum and interim payments.
52. Purchase of annuities.

Reconsideration of decisions

53. Final payment not yet made.
54. Decision already notified to applicant.
55. Decision in accordance with direction by adjudicators.

Re-opening of cases

56. Change in victim's medical condition.
57. Time limit.

Review of decisions

58. Decisions open to review.
59. Written application within time limit.
60. Procedure on review.

Appeals against review decisions

61. Written notice within time limit.
62. Waiver of time limit.
63. Procedure for appeals.
64. Onus on appellant.
65. Inspection of injury.

Appeals concerning time limits and re-opening of cases

66. Single adjudicator.
67. Determination of appeal.
68. Direction to Authority.

Appeals concerning awards

69. Referral for oral hearing.
70. Referral to adjudicator.
71. Dismissal of appeal.

Oral hearing of appeals

72. More than one adjudicator.

73. Notice of hearing and disclosure of documents.
74. Attendance at hearing.
75. Procedure at hearing.
76. Observers.
77. Determination of appeal.
78. Failure to attend.

Rehearing of appeals

79. Written application within time limit.
80. Waiver of time limit.
81. Decision on application for rehearing.
82. Procedure at rehearing.

Implementation and transitional provisions

83. Scheme in force from 1 April 1996.
84. Earlier applications dealt with under old Scheme.
85. Transfer of Board's cases.
86. Adaptation of Board's powers.
87. Re-opening of old Scheme cases.

Notes to the Scheme

Note 1. Definition of Great Britain.
Note 2. Definition of British craft.
Note 3. Table of Illustrative Multipliers.

Tariff of injuries and standard amounts of compensation

Levels of compensation.
Descriptions of injury.
Notes to the Tariff.

The Criminal Injuries Compensation Scheme

1. This Scheme is made by the Secretary of State under the Criminal Injuries Compensation Act 1995. Applications received on or after 1 April 1996 for the payment of compensation to, or in respect of, persons who have sustained criminal injury will be considered under this Scheme.

Administration of the Scheme

2. Claims officers in the Criminal Injuries Compensation Authority ('the Authority') will determine claims for compensation in accordance with this Scheme. Appeals against decisions taken on reviews under this Scheme will be determined by adjudicators. Persons appointed as adjudicators are appointed as members of the Criminal Injuries Compensation Appeals Panel ('the Panel'). The Secretary of State will appoint one of the adjudicators as Chairman of the Panel. The Secretary of State will also appoint persons as staff of the Panel to administer the provisions of this Scheme relating to the appeal system.

3. Claims officers will be responsible for deciding, in accordance with this

Scheme, what awards (if any) should be made in individual cases, and how they should be paid. Their decisions will be open to review and thereafter to appeal to the Panel, in accordance with this Scheme. No decision, whether by a claims officer or the Panel, will be open to appeal to the Secretary of State.

4. The general working of this Scheme will be kept under review by the Secretary of State. The Accounting Officer(s) for the Authority and the Panel must each submit reports to the Secretary of State as soon as possible after the end of each financial year, dealing with the operation of this Scheme and the discharge of function's under it. The Accounting Officer(s) must each keep proper accounts and proper records in relation to those accounts, and must each prepare a statement of accounts in each financial year in a form directed by the Secretary of State. These statements of accounts must be submitted to the Secretary of State as soon as possible after the end of each financial year.

5. The Panel will advise the Secretary of State on matters on which he seeks its advice, as well as on such other matters and at such time as it considers appropriate. Any advice given by the Panel will be referred to by the Accounting Officer for the Panel in his annual report made under the preceding paragraph.

Eligibility to apply for compensation

6. Compensation may be paid in accordance with this Scheme:

(a) to an applicant who has sustained a criminal injury on or after 1 August 1964;

(b) where the victim of a criminal injury sustained on or after 1 August 1964 has since died, to an applicant who is a qualifying claimant for the purposes of paragraph 38 (compensation in fatal cases).

For the purposes of this Scheme, 'applicant' means any person for whose benefit an application for compensation is made, even where it is made on his behalf by another person.

7. No compensation will be paid under this Scheme in the following circumstances:

(a) where the applicant lodged a claim before 1 April 1996 for compensation in respect of the same criminal injury under any scheme for the compensation of the victims of violent crime in operation in Great Britain before that date; or

(b) where the criminal injury was sustained before 1 October 1979 and the victim and the assailant were living together at the time as members of the same family.

8. For the purposes of this Scheme, 'criminal injury' means one or more personal injuries as described in the following paragraph, being an injury sustained in Great Britain (see Note 1) and directly attributable to:

(a) a crime of violence (including arson, fire-raising or an act of poisoning); or

(b) an offence of trespass on a railway; or

(c) the apprehension or attempted apprehension of an offender or a suspected offender, the prevention or attempted prevention of an offence, or the giving of help to any constable who is engaged in any such activity.

9. For the purposes of this Scheme, personal injury includes physical injury (including fatal injury), mental injury (that is, a medically recognised psychiatric or psychological illness) and disease (that is, a medically recognised illness or condition). Mental injury or disease, may either result directly from the physical injury or occur without any physical injury, but compensation will not be payable for mental injury alone unless the applicant:

(a) was put in reasonable fear of immediate physical harm to his own person; or

(b) had a close relationship of love and affection with another person at the time when that person sustained physical (including fatal) injury directly attributable to conduct within paragraph 8(a), (b) or (c), and

  (i) that relationship still subsists (unless the victim has since died), and

  (ii) the applicant either witnessed and was present on the occasion when the other person sustained the injury, or was closely involved in its immediate aftermath; or

(c) was the non-consenting victim of a sexual offence (which does not include a victim who consented in fact but was deemed in law not to have consented); or

(d) being a person employed in the business of a railway, either witnessed and was present on the occasion when another person sustained physical (including fatal) injury directly attributable to an offence of trespass on a railway, or was closely involved in its immediate aftermath. Paragraph 12 below does not apply where mental injury is sustained as described in this sub-paragraph.

10. It is not necessary for the assailant to have been convicted of a criminal offence in connection with the injury. Moreover, even where the injury is attributable to conduct within paragraph 8(a) in respect of which the assailant cannot be convicted of an offence by reason of age, insanity or diplomatic immunity, the conduct may nevertheless be treated as constituting a criminal act.

11. A personal injury is not a criminal injury for the purposes of this Scheme where the injury is attributable to the use of a vehicle, except where the vehicle was used so as deliberately to inflict, or attempt to inflict, injury on any person.

12. Where an injury is sustained accidentally by a person who is engaged in:

(a) any of the law-enforcement activities described in paragraph 8(c), or

(b) any other activity directed to containing, limiting or remedying the consequences of a crime,

compensation will not be payable unless the person injured was, at the time he sustained the injury, taking an exceptional risk which was justified in all the circumstances.

Eligibility to receive compensation

13. A claims officer may withhold or reduce an award where he considers that:

(a) the applicant failed to take, without delay, all reasonable steps to inform the police, or other body or person considered by the Authority to be appropriate for the purpose, of the circumstances giving rise to the injury; or

(b) the applicant failed to co-operate with the police or other authority in attempting to bring the assailant to justice; or

(c) the applicant has failed to give all reasonable assistance to the Authority or other body or person in connection with the application; or

(d) the conduct of the applicant before, during or after the incident giving rise to the application makes it inappropriate that a full award or any award at all be made; or

(e) the applicant's character as shown by his criminal convictions (excluding convictions spent under The Rehabilitation of Offenders Act 1974) or by evidence available to the claims officer makes it inappropriate that a full award or any award at all be made.

14. Where the victim has died since sustaining the injury (whether or not in consequence of it), the preceding paragraph will apply in relation both to the deceased and to any applicant.

15. A claims officer will make an award only where he is satisfied:

(a) that there is no likelihood that an assailant would benefit if an award were made; or

(b) where the applicant is under 18 years of age when the application is determined, that it would not be against his interest for an award to be made.

16. Where a case is not ruled out under paragraph 7(b) (injury sustained before 1 October 1979) but at the time when the injury was sustained, the victim and any assailant (whether or not that assailant actually inflicted the injury) were living in the same household as members of the same family, an award will be withheld unless:

(a) the assailant has been prosecuted in connection with the offence, except where a claims officer considers that there are practical, technical or other good reasons why a prosecution has not been brought; and

(b) in the case of violence between adults in the family, a claims officer is satisfied that the applicant and the assailant stopped living in the same household before the application was made and are unlikely to share the same household again.

For the purposes of this paragraph, a man and woman living together as husband and wife will be treated as members of the same family.

Consideration of applications

17. An application for compensation under this Scheme in respect of a criminal injury ('injury' hereafter in this Scheme) must be made in writing on a form

obtainable from the Authority. It should be made as soon as possible after the incident giving rise to the injury and must be received by the Authority within two years of the date of the incident. A claims officer may waive this time limit where he considers that, by reason of the particular circumstances of the case, it is reasonable and in the interests of justice to do so.

18. It will be for the applicant to make out his case including, where appropriate:

(a) making out his case for a waiver of the time limit in the preceding paragraph; and

(b) satisfying the claims officer dealing with his application (including an officer reviewing a decision under paragraph 60) that an award should not be reconsidered, withheld or reduced under any provision of this Scheme.

Where an applicant is represented, the costs of representation will not be met by the Authority.

19. A claims officer may make such directions and arrangements for the conduct of an application, including the imposition of conditions, as he considers appropriate in all the circumstances. The standard of proof to be applied by a claims officer in all matters before him will be the balance of probabilities.

20. Where a claims officer considers that an examination of the injury is required before a decision can be reached, the Authority will make arrangements for such an examination by a duly qualified medical practitioner. Reasonable expenses incurred by the applicant in that connection will be met by the Authority.

21. A Guide to the operation of this Scheme will be published by the Authority. In addition to explaining the procedures for dealing with applications, the Guide will set out, where appropriate, the criteria by which decisions will normally be reached.

Types and limits of compensation

22. Subject to the other provisions of this Scheme, the compensation payable under an award will be:

(a) a standard amount of compensation determined by reference to the nature of the injury in accordance with paragraphs 25–29;

(b) where the applicant has lost earnings or earning capacity for longer than 28 weeks as a direct consequence of the injury (other than injury leading to his death), an additional amount in respect of such loss of earnings, calculated in accordance with paragraphs 30–34;

(c) where the applicant has lost earnings or earning capacity for longer than 28 weeks as a direct consequence of the injury (other than injury leading to his death) or, if not normally employed, is incapacitated to a similar extent, an additional amount in respect of any special expenses, calculated in accordance with paragraphs 35–36;

(d) where the victim has died in consequence of the injury, the amount or amounts calculated in accordance with paragraphs 37–43;

(e) where the victim has died otherwise than in consequence of the injury, a supplementary amount calculated in accordance with paragraph 44.

23. The total maximum amount payable in respect of the same injury will not exceed £500,000. For these purposes, where the victim has died in consequence of the injury, any application made by the victim before his death and any application made by any qualifying claimant or claimants after his death will be regarded as being in respect of the same injury.

24. The injury must be sufficiently serious to qualify for an award equal at least to the minimum amount payable under this Scheme in accordance with paragraph 25.

Standard amount of compensation

25. The standard amount of compensation will be the amount shown in respect of the relevant description of injury in the Tariff appended to this Scheme, which sets out:

(a) a scale of fixed levels of compensation; and

(b) the level and corresponding amount of compensation for each description of injury.

Level 1 represents the minimum amount payable under this Scheme, and Level 25 represents the maximum amount payable for any single description of injury. Where the injury has the effect of accelerating or exacerbating a pre-existing condition, the compensation awarded will reflect only the degree of acceleration or exacerbation.

26. Minor multiple injuries will be compensated in accordance with Note 1 to the Tariff. The standard amount of compensation for more serious but separate multiple injuries will be calculated as:

(a) the Tariff amount for the highest-rated description of injury; plus

(b) 10 per cent of the Tariff amount for the second highest-rated description of injury; plus, where there are three or more injuries,

(c) 5 per cent of the Tariff amount for the third highest-rated description of injury.

27. Where a woman has become pregnant as a result of rape and an award is made to her in respect of non-consensual vaginal intercourse, an additional amount will be payable equal to Level 10 of the Tariff in respect of each child born alive which she intends to keep.

28. Where the Authority considers that any description of injury for which no provision is made in the Tariff is sufficiently serious to qualify for at least the minimum amount payable under this Scheme, it will, following consultation with the Panel, refer the injury to the Secretary of State. In doing so the Authority will recommend to the Secretary of State both the inclusion of that description of injury in the Tariff and also the amount of compensation for which it should qualify. Any such consultation with the Panel or reference to the Secretary of State must not refer to the circumstances of any individual application for compensation under this Scheme other than the relevant medical reports.

29. Where an application for compensation is made in respect of an injury for which no provision is made in the Tariff and the Authority decides to refer the

injury to the Secretary of State under the preceding paragraph, an interim award may be made of up to half the amount of compensation for which it is recommended that such description of injury should qualify if subsequently included in the Tariff. No part of such an interim award will be recoverable if the injury is not subsequently included in the Tariff or, if included, qualifies for less compensation than the interim award paid.

Compensation for loss of earnings

30. Where the applicant has lost earnings or earning capacity for longer than 28 weeks as a direct consequence of the injury (other than injury leading to his death), no compensation in respect of loss of earnings or earning capacity will be payable for the first 28 weeks of loss. The period of loss for which compensation may be payable will begin 28 weeks after the date of commencement of the applicant's incapacity for work and continue for such period as a claims officer may determine.

31. For a period of loss ending before or continuing to the time the claim is assessed, the net loss of earnings or earning capacity will be calculated on the basis of:

(a) the applicant's emoluments (being any profit or gain accruing from an office or employment) at the time of the injury and what those emoluments would have been during the period of loss; and

(b) any emoluments which have become payable to the applicant in respect of the whole or part of the period of loss, whether or not as a result of the injury; and

(c) any changes in the applicant's pension rights; and

(d) in accordance with paragraphs 45–47 (reductions to take account of other payments), any social security benefits, insurance payments and pension which have become payable to the applicant during the period of loss; and

(e) any other pension which has become payable to the applicant during the period of loss, whether or not as a result of the injury.

32. Where, at the time the claim is assessed, a claims officer considers that the applicant is likely to suffer continuing loss of earnings or earning capacity, an annual rate of net loss (the multiplicand) or, where appropriate, more than one such rate will be calculated on the basis of:

(a) the current rate of net loss calculated in accordance with the preceding paragraph; and

(b) such future rate or rates of net loss (including changes in the applicant's pension rights) as the claims officer may determine; and

(c) the claims officer's assessment of the applicant's future earning capacity; and

(d) in accordance with paragraphs 45–47 (reductions to take account of other payments), any social security benefits, insurance payments and pension which will become payable to the applicant in future; and

(e) any other pension which will become payable to the applicant in future, whether or not as a result of the injury.

The compensation payable in respect of such continuing loss will be a lump sum which is the product of that multiplicand and an appropriate multiplier. The summary table given in Note 3 illustrates the multipliers applicable to various periods of future loss to allow for the accelerated receipt of compensation. In selecting the multiplier, the claims officer may refer to the Actuarial Tables for use in Personal Injury and Fatal Accident Cases published by the Government Actuary's Department, and take account of any factors and contingencies which appear to him to be relevant.

33. Where a claims officer considers that the approach in the preceding paragraph is impracticable, the compensation payable in respect of continuing loss of earnings or earning capacity will be such other lump sum as he may determine.

34. Any rate of net loss of earnings or earning capacity (before any reduction in accordance with this Scheme) which is to be taken into account in calculating any compensation payable under paragraphs 30–33 must not exceed one and a half times the gross average industrial earnings at the time of assessment according to the latest figures published by the Department of Education and Employment.

Compensation for special expenses

35. Where the applicant has lost earnings or earning capacity for longer than 28 weeks as a direct consequence of the injury (other than injury leading to his death), or, if not normally employed, is incapacitated to a similar extent, additional compensation may be payable in respect of any special expenses incurred by the applicant from the date of the injury for:

(a) loss of or damage to property or equipment belonging to the applicant on which he relied as a physical aid, where the loss or damage was a direct consequence of the injury;

(b) costs (other than by way of loss of earnings or earning capacity) associated with National Health Service treatment for the injury;

(c) the cost of private health treatment for the injury, but only where a claims officer considers that, in all the circumstances, both the private treatment and its cost are reasonable;

(d) the reasonable cost, to the extent that it falls to the applicant, of

  (i) special equipment, and/or

  (ii) adaptations to the applicant's accommodation, and/or

  (iii) care, whether in a residential establishment or at home, which are not provided or available free of charge from the National Health Service, local authorities or any other agency, provided that a claims officer considers such expense to be necessary as a direct consequence of the injury.

In the case of (d)(iii), the expense of unpaid care provided at home by a relative or friend of the victim will be compensated by assessing the carer's loss of earnings or earning capacity and/or additional personal and living expenses, as calculated on such basis as a claims officer considers appropriate in all the circumstances. Where the foregoing method of assessment is considered by the claims officer not to be relevant in all the circumstances, the compensation payable will be such sum as he may determine having regard to the level of care provided.

36. Where, at the time the claim is assessed, a claims officer is satisfied that the need for any of the special expenses mentioned in the preceding paragraph is likely to continue, he will determine the annual cost and select an appropriate multiplier in accordance with paragraph 32 (future loss of earnings), taking account of any other factors and contingencies which appear to him to be relevant.

Compensation in fatal cases

37. Where the victim has died in consequence of the injury, no compensation other than funeral expenses will be payable for the benefit of his estate. Such expenses will, subject to the application of paragraph 13 in relation to the actions, conduct and character of the deceased, be payable up to an amount considered reasonable by a claims officer, even where the person bearing the cost of the funeral is otherwise ineligible to claim under this Scheme.

38. Where the victim has died since sustaining the injury, compensation may be payable, subject to paragraph 14 (actions, conduct and character), to any claimant (a 'qualifying claimant') who at the time of the deceased's death was:

(a) the spouse of the deceased, being only, for these purposes:

(i) a person who was living with the deceased as husband and wife in the same household immediately before the date of death and who, if not formally married to him, had been so living throughout the two years before that date, or

(ii) a spouse or former spouse of the deceased who was financially supported by him immediately before the date of death; or

(b) a parent of the deceased, whether or not the natural parent, provided that he was accepted by the deceased as a parent of his family; or

(c) a child of the deceased, whether or not the natural child, provided that he was accepted by the deceased as a child of his family or was dependent on him.

Where the victim has died in consequence of the injury, compensation may be payable to a qualifying claimant under paragraphs 39–42 (standard amount of compensation, dependency, and loss of parent). Where the victim has died otherwise than in consequence of the injury, compensation may be payable to a qualifying claimant only under paragraph 44 (supplementary compensation).

39. In cases where there is only one qualifying claimant, the standard amount of compensation will be Level 13 of the Tariff. Where there is more than one qualifying claimant, the standard amount of compensation for each claimant will be Level 10 of the Tariff. A former spouse of the deceased is not a qualifying claimant for the purposes of this paragraph.

40. Additional compensation calculated in accordance with the following paragraph may be payable to a qualifying claimant where a claims officer is satisfied that the claimant was financially dependent on the deceased. A dependency will not be established where the deceased's only normal income was from:

(a) United Kingdom social security benefits; or

(b) social security benefits or similar payments from the funds of other countries.

41. The amount of compensation payable in respect of dependency will be calculated on a basis similar to paragraphs 31–34 (loss of earnings). The period of loss will begin from the date of the deceased's death and continue for such period as a claims officer may determine, with no account being taken, where the qualifying claimant was formally married to the deceased, of remarriage or prospects of remarriage. In assessing the dependency, the claims officer will take account of the qualifying claimant's income and emoluments (being any profit or gain accruing from an office or employment), if any. Where the deceased had been living in the same household as the qualifying claimant before his death, the claims officer will, in calculating the multiplicand, make such proportional reduction as he considers appropriate to take account of the deceased's own personal and living expenses.

42. Where a qualifying claimant was under 18 years of age at the time of the deceased's death and was dependent on him for parental services, the following additional compensation may also be payable:

(a) a payment for loss of that parent's services at an annual rate of level 5 of the Tariff; and

(b) such other payments as a claims officer considers reasonable to meet other resultant losses.

Each of these payments will be multiplied by an appropriate multiplier selected by a claims officer in accordance with paragraph 32 (future loss of earnings), taking account of the period remaining before the qualifying claimant reaches age 18 and of any other factors and contingencies which appear to the claims officer to be relevant.

43. Application may be made under paragraphs 37–42 (compensation in fatal cases) even where an award had been made to the victim in respect of the same injury before his death. Any such application will be subject to the conditions set out in paragraphs 56–57 for the re-opening of cases, and any compensation payable to the qualifying claimant or claimants, except payments made under paragraphs 37 and 39 (funeral expenses and standard amount of compensation), will be reduced by the amount paid to the victim. The amounts payable to the victim and the qualifying claimant or claimants will not in total exceed £500,000.

44. Where a victim who would have qualified for additional compensation under paragraph 22(b) (loss of earnings) and/or paragraph 22(c) (special expenses) has died, otherwise than in consequence of the injury, before such compensation was awarded, supplementary compensation under this paragraph may be payable to a qualifying claimant who was financially dependent on the deceased within the terms of paragraph 40 (dependency), whether or not a relevant application was made by the victim before his death. Payment may be made in accordance with paragraph 31 in respect of the victim's loss of earnings (except for the first 28 weeks of such loss) and in accordance with paragraph 35 in respect of any special expenses incurred by the victim before his death. The amounts payable to the victim and the qualifying claimant or claimants will not in total exceed £500,000.

Effect on awards of other payments

45. All awards payable under this Scheme, except those payable under paragraphs 25, 27, 39 and 42(a) (Tariff-based amounts of compensation), will be subject to a

reduction to take account of social security benefits or insurance payments made by way of compensation for the same contingency. The reduction will be applied to those categories or periods of loss or need for which additional or supplementary compensation is payable, including compensation calculated on the basis of a multiplicand or annual cost. The amount of the reduction will be the full value of any relevant payment which the applicant has received, or to which he has any present or future entitlement, by way of:

(a) United Kingdom social security benefits;

(b) social security benefits of similar payments from the funds of other countries;

(c) payments under insurance arrangements, including, where a claim is made under paragraphs 35(c) and (d) and 36 (special expenses), insurance personally effected, paid for and maintained by the personal income of the victim of, in the case of a person under 18 years of age, by his parent. Insurance so personally effected will otherwise be disregarded.

In assessing the value of any such benefits and payments, account may be taken of any income tax liability likely to reduce their value.

46. Where, in the opinion of a claims officer, an applicant may be eligible for any of the benefits and payments mentioned in the preceding paragraph, an award may be withheld until the applicant has taken such steps as the claims officer considers reasonable to claim them.

47. Where the victim is alive, any compensation payable under paragraphs 30–34 (loss of earnings) will be reduced to take account of any pension accruing as a result of the injury. Where the victim has died in consequence of the injury, any compensation payable under paragraphs 40–41 (dependency) will similarly be reduced to take account of any pension payable, as a result of the victim's death, for the benefit of the applicant. Where such pensions are taxable, one half of their value will be deducted, but they will otherwise be deducted in full (where, for example, a lump sum payment not subject to income tax is made). For the purposes of this paragraph, 'pension' means any payment payable as a result of the injury or death in pursuance of pension or any other rights connected with the victim's employment, and includes any gratuity of that kind and similar benefits payable under insurance policies paid for by the victim's employers. Pension rights accruing solely as a result of payments by the victim or a dependant will be disregarded.

48. An award payable under this Scheme will reduced by the full value of any payment in respect of the same injury which the applicant has received by way of:

(a) any criminal injury compensation award made under or pursuant to arrangements in force at the relevant time in Northern Ireland;

(b) any compensation award or similar payment from the funds of other countries;

(c) any award where:
   (i) a civil court has made an order for the payment of damages;
   (ii) a claim for damages and/or compensation has been settled on terms providing for the payment of money;

(iii) payment of compensation has been ordered by a criminal court in respect of personal injuries.

In the case of (a) or (b), the reduction will also include the full value of any payment to which the applicant has any present or future entitlement.

49. Where a person in whose favour an award under this Scheme is made subsequently receives any other payment in respect of the same injury in any of the circumstances mentioned in the preceding paragraph, but the award made under this Scheme was not reduced accordingly, he will be required to repay the Authority in full up to the amount of the other payment.

Determination of applications and payment of awards

50. An application for compensation under this Scheme will be determined by a claims officer, and written notification of the decision will be sent to the applicant or his representative. The claims officer may make such directions and arrangements, including the imposition of conditions, in connection with the acceptance, settlement, payment, in payment and/or administration of an award as he considers appropriate in all the circumstances. Subject to any such arrangements, including the special procedure in paragraph 52 (purchase of annuities), and to paragraphs 53–55 (reconsideration of decisions), title to an award offered will be vested in the applicant when the Authority has received notification in writing that he accepts the award.

51. Compensation will normally be paid as a single lump sum, but one or more interim payments may be made where a claims officer considers this appropriate. Once an award has been paid to an applicant or his representative, the following paragraph does not apply.

52. Where prior agreement is reached between the Authority and the applicant or his representative, an award may consist in whole or in part of an annuity or annuities, purchased for the benefit of the applicant or to be held on trust for his benefit. Once that agreement is reached, thc Authority will take the instructions of the applicant or his representative as to which annuity or annuities should be purchased. Any expense incurred will be met from the award.

Reconsideration of decisions

53. A decision made by a claims officer (other than a decision made in accordance with a direction by adjudicators on determining an appeal under paragraph 77) may be reconsidered at any time before actual payment of a final award where there is new evidence or a change in circumstances. In particular, the fact that an interim payment has been made does not preclude a claims officer from reconsidering issues of eligibility for an award.

54. Where an applicant has already been sent written notification of the decision on his application, he will be sent written notice that the decision is to be reconsidered, and any representations which he sends to the Authority within 30 days of the date of such notice will be taken into account in reconsidering the decision. Whether or not any such representations are made, the applicant will be sent written notification of the outcome of the reconsideration, and where the original decision is not confirmed, such notification will include the revised decision.

55. Where a decision to make an award has been made by a claims officer in accordance with a direction by adjudicators on determining an appeal under paragraph 77, but before the award has been paid the claims officer considers that there is new evidence or a change in circumstances which justifies reconsidering whether the award should be withheld or the amount of compensation reduced, the Authority will refer the case to the Panel for rehearing under paragraph 82.

Re-opening of cases

56. A decision made by a claims officer and accepted by the applicant, or a decision made by the Panel, will normally be regarded as final. The claims officer may, however, subsequently re-open a case where there has been such a material change in the victim's medical condition that injustice would occur if the original assessment of compensation were allowed to stand, or where he has since died in consequence of the injury.

57. A case will not be re-opened more than two years after the date of the final decision unless the claims officer is satisfied, on the basis of evidence presented in support of the application to re-open the case, that the renewed application can be considered without a need for further extensive enquiries.

Review of decisions

58. An applicant may seek a review of any decision under this Scheme by a claims officer:

(a) not to waive the time limit in paragraph 17 (application for compensation) or paragraph 59 (application for review); or

(b) not to re-open a case under paragraphs 56–57; or

(c) to withhold an award, including such decision made on reconsideration of an award under paragraphs 53–54; or

(d) to make an award, including a decision to make a reduced award whether or not on reconsideration of an award under paragraphs 53–54; or

(e) to seek repayment of an award under paragraph 49.

An applicant may not, however, seek the review of any such decision where the decision was itself made on a review under paragraph 60 and either the applicant did not appeal against it or the appeal was not referred for determination on an oral hearing, or where the decision was made in accordance with a direction by adjudicators on determining an appeal under paragraph 77.

59. An application for the review of a decision by a claims officer must be made in writing to the Authority and must be supported by reasons together with any relevant additional information. It must be received by the Authority within 90 days of the date of the decision to be reviewed, but this time limit may, in exceptional circumstances, be waived where a claims officer more senior than the one who made the original decision considers that:

(a) any extension requested by the applicant within the 90 days is based on good reasons; or

(b) it would be in the interests of justice to do so.

60. All applications for review will be considered by a claims officer more senior than any claims officer who has previously dealt with the case. The officer conducting the review will reach his decision in accordance with the provisions of this Scheme applying to the original application, and he will not be bound by any earlier decision either as to the eligibility of the applicant for an award or as to the amount of an award. The applicant will be sent written notification of the outcome of the review, giving reasons for the review decision, and the Authority will, unless it receives notice of an appeal, ensure that a determination of the original application is made in accordance with the review decision.

Appeals against review decisions

61. An applicant who is dissatisfied with a decision taken on a review under paragraph 60 may appeal against the decision by giving written notice of appeal to the Panel on a form obtainable from the Authority. Such notice of appeal must be supported by reasons for the appeal together with any relevant additional material which the appellant wishes to submit, and must be received by the Panel within 30 days of the date of the review decision. The Panel will send to the Authority a copy of the notice of appeal and supporting reasons which it receives and of any other material submitted by the appellant. Where the applicant is represented for the purposes of the appeal, the costs of representation will not be met by the Authority or the Panel.

62. A member of the staff of the Panel may, in exceptional circumstances, waive the time limit in the preceding paragraph where he considers that:

(a) any extension requested by the appellant within the 30 days is based on good reasons; or

(b) it would be in the interests of justice to do so.

Where, on considering a request to waive the time limit, a member of the staff of the Panel does not waive it, he will refit the request to the Chairman of the Panel or to another adjudicator nominated by the Chairman to decide requests for waiver, and a decision by the adjudicator concerned not to waive the time limit will be final. Written notification of the outcome of the waiver request will be sent to the appellant and to the Authority, giving reasons for the decision where the time limit is not waived.

63. Where the Panel receives notice of an appeal against a review decision relating to a decision mentioned in paragraph 58(a) or (b), the appeal will be dealt with in accordance with paragraphs 66–68 (appeals concerning time limits and re-opening of cases). Where the Panel receives notice of an appeal against a review decision relating to a decision mentioned in paragraph 58(c), (d) or (e), the appeal will be dealt with in accordance with paragraphs 69–71 (appeals concerning awards) and may under those provisions be referred for an oral hearing in accordance with paragraphs 72–78. The Panel may publish information in connection with individual appeals, but such information must not identify any appellant or other person appearing at an oral hearing or referred to during an appeal, or enable identification to be made of any such person.

64. The standard of proof to be applied by the Panel in all matters before it will be the balance of probabilities. It will be for the appellant to make out his case including, where appropriate:

(a) making out his case for a waiver of the time limit in paragraph 61 (time limit for appeals); and

(b) satisfying the adjudicator or adjudicators responsible for determining his appeal that an award should not be reconsidered, withheld or reduced under any provision of this Scheme. Subject to paragraph 78 (determination of appeal in appellant's absence), the adjudicator or adjudicators concerned must ensure, before determining an appeal, that the appellant has had an opportunity to submit representations on any evidence or other material submitted by or on behalf of the Authority.

65. The Panel may make such arrangements for the inspection of the injury as it considers appropriate. Reasonable expenses incurred by the appellant in that connection will be met by the Panel.

Appeals concerning time limits and re-opening of cases

66. The Chairman of the Panel or another adjudicator nominated by him will determine any appeal against a decision taken on a review:

(a) not to waive the time limit in paragraph 17 (application for compensation) or paragraph 59 (application for review); or

(b) not to re-open a case under paragraphs 56–57.

Where the appeal concerns a decision not to re-open a case and the application for re-opening was made more than two years after the date of the final decision, the adjudicator must be satisfied that the renewed application can be considered without a need for further extensive enquiries by the Authority.

67. In determining an appeal under the preceding paragraph, the adjudicator will allow the appeal where he considers it appropriate to do so. Where he dismisses the appeal, his decision will be final. Written notification of the outcome of the appeal, giving reasons for the decision, will be sent to the appellant and to the Authority.

68. Where the adjudicator allows an appeal in accordance with the preceding paragraph, he will direct the Authority:

(a) in a case where the appeal was against a decision not to waive the time limit in paragraph 17, to arrange for the application for compensation to be dealt with under this Scheme as if the time limit had been waived by a claims officer;

(b) in a case where the appeal was against a decision not to waive the time limit in paragraph 59, to conduct a review under paragraph 60;

(c) in a case where the appeal was against a decision not to re-open a case, to re-open the case under paragraphs 56–57.

Appeals concerning awards

69. A member of the staff of the Panel may refer for an oral hearing in accordance with paragraphs 72–78 any appeal against a decision taken on a review:

(a) to withhold an award, including such decision made on reconsideration of an award under paragraphs 53–54; or

(b) to make an award, including a decision to make a reduced award whether or not on reconsideration of an award under paragraphs 53–54; or

(c) to seek repayment of an award under paragraph 49.

A request for an oral hearing in such cases may also be made by the Authority.

70. Where a member of the staff of the Panel does not refer an appeal for an oral hearing under the preceding paragraph, he will refer it to an adjudicator. The adjudicator will refer the appeal for determination on an oral hearing in accordance with paragraphs 72–78 where, on the evidence available to him, he considers:

(a) in a case where the review decision was to withhold an award on the ground that the injury was not sufficiently serious to qualify for an award equal to at least the minimum amount payable under this Scheme, that an award in accordance with this Scheme could have been made; or

(b) in any other case, that there is a dispute as to the material facts or conclusions upon which the review decision was based and that a different decision in accordance with this Scheme could have been made.

He may also refer the appeal for determination on an oral hearing in accordance with paragraphs 72–78 where he considers that the appeal cannot be determined on the basis of the material before him or that for any other reason an oral hearing would be desirable.

71. Where an appeal is not referred under paragraphs 69 or 70 for an oral hearing, the adjudicator's dismissal of the appeal will be final and the decision taken on the review will stand. Written notification of the dismissal of the appeal, giving reasons for the decision, will be sent to the appellant and to the Authority.

Oral hearing of appeals

72. Where an appeal is referred for determination on an oral hearing, the hearing will take place before at least two adjudicators. Where the referral was made by an adjudicator under paragraph 70, that adjudicator will not take part in the hearing. Subject to the provisions of this Scheme, the procedure to be followed for any particular appeal will be a matter for the adjudicators hearing the appeal.

73. Written notice of the date proposed for the oral hearing will normally be sent to the appellant and the Authority at least 21 days beforehand. Any documents to be submitted to the adjudicators for the purposes of the hearing by the appellant, or by or on behalf of the Authority, will be made available at the hearing, if not before, to the Authority or the appellant respectively.

74. It will be open to the appellant to bring a friend or legal adviser to assist in presenting his case at the hearing, but the costs of representation will not be met by the Authority or the Panel. The adjudicators may, however, direct the Panel to meet reasonable expenses incurred by the appellant and any person who attends to give evidence at the hearing.

75. The procedure at hearings will be as informal as is consistent with the proper determination of appeals. The adjudicators will not be bound by any rules of evidence which may prevent a court from admitting any document or other matter

or statement in evidence. The appellant, the claims officer presenting the appeal and the adjudicators may call witnesses to give evidence and may cross-examine them.

76. Hearings will take place in private. The Panel may, however, subject to the consent of the appellant, give permission for the hearing to be attended by observers such as representatives of the press, radio and television. Any such permission will be subject to written undertakings being given:

(a) that the identity of the appellant and of any other persons appearing at the hearing or referred to during the appeal will be kept confidential and will not be disclosed in any account of the proceedings which is broadcast or in any way published; and

(b) that no material will be disclosed or in any other way published from which those identities could be discovered.

77. Where the adjudicators adjourn the hearing, they may direct that an interim payment be made. On determining the appeal, the adjudicators will, where necessary, make such direction as they think fit as to the decision to be made by a claims officer on the application for compensation, but any such direction must be in accordance with the relevant provisions of this Scheme. Where they are of the opinion that the appeal was frivolous or vexatious, the adjudicators may reduce the amount of compensation to be awarded by such amount as they consider appropriate. The appellant and the Authority will be informed of the adjudicators' determination of the appeal and the reasons for it, normally at the end of the hearing, but otherwise by written notification as soon as is practicable thereafter.

78. Where an appellant who fails to attend a hearing gives no reasonable excuse for his non-attendance, the adjudicators may determine the appeal in his absence.

Rehearing of appeals

79. Where an appeal is determined in the appellant's absence, he may apply to the Panel in writing for his appeal to be reheard, giving the reasons for his non-attendance. Any such application must be received by the Panel within 30 days of the date of notification to the appellant of the outcome of the hearing which he failed to attend. The Panel will send a copy of the application to the Authority.

80. A member of the staff of the Panel may waive the time limit in the preceding paragraph where he considers that it would be in the interests of justice to do so. Where he does not waive the time limit, he will refer the application to the Chairman of the Panel or to another adjudicator nominated by the Chairman to decide such applications, and a decision by the adjudicator concerned not to waive the time limit will be final. Written notification of the waiver decision will be sent to the appellant and to the Authority, giving reasons for the decision where the time limit is not waived.

81. Where a member of the staff of the Panel considers that there are good reasons for an appeal to be reheard, he will refer it for a rehearing. Where he does not refer it for a rehearing, he will refer the application to the Chairman of the Panel or to another adjudicator nominated by the Chairman to decide such applications,

and a decision by the adjudicator concerned not to rehear the appeal will be final. Written notification of the decision on the application for a rehearing will be sent to the appellant and to the Authority, giving reasons for the decision where the application is refused.

82. Where an appeal is to be reheard, the adjudicators who determined the appeal originally will not take part in the rehearing, and paragraphs 64 (onus on appellant), 65 (inspection of injury), and 72–78 (oral hearings) will apply.

Implementation and transitional provisions

83. The provisions of this Scheme come into force on 1 April 1996. All applications for compensation received by the Criminal Injuries Compensation Board ('the Board') on or after that date will be passed to the Authority to be dealt with under this Scheme.

84. Subject to paragraphs 85–87, applications for compensation received by the Board before 1 April 1996 will be dealt with according to the provisions of the non-statutory Scheme which came into operation on 1 February 1990 ('the old Scheme'), which includes the earlier Schemes mentioned therein insofar as they continue to have effect immediately before 1 April 1996 by virtue of the old Scheme or corresponding provisions in an earlier Scheme.

85. The Board will cease to exist on such date ('the transfer date') as the Secretary of State may direct. Immediately before the transfer date, the Board will transfer to the Authority all its records of current and past applications.

86. On and after the transfer date, applications required by paragraph 84 to be dealt with according to the provisions of the old Scheme will be so dealt with by the Authority, and:

(a) any decision authorised under the old Scheme to be made by a Single Member of the Board may be made by a single legally qualified member of the Panel appointed for the purposes of this Scheme;

(b) any decision authorised under the old Scheme to be made by at least two Members of the Board may be made by at least two legally qualified members of the Panel;

(c) any decision authorised under the old Scheme to be made by the Chairman of the Board may be made by the Chairman of the Panel.

In this paragraph 'legally qualified' means qualified to practise as a solicitor in any part of Great Britain, or as a barrister in England and Wales, or as an advocate in Scotland.

87. On and after the transfer date, any application to re-open a case under paragraph 13 of the old Scheme (or any corresponding provision in any of the earlier Schemes) must be addressed to the Authority, which will deal with it according to the provisions of the old Scheme, applying paragraphs 84 and 86 above as appropriate.

Notes to the Scheme
(see paragraph 8)

Note 1 Definition of Great Britain

(a) For the purposes of paragraph 8 of this Scheme, an injury is sustained in Great Britain where it is sustained:

   (i) on a British aircraft, hovercraft or ship (see Note 2); or

   (ii) on, under or above an installation in a designated area within the meaning of section 1(7) of the Continental Shelf Act 1964 or any waters within 500 metres of such an installation; or

   (iii) in a lighthouse off the coast of Great Britain.

(b) For the purposes of paragraph 8 of this Scheme, Great Britain includes that part of the Channel Tunnel designated part of Great Britain by the Channel Tunnel Act 1987. Within that part of the Tunnel or in the control zones within the meaning of the Channel Tunnel (International Arrangements) Order 1993 (SI No 1813), this Scheme applies to:

   (i) anyone injured by a UK 'officer' (as defined by Article 1(d) of the Protocol made under the Channel Tunnel Treaty signed at Sangette on 25 November 1991) in the exercise of his duties, and

   (ii) any UK 'officer' injured in the exercise of his duties, but it does not apply to:

   (iii) anyone (except a UK 'officer' in the exercise of his duties) injured by a non-UK 'officer' in the exercise of his duties, and

   (iv) any non-UK 'officer' injured in the exercise of his duties, and such persons must pursue their remedy under the relevant national law.

Note 2 Definition of British craft

In Note 1 above:

(a) 'British aircraft' means a British controlled aircraft within the meaning of section 92 of the Civil Aviation Act 1982 (application of criminal law to aircraft), or one of Her Majesty's aircraft;

(b) 'British hovercraft' means a British controlled hovercraft within the meaning of that section (as applied in relation to hovercraft by virtue of provision made under the Hovercraft Act 1968), or one of Her Majesty's hovercraft; and

(c) 'British ship' means any vessel used in navigation which is owned wholly by persons of the following descriptions, namely:

   (i) British citizens, or

   (ii) bodies corporate incorporated under the law of some part of, and having their principal place of business in, the United Kingdom, or

   (iii) Scottish partnerships, or one of Her Majesty's ships.

The references in this Note to Her Majesty's aircraft, hovercraft or ships are references to aircraft, hovercraft or ships which belong to, or are exclusively used in the service of, Her Majesty in right of the government of the United Kingdom.

Note 3 Illustrative Multipliers
(see paragraph 32)

Years of Loss	*Multiplier*	*Years of Loss*	*Multiplier*
5	5	15	10.5
6	5.5	16	11
7	6	17	11.5
8	7	18	12
9	7.5	19	12.5
10	8	20	13
11	8.5	25	15
12	9	30	16
13	9.5	35	17
14	10	40	18

Criminal Injuries Compensation Scheme

Levels of compensation

Level 1	£1,000
Level 2	£1,250
Level 3	£1,500
Level 4	£1,750
Level 5	£2,000
Level 6	£2,500
Level 7	£3,000
Level 8	£3,500
Level 9	£4,000
Level 10	£5,000
Level 11	£6,000
Level 12	£7,500
Level 13	£10,000
Level 14	£12,500
Level 15	£15,000
Level 16	£17,500
Level 17	£20,000
Level 18	£25,000
Level 19	£30,000
Level 20	£40,000
Level 21	£50,000
Level 22	£75,000
Level 23	£100,000
Level 24	£175,000
Level 25	£250,000

Appendix 3

Tariff of Injuries

Description of Injury	Level	Standard Amount £
Bodily functions: hemiplegia (paralysis of one side of the body)	21	50,000
Bodily functions: paraplegia (paralysis of the lower limbs)	24	175,000
Bodily functions: quadriplegia/tetraplegia (paralysis of all 4 limbs)	25	250,000
Brain damage: moderate impairment of social/intellectual functions	15	15,000
Brain damage: serious impairment of social/intellectual functions	20	40,000
Brain damage: permanent – extremely serious (no effective control of functions)	25	250,000
Burns: multiple first degree: covering at least 25% of body	19	30,000
(For other burn injuries see under individual parts of the body)		
Epilepsy: serious exacerbation of pre-existing condition	10	5,000
Epilepsy: fully controlled	12	7,500
Epilepsy: partially controlled	14	12,500
Epilepsy: uncontrolled	20	40,000
Fatal injury (one qualifying claimant)	13	10,000
Fatal injury (each qualifying claimant if more than one):	10	5,000
Head: burns: minor	3	1,500
Head: burns: moderate	9	4,000
Head: burns: severe	13	10,000
Head: ear: fractured mastoid	1	1,000
Head: ear: temporary partial deafness – lasting 6 to 13 weeks	1	1,000
Head: ear: temporary partial deafness – lasting more than 13 weeks	3	1,500
Head: ear: partial deafness (one ear) – remaining hearing socially useful	8	3,500
Head: ear: partial deafness (both ears) – with hearing aid if necessary	12	7,500
Head: ear: total deafness (one ear)	15	15,000
Head: ear: total deafness (both ears)	20	40,000
Head: ear: partial loss of ear(s)	9	4,000
Head: ear: loss of ear	13	10,000
Head: ear: loss of both ears	16	17,500
Head: ear: perforated ear drum	4	1,750

Head: ear: tinnitus (ringing noise in ears) – lasting 6 to 13 weeks	1	1,000
Head: ear: tinnitus – lasting more than 13 weeks	7	3,000
Head: ear: tinnitus – permanent (moderate)	12	7,500
Head: ear: tinnitus – permanent (very serious)	15	15,000
Head: eye: blow out fracture of orbit bone cavity containing eyeball	7	3,000
Head: eye: blurred or double vision – lasting 6 to 13 weeks	1	1,000
Head: eye: blurred or double vision – lasting more than 13 weeks	4	1,750
Head: eye: blurred or double vision – permanent	12	7,500
Head: eye: cataracts one eye (requiring operation)	7	3,000
Head: eye: cataracts both eyes (requiring operation)	12	7,500
Head: eye: cataracts one eye (permanent/inoperable)	12	7,500
Head: eye: cataracts both eyes (permanent/inoperable)	16	17,500
Head: eye: corneal abrasions	5	2,000
Head: eye: damage to iris resulting in hyphaema (bleeding in ocular chamber)	6	2,500
Head: eye: damage to irises resulting in hyphaema (bleeding in ocular chamber)	11	6,000
Head: eye: detached retina	10	5,000
Head: eye: detached retinas	14	12,500
Head: eye: degeneration of optic nerve	5	2,000
Head: eye: degeneration of optic nerves	10	5,000
Head: eye: dislocation of lens	10	5,000
Head: eye: dislocation of lenses	14	12,500
Head: eye: glaucoma	6	2,500
Head: eye: residual floaters	10	5,000
Head: eye: traumatic angle recession of eye	6	2,500
Head: eye: loss of one eye	18	25,000
Head: eye: loss of both eyes	23	100,000
Head: eye: loss of sight of one eye	17	20,000
Head: eye: loss of sight of both eyes	22	75,000
Head: eye: partial loss of vision – 6/9	12	7,500
Head: eye: partial loss of vision – 6/12	13	10,000
Head: eye: partial loss of vision – 6/24	14	12,500
Head: eye: partial loss of vision – 6/36	15	15,000
Head: eye: partial loss of vision – 6/60	16	17,500
Head: face: burns – minor	5	2,000
Head: face: burns – moderate	10	5,000
Head: face: burns – severe	18	25,000
Head: face: scarring: minor disfigurement	3	1,500
Head: face: scarring: significant disfigurement	8	3,500
Head: face: scarring: serious disfigurement	12	7,500
Head: facial: dislocated jaw	5	2,000
Head: facial: permanently clicking jaw	10	5,000
Head: facial: fractured malar and/or zygomatic – cheek bones	5	2,000

Head: facial: fractured mandible and/or maxilla – jaw bones	7	3,000
Head: facial: multiple fractures to face	13	10,000
Head: facial: temporary numbness/loss of feeling, lasting 6–13 weeks	1	1,000
Head: facial: temporary numbness/loss of feeling (lasting more than 13 weeks) – recovery expected	3	1,500
Head: facial: permanent numbness/loss of feeling	9	4,000
Head: nose: deviated nasal septum	1	1,000
Head: nose: deviated nasal septum requiring septoplastomy	5	2,000
Head: nose: undisplaced fracture of nasal bones	1	1,000
Head: nose: displaced fracture of nasal bones	3	1,500
Head: nose: displaced fracture of nasal bones requiring manipulation	5	2,000
Head: nose: displaced fracture of nasal bones requiring rhinoplasty	5	2,000
Head: nose: displaced fracture of nasal bones requiring turbinectomy	5	2,000
Head: nose: partial loss (at least 10%)	9	4,000
Head: nose: loss of smell and/or taste (partial)	10	5,000
Head: nose: loss of smell or taste	13	10,000
Head: nose: loss of smel! and taste	15	15,000
Head: scarring: visible, minor disfigurement	3	1,500
Head: scarring: significant disfigurement	7	3,000
Head: scarring: serious disfigurement	10	5,000
Head: skull: balance impaired – permanent	12	7,500
Head: skull: concussion (lasting at least one week)	3	1,500
Head: skull: simple fracture (no operation)	6	2,500
Head: skull: depressed fracture (no operation)	9	4,000
Head: skull: depressed fracture (requiring operation)	11	6,000
Head: skull: subdural haematoma – treated conservatively	9	4,000
Head: skull: subdural haematoma – requiring evacuation	12	7,500
Head: skull: brain haemorrhage (full recovery)	9	4,000
Head: skull: brain haemorrhage (residual minor impairment of social/intellectual functions)	12	7,500
Head: skull: stroke (full recovery)	10	5,000
Head: teeth: fractured/chipped tooth/teeth requiring treatment	1	1,000
Head: teeth: chipped front teeth requiring crown	1	1,000
Head: teeth: fractured tooth/teeth requiring crown	1	1,000
Head: teeth: fractured tooth/teeth requiring apicectomy (surgery to gum to reach root – root resection)	5	2,000
Head: teeth: damage to tooth/teeth requiring root-canal treatment	1	1,000
Head: teeth: loss of crowns	2	1,250
Head: teeth: loss of one front tooth	3	1,500
Head: teeth: loss of two or three front teeth	5	2,000
Head: teeth: loss of four or more front teeth	7	3,000
Head: teeth: loss of one tooth other than front	1	1,000
Head: teeth: loss of two or more teeth other than front	3	1,500

Head: teeth: slackening of teeth requiring dental treatment	1	1,000
Head: tongue: impaired speech: slight	5	2,000
Head: tongue: impaired speech: moderate	10	5,000
Head: tongue: impaired speech: serious	13	10,000
Head: tongue: impaired speech: severe	16	17,500
Head: tongue: loss of speech: permanent	19	30,000
Head: tongue: loss of tongue	20	40,000
Lower limbs: burns – minor	3	1,500
Lower limbs: burns – moderate	9	4,000
Lower limbs: burns – severe	13	10,000
Lower limbs: fractured ankle (full recovery)	7	3,000
Lower limbs: fractured ankle (with continuing disability)	10	5,000
Lower limbs: fractured ankle (full recovery)	12	7,500
Lower limbs: fractured ankles (with continuing disability)	13	10,000
Lower limbs: fractured femur – thigh bone (full recovery)	7	3,000
Lower limbs: fractured femur (with continuing disability)	10	5,000
Lower limbs: fractured femur – both legs (full recovery)	12	7,500
Lower limbs: fractured femur – both legs (with continuing disability)	13	10,000
Lower limbs: fractured fibula – slender bone from knee to ankle (full recovery)	7	3,000
Lower limbs: fractured fibula (with continuing disability)	10	5,000
Lower limbs: fractured fibula – both legs (full recovery)	12	7,500
Lower limbs: fractured fibula – both legs (with continuing disability)	13	10,000
Lower limbs: fractured great toe	6	2,500
Lower limbs: fractured great toe – both feet	10	5,000
Lower limbs: fractured phalanges – toes	3	1,500
Lower limbs: fractured heel bone (full recovery)	6	2,500
Lower limbs: fractured heel bone (with continuing disability)	10	5,000
Lower limbs: fractured heel bone – both feet (full recovery)	10	5,000
Lower limbs: fractured heel bone – both feet (with continuing disability)	13	10,000
Lower limbs: fractured patella – knee cap (full recovery)	12	7,500
Lower limbs: fractured patella (with continuing disability)	13	10,000
Lower limbs: fractured patella – both legs (full recovery)	15	15,000
Lower limbs: fractured patella – both legs (with continuing disability)	17	20,000
Lower limbs: dislocated patella – both legs (full recovery)	5	2,000
Lower limbs: dislocated patella – both legs (with continuing disability)	16	17,500
Lower limbs: arthroscopy (investigative surgery/ repair to knees) – no fracture	5	2,000
Lower limbs: fractured metatarsal bones (full recovery)	6	2,500
Lower limbs: fractured metatarsal bones (with continuing disability)	12	7,500
Lower limbs: fractured metatarsal bones – both feet (full recovery)	10	5,000
Lower limbs: fractured metatarsal bones – both feet (with continuing disability)	15	15,000
Lower limbs: fractured tarsal bones (full recovery)	6	2,500

Lower limbs: fractured tarsal bones (with continuing disability)	12	7,500
Lower limbs: fractured tarsal bones – both feet (full recovery)	10	5,000
Lower limbs: fractured tarsal bones – both feet (with continuing disability)	10	15,000
Lower limbs: fractured tibia – shin bone (full recovery)	7	3,000
Lower limbs: fractured tibia (with continuing disability)	10	5,000
Lower limbs: fractured tibia – both legs (full recovery)	12	7,500
Lower limbs: fractured tibia – both legs (with continuing disability)	13	10,000
Lower limbs: paralysis of leg	18	25,000
Lower limbs: loss of leg below knee	19	30,000
Lower limbs: loss of leg above knee	20	40,000
Lower limbs: loss of both legs	23	100,000
Lower limbs: minor damage to tendon(s)/ligament(s) (full recovery)	1	1,000
Lower limbs: minor damage to tendon(s)/ligament(s) (with continuing disability)	7	3,000
Lower limbs: moderate damage to tendon(s)/ligament(s) (full recovery)	5	2,000
Lower limbs: moderate damage to tendon(s)/ligament(s) (with continuing disability)	10	5,000
Lower limbs: severe damage to tendon(s)/ligaments(s) (full recovery)	7	3,000
Lower limbs: severe damage to tendon(s)/ligaments(s) (with continuing disability)	12	7,500
Lower limbs: scarring: minor disfigurement	2	1,250
Lower limbs: scarring: significant disfigurement	4	1,750
Lower limbs: scarring: serious disfigurement	10	5,000
Lower limbs: sprained ankle – disabling for at least 6–13 weeks	1	1,000
Lower limbs: sprained ankle – disabling for more than 13 weeks	6	2,500
Lower limbs: sprained ankle – both feet – disabling for at least 6–13 weeks	5	2,000
Lower limbs: sprained ankle – both feet – disabling for more than 13 weeks	8	3,500
Medically recognised illness/condition (not psychiatric or psychological). Significantly disabling disorder where the symptoms and disability persist for more than 6 weeks from the incident/date of onset		
lasting 6 to 13 weeks	1	1,000
lasting up to 28 weeks	9	4,000
lasting over 28 weeks – but not permanent	12	7,500
permanent disability	17	20,000
Minor injuries: multiple (see notes)	1	1,000
Neck: burns: minor	3	1,500
Neck: burns: moderate	9	4,000

Neck: burns: severe	13	10,000
Neck: scarring: minor disfigurement	3	1,500
Neck: scarring: significant disfigurement	7	3,000
Neck: scarring: serious disfigurement	9	4,000
Neck: strained neck – disabling for 6–13 weeks	1	1,000
Neck: strained neck – disabling for more than 13 weeks	4	1,750
Neck: strained neck – seriously disabling – but not permanent	10	5,000
Neck: strained neck – seriously disabling – permanent	13	10,000
Neck: whiplash injury: effects lasting 6–13 weeks	1	1,000
Neck: whiplash injury: effects lasting more than 13 weeks	4	1,750
Neck: whiplash injury: seriously disabling – but not permanent	10	5,000
Neck: whiplash injury: seriously disabling – permanent	13	10,000
Physical Abuse of Children (where individual injuries do not otherwise qualify)		
Minor abuse – isolated or intermittent assault(s) beyond ordinary chastisement resulting in bruising, weals, hair pulled from scalp etc	1	1,000
Serious abuse – intermittent physical assaults resulting in an accumulation of healed wounds, burns or scalds, but with no appreciable disfigurement	5	2,000
Severe abuse – pattern of systematic violence against the child resulting in minor disfigurement	7	3,000
Persistent pattern of severe abuse over a period exceeding 3 years	11	6,000
Sexual Abuse of Children (not otherwise covered by sexual assault)		
Minor isolated incidents – non-penetrative indecent acts	1	1,000
Pattern of serious abuse – repetitive, frequent non-penetrative indecent acts	5	2,000
Pattern of severe abuse – repetitive, frequent indecent acts involving digital or other non-penile penetration and/or oral genital contact	7	3,000
Pattern of severe abuse over a period exceeding 3 years	11	6,000
Repeated non-consensual vaginal and/or anal intercourse over a period up to 3 years	13	10,000
Repeated non-consensual vaginal and/or anal intercourse over a period exceeding 3 years	16	17,500
Sexual Assault (single incident – victim any age)		
Minor indecent assault – non-penetrative indecent physical act over clothing	1	1,000
Serious indecent assault – non-penetrative indecent act under clothing	5	2,000
Severe indecent assault – indecent act involving digital, or other non-penile penetration, and/or oral/genital contact	7	3,000
Non-consensual vaginal and/or anal intercourse	12	7,500

Non-consensual vaginal and/or anal intercourse by two or more attackers	13	10,000
Non-consensual vaginal and/or anal intercourse with other serious bodily injuries	16	17,500
Shock (see notes)		
Disabling, but temporary mental anxiety, medically verified	1	1,000
Disabling mental disorder, confirmed by psychiatric diagnosis:		
lasting up to 28 weeks	6	2,500
lasting over 28 weeks to one year	9	4,000
lasting over one year but not permanent	12	7,500
Permanently disabling mental disorder confirmed by psychiatric prognosis	17	20,000
Torso: back: fracture of vertebra (full recovery)	6	2,500
Torso: back: fracture of vertebra (continuing disability)	10	5,000
Torso: back: fracture of more than one vertebra (full recovery)	9	4,000
Torso: back: fracture of more than one vertebra (continuing disability)	12	7,500
Torso: back: prolapsed invertebral disc(s) – seriously disabling – not permanent	10	5,000
Torso: back: prolapsed invertebral disc(s) – seriously disabling – permanent	12	17,500
Torso: back: ruptured invertebral disc(s) requiring surgical removal	13	10,000
Torso: back: strained back – disabling for 6 – 13 weeks	1	1,000
Torso: back: strained back – disabling for more than 13 weeks	6	2,500
Torso: back: strained back – seriously disabling – but not permanent	10	5,000
Torso: back: strained back – seriously disabling – permanent	12	7,500
Torso: burns: minor	3	1,500
Torso: burns: moderate	9	4,000
Torso: burns: severe	13	10,000
Torso: punctured lung	7	3,000
Torso: two punctured lungs	11	6,000
Torso: collapsed lung	8	3,500
Torso: two collapsed lungs	12	7,500
Torso: permanent and disabling damage to lungs from smoke inhalation	10	5,000
Torso: loss of spleen	9	4,000
Torso: damage to testes	4	1,750
Torso: dislocated hip (full recovery)	4	1,750
Torso: dislocated hip (with continuing disability)	12	7,500
Torso: fractured hip	12	7,500
Torso: dislocated shoulder (full recovery)	4	1,750
Torso: dislocated shoulder (with continuing disability)	10	5,000

Torso: fractured rib	1	1,000
Torso: fractured rib(s) (two or more)	3	1,500
Torso: fractured clavicle – collar bone	5	2,000
Torso: two fractured clavicles	10	5,000
Torso: fractured coccyx – tail bone	6	2,500
Torso: fractured pelvis	12	7,500
Torso: fractured scapula – shoulder blade	6	2,500
Torso: two fractured scapula	11	6,000
Torso: fractured sternum – breast bone	6	2,500
Torso: frozen shoulder	8	3,500
Torso: hernia	8	3,500
Torso: injury requiring laparotomy	8	3,500
Torso: injury to genitalia requiring medical treatment – no permanent damage	4	1,750
Torso: injury to genitalia requiring medical treatment – permanent damage	10	5,000
Torso: loss of fertility	21	50,000
Torso: loss of kidney	17	20,000
Torso: loss of testicle	10	5,000
Torso: scarring: minor disfigurement	2	1,250
Torso: scarring: significant disfigurement	6	2,500
Torso: scarring: serious disfigurement	10	5,000
Upper limbs: burns: minor	3	1,500
Upper limbs: burns: moderate	9	4,000
Upper limbs: burns: severe	13	10,000
Upper limbs: dislocated/fractured elbow (with full recovery)	7	3,000
Upper limbs: dislocated/fractured elbow (with continuing disability)	12	7,500
Upper limbs: two dislocated/fractured elbows (with full recovery)	12	7,500
Upper limbs: two dislocated/fractured elbows (with continuing disability)	13	10,000
Upper limbs: dislocated finger(s) or thumb – one hand (full recovery)	2	1,250
Upper limbs: dislocated finger(s) or thumb – one hand (with continuing disability)	6	2,500
Upper limbs: dislocated finger(s) or thumb(s) – both hands (full recovery)	7	3,000
Upper limbs: dislocated finger(s) or thumb(s) – both hands (with continuing disability)	12	7,500
Upper limbs: fractured finger(s) or thumb – one hand (full recovery)	3	1,500
Upper limbs: fractured finger(s) or thumb – one hand (with continuing disability)	8	3,500
Upper limbs: fractured finger(s) or thumb(s) – both hands (full recovery)	9	4,000
Upper limbs: fractured finger(s) or thumb(s) – both hands (with continuing disability)	12	7,500
Upper limbs: fractured hand (full recovery)	5	2,000

Upper limbs: fractured hand (with continuing disability)	10	5,000
Upper limbs: two fractured hands (full recovery)	8	3,500
Upper limbs: two fractured hands (with continuing disability)	12	7,500
Upper limbs: fractured humerus – upper arm bone (full recovery)	7	3,000
Upper limbs: fractured humerus (with continuing disability)	10	5,000
Upper limbs: fractured humerus – both arms (full recovery)	12	7,500
Upper limbs: fractured humerus – both arms (with continuing disability)	13	10,000
Upper limbs: fractured radius – smaller forearm bone (full recovery)	7	3,000
Upper limbs: fractured radius (with continuing disability)	10	5,000
Upper limbs: fractured radius – both arms (full recovery)	12	7,500
Upper limbs: fractured radius – both arms (with continuing disability)	13	10,000
Upper limbs: fractured ulna – inner forearm bone (full recovery)	7	3,000
Upper limbs: fractured ulna (with continuing disability)	10	5,000
Upper limbs: fractured ulna – both arms (full recovery)	12	7,500
Upper limbs: fractured ulna – both arms (with continuing disability)	13	10,000
Upper limbs: fractured wrist – including scaphoid fracture (full recovery)	7	3,000
Upper limbs: fractured wrist – including scaphoid fracture (with continuing disability)	11	6,000
Upper limbs: two fractured wrists – including scaphoid fracture (full recovery)	11	6,000
Upper limbs: two fractured wrists – including scaphoid fracture (with continuing disability)	13	10,000
Upper limbs: fractured wrist – colles type (full recovery)	9	4,000
Upper limbs: fractured wrist – colles type (with continuing disability)	12	7,500
Upper limbs: two fractured wrists – colles type (full recovery)	12	7,500
Upper limbs: two fractured wrists – colles type (with continuing disability)	13	10,000
Upper limbs: partial loss of finger (other than thumb/index) (one joint)	6	2,500
Upper limbs: partial loss of thumb or index finger (one joint)	9	4,000
Upper limbs: loss of one finger other than index	10	5,000
Upper limbs: loss of index finger	12	7,500
Upper limbs: loss of two or more fingers	13	10,000
Upper limbs: loss of thumb	15	15,000
Upper limbs: loss of hand	20	40,000
Upper limbs: loss of both hands	23	100,000
Upper limbs: loss of arm	20	40,000
Upper limbs: loss of both arms	23	100,000
Upper limbs: paralysis of arm	19	30,000
Upper limbs: paralysis of both arms	22	75,000
Upper limbs: permanently & seriously impaired grip – one arm	12	7,500

Upper limbs: permanently & seriously impaired grip – both arms	15	15,000
Upper limbs: scarring: minor disfigurement	2	1,250
Upper limbs: scarring: significant disfigurement	6	2,500
Upper limbs: scarring: serious disfigurement	9	4,000
Upper limbs: minor damage to tendon(s)/ligament(s) (full recovery)	1	1,000
Upper limbs: minor Image to tendon(s)/ligament(s) (with continuing disability)	7	3,000
Upper limbs: moderate damage to tendon(s)/ligament(s) (full recovery)	5	2,000
Upper limbs: moderate damage to tendon(s)/ligament(s) (with continuing disability)	10	5,000
Upper limbs: severely damaged tendon(s)/ligaments(s) (full recovery)	7	3,000
Upper limbs: severely damaged tendon(s)/ligaments(s) (with permanent disability)	12	7,500
Upper limbs: sprained wrist – disabling for 6 – 13 weeks	1	1,000
Upper limbs: sprained wrist – disabling for more than 13 weeks	3	1,500
Upper limbs: two sprained wrists – disabling for 6 – 13 weeks	5	2,000
Upper limbs: two sprained wrists – disabling for more than 13 weeks	7	3,000

Notes to the Tariff

1. Minor multiple injuries will only qualify for compensation where the applicant has sustained at least three separate injuries of the type illustrated below, at least one of which must still have had significant residual effects six weeks after the incident. The injuries must also have necessitated at least two visits to or by a medical practitioner within that six-week period. Examples of qualifying injuries are:

(a) grazing, cuts, lacerations (no permanent scarring)
(b) severe and widespread bruising
(c) severe soft tissue injury (no permanent disability)
(d) black eye(s)
(e) bloody nose
(f) hair pulled from scalp
(g) loss of fingernail

2. Shock or 'nervous shock' may be taken to include conditions attributed to post-traumatic stress disorder, depression and similar generic terms covering:

(a) such psychological symptoms as anxiety, tension, insomnia, irritability, loss of confidence, agoraphobia and preoccupation with thoughts of guilt or self-harm; and

(b) related physical symptoms such as alopecia, asthma, eczema, enuresis and psoriasis. Disability in this context will include impaired work (or school) performance, significant adverse effects on social relationships and sexual dysfunction.

Index

page

Accidental injuries,
  apprehension of offender, ... 45–51
  exceptional risk, ... 6
  justification, ... 6
  proving claim, ... 6
  reform of law, ... 6
Administration of Scheme, ... 4
  see also Procedure
Adoption,
  death of victim (1996 Scheme), ... 204–205
Aircraft, injury sustained on, ... 8, 9
Appeals,
  CICB hearing, ... 5
  jurisdiction, ... 5
  Panel – *see* Appeals Panel
  review decision, ... 247–256
  structure of Scheme, ... 4
  transfer date, ... 5
Appeals Panel,
  appeal from, ... 5
  creation, ... 4
  finality of decision, ... 5
  independence, ... 4
  introduction, ... 4
  jurisdiction, ... 5
  membership, ... 4
  review decision, ... 247–256
Applicant,
  character – *see* Character of applicant
  conduct – *see* Conduct of applicant
  criminal convictions, ... 82–91
  death, generally, ... 7
  nationality, ... 8
  residence of applicant, ... 8
Application,
  pre- 1 April 1996, ... 1, 3
  procedure – *see* Procedure
  reform to Scheme, ... 1
  time limits – *see* Time limits

Apportionment of awards,
death of victim (1990 Scheme), ... 199–200
Apprehension of offender,
1990 Scheme, ... 45–51
1996 Scheme, ... 45–51
accidental injury, ... 45–51
assault on police officer, ... 47–48
civilian claims, ... 45
examples, ... 49–51
exceptional risk, ... 48, 49, 50
generally, ... 45
illustrations, ... 49–51
innocent bystanders, ... 46–47
justification, ... 48, 49
law enforcement activities, ... 45–51
police officers' applications, ... 45
Arson,
1990 Scheme, ... 22–25
1996 Scheme, ... 23, 25–26
accidental injuries, ... 23, 26
crime of violence, ... 22–23
exceptional risk, ... 23, 25
Assailant – *see* Offender
Assessment of compensation,
1990 Scheme – *see* Assessment of compensation (1990 Scheme)
1996 Scheme – *see* Assessment of compensation (1996 Scheme)
alteration of basis, ... 1
basis, ... 1
common law damages, ... 1
general rule, ... 1
reforms, ... 1
simplification, ... 1
tariffs,
example, ... 1
introduction, ... 1
Assessment of compensation (1990 Scheme),
1994 Tariff Scheme and, ... 121
1996 Scheme and, ... 121
account, payment on, ... 125
amenity, loss of, ... 123–124
basis, ... 122–125
Board,
jurisdiction, ... 122
precedents, use of, ... 123
career loss, ... 128
carers, ... 127
common law damages basis, ... 122–125
consultant's report, ... 126
costs, ... 125

earnings, loss of, ... 122, 124–125, 128–131
  see also Earnings, loss of
example,.. 124–125
extinguished awards,.. 135
future loss,.. 126–127
future loss of earnings,... 128–131
  see also Earnings, loss of
general damages, ... 124
generally,.. 121–122
hearings,... 135, 136
injury, award for, ... 123
interest,... 136
interim payments, ... 125
jurisdiction of Board, ... 122
labour market, prejudice in,.. 125
legal costs,.. 125
loss of earnings, ... 122, 124–125, 128–131
  see also Earnings, loss of
lump sum payments, ... 134
medical evidence,... 126
  see also Medical evidence
objectives,... 121–122
pain and suffering, ... 123–124
permanent disability,... 126
precedents,... 123
prejudice in labour market,... 125
preparation of case, ... 125
principles,... 122–125
reconsideration provisions,....................................... 135, 136
reduced awards,... 135
serious injury,... 125–128
special damages, ... 124, 126–127
terminology,.. 124
title to award, ... 136–137
Assessment of compensation (1996 Scheme),
  earnings, loss of,
    calculation,.. 154
    continuing loss,...................................... 155, 162–164
    deductions,.. 155–156
    emoluments, ... 159–160
    financial benefits,... 158
    future loss, ... 155, 162–164
    health insurance,... 159
    impracticable para 32 calculation,........................... 164–166
    insurance arrangements, ... 158–159, 161
    maximum award, ... 155
    method of calculation, ... 154
    multipliers,.. 155
    other payments, effect of,.................................. 156–158

pensions, ... 160
period covered by, ... 154
protection from reductions, ... 158
reductions, ... 155–156
repayment to Authority, ... 156
social security benefits, ... 156, 161
withholding award, ... 156
limits of compensation, ... 153–154
maximum amounts, ... 154
minimum award, ... 154
possible heads of claim, ... 153–154
special expenses, ... 166–173
standard amount, ... 173–180
see also Tariffs
tariffs - *see* Tariffs
types of compensation, ... 153–154
Assistance to Authority/Board, ... 80–81
Authority - *see* CICA
Award - *see* Compensation; Maximum award; Minimum award

Benefiting offender, ... 98–99
Bereavement award (1990 Scheme), ... 191–192
Broken nose, ... 55
Burden of proof, ... 6
crime of violence, ... 16
hearing, ... 233, 239
procedure (1996 Scheme), ... 244

Careless driving, ... 118
Cars - *see* Traffic offences
Channel Tunnel, injury sustained in, ... 9
Character of applicant,
1987 Statement, ... 84
1990 Guide, ... 84
1990 Scheme, ... 82, 84
1996 Guide, ... 84, 85
1996 Scheme, ... 84, 90
appropriateness, ... 83
burglary, ... 88–89
challenging decisions, ... 83
criminal convictions, ... 82–91
date of conviction, ... 88
discretionary powers, ... 85–88
drug dealing, ... 89
effect of, ... 82–91
evaluation, ... 83
fraud, ... 89
gangs, ... 90
judicial review, ... 83

penalty points system, ... 84–85
prostitution, ... 90
reasonable exercise of discretionary power, ... 89
reduction in award, ... 83, 85
subsequent convictions, ... 88
worthiness, ... 84

Child(ren),
awards to,
1990 Scheme, ... 104–106
1996 Scheme, ... 106–107
abuse victims, ... 106
Court of Protection, ... 106, 107
guardian consent, ... 105
investment account, ... 105–106
special arrangements, ... 107
trusts, ... 106
co-operation with police, ... 73–75
Court of Protection, ... 106, 107
dangerous games played by, ... 97
death of victim (1990 Scheme), ... 184
games played by, ... 97
guardian consent to payment, ... 105
investment accounts, ... 105–106
members of same household, ... 102–103
offenders, as, ... 18–19
playground injuries, ... 19
sexual abuse of, ... 78–79, 113–116
time limit for application, ... 10–11
trusts, ... 106

CICA,
administration, ... 4
assistance to, ... 80–81
CICB, relationship with, ... 4
claims officers,
discretionary powers, ... 12–13
duty, ... 12–13
composition, ... 4
determination of claim, ... 12
discretionary powers, ... 6–7
reduction of award, ... 6
refusal of award, ... 6
responsibility, ... 4
staffing, ... 4

CICB,
assessment of compensation – *see* Assessment of compensation (1990 Scheme)
assistance to, ... 80–81
caseload, ... 3
cessation, ... 216–217

CICA, relationship with, ... 4
composition, ... 4
delegation by, ... 3
membership, ... 4
old cases, ... 3
responsibility, ... 3, 4
transfer date, ... 216, 217, 219
White Paper on, ... 3

Cohabitees,
death of victim (1996 Scheme), ... 203

Common law damages, ... 1, 2

Compensation,
alternative arrangements, ... 134–135
assessment – *see* Assessment of compensation; Assessment of compensation (1990 Scheme); Assessment of compensation (1996 Scheme)
benefiting offender, ... 98–99
character of applicant – *see* Character of applicant
damages, ... 151–152
duplication of payment from public funds, ... 144–147
eligibility for – *see* Eligibility for compensation
generally, ... 54
household, members of same – *see* Members of same household
interest, ... 136–137
limitations on, ... 138 *et seq*
lump sum payments, ... 134–135
maximum award – *see* Maximum award
minimum award – *see* Minimum award
offender benefiting, ... 98–99
pension payments, ... 148–150
public funds, duplication of payments from, ... 144–147
structure of Scheme, ... 3–4
tariffs – *see* Tariffs
title to award, ... 136–137

Conduct of applicant,
1990 Scheme, ... 91–92
1996 Scheme, ... 91–92
accidents, ... 95
after event, ... 94–95
appropriateness, ... 91–92
causation issues, ... 92–94
children, ... 97
dangerous games played by children, ... 97
discretion of Board, ... 91–92
during incident, ... 93–94
effect of, ... 91
fighting, ... 92
football supporters, ... 93
gangs, ... 95

glassing, 92
ill-judged conduct, 95
length of confrontation, 93–94
provocative conduct, 7, 92, 93
reasonableness test, 96
rescue cases, 95–96
retreat, duty to, 94–95
self-defence argument, 16–17, 96
stabbing, 92
Conviction,
crime of violence, 18
offender, of, 6
Co-operation with police,
1996 Scheme procedure, 72
authority, report to, 77
children, 73–75
documents required, 68–69
effect of failure, 68
employment, injury during, 78
evidence, 72
examples, 69–71
failure, meaning of, 68
family violence, 79–80
hearing, 72–73
hospital attendance preventing, 69
ignorance of Scheme, 71
length of delay, 70
meaning of failure, 68
medical reports, 69
mental hospitals, injuries in, 77–78
minors, 73–75
pointlessness of report, 71, 76
prisons, injuries in, 77, 78
rationale, 69, 71
reasons for reporting, 76
report from police to Board, 68
reprisals from assailant, 68
requirement, 68
retraction statements, 70
schools, injuries in, 78
seriously injured applicant, 73
sexual abuse of children, 78–79
time-scale, 69
trade union official, report to, 77
trial, failure to attend, 68
'without delay', 71
Costs, 125, 242, 244
Court of Protection, 106, 107
Crime of violence,

1990 Scheme, 12, 16
1996 Scheme, 12, 16
absence of information, 17
arson, 22–26
see also Arson
assault occasioning actual bodily harm, 15–16
burden of proof, 16
children, 18–19
conduct of applicant, 16–17
conviction of assailant, 18
definition, 12
directly attributable injury – *see* Directly attributable injury
dog bites, 22
evidence, 16–17
hospital staff, 20–21
identifying, 14
immunity of offender, 18–21
information available, 17
insanity, 19, 20
intent, 14, 16
judicial interpretation, 13–14
meaning, 13–14
minors, 18–19
motoring offences, 22
nurses, 20–21
recklessness, 14–16
self-defence, 16–17, 96
sporting injuries, 17–18
Criminal Injuries Compensation Authority – *see* CICA
Criminal Injuries Compensation Board – *see* CICB
Criminal injury,
1996 Scheme, 12
definition, 12

Damages, 151–152
common law, 1, 2
receipt of damages, 151
reduction in award, 151, 152
undertaking to repay compensation, 151
Death,
victim,
1990 Scheme – *see* Death of victim (1990 Scheme)
1996 Scheme – *see* Death of victim (1996 Scheme)
generally, 7
Death of victim (1990 Scheme),
1996 Scheme and, 201
acquittal of assailant, 185
apportionment of awards, 199–200
bereavement award, 191–192

calculation of financial support, ... 185–186
character of deceased, ... 184
child(ren), ... 184
cohabitees, claims by, ... 182–183
conduct of deceased, ... 184
consequence of injury, ... 181–195
crime of violence, death attributable to, ... 185
deductible benefits, ... 196–198
deductions, ... 199–200
dependants, claims by, ... 182–191
earning capacity of wife, ... 186
expectation of life, loss of, ... 193–194
financial support claims, ... 182–191
funeral expenses, ... 185, 194–195
generally, ... 181
high earners, ... 187
immediate death after attack, ... 183–184
loss of society, ... 192–194
measuring dependency, ... 185–186
medical evidence, ... 186
minors as applicants, ... 184
mother, death of, ... 188–191
otherwise than in consequence of injury, ... 196
pensions, ... 198–199
police investigation, ... 185
relatives, claims by, ... 182
Scotland, ... 182, 192–194
test for financial dependency, ... 183
wife/mother, death of, ... 188–191
Death of victim (1996 Scheme),
1990 Scheme and, ... 201
adoption, ... 204–205
amount of compensation, ... 206–214
award received before death, ... 211–212
calculation, ... 207–208
cohabitees, ... 208–209
dependency, ... 206–210
financial dependency, ... 207
loss of parental services, ... 210–211
multipliers, ... 209–210
'only normal income', ... 207
otherwise than in consequence of injury, death, ... 212–214
proportional reduction, ... 208–209
reductions, ... 208–210
remarriage, ... 208
standard amount, ... 206
child of deceased, ... 205, 210–211
cohabitees, ... 203, 208–209
conditions for claim, ... 202

dependency, amount payable in respect of, 206–210
divorce, 203
formally married claimants, 203
funeral expenses, 201–202
generally, 201
loss of parental services, 210–211
otherwise than in consequence of injury, death, 212–214
parent of deceased, 204–205
qualifying claimant, 202–203
same sex partners, 203
spouse of deceased, 203
standard amount, 206
step-parents, 204
Determination of application – *see* Procedure
Directly attributable injury,
1990 Scheme, 30–33, 33–39
1996 Scheme, 31
common law test, 32
'directly', 32–33
foreseeability of damage, 32
guidance statement, 31
intervening factors, 31–32
meaning, 30
medical treatment, 31–32
mental injury cases, 40–44
1990 Scheme, 33–39
novus actus interveniens, 31–32
reform proposals, 31
remoteness of damage, 32
requirement for, 30
Disability, persons under,
awards to,
1990 Scheme, 104–106
1996 Scheme, 106–107
Divorce, 101–102
death of victim (1996 Scheme), 203
Dog bites,
crime of violence, 22
Duplication of payment from public funds (1990 Scheme), 144–147

Earnings, loss of,
1969 Scheme, 141–143
1990 Scheme, 122, 124–125, 128–131, 138–144
1996 Scheme – *see* Assessment of compensation (1996 Scheme)
average industrial earnings, 142
evidence, 143–144
example, 140–141
exemplary damages, 144
future loss, 128–131

maximum limits, ... 138–139
net loss, ... 139–142
occupational pensions, ... 143
rate of net loss of earnings, ... 140–141
Ears, injuries to, ... 60
Eligibility for compensation,
1990 Scheme, ... 63–64
1996 Scheme, ... 63
co-operation with police – *see* Co-operation with police
criteria, ... 65
determination of claim, ... 65
discretion of Board, ... 65
ex gratia payments, ... 64–65
informing police, ... 66–68
person informing police, ... 67
rationale, ... 64
reasonableness, ... 64
reduction in award, ... 63–64
withholding award, ... 63–64
European Convention on the Compensation of Victims of Violent Crime, ... 8
Evidence,
burden of proof, ... 6
crime of violence, ... 16–17
earnings, loss of, ... 143–144
reconsideraton of a case as a result of new evidence, ... 262–265, 266–267
standard of proof, ... 6
see also Medical evidence
Exceptional risk,
apprehension of offender, ... 47, 48, 49–51
Eyes, injuries to, ... 60

Facial injuries, ... 60
Facial scarring, ... 133
Family violence, ... 79–80
Fatal cases – *see* Death of victim (1990 Scheme); Death of victim (1996 Scheme)
Fighting, ... 92
Football supporters, ... 93
Foreseeability of damage, ... 32
Fraud, ... 89
Funeral expenses,
1990 Scheme, ... 185, 194–195
1996 Scheme, ... 201–202

Gangs, ... 95

Harassment,

mental injury, ... 29–30
Hearing aids, ... 26
Hearing – *see* Procedure (1990 Scheme); Procedure (1996 Scheme)
Hearsay, ... 238
Hospital staff,
crime of violence, ... 20–21
Household, membership of same – *see* Members of same household
Hovercraft, injury sustained on, ... 8, 9

Ignorance of Scheme, ... 71
Indecent assault, ... 11
Injury,
directly attributable – *see* Directly attributable injury
mental – *see* Mental injury
personal – *see* Personal injury
Insanity,
crime of violence, ... 19, 20
Intent,
crime of violence, ... 14, 16
Interest, ... 136–137
Interim awards, ... 125, 133, 135, 234
Investment accounts,
children, awards to, ... 105–106

Judicial review, ... 83, 242, 268–306
Jurisdiction,
1990 Scheme, ... 8
1996 Scheme, ... 8–9
Great Britain, ... 9
nationality, ... 8
Northern Ireland, ... 8
place of injury, ... 8–9
residence, ... 8
'sustained in Great Britain', injury, ... 8
visitors to Great Britain, ... 8

Legal costs, ... 125, 242
Levels of award,
1996 Scheme, ... 54
see also Maximum award; Minimum award
Lighthouses, injury sustained on, ... 9
Limbs, injuries to, ... 60
Loss of parental services,
death of victim (1996 Scheme), ... 210–211
Loss of society, ... 192–194
Lost earnings – *see* Earnings, loss of

Maximum award,
1996 Scheme, ... 54

introduction of, ... 54
see also Tariffs
Medical evidence,
application form, ... 132
assessment of compensation (1990 Scheme), ... 132–137
contents, ... 132
disagreement in medical profession, ... 134
facial scarring, ... 133
interim awards, ... 133
mental injury, ... 132
minor injuries, ... 132–133
nervous shock cases, ... 132
orthopaedic disorders, ... 134
pre-existing conditions, ... 134
request for report, ... 132
requirement, ... 132
scope, ... 132
serious injury ... 125–128
tariffs, ... 174–180
Members of same household, ... 99–103
1990 Scheme, ... 99–100, 103
1996 Scheme, ... 100, 103
absence of prosecution, ... 102
cessation of cohabitation, ... 101
child(ren), ... 102–103
co-operation with police, ... 100–101
divorce, ... 101–102
historical background, ... 101
minors, ... 102–103
prosecution requirement, ... 101
retraction statements, ... 101
withdrawal of complaint, ... 101
Mental hospitals, injuries in, ... 20–21, 77–78
Mental injury,
1990 Scheme, ... 27, 28–30, 33–39
1996 Scheme, ... 27–28, 30, 40–44
basic rule, ... 26
directly attributable injury,
1990 Scheme, ... 33–39
1996 Scheme, ... 40–44
establishing claim, ... 6, 58
harassment, ... 29–30
medical test, ... 30
psychiatric illness, ... 29, 58
reform of law, ... 6
secondary victim, ... 40–44
self-confidence, diminution in, ... 29
sexual offences, ... 43–44
stalking, ... 30

'survivor guilt', ... 29
symptoms, ... 29
tariff, ... 61, 179
test for,
1990 Scheme, ... 27, 28–30, 33–39
1996 Scheme, ... 27–28, 30, 40–44
Mentally ill persons,
awards to,
1990 Scheme, ... 104–106
1996 Scheme, ... 106–107
Minimum award,
1990 Scheme, ... 54–60
1996 Scheme, ... 54, 60–62, 173
amount, ... 54, 60
calculations, ... 57
elderly applicants, ... 59
generally, ... 54, 60
importance of provisions, ... 56
individual consideration of cases, ... 59–60
mental injuries, ... 58
nose, broken, ... 55–56, 60
special expenses, ... 56
tariff – *see* Tariffs
total amount of compensation, ... 56–57
Motoring offences,
crime of violence, ... 22
see also Traffic offences

Nationality,
applicant, ... 8
Neck injuries, ... 60
Nervous shock – *see* Mental injury
Northern Ireland,
jurisdiction, ... 8
Nose, broken, ... 55–56, 60
Nurses,
crime of violence, ... 20–21

Offence,
violent – *see* Crime of violence
Offender,
apprehension of – *see* Apprehension of offender
benefiting, ... 98–99
children, ... 18–19
conviction, ... 6
insanity, ... 18–19, 20–21
minors, ... 18–19
Oil rigs, injury sustained on, ... 8
Orthopaedic disorders, ... 134

Pension payments, ... 148–150
Pensions,
death of victim (1990 Scheme), deductible benefits, ... 198–199
Personal injury,
1990 Scheme, ... 26, 27
1996 Scheme, ... 26–27
directly attributable - *see* Directly attributable injury
meaning, ... 26
mental - *see* Mental injury
sustained, ... 26–30
see also Mental injury
vehicles, attributable to - *see* Motoring offences; Traffic offences; Vehicles
Playground injuries, ... 19
dangerous games, ... 97
Police officers,
apprehension of offenders, claims arising from, ... 45–51
co-operation with - *see* Co-operation with police
informing without delay, ... 66–68
reporting crime to, ... 66–68
Prejudice in labour market, ... 125
Prisons, injuries in, ... 77, 78
Procedure,
1990 Scheme - *see* Procedure (1990 Scheme)
1996 Scheme - *see* Procedure (1996 Scheme)
generally, ... 215–216
importance, ... 215
Procedure (1990 Scheme),
acceptance of offer, ... 225
administration, ... 219
applications, ... 221–242
chairman, ... 220
changes to Scheme, ... 218–219
commencement of application, ... 221–223
conditional grant of oral hearing, ... 222
criminal convictions, ... 226
death of claimant, ... 225, 226
delegation of determination, ... 222
eligibility decisions, ... 221
entitlement to award, ... 225–227
generally, ... 215–216
hearing,
adjournment, ... 242
alteration in award, ... 231
application, ... 227–229
attendance at, ... 238, 240
availability, ... 227
'broad justice' approach, ... 223

bundles, ... 235
burden of proof, ... 233, 238–239
conditional grant, ... 222
confidential nature, ... 240–241
coroners report, ... 240
costs, ... 242
cross-examination, ... 237, 238
decision, ... 241–242
disallowance of request, ... 230
entitlement to, ... 229–233
erroneous information, ... 227–229
evidence, laws of 241
facts disputed, ... 232–233
finality of decision, ... 223, 242
fresh start, as 234
hearsay, ... 238
incomplete information, ... 227–229
informality, ... 241–242
interim award, ... 234
see also Interim awards
intermediate stage, ... 230–231
judicial review, ... 242, 268–306
larger award possible, ... 230–231
limitation period, ... 222–223, 229
listing, ... 235, 237
material facts disputed, ... 232–233
medical evidence, incomplete 228–229
members of Board, ... 222
observing at, ... 240–241
papers available for, ... 235–236
preparation for, ... 235–236
procedure at, ... 233–242
referral straight to oral hearing, ... 224–225
representations, ... 231
requesting, ... 222, 226–227
summary of issues, ... 235
time limits, ... 222–223, 229
witnesses, ... 235–242
inappropriate original offer, ... 226–227
infirm applicants, ... 226
offer of compensation, ... 222, 225–227
pre- 1979 injuries, ... 218
preservation of 'old' Scheme rights, ... 217–220
refusal of award, ... 222, 226–227
reopening cases, ... 219
1990 Scheme, ... 262–264
sexual abuse of children cases, ... 218
title to award, ... 225–227
transfer date, ... 216, 217, 219

Procedure (1996 Scheme), ... 243–261
  appeals against review decisions, ... 247–256
  application for review, ... 243–247
  burden of proof, ... 244
  costs of representation, ... 244
  extension of time limit, ... 245
  generally, ... 243
  initial decision, ... 243–244
  nature of Scheme, ... 250
  oral hearing of appeals, ... 256–259
  passed up cases, ... 249
  rehearing of appeals, ... 259–261
  reopening cases, ... 249
  1996 Scheme, ... 264–265
  review of decision, ... 244–247
  risks of review application, ... 246
  standard of proof, ... 244
  time limits, ... 245
Property damage,
  1990 Scheme, ... 26
  hearing aids, ... 26
  physical aids, ... 26
  spectacles, ... 26
Prostitution, ... 90
Provocation, ... 7, 92, 93

Railway,
  1990 Scheme, ... 51–53
  1996 Scheme, ... 12, 44, 51–53
  trespass on, ... 12, 44, 51–53
Rape, ... 43–44, 108–113
  1990 Scheme, ... 108–113
  1996 Scheme, ... 108–113, 175–176
  acquittal, ... 111–112
  additional award, ... 112–113
  co-operation with police, ... 111
  crime of violence, as, ... 108
  definition, ... 110
  evidence, ... 109, 110–112, 113
  pregnancy, consequent, ... 112–113
  reporting, ... 109
  support organisations, ... 109–110
  tariff levels, ... 108, 111, 112
  time limit, ... 11, 109, 111
Recklessness,
  crime of violence, ... 14–16
  traffic offences, ... 117–119
Reconsideration of case,
  1990 Scheme, ... 262–264, 266–267

1996 Scheme, ... 264–265, 266–267
generally, ... 262
Reduction of award, ... 6–7, 135, 155–156
Remoteness of damage, ... 32
Reopening cases,
1990 Scheme, ... 219, 262–264
1996 Scheme, ... 249, 264–265
see also Reconsideration of case
Residence,
applicant, ... 8
Retraction statements,
members of same household, ... 101

Same sex partners,
death of victim (1996 Scheme), ... 203
Scar, facial, ... 133
Schools, injuries in, ... 19, 78
Scotland,
death of victim (1990 Scheme), ... 182, 192–194
loss of society, ... 192–194
Self-defence,
crime of violence, ... 16–17, 96
Sexual offences,
1990 Scheme, ... 108–113
1996 Scheme, ... 108–113, 175–176
crime of violence, as, ... 108
mental injury, ... 43–44
minors, against, ... 43–44, 61, 113–116
rape – *see* Rape
Ships, injury sustained on, ... 8, 9
Spectacles, ... 26
Sporting injuries,
crime of violence, ... 17–18
Stabbing, as a response to an insult, ... 92
Stalking,
mental injury, ... 30
Standard of proof, ... 6
procedure (1996 Scheme), ... 244
Step-parents,
death of victim (1996 Scheme), ... 204, 205
Sustained personal injury, ... 26–30
see also Mental injury; Personal injury

Tariff,
1994 Scheme, ... 26–27, 62, 153
1996 Scheme, ... 60–62, 153–180
child abuse, ... 61
combined injuries, ... 176–177
ears, injuries to, ... 60

eyes, injuries to, ... 60
facial injuries, ... 60
introduction, ... 1, 54
medical evidence, ... 174, 175
mental injury, ... 179
minimum award, ... 54, 60–62, 173
minor injuries, ... 61–62, 173–174
multiple injuries, ... 61, 173–174, 176–177
purpose, ... 2–3
rape, ... 108, 111, 112
sexual assaults, ... 108–111, 175–176
shock, ... 61, 179
standard amount, ... 173–180
terminology, ... 174–176
unlisted injury, ... 61–62
Teeth, injuries to, ... 60
Time limit,
1990 Scheme, ... 10–11
1996 Scheme, ... 9–10, 11
ignorance of Scheme, ... 11
indecent assault, ... 11
interpretation, ... 5–6, 10
late applications, ... 10
minors, ... 10–11
rape, ... 11
reform, ... 5
waiver, ... 5–6, 10
Traffic offences,
attempts to run down, ... 117–119
careless driving, ... 118
deliberate running down, ... 117–119
general rule, ... 117
recklessness, ... 117–119
Trespass on a railway, ... 12, 44, 51–53
Trusts,
child(ren) and person(s) under disability, awards to, ... 106

Undisplaced nasal fractures, ... 55

Vehicles,
1990 Scheme – *see* Traffic offences
1996 Scheme, ... 120
traffic offences – *see* Traffic offences
use of, injury attributable to, ... 120
Victim – *see* Applicant; Child(ren)
Violence,
crime of – *see* Crime of Violence

NOTES

NOTES

NOTES